The New York Times

ABCs OF CROSSWORDS

THE NEW YORK TIMES ABCs OF CROSSWORDS.

Printed in the United States of America. For information, address
St. Martin's Press, 175 Fifth Avenue, New York, NY 10010.

www.stmartins.com

ISBN 978-1-250-00922-7

First Edition: May 2012

10 9 8 7 6 5 4 3 2 1

The New York Times

ABCs OF CROSSWORDS

200 Easy to Hard Puzzles

Edited by Will Shortz

ST. MARTIN'S GRIFFIN NEW YORK

ACROSS

1 French-speaking nation in the Americas
6 Network with an eye logo
9 ___ colada
13 *Eloquent
16 "Crazy" bird
17 *British novelist who wrote "London Fields"
18 Liter or meter
19 Crafty
20 *College near Philadelphia
22 Mets' ballpark until 2008
24 Symbol on Superman's chest
25 *Having both Republican and Democratic support
30 Degree after an M.A., perhaps
33 "___ do" ("Not possible")
34 Hot cocoa container, maybe
35 Japanese "yes"
36 Unfinished project . . . or, literally, what the answers to the eight starred clues contain?
41 Where a bear hibernates
42 Go kaput
43 See 40-Down
44 Kerfuffle
45 *National discount store chain
48 Dove's sound
50 Whacked-out mental state
51 *Container next to a bowl of cereal
56 The last "w" in www
59 Morales of "NYPD Blue"
60 *Like some checks and vendors
63 "Or ___!" (threat)
64 *Gradually separated
65 Pictures inked on the body, in slang
66 Lawn base
67 Wigwam relative

DOWN

1 Easter roasts
2 Asia's shrinking ___ Sea
3 Humble response to a compliment
4 Palindromic bird
5 Here in 1-Across
6 Scratch, as a cat might a sofa
7 Crimson Tide school, for short
8 Start to wake up
9 Prunes, originally
10 Where the Northern Lights occur
11 Dark film genre
12 ___ meridiem (morning: Lat.)
14 Al who won four Indy 500s
15 D.C. winter hrs.
21 Rooster's mate
22 Train for a boxing match
23 Baseball's Hammerin' ___
25 Bent at a curtain call
26 Antiestablishment figure
27 Urge
28 Spanish "south"
29 In the past
31 Hurry
32 What everyone brings to a potluck dinner
33 Nothing
37 Words before "You may kiss the bride"
38 Nothing
39 Saxophonist Stan
40 With 43-Across, yttrium or scandium
45 ___ Martens (shoes)
46 Loved to pieces
47 Corp. creativity department
49 Dust Bowl migrants
51 Encounter
52 Jamaica, por ejemplo
53 Place to enter a PIN
54 Letters after pis
55 Record for later viewing, in a way
56 Shawl, e.g.
57 French "to be"
58 Tiny part of a computer's memory
61 Congratulate nonverbally
62 King Kong, e.g.

by Joel Fagliano

2

ACROSS

1 "Ars gratia artis" studio
4 Had a hunch
8 Attack via plane, in a way
14 Fair-hiring letters
15 Toast topper
16 Manny of 1970s-'80s baseball
17 Performer with a self-titled HBO special in 2006
19 Fire & Ice cosmetics company
20 Tabriz native
21 Yalie
23 Part of E.U.: Abbr.
24 Green machines?
25 Performer with a self-titled ABC series in 1996
29 Bottom of a crankcase
31 "Senses Working Overtime" band
32 Suffix with elephant
33 Main line
35 Perform as one
37 Performer with a self-titled Comedy Central series from 2003 to 2006
41 Fundamental belief
42 Lend ___ (help)
43 In the manner of
44 The Beatles' "___ Loser"
47 Like Dickens's Dodger
50 Performer with a self-titled PBS series from 1977 to 1982
53 Fit to serve
55 Many a federal holiday: Abbr.
56 Perfection, in some sports
57 Big name in pest control
58 Subject of scientific mapping
60 "Captain Marvel" publisher . . . and a hint to 17-, 25-, 37- and 50-Across
63 Recipient of coal for Christmas
64 The whole kit and caboodle
65 Scot's refusal
66 Equilibrium
67 City tricked with a wooden horse
68 Alternative to cable

DOWN

1 Newspaper, television, etc.
2 Customize for, as an audience
3 "My friend," in Marseille
4 Centers of attention
5 "Don't Bring Me Down" band, informally
6 1-Across's roarer
7 Straphanger's buy, once
8 Inflexible about rules
9 Uno+due
10 Styx, for one
11 Like soil in a delta
12 City on the Arno
13 Ages and ages
18 Place in shackles
22 Flexible about rules
25 Ste. Jeanne ___
26 Literary collection: Abbr.
27 One way to tell where someone is from
28 As of now
30 Word before license or justice
34 Energizer letters
36 What one might return to after a slump
37 Bologna or salami
38 Crushing snake
39 Excellent, in slang
40 Thespian's aim
41 Tiny bit
45 Buccaneer's buddies
46 N.Y.C.'s Park or Lex
48 Mean-spirited
49 Some German cameras
51 Turners on tuners
52 Conclude by
54 Photographer Adams
57 Like mud between one's toes, say
58 "Pygmalion" monogram
59 Facetious "Who, me?"
61 Pigskin snapper: Abbr.
62 Whisper sweet nothings

by Albert R. Picallo

3

ACROSS

1 With 69-Across where to find the ends of 17-, 22-, 32-, 43-, 54- and 61-Across
5 Organization for the supersmart
10 ___-in-the-blank
14 Most eligible for military service
15 State in NE India
16 Not working
17 Q-tip, e.g.
19 Hall-of-Famer Musial
20 Whole ___ and caboodle
21 Tetley product
22 It points to the minutes
24 Terse four-star review
27 Danish toy blocks
28 Prefix with plunk or plop
29 French notions
32 Presidential candidate's #2
36 Letter after chi
39 The Bard of ___ (Shakespeare)
40 Lifeless
41 Arkin of Hollywood
42 Part of the head that moves when you talk
43 Excellent, slangily
45 Snapshot
46 007 creator Fleming
47 Reproductive part of a fungus
50 Tire-changing group at a Nascar race
54 Sticky stuff on a baseball bat
57 Middling grade
58 ___ Newton (Nabisco treat)
60 W.W. II foe, with "the"
61 Condiment that's O.K. for observant Jews
64 Hysterically funny sort
65 Letter-shaped construction piece
66 Folkie Guthrie
67 Casino game with numbers
68 Slender amphibians
69 See 1-Across

DOWN

1 Sell at a pawnshop
2 How French fries are fried
3 Become friendly with
4 Dr. Seuss's "The Cat in the ___"
5 Like a lion or horse
6 Piece of French writing
7 Australian state whose capital is Sydney: Abbr.
8 Volvo rival
9 Prefix with dextrous
10 Uses a rod and reel
11 Item on a dog collar
12 Grassy plain of the Southwest
13 Gives for a time
18 Onetime "S.N.L." regular Cheri
23 Great happiness
25 ___ diagram (logic tool)
26 1994 Jean-Claude Van Damme sci-fi film
30 Unlit
31 Suffix with Rock
32 British rule in colonial India
33 The Cavaliers of the A.C.C.
34 Actor Robert De ___
35 Pesky insect
36 Airline ticket cost
37 Holder of a squid's 38-Down
38 It's held in a squid's 37-Down
41 Slightly open
43 Guitarist Atkins
44 Kitchen gadget for processing potatoes
45 Magician's cry
47 Start of a fire
48 Mischievous fairy
49 Weekly satirical paper, with "The"
51 Instant-messaging program for Macs
52 Swarms (with)
53 Cather who wrote "O Pioneers!"
55 Similar (to)
56 Judge's attire
59 Old Pontiac muscle cars
62 Make clothes
63 Carrier to Oslo

by Ian Livengood

4

ACROSS

1 One of the Pleiades
5 Q.: When is a door not a door? A.: When it's ___
9 Pickpocket, e.g.
14 ID in a library vol.
15 Dunce cap shape
16 Three-wheeled Asian cab
17 "Peanuts" figure . . . or some fabulous fall soup?
20 "For rent"
21 Figure in academia
22 Nein : German :: ___ : Russian
23 Subway turners
25 Much-derided 1980s-'90s car
27 Calif. setting for "Stand and Deliver"
30 Words to swear by
34 Off-road wheels, for short
36 Rhyme scheme for Frost's "Stopping By Woods on a Snowy Evening"
38 Onion-flavored roll
39 Early 1970s dance . . . or some smelly soup?
43 Kenyan tribesman
44 Suffix with opal
45 Key to get out of a jam?
46 At a chop shop, perhaps
48 Tennis's Graf
51 Exam for an aspiring Esq.
53 Ray of "GoodFellas"
56 Ways to the Web: Abbr.
59 It may be put on a pedestal
62 Gloomy, in verse
63 Nickname for snowboarder Shaun White . . . or some airborne soup?
66 Paddled craft
67 Canceled
68 Old camera settings, for short
69 Many-headed challenge for Hercules
70 Like flicks seen without special glasses
71 Instrument played with a plectrum

DOWN

1 Baseball gloves
2 "Give it ___!" ("Try!")
3 "Yes, if you ask me"
4 German chancellor Merkel
5 Score 100% on
6 "The Grapes of Wrath" family name
7 The "a" in a.m.
8 Compensate for loss
9 Channel for old films
10 Like a swinging pendulum, say
11 "Eww! Gross!"
12 "Night" author Wiesel
13 Helvetica, e.g.
18 Hwys.
19 "One" on a penny
24 Lee of Marvel Comics
26 Mongolian desert
28 Okeechobee, e.g.
29 Chasm
31 "Calm down!"
32 Shouts at a fútbol game
33 Harmony
34 $20 dispensers
35 "What's ___?"
37 No. at a brokerage
40 Becomes smitten by
41 Sometimes-illegal turns, in slang
42 Dog command
47 The Midshipmen
49 Relative of Rex
50 Not casual
52 Corrupt
54 One of a Turkic people
55 Got out of bed
56 Allergic reaction
57 One-horse carriage
58 Be in limbo
60 Author C. P. ___
61 Frozen waffle brand
64 Grazing ground
65 Thomas Mann's "Der ___ in Venedig"

1	2	3	4	■	5	6	7	8	■	9	10	11	12	13
14				■	15				■	16				
17				18					19					
20					■	21				■	22			
23					24	■	■	25		26		■	■	■
■	■	27				28	29	■	30			31	32	33
34	35		■	■	36			37	■	38				
39			40	41					42					
43					■	44				■	■	45		
46					47	■	48			49	50		■	■
■	■	■	51			52	■	■	53				54	55
56	57	58		■	59		60	61	■	62				
63				64					65					
66					■	67				■	68			
69					■	70				■	71			

by Tony Orbach

ACROSS

1 Ice cream utensil
6 Sea creature that moves sideways
10 "But wait! There's more . . ."
14 Cuban "line" dance
15 Lasso
16 Italian "bye"
17 Crowd sounds
18 Baldwin of "30 Rock"
19 Bullets
20 Buffalo wings or bruschetta, e.g.
23 Kid's "shooter" projectile
24 Formula ___ racing
25 Overly
26 Kanye West's genre
28 "E" on a baseball scoreboard
30 Sylvania product
31 Rightmost number on a grandfather clock
32 Dish under a teacup
34 High point
35 Pittsburgh Pirates hero of the 1960 World Series
39 Perry with the 1956 #1 hit "Hot Diggity"
40 Winners' opposites
41 Auto additive brand
42 Hole-punching tools
44 Swung and missed
48 Equal: Prefix
49 W. Hemisphere alliance
50 Allow
51 "___ Baba and the 40 Thieves"
52 Music source on many an old fairground
56 Western writer Grey
57 Heading into overtime
58 Source of amber
59 ___-European languages
60 Prefix with potent or present
61 Ridiculous
62 "No bid"
63 Noble gas
64 Weasel family member

DOWN

1 Predicament
2 "The Last of the Mohicans" author
3 Commensurate (with)
4 Shrek, for one
5 Rustic
6 Hula hoops in the 1950s, e.g.
7 Part to play
8 Camera openings
9 "Take a chill pill!"
10 Military sch.
11 Verse often beginning "There once was a . . ."
12 "Spider-Man" series director
13 Tic-tac-toe victory
21 All together
22 Burgle
27 Baked dessert
29 Norway's capital
30 Jeff who founded Amazon.com
33 Gives teams a short break
34 Professional org.
35 Neighbor of South Africa
36 Seizes, as a car
37 Direct elsewhere
38 Handel's "Messiah," e.g.
39 CBS forensic series
42 Time Warner spinoff of '09
43 Serve attentively
45 Pesters
46 Jerry's ex on "Seinfeld"
47 Supper
50 Ushered
53 Old-fashioned Speed Wagons
54 Greek philosopher known for paradoxes
55 Landlord's due
56 Nothing . . . or a hint to what's hidden in 20-, 35- and 52-Across

by Stan Newman

6

ACROSS

1 Cut down, as a photo
5 Big Apple?
9 Like many bathroom floors
14 Poland's Walesa
15 It gets hammered
16 Rub out
17 Brainstorm
18 Be rewarded for a pious life, as the devout believe
20 Abyss
22 Shipping container
23 Stereotypical sitcom greeting
26 Hypotheticals
29 U.F.O. crew
30 Roman "I"
31 Satellite-based car option
33 Former Japanese capital
35 "The Flintstones" pet
36 Castle on the Thames
41 Doll call
42 Spanish finger food
43 A girl was from there in a 1964 hit song
47 His big day is in June
48 Rx watchdog
51 Finger count
52 Pet store purchase
55 Big, big, big
56 Aired again
57 Invisible writing on a computer screen . . . or a component of 18-, 23-, 36- and 52-Across?
62 All's counterpart
63 "Doe, ___ . . ."
64 Les États-___
65 Puts on
66 Chinese restaurant request
67 Force unit
68 Apt rhyme of "aahs"

DOWN

1 Overused expression
2 In very high demand
3 "___ Eleven"
4 Developmental period
5 Suffix with seem or teem
6 Chinese chairman
7 Gee follower
8 Laundry brand
9 Be on the brink of toppling
10 "Dies ___"
11 Restroom, informally
12 WNW's opposite
13 Room for trophies, maybe
19 Soccer great Mia
21 "Balderdash!"
24 Inventor Sikorsky
25 Mr. ___, Japanese sleuth
26 Peculiar: Prefix
27 Neighbor of a Swede
28 ___ Canals
32 Tacks on
33 Skater Michelle
34 Frequently, to a bard
36 Mending aid
37 Muscat's land
38 Disney dog
39 Memorable 1995 hurricane with a gem of a name?
40 Low point
41 Cambridge univ.
44 Anita of "La Dolce Vita"
45 Appearance
46 Available for breeding
48 Farcical 1960s sitcom with the Indian character Roaring Chicken
49 Troi on "Star Trek: T.N.G."
50 "Gunsmoke" star James
53 Minuscule
54 Minds, as a fire
55 Laudatory poems
57 Solo of "Star Wars"
58 Vow at an altar
59 Those people, in Brooklyn
60 Mark, as a ballot
61 Syllable after 6-Down

by David Steinberg

7

ACROSS

1 Handkerchief stuffed in the mouth, e.g.
4 "The 59th Street Bridge Song (___ Groovy)" (1967 hit)
10 Start for a plant
14 Hwy.
15 Provide with the latest info
16 Friend in war
17 Giant Mel
18 Anti-abortion position
20 Cry to a horse that's the opposite of "Giddyup!"
22 Allow
23 Place to get a facial
24 Abandoned, in a way
27 Incorporate, as a picture in a blog
31 Kermit, e.g.
32 Ice cream flavor that's a synonym for "boring"
34 Up and about
36 Announced
38 Landon who lost to F.D.R. in 1936
39 Not shown in theaters
43 Suffix with plug
44 Not feral
45 2000 comedy "Me, Myself & ___"
46 Place to play foosball or Ping-Pong
49 Wall Street pessimist
50 Arcade coin
51 Satisfactory
56 Josh
58 Meadow
59 Concerning
60 Having no illusions or pretensions
65 Singer ___ King Cole
66 Little of this and that
67 Fiat
68 Big Australian bird
69 Move text around
70 Mrs. with a famous cow
71 Lo-___ screen

DOWN

1 Canine threat
2 "Casey ___ Bat"
3 Go astray
4 Wearing this is a PETA peeve
5 Afterword
6 Barely beaten
7 Christine of "Chicago Hope"
8 Hairy TV cousin
9 Fishermen cast them
10 Deli meat
11 Football's Manning
12 Rice Krispies' Snap, Crackle or Pop
13 Change from brunette to blonde, say
19 "___ sesame"
21 Heart parts
25 Doughnuts, topologically speaking
26 What you might R.S.V.P. to via a computer
28 1982 Harrison Ford sci-fi film
29 Funny DeGeneres
30 Actor Willem
33 Hubbub
34 Of ___ (somewhat)
35 Canonized fifth-century pope
36 SeaWorld whale
37 Green machine?
40 Sporty Pontiac of years past
41 Competes (for)
42 Tehran native
47 Tie again, as a necktie
48 "I'm working ___"
49 Yachtsman, e.g.
52 Come in second
53 ___ cotta
54 Box on a bowling scoresheet
55 Baby-to-be
57 Dumb ox
60 Mother of a fawn
61 Superannuated
62 Nintendo console with a remote
63 Snaky fish
64 "You there!"

by Milo Beckman

8

ACROSS

1 Handled, as a matter
6 Sleepaway, e.g.
10 Wood strip
14 "Er . . . um . . ."
15 Instrument heard in Sonny & Cher's "I Got You Babe"
16 Currency that replaced the drachma
17 "Spitting" snake
18 Roller coaster, e.g.
19 Rigging support
20 Bolt
23 Cousin of Muhammad
25 Sharer of an exclamation point on a keyboard
26 Locale of the Île de la Cité
27 Bolt
32 Tatum of "Paper Moon"
33 The "she" in the lyric "She walked up to me and she asked me to dance"
34 Window part
35 Unlikely to hug, say
37 Frozen dessert franchise
41 Part of the Old World
42 Wipe the slate clean
43 Bolt
47 Marble, for one
49 What "-" may mean: Abbr.
50 511, to Caesar
51 Bolt
56 Wrist/elbow connector
57 Every family has one
58 Energy
61 Toy sometimes pulled with a rope
62 Leer
63 It's a blessing
64 Half of a famous split personality
65 Unite under fire?
66 Smarts

DOWN

1 Word to an attack dog
2 ___, amas, amat . . .
3 They have homes that many people visit
4 Protective covering
5 Hot, scoring-wise
6 Pupil coverer
7 Somewhat
8 Number in statistics
9 ___ review
10 Renter
11 Foreign domestic
12 Choo-choo
13 See 24-Down
21 Like Brahms's Symphony No. 3
22 Jimmy Carter's alma mater: Abbr.
23 Famous ___ cookies
24 With 13-Down, "Stormy Weather" singer
28 Sound from a weary person sinking into a hot tub
29 ___-Kettering Institute
30 Also
31 Figure in Santa's workshop
35 Result of a fire
36 On fire
37 Play about Capote
38 1972 #1 hit for Sammy Davis Jr., with "The"
39 Vitamin whose name sounds like a bingo call
40 Mountain sighting
41 Writer James
42 Drinks that are often ladled
43 Given for a time
44 Attack, as across a boundary
45 "Absolutely!"
46 Born as
47 Snow when it's around 32°F
48 British boob tube
52 Store
53 Persuade
54 Big maker of 59-Down
55 Folk tales and such
59 Office staples, for short
60 ___-haw

by Michael Farabaugh

9

ACROSS

1 You can stick them in your ear
6 "Planet of the ___"
10 Soft, thick lump
14 Sum
15 Leap
16 Learning by memorization
17 Bolivian capital
18 Mideast leader: Var.
19 The "a" in a.m.
20 Legendary San Francisco music/comedy club where Lenny Bruce and Woody Allen have performed
23 To the ___ degree
24 Extremity
25 Got rid of some tobacco juices, say
28 Ali Baba's magic words
35 Counterpart of hers
36 Puppeteer Lewis
37 High-end watchmaker
38 Bonus
40 Quarry, e.g.
41 Amalgamate
42 Poet/playwright Jones
43 ___ self-defense
45 Tavern
46 Bad place to live when the river rises
48 Deposit around a river's mouth
49 Road surfacing material
50 Cartoon frame
52 Everything . . . or what might cover an everything 62-Across?
60 The "A" in U.A.W.
61 Group of birds
62 Item whose varieties include the endings of 20-, 28- and 46-Across
64 Deborah of "The King and I"
65 50-50
66 Online-only publication
67 Sized up visually
68 45 or 78
69 Results of bumps to a bumper

DOWN

1 Ice cream amts.
2 Brazenly promote
3 "The Seven Year ___"
4 Mother or father
5 Caught some Z's
6 Not fully shut
7 The heart, essentially
8 Actor Jannings who won the first Best Actor Oscar
9 Wild shopping sessions
10 Junior's junior
11 Actress Anderson
12 "Beetle Bailey" bulldog
13 "___ there, done that"
21 "This isn't looking good"
22 Minimal lead in baseball
25 Bookcase part
26 Dot on a computer screen
27 Houston baseballer
29 Vatican-related
30 "Fear of Fifty" writer Jong
31 Capone henchman
32 What a murder suspect needs
33 Zinc or zirconium
34 Apply, as pressure
36 Got ready for a tongue depressor, say
39 The Greek "khalix" (pebble) for the English "calculus," e.g.
44 Ruler part
47 Examined deeply
48 Schlock
51 Fix deeply and tightly
52 Seize
53 ___ Lewis and the News
54 To live, to Lévy
55 ___ Strauss jeans
56 After-work times, in classifieds
57 Harmony
58 Opposed to, in dialect
59 Check for a landlady
63 "___ Misérables"

by Andrea Carla Michaels and Michael Blake

10

ACROSS

1 Hungry mouth
4 Person assisting a worship service
10 Jockey's whip
14 Lincoln, the Rail-Splitter
15 Place for a bookcase
16 Auto company whose name is Latin for "listen"
17 Title of respect
18 Longtime New York theater critic
20 Emphatic follow-up to yes or no
22 Corporate dept. that may include labs
23 Actor in 1960s TV's "77 Sunset Strip"
26 Nary a soul
29 Tropical citrus fruit
30 Fleischmann's product
32 Wilson of "Midnight in Paris"
33 Spanish king
34 Popular card game since 1954
37 Speck
38 Org. issuing many refunds
39 TV/film/stage actor once married to actress Meredith Baxter
45 Informer
48 International furniture retailer
49 Facility
50 Madame Chanel
51 Italian city famous for its cheese
53 Big dog
56 Yankee great Roger
58 Came ashore
59 Prime cooking spot
63 ___ de mer
64 "___ She Sweet"
65 "That's it for me"
66 Get along in years
67 Memo
68 Conflict waged between navies
69 ___ diem

DOWN

1 Rubber man?
2 Cut
3 In an odd manner
4 ___ Davenport, long-running "Doonesbury" character
5 Aunt ___ of "Oklahoma!"
6 Start of the third century
7 "Mazel ___!"
8 Be in charge of
9 Singer McEntire
10 Nowadays they usually have power locks and windows
11 Decrepit
12 Pindar creation
13 Fraternity letters
19 The Atlantic's Cape ___
21 Baseball stat
24 ___ pros. (court record abbr.)
25 Building extension
27 Born, in Brittany
28 Naval officer below lieut.
31 Annual theater award
34 Quaintly stylish
35 Barry Manilow's "Could ___ Magic"
36 Suffix with contradict
37 Old Mitsubishi model
39 Fondue feature
40 Alias
41 First U.S. state to abolish slavery
42 "It seems evident that . . ."
43 Alphabet trio
44 Beak
45 Motorist's guide
46 Farmland spread
47 Real young 'un
50 Piers Morgan's channel
52 Realm of beauty
54 Justice Kagan
55 Less done, as steak
57 Long-legged wader
59 Ceiling addition
60 ___ de la Plata
61 Nutritional allotment, for short
62 At once

by Bernice Gordon

ACROSS

1 Necklace fasteners
7 "Entourage" cable channel
10 Talks like this in "Star Wars" films he does
14 Cut the mustard
15 Dada artist Jean
16 Landed
17 Property with a mansion
18 "Fat chance, laddie"
19 Griffin who created "Wheel of Fortune"
20 Charleston is its capital
23 "All seats have been sold" sign
24 First part of a ski jump
25 Longest river in Deutschland
29 ___, Crackle and Pop
31 Trumpet's saliva-draining key
33 Skirt's edge
35 ___ Paulo, Brazil
36 Perry Mason's field
37 Kitchen cleanup cloth
41 Samuel Langhorne ___
44 Simile's center
45 Author Asquith of children's books
47 511, in old Rome
48 Not a unanimous ruling
52 Role in "Young Frankenstein"
55 "Laughing" animal
56 Biblical word with "thou"
58 Deposit, as an egg
60 Swedish liquor with memorable ads
63 Melt
66 Qty.
67 Jack the ___
68 Elvis's "___ Las Vegas"
69 Doctor's charge
70 Log-in info
71 Fix, as a cat
72 Finish
73 Eagle's grabbers

DOWN

1 Masticates
2 Focused-beam emitters
3 Takes steps in response to
4 32-card game
5 Venomous snake
6 Oktoberfest vessel
7 Abrupt finishes to phone conversations
8 Genius
9 Ready for business
10 Japanese motorcycle maker
11 Bullfight cheer
12 North, east, west or south: Abbr.
13 Off-road transport, briefly
21 Four Monopoly properties: Abbr.
22 Chicago columnist Kupcinet
26 Fashion magazine founded in France
27 ___ the Terrible
28 What literally comes from the north, east, west and south?
30 "Feels great!"
32 Informed
34 Sportscaster Albert
37 Bit of Morse code
38 Look-for-it children's game
39 Common event the day after Thanksgiving
40 Favorable sign
42 Permit for leaving a country
43 Russian fighter jet
46 Stiffly phrased
49 Sort of
50 Indenting key
51 College Web site suffix
53 One who knows the ropes
54 Earn tons of, as dough
57 Walk proudly
59 Distance units on a football field
61 Not threatened
62 German car
63 Appliances hidden in seven answers in this puzzle
64 It's rotated when doing the twist
65 Palindromic girl

by Patrick Merrell

12

ACROSS

1 It gets patted on the bottom
5 Tableland
9 Lead-in to boy or girl
13 Surveyor's calculation
14 Raring to go
15 Gershwin and Glass
16 Ticket usable on more than one trip
18 Basketball hoops
19 Gerund's finish
20 When repeated, cry to a vampire
21 ___ accompli
22 They make a king laugh
26 Available if needed
28 One who's supposed to be available if needed
29 End-of-list abbr.
31 Diamond cover
32 Life, in short
33 Neck cover
35 Smells bad
38 Mel who batted left and threw right
39 Become oblivious to one's surroundings
41 Completely untrained
42 Home of Arizona State University
44 Stir up, as a fire
45 Suffix with brigand
46 "___ well"
48 Alternative to .com or .org
49 Bean type
50 Like maps, iguanas and rock walls
52 Bad-mouth
54 Counterparts of dits
55 Cut with a sweeping motion
57 Greek H
58 Theater sign
59 Fast marching pace . . . or a hint to 16- and 39-Across and 10- and 24-Down
64 Dairy Queen purchase
65 Shortstop Smith who won 13 consecutive Gold Glove Awards
66 Cajole
67 Lollapalooza
68 "Butt out," briefly
69 Novelist Victor

DOWN

1 Bit of body art, for short
2 Train schedule abbr.
3 Meadow
4 Dentist's target
5 Apple on a table
6 "My word!"
7 Prefix with comic
8 Raring to go
9 Expedia calculation
10 Interval in which something is tested
11 Indian tongue
12 Helper: Abbr.
14 Artist born in 30-Down
17 WSW's opposite
22 Frilly neckwear
23 Type of type
24 Las Vegas staple
25 Nixon aide Maurice
27 ___ blanche
30 Minotaur's home
33 Former Cleveland Orchestra conductor George
34 General ___, former maker of Jell-O and Sanka
36 Rapper West
37 Promise
40 Luau instrument
43 Wall cover
47 Rarely
49 Grab
50 Anglo-___
51 Lollapalooza
53 Noshed
54 Art ___
56 "The Godfather" author
60 Drool catcher
61 Debtor's letters
62 O or Cosmo
63 Prefix with skeleton

by Susan Gelfand

ACROSS

1 One of the "hands" in the command "shake hands"
4 Result of a burst dike
9 "O.K., O.K. . . . tell me!"
14 "So that's it!"
15 Caffè ___
16 Healing plants
17 Unused parts of a cell phone plan
20 Youngster
21 Encircle
22 Stun, as with a police gun
23 British lockup
26 Wander
28 Formal meal at a table
33 "One more time!"
35 Hops kiln
36 Lab eggs
37 X-rated flick
38 Arid
39 What a soldier wears that has a serial no.
41 Any port ___ storm
42 Letters before omegas
44 Hammerin' Hank and others
45 Question that's a classic pickup line
48 Instrument for a Muse
49 La ___ Tar Pits
50 Mountain lion
53 Chemical suffixes
55 Three Wise Men
59 Death row inmate's hope
63 Finnish bath
64 Big name in printers
65 See 57-Down
66 Person who uses the "five-finger discount"
67 Medicinal amounts
68 Juice suffix

DOWN

1 Segment
2 "___, matey!"
3 Send to base on balls
4 Pop music's ___ & Eddie
5 Restroom, informally
6 Verdi opera
7 Other: Sp.
8 Actress Rebecca
9 Novelist Fleming
10 Substance in wheat flour
11 Minuscule amount
12 Flying geese formations
13 To be, in old Rome
18 American ___ (veterans' group)
19 Apple devices with earbuds
24 Wither
25 "___ to a Nightingale"
27 Impair the quality of
28 "Git!"
29 Less favorable
30 Off
31 2007 film "___ Almighty"
32 ___-to-riches
33 Heroic tale
34 It's prohibited
38 Exigency
40 Had visions during sleep
43 Letter flourish
44 Where Nigeria is: Abbr.
46 Comic Boosler
47 Keep thinking about, with "on"
50 Whispered attention-getter
51 Salt Lake City's state
52 Hawaiian island
54 Int'l fair
56 Verdi opera
57 With 65-Across, comment that might be heard after the start of 17-, 28-, 45- or 59-Across
58 Playwright William
60 Clumsy sort
61 Iowa college
62 Young ___ (kids)

by Keith Talon

14

ACROSS

1 Nile bird
5 A ditz hasn't one
9 ___ Downs
14 "High Hopes" lyricist
16 Slightest amount
17 Guilty plea, say
18 Lilylike garden plant
19 It might make the nose wrinkle
20 Singer with the #1 R&B hit "I Feel for You"
22 Suffix with ox- or sulf-
23 "Paper Moon" father and daughter
24 Biscotti flavor
26 Like Batman, the Lone Ranger, etc.
29 Hagen of stage and screen
30 Japan's "way of the gods" religion
32 Eurasian duck
36 Pre-K child
37 Scam . . . or an apt title for this puzzle?
39 Useless tic-tac-toe line
40 Certain blood type, for short
42 Economist Friedman
43 Suffix with no-good
44 ___ Pieces
46 Aides: Abbr.
48 Dead Sea Scrolls ascetic
51 Grafton's "___ for Outlaw"
52 He was Sonny to Marlon Brando's Vito
56 Chilly
58 54-Down by Verdi
59 Allowed to wander, as a chicken
61 Handle the fixin's for a party, say
62 Boxer who almost upset Joe Louis in 1941
63 "I'm done!"
64 Jonas who developed a polio vaccine
65 Formerly, once

DOWN

1 "A miss ___ good . . ."
2 Sport with a birdie
3 Having no delay
4 Says "Cheese!"
5 Hypo meas.
6 Nonclerical
7 "Looks like I goofed"
8 City of central Sicily
9 Gaseous hydrocarbon
10 Sneakers brand sported by Abdul-Jabbar
11 The younger Obama girl
12 Of base 8
13 Intends
15 Fashion monogram
21 Indiana University campus site
24 Grand Theft ___
25 Upper-left key
26 Cooper cars
27 Protractor measure
28 Field goal percentages and such
31 Class for cooking, sewing, etc.
33 Priest's honorific
34 Illuminated notices above theater doors
35 Stir-fry vessels
38 Bambi's aunt
41 Welcomer at Walmart, e.g.
45 Make certain
47 Give comfort to
48 Give the heave-ho
49 Politico Palin
50 Strike down
53 Place for B-2s and B-52s: Abbr.
54 Operatic highlight
55 Dudley Do-Right's heartthrob
56 Mission conclusion?
57 Car ding
60 Yellowstone beast

by Patrick McIntyre

ACROSS

1 Common interjection on 27-/44-Across
5 Corn, wheat or soybeans
9 Mobile downloadables
13 Ark builder
14 Amours
16 Underground part of a plant
17 Where plank-walkers end up on 27-/44-Across
20 Often-purple flowers
21 500 sheets
22 Big bird Down Under
23 "It's the ___ I can do"
25 "Hold it!," on 27-/44-Across
27 With 44-Across, annual celebration on 9/19
31 That woman
32 Yours, in Tours
33 Never, in Nuremberg
34 Gog and ___ (enemies of God, in Revelation)
36 Deep-toned woodwind
38 Bird in a "tuxedo"
40 Malevolent spirit
41 Cushion
42 Actress Swenson of "Benson"
43 Asian electronics giant
44 See 27-Across
46 Treasure on 27-/44-Across
48 Sometimes-sprained joint
49 Pretend
50 Watch sound
52 Playmate of Tinky Winky, Dipsy and Po
57 "I don't believe it!," on 27-/44-Across
60 "___ la Douce"
61 Ultimate authority
62 "The Art of Fugue" composer
63 Onetime competitor of Nair
64 Glowing gas
65 Hello, on 27-/44-Across

DOWN

1 "I've fallen . . . ___ can't get up!"
2 Surf sound
3 Sitar player Shankar
4 John ___-Davies of the "Lord of the Rings" trilogy
5 Get near to
6 Harry Potter's best friend
7 Be a foreman of
8 Onetime money in Spain
9 Curve
10 Do some investigating
11 Sonnets and haikus
12 Peacock's walk
15 1970s radical org.
18 Set, as mousse
19 Resident of Nebraska's largest city
24 Related (to)
26 ___ burger (meatless dish)
27 Key on the far left of a keyboard
28 Not much
29 Take immediate steps
30 Destiny
34 Award hung on a chain or ribbon
35 Prefix with byte
37 Immature egg cell
38 The "P" of PRNDL
39 Aye's opposite
41 Ocular inflammation also known as conjunctivitis
44 Dot-chomping character in a classic arcade game
45 What there's no "I" in
46 Place to wash up
47 Autumn hue
51 1040 org.
53 "Mamma Mia" group
54 Jacob's first wife
55 California-based oil giant
56 Like a used barbecue pit
58 Winery container
59 General on a Chinese menu

by Julian Lim

16

ACROSS

1 PC hearts
5 Capital ENE of Fiji
9 "Star Wars" director George
14 Mont Blanc, par exemple
15 Table salt, chemically
16 Chip away
17 Way to reduce spending
19 Broadcaster
20 Coach Parseghian
21 URL ending
22 ___ instant
23 Pre-sporting-event songs
29 Baldwin of "30 Rock"
30 Genesis mariner
31 Deli side
32 Fabergé collectible
35 River to the Caspian
37 Author Levin
38 President Taft's foreign policy
43 N.Y.C.'s Park or Lex
44 Union collections
45 "Alice" spinoff
46 Nimble-fingered
48 Long skirt
50 Malone of "Into the Wild"
54 Areas targeted for economic revitalization
58 Part of Miss Muffet's meal
59 Kitchen gadget brand
60 "Mighty ___ a Rose"
61 Director Kurosawa
63 Some vacation expenses . . . or a hint to the starts of 17-, 23-, 38- and 54-Across
66 Echolocation acronym
67 Kind of sax
68 Play opener
69 Speaks silently
70 One pitied by Mr. T
71 McJob doer

DOWN

1 Poolside enclosure
2 Mice or men
3 "This just in . . ." announcement
4 Line part: Abbr.
5 Composer Bruckner
6 Game with four "ghosts"
7 Post-O.R. stop
8 PC key near the space bar
9 Was biased
10 Heep and others
11 First wife of Julius Caesar
12 Suffix with block or cannon
13 Sun. speech
18 Prefix with friendly
22 Divided 50/50
24 Reykjavik's land: Abbr.
25 15th-century French king nicknamed "the Prudent"
26 Seniors' org.
27 Painter Chagall
28 Have influence on
33 Wander, with "about"
34 In a mood to complain
36 Follower of a chat room joke
38 Miami-___ County
39 Place for a roast
40 More than liberal
41 Very expensive
42 Voodoo charm
47 Persian Gulf capital
49 Sees through, in a way
51 Intertwine
52 On the verge of
53 Invites to enter one's home
55 Brings up
56 Heap kudos on
57 Suffix meaning "animals"
61 Balaam's beast
62 Fish in backyard pools
63 U.K. fliers
64 "Xanadu" rock grp.
65 Salary ceiling

by Daniel Raymon

ACROSS

1 Little argument
5 Result of a mosquito bite
9 /
14 Gas company famous for its toy trucks
15 Classic soda brand
16 Acknowledge as true, as a crime
17 Operatic solo
18 Signal, as a cab
19 Common mirage image
20 Some McDonald's burgers
23 Four-baggers: Abbr.
24 View
25 Look up to
29 It might make you go "Achoo!"
31 January 1 for the Rose Bowl, e.g.
35 Good, in Guatemala
36 Wild pig
37 ___ exhaust
38 Part of a 2005 Harry Potter title
41 "That's ___ haven't heard"
42 Paris airport
43 Be a cast member of
44 Double-___ (oboe, e.g.)
45 Bus. opposite
46 Party south of the border
47 Years on end
49 Partners for mas
50 1987 Stanley Kubrick classic
59 Lightning-fast Bolt
60 Actor Morales
61 ___ avis
62 Tooth: Prefix
63 For fear that
64 French friends
65 Heavy carts
66 Tibetan priest
67 Word that can follow the start of 20-, 38- or 50-Across

DOWN

1 N.B.A. nickname until 2011
2 Llama land
3 It's north of the Indian Ocean
4 Former Russian royal
5 "Yoo-hoo" response
6 They may stream down the cheeks
7 Chocolate-___
8 Hawaiian port
9 English biscuit served with tea
10 Items for gamblers who cheat
11 Area that may have stained-glass windows
12 Use a teaspoon in tea, e.g.
13 "Bonanza" brother
21 Pulsate painfully
22 Improperly seize
25 Despise
26 One of the Allman Brothers
27 Brawl
28 Cheating on a spouse
29 April 1 victims
30 ___ Gaga
32 Female relations
33 Not said explicitly
34 1941 chart-topper "Maria ___"
36 Drill a hole
39 Michaels of "S.N.L."
40 Mrs. Gorbachev
46 Tex-Mex wrap
48 Old Dodges
49 Ecto- or proto- ending
50 Elmer with a double-barreled shotgun
51 Manipulator
52 Actress Turner
53 Explain to
54 On an ocean voyage
55 Creature that sidles
56 ___ Sutra
57 Attorney General Holder
58 Work to do

by David Gray

18

ACROSS

1 Medicine holder
5 Walk ungracefully
11 Nick, say
14 Rights advocacy grp.
15 This point forward
16 Bon ___
17 *Area in front of a coop
19 Grand Canyon part
20 Cornfield call
21 Sea eagle
22 Some Saturns
23 *Modern school memento
28 Beatle lover
29 More clever
30 Wee, informally
31 Baseball's Blue Moon
33 O.R. figures
34 One working with checks and balances, for short
35 *Braided floor covering
37 *More than enough
41 "___ the season"
42 Play about Capote
43 Bosnian, e.g.
44 Larklike bird
47 Ore-Ida parent company
49 Language suffix
50 *Elemental parts of human nature
53 Posh
54 Letter from Homer?
55 ___ v. Wade
56 Former White House press secretary Fleischer
57 *Discover to be fibbing
62 Bee follower
63 Opposed (to)
64 Hobbling, say
65 Actors Burns and Wynn
66 Guardian Angels' toppers
67 Event with booths

DOWN

1 Hoover or Oreck, for short
2 German "I"
3 Noted 1964 convert to Islam
4 Susan of soaps
5 Character in a Beatles song
6 Wine: Prefix
7 They may be hard to find at a tearjerker
8 More loved
9 "___ Doone"
10 Knock off
11 Strand
12 Some acids
13 Composer ___-Korsakov
18 Kit ___ (chocolate bars)
22 Metal supports in skyscrapers
23 Opportunity, metaphorically
24 ___-European
25 Sticky stuff
26 When repeated, a noted panda
27 Takeback, briefly
32 Break from responsibilities, informally
34 Sovereign lands . . . or what are hidden in the answers to the six starred clues
36 "Lovely" Beatles girl
37 Baseball Hall-of-Famer Speaker
38 Actor Baldwin
39 Creator of the G.O.P. elephant
40 The "Y" in Y.S.L.
42 Like a small farm, perhaps
44 France's Élysée, for one
45 Hardened
46 Fairies
47 One getting lots of doubles and home runs, say
48 The Jewish people
51 It might be taken by a sailor
52 Author Zora ___ Hurston
57 Request inside (or outside?) a wine bar
58 Pres. when NATO was formed
59 Loosey-goosey
60 Mischief-maker
61 Fair-hiring inits.

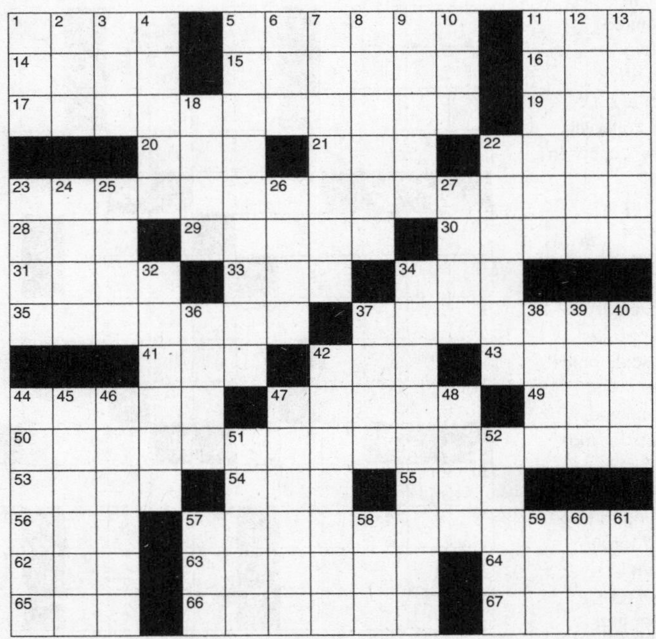

by Peter A. Collins

ACROSS

1 Teenage Mutant ___ Turtles
6 Perfect school grade
11 Bar bill
14 Spring zodiac sign
15 Promote
16 When a plane is due in, for short
17 Wins a dispute
19 Some "General Hospital" roles, in brief
20 Sci-fi vehicle
21 Cry between "ready" and "go"
22 I.R.S. experts
23 Microscope part
26 Pompous pronoun
29 Clean air org.
30 Recent: Prefix
31 Pretty good
32 You Tube upload
34 Andy Warhol genre
37 "It's a mystery to me"
42 Two-front, as a Coast Guard rescue
43 Practical application
44 Italian shrimp dish
47 Blaster's buy
49 Call ___ day
50 Sob stories
53 Off-road bikes, for short
54 Cameo shape
55 Numeral at the top of grandfather clocks
56 Yonder yacht
58 "___ Misérables"
59 In romantic pursuit
64 Annoy
65 Draw forth
66 43rd president's nickname
67 Crime lab evidence
68 Satisfy, as a mortgage
69 Shuts tightly

DOWN

1 Remind too often
2 Wrath
3 Trivial complaint
4 Subject of Handel's "Messiah"
5 Beginning on
6 16th president's nickname
7 Rap artist's entourage
8 Less lofty
9 National paper
10 Home for hogs
11 Place of worship
12 When many duels were held
13 Long-eared hound
18 Make mention of
22 Bit of desert flora
23 ___ Strauss jeans
24 Grand-scale
25 Zilch
27 Optimistic feelings
28 Umpire's yell
30 Vacation resort policy, perhaps
33 Tooth covering
35 Soccer spectator's shout
36 Student of Socrates
38 Compound containing O3
39 Hang around (for)
40 "House Hunters" cable channel
41 Thumbs-up votes
44 Unemotional
45 Where to find stalactites and stalagmites
46 Fairbanks's home
48 "M*A*S*H" soft drink
51 Equip
52 So-called "white magic"
53 Put up a fuss
57 Discontinues
59 The "p" in m.p.h.
60 "Just a cotton-pickin' minute!"
61 Bout-sanctioning org.
62 Olive ___ (Popeye's sweetie)
63 W. Hemisphere alliance

by Stanley Newman

20

ACROSS

1 Band with the 22× platinum album "Black in Black"
5 Second-in-command to Captain Kirk
10 State south of Manitoba: Abbr.
14 Mythological hammer thrower
15 Bejeweled headgear
16 River to the Seine
17 Make gentle
18 Innocent ___ proven guilty
19 TV show for which Bill Cosby won three Emmys
20 Squelches early
23 Immigrant's course: Abbr.
24 Donkey
25 Ones dealing in futures?
29 Like the sound of a teakettle
32 Move so as to hear better, say
33 Took care of, as a bill
34 Got the wrinkles out
38 Mai ___
39 Capital of Latvia
40 Queen, en Español
41 Edible seaweed
42 Raptorial seabird
43 Syrup sources
44 Pseudonym of the artist Romain de Tirtoff
45 Likes a whole lot
47 Caveat ___
49 Stanley who co-directed "Singin' in the Rain"
50 Bit of song and dance, e.g.
53 "Ain't ___ shame?"
54 51-Down's talent . . . or what the circled squares represent?
59 Puzzle with a start and a finish
62 Scent
63 Once again
64 Smart ___
65 Drainage system
66 Michael of "Arrested Development"
67 Half-and-half carton, often
68 Name of eight English kings
69 Water whirled

DOWN

1 Envelope abbr.
2 Spiced Indian tea
3 Pricey bubbly
4 Lover of Troilus in a Shakespeare play
5 Gobsmack
6 Vessel of 1492
7 "#@*!" and such
8 Breaks down, in a way
9 Former "Meet the Press" host Marvin
10 "Beats me!"
11 Insult, slangily
12 Nile reptile
13 Critical
21 "___ be back!"
22 Like many items listed on eBay
26 Put on a show
27 Theater district
28 One taking potshots
29 Butter or mayo
30 Weave, shag or braids
31 Turkish "dollars"
32 Tenancy document
35 What people think of you, for short
36 Word with baby, bath or banana
37 Uptown dir. in N.Y.C.
41 Stayed with the leader
43 Computer list
46 Turn down, as a manuscript
48 Russian fighter jet
50 Say "O.K."
51 Circus performer
52 Official with a stopwatch
55 Deep cut
56 ___ a one
57 Anyone who can speak Klingon, e.g.
58 Go to and fro
59 "The Amazing Race" necessity
60 "Prince ___" ("Aladdin" song)
61 Buddhist state

by Dan Feyer

ACROSS

1 Scratch
4 Cries out loud
8 Football team with a blue horseshoe on its helmet
13 ___-Wan Kenobi
14 Annoying computer message
16 Nail a test
17 Stogie holder
19 Letter after eta
20 Kitchen range
21 Florida city on the Gulf
23 Singer Horne
25 "___ the Explorer" (Nickelodeon show)
26 NBC skit show since '75
27 What a TV host often reads from
30 Type
32 "The buck stops here" pres.
33 Place to hang a jacket
39 Words in an analogy
41 Thurman of Hollywood
42 Pet lovers' org.
43 Sign of alien life, some say
47 Chihuahua's bark
48 Tiny amount
49 Army do
52 HBO alternative
55 Fishing sticks
58 "I cannot tell ___"
59 Fessed up
62 Follow
65 Japanese port
66 The French Open is the only Grand Slam tournament played on this
68 "On the ___ hand . . ."
69 Completely dead, as an engine
70 "Here ___ Again" (1987 Whitesnake hit)
71 Razz
72 Projects for beavers
73 Card below a jack

DOWN

1 Footwear that may be worn with PJs
2 Somewhat
3 Verdi opera
4 Venus's sister with a tennis racket
5 "The Lord of the Rings" creature
6 Bric-a-___
7 "'Tis a pity"
8 Bit of razzing
9 Cinco + tres
10 Lecherous looks
11 Mythical giant
12 Play for time
15 Seized vehicle
18 With: Fr.
22 Clapton of rock
24 Path of a fly ball
27 Trendy
28 The Beatles' "Back in the ___"
29 Gloomy
31 Dramatic boxing results, briefly
34 "Mad Men" network
35 Soft powder
36 Astronaut's attire
37 Off-white shade
38 President whose father co-founded Yale's Skull and Bones
40 Choose (to)
44 Auto maintenance
45 One who's worshiped
46 ___ of Good Feelings
50 Chooses for office
51 Excessive lover of the grape
52 Get a move on
53 Waste maker, in a proverb
54 Midwest city whose name is a poker variety
56 All 52 cards
57 Leafy course
60 Just manages, with "out"
61 California's ___ Valley
63 Longing
64 School on the Thames
67 "Dee-lish!"

by Ian C. Livengood

22

ACROSS

1 Convenience for working travelers
7 The latest
11 The holder
14 Dog that merits "Good boy!"
15 Score all over
16 Hoppy brew
17 Tumblers
19 Coal holder
20 Perry of "Beverly Hills 90210"
21 Flu symptom
22 Execs' degs.
23 /, to a bowler
25 Beethoven's Third
27 Frank's wife before Mia
30 N.F.L. ball carriers
31 Result of pushing too hard?
32 Tumblers
37 PC whizzes
38 Miler Sebastian
39 Crinkly sole material
41 Tumblers
44 "Would ___ to you?"
45 Bailed-out insurance co.
46 Scores for 30-Across
47 Money spent
49 Stomach problem
51 Mice, to owls
52 Marie with two Nobels
54 "Woe is me!"
58 First of three X's or O's
59 Tumblers
61 "Dig in!"
62 ___ of Man
63 Garlicky shrimp dish
64 Nonfielding A.L. players
65 Rare airline offering, nowadays
66 Repeated

DOWN

1 Lounge around
2 "___ Ben Adhem"
3 Hunt-and-___ (typing method)
4 Little squirts
5 U.K. wordsmith's ref.
6 Quick-to-erect homes
7 Born yesterday, so to speak
8 "Behold," to Caesar
9 Cabbie's query
10 The "S" in CBS: Abbr.
11 Old-fashioned pregnancy check
12 Hipbone-related
13 Good problem solvers, as a group
18 Big name in Italian fashion
22 Wisdom teeth, e.g.
24 Otto von Bismarck's realm
26 Protective part of a trunk
27 Play a role
28 Penthouse perk
29 Ones making plans
33 Unfriendly, as a greeting
34 Playfully shy
35 King's trappings
36 Went flat-out
40 Problem for lispers
42 Jingly pocket item
43 Requirement to hunt or drive
47 Made a choice
48 Dickens's ___ Heep
49 "Family Matters" dweeb
50 Big Indian
53 The Bruins' sch.
55 Long wheels
56 Mont Blanc, par exemple
57 Lost traction
59 Huck's raftmate
60 700, to Caesar

by Ed Sessa

ACROSS

1 Fateful day for Caesar
5 All-night dance party
9 Laboratory maze runners
13 Scrabble draw
14 Completely confused
16 The "E" in Q.E.D.
17 Stratford-upon-___
18 Manicurists treat them
19 Sluggish from sedatives
20 Catch Groucho while fishing?
22 Blues player's instrument?
24 18-wheeler
25 Chaotic battles
26 French farewell
28 Falafel holders
29 Cereal that doesn't really taste like anything?
31 Period of duty
35 1930s-'40s prez
36 Beyond repair
38 Expected to arrive
39 Islamic decree
42 Wildcat that can't sit still?
45 Dances to Hawaiian music
47 Astronaut Armstrong and others
48 Burning emergency signals
50 New ___ (35-Across's program)
51 Levy paid by white-collar workers?
52 Formal wear for one's belly?
56 Cupid, to the Greeks
57 What an electric meter indicates
59 Corn bread
60 "99 Luftballons" singer
61 Fabric that's glossy on one side
62 Feudin' with, say
63 June 6, 1944
64 Left the scene
65 Numbers to be crunched

DOWN

1 Type used for emphasis: Abbr.
2 Hard-to-please celeb
3 North Carolina university
4 Submits, as a manuscript
5 Rampaged
6 Creator of the game Missile Command
7 Engine type pioneered by the Buick Special
8 Snakelike fish
9 Most sunburned
10 Got out of bed
11 Spanish finger food
12 River of Hades
15 Plus column entry
21 Easily cowed
23 "Regrettably . . ."
25 Scramble
26 Alan who played Hawkeye
27 Object thrown in a pub
28 17th-century diarist Samuel
29 Teen girl's close chum, for short
30 Laugh track sounds
32 Pastoral poem
33 Convent residents
34 Common cowboy nickname
37 Slumlord's building
40 "How about it?"
41 Otherworldly glow
43 500 sheets of paper
44 Large leaf on which a frog may repose
46 Upscale marquee owned by Toyota
48 Dismissed from "The Apprentice"
49 Helmsley known as the Queen of Mean
50 Began eating
51 Look after, as a bar
52 London art gallery
53 "Animal House" party costume
54 Peck, pint or pound
55 Leather-wearing TV princess
58 Lumberjack's tool

by Patrick Berry

24

ACROSS

1 Elba or Capri
5 Pleasant, weatherwise
10 Measure of sugar: Abbr.
14 Reduction of sugar intake, e.g.
15 Trojan War epic
16 Pro ___ (proportionately)
17 Where sad trash collectors get together?
19 Savings options for the golden yrs.
20 Stadium area
21 Cow sound
22 Mends, as socks
23 The "P" of PT boat
25 Put to good effect
27 Rock's ___ Rose
28 Where future motorists get together?
31 Architect I. M. ___
32 Fencer's sword
33 End of a student's e-mail address
34 Living off the land?
36 Smidgen
38 Org. for a Big Apple cop
42 Sir ___ McKellen
45 Snap up
48 Rousing cry at a ring
49 Where elderly picnickers get together?
53 Hair spiffer-upper
54 Holey brewing gadget
55 Spa treatment that might include two cucumber slices
57 Group of eight
58 Cries of surprise
61 Arrests
62 Soul singer Redding
63 Where stranded canoeists get together?
66 Lacking company
67 "I feel the same"
68 Gentleman's partner
69 Basic work units
70 Colorado skiing town
71 Yankee superslugger, to fans

DOWN

1 Coup leader ___ Amin
2 Extra costs of smoking and drinking
3 "Just forget about this"
4 Once-popular anesthetic
5 Offer on eBay
6 Grad
7 Chauffeur-driven auto
8 Plan, as an itinerary
9 Fabric amts.
10 Preliminary test
11 Hispanic neighborhood
12 One of four for "The Star-Spangled Banner"
13 Got a D or better
18 Wash away, as soil
22 Conked out
23 Elderly Smurf
24 Cut (off)
26 French tea
29 Spider's creation
30 Whinny
35 Sites for military flights
37 Prefix with athlete
39 Boo Boo's buddy in Jellystone Park
40 "Go right ahead"
41 Texas computer giant started in a dorm room
43 Not much
44 Stanley Cup org.
46 Furry extraterrestrial in a 1980s sitcom
47 Mel with "1,000 voices"
49 Actor Peter of "Becket"
50 Course taken by a plane or missile
51 Dining
52 Gets hitched in haste
56 French president Nicolas Sarkozy's wife
59 URL starter
60 Pump or loafer
63 "Kill Bill" co-star Thurman
64 Seemingly forever
65 Elizabethan dramatist Thomas

by Lynn Lempel

ACROSS

1 Nurses at the bar
5 "Pipe down!"
9 Derive logically
14 Bad child's stocking filler
15 Indiana/Kentucky border river
16 Sound from a stable
17 Kendrick of "Up in the Air"
18 ___ contendere
19 North Dakota city
20 Time in the title of a 1965 Wilson Pickett hit
23 Skedaddles
24 Trial fig.
25 Doo-woppers ___ Na Na
28 TV oilman-turned-private eye
33 Doll's cry
37 Aussie bounder
38 Friars Club event
39 Multiple-dwelling buildings
43 Chop finely
44 Light bulb inventor's inits.
45 Light carriage
46 Droopy-eared dog
50 Small bill
51 ___-wolf
52 Perform better than
57 Question that follows "O Brother" in film . . . and a hint to this puzzle's theme
61 Grotto isle of Italy
64 Grotto color at 61-Across
65 Java servers
66 Say "#%@!"
67 Calls upon
68 20-0 baseball score, say
69 Ill-suited
70 "___ we forget . . ."
71 Keeps after taxes

DOWN

1 Con jobs
2 Greek column style
3 Bamboo-munching critter
4 Way of looking at things
5 ___ Kong
6 "We're in trouble!"
7 Delta deposit
8 Commotion
9 Yet to happen, at law
10 In the vicinity
11 Douglas ___
12 Cadbury confection
13 Letter before sigma
21 Suffix in poli sci
22 Ear-related prefix
25 Squirrel away
26 Minor prophet of the Old Testament
27 Prone to fidgeting
29 Prepare for combat
30 Tip of a boot
31 Scout's rider of early TV
32 ___-chef (kitchen's number two)
33 Cuban musical form
34 Bee-related
35 Parson's home
36 Circle segments
40 Vacation souvenir wear
41 Letter after sigma
42 Old biddy
47 Everyday article
48 Like some teas
49 Part of a pointillist painting
53 Driver's one-eighty
54 Severe pang
55 Glazed or powdered item
56 Gives the boot
57 Cylindrical sandwich
58 Threat-ending word
59 Razor-billed birds
60 Take five
61 CBS drama with DNA testing
62 Bristle on barley
63 Split ___

by C. W. Stewart

26

ACROSS

1 "Now!," in a memo
5 Prefix with morphosis
9 Knight's protection
14 Colorado skiing mecca
15 Man from Oman, e.g.
16 Jeweler's magnifying tool
17 Simultaneously
19 Beatnik's "Gotcha"
20 "Damn!," e.g.
21 Minnesota's capital
22 Like many itchy mutts
26 Oscar : film :: ___ : TV
27 "Get ___ here! ("Scram!")
28 Get guns again
30 Yellow, as a banana
31 Art of "The Honeymooners"
34 Star pitcher
37 Likely reaction to fried ants
38 Creature who might disagree with the saying at the ends of 17-, 22-, 48- and 56- Across
39 Opposite of mult.
40 "O Sole ___"
41 Perjury and piracy, for two
42 Vena ___ (passage to the heart)
43 Author Ephron and others
45 Not liquid or gaseous
46 Honey makers
48 Be deliberative
52 Moral standards
54 Bar mitzvah scroll
55 "Now!," in Nicaragua
56 Not wanting to be shot?
60 Send, as payment
61 Paradigm of happiness
62 Final Four org.
63 Gown
64 ___ Ranger
65 Airhead

DOWN

1 Actress Gardner
2 "I've got a mule, and her name is ___"
3 Be under the weather
4 Throw a bone to
5 Indigenous New Zealanders
6 Young's partner in accounting
7 "Be silent," musically
8 Honest ___ (presidential moniker)
9 Came down to earth
10 TV's "___ Room"
11 "It's hard to be humble when you're as great as I am" speaker
12 Drug from poppies
13 Answer
18 Oom-pah-pah instrument
21 Derisive looks
22 Discussion site
23 One of the Mario Brothers
24 Classic 1982 movie line spoken with an outstretched finger
25 Bert's pal on "Sesame Street"
29 Affirmative vote
31 Gem units
32 Like the witness in "Witness"
33 Meas. of engine speed
35 Honda model with a palindromic name
36 Circumvent
38 Passé TV hookup
42 Ranch worker
44 Egyptian god of the underworld
45 Proxima Centauri, for one
46 Feature of Dumbledore or Merlin
47 Old-time anesthetic
49 Author Calvino
50 "___ is an island . . ."
51 Krispy ___ doughnuts
53 Meowers
56 250, in old Rome
57 Chem., for one
58 Fedora or fez
59 Big name in Bosox history

by Jeff Chen

ACROSS

1 Healthful retreats
5 Suitcases
9 Minor quarrel
13 Result of four balls, in baseball
14 Ear-related
15 Nothin'
16 "A Death in the Family" author
17 1964 Beatles hit
19 Part of school that includes push-ups and sit-ups
21 Hive dweller
22 Alternative rock genre
23 Showman associated with the quote "There's a sucker born every minute"
28 Religious observance
30 Illustrator Edward
31 WSW's opposite
32 Determined to do
33 Ski lift
34 Somewhat
35 Family groups
36 Gangster's gun
37 "Et tu, ___?"
38 Is bedridden, say
39 Sumptuous
40 More fit
41 Hawaiian souvenir
42 Any of the Seven Dwarfs, by profession
43 Constricting snakes
44 Chinese restaurant chain
46 "___ the ramparts . . ."
47 Superannuated
48 Acidity of alkalinity
52 Rating of "Avatar"
57 Neat
58 Hawaiian island
59 Expenditures
60 Consumer
61 Collector's ___
62 Seven things for a sailor
63 Stable locks?

DOWN

1 Exchange
2 Call on an intercom, as a doctor
3 Baldwin who has hosted "S.N.L." more times than anyone else
4 Some Halloween costumes
5 Kiss
6 "Exodus" hero
7 Rodeo female
8 Drool
9 Expression that includes a lip curl
10 Salary
11 Brouhaha
12 Sigma's follower
14 Lhasa ___ (dog)
18 Calf's meat
20 Prayer enders
23 U.S. mail holders
24 Merchant
25 Part of a galaxy
26 Brings together
27 Something that's fed along a street
28 What the Red Cross provides
29 Slanted type
30 Like tennis rackets and harps
32 Where dandruff accumulates
34 Place where trees are studied
37 Tower of ___
39 Retired hockey great Eric
42 West African land
45 Dull
46 Cry of panic
48 Things to hang hats on
49 MasterCard competitor
50 Place of bliss
51 Bard's instrument
52 Hawaiian dish
53 Gangster's gun
54 Article seen in many places
55 Election day: Abbr.
56 Pilot's approximation, for short

by David Steinberg

28

ACROSS

1 "Mamma Mia" singers
5 Sheath of connective tissue
11 Buddy, for short
14 Object of pity for Mr. T
15 Parthenon goddess
16 Sock-in-the-gut reaction
17 1960 Jerry Lewis fairy tale spoof
19 UV ray-blocking stat
20 Once known as
21 Stephen of "Still Crazy"
22 Suit to ___
23 Reality show featuring Whitney Houston and her then-husband
28 Help pull off a crime
29 $5 bills, slangily
30 Radius neighbors
31 Judge's wear
32 Poppycock
33 "Ciao for now!"
34 NBC show with skits, in brief
35 Part of a bray
36 Mrs. Gorbachev
37 Eurasian range
39 M.D. concerned with tonsils
40 Backyard pond fish
43 Great Chicago Fire scapegoat Mrs. ___
45 "Just as I suspected!"
46 "Hor." neighbor, on old TVs
47 Second offer, as on eBay
48 Flair
49 Poems of praise
50 Healthy delivery, perhaps
53 Some QB turnovers: Abbr.
54 Rap's Dr. ___
55 Norma ___ (Sally Field role)
56 Up to, in ads
57 Bowl over
62 Suffix with ethyl
63 Got back, as hair by a Rogaine user
64 Nephew of Abel
65 ___ Bingle (Crosby)
66 Think creatively
67 Invitation letters

DOWN

1 N.Y. Jets' org.
2 Avril Lavigne's "Sk8er ___"
3 Rhett and Scarlett's child
4 Firm, as pasta
5 A way off
6 Antismuggling org.
7 Cold dessert
8 People profiled in People
9 Furniture decoration
10 Small battery
11 Dish often served with franks
12 Suspended ore conveyor, e.g.
13 Side with the ball
18 Brain wave monitor, briefly
22 Van Gogh's "Sunflowers" setting
23 Granola servings
24 Black, in poetry
25 With no room to spare
26 High-pitched double-reeds
27 Salesman's exhortation
33 Daiquiri fruit
35 Corporate head?
36 Post-op program
38 Claude of "Casablanca"
41 Cookie with crème in the middle
42 ___-bitsy
43 Traveled like Sputnik
44 Like Simba or Nala
45 "Solve for x" subject
46 First spacecraft to reach Uranus and Neptune
48 Cause to see red
51 Sat
52 Comment during a cold snap
57 Popular party day: Abbr.
58 Vegas action
59 Meadow mother
60 Part of U.S.S.R.: Abbr.
61 Recipe amt.

by Scott Atkinson

ACROSS

1 Sailing
5 "Remember the ___!" (Texan's cry)
10 "___ and Circumstance"
14 Mideast royal name
15 "She loves me, she loves me not . . ." flower part
16 Memento of an old wound
17 Acquire sudden riches
19 Capture
20 Boxing venue
21 Alter, as the Constitution
23 Slowing, in music: Abbr.
24 Talk, talk and talk some more
25 Groove
27 Tincture of ___
29 Help out a panhandler
33 Suffix with ethyl
34 Make peeved
35 Central street name
36 Big stingers
39 Cheer for a toreador
40 Bridge positions
41 Capital of Samoa
42 Charged particle
43 Greyhound, e.g.
44 What multiple winners of a lottery must do
50 Equipment next to swings and seesaws
51 Popeye's Olive ___
52 ___ out a living
53 Old nuclear regulatory org.
54 Bigwig
57 Florida key, e.g.
59 Portable product for music lovers
61 Absolutely amazed
63 Queue
64 Black-and-white cookies
65 Classic name for a French poodle
66 Observes
67 Busybody
68 One-spot cards

DOWN

1 Tests, as ore
2 Minor despot
3 "I've got it!"
4 Deuce follower, in tennis
5 Human's hairy cousin
6 Smooth, in music
7 Proton's place
8 Y chromosome carrier
9 Satan
10 Winter clock setting in L.A.
11 Flutelike instruments
12 Achieving success
13 Fifth and sixth graders, typically
18 Actresses Allen and Black
22 Cry from Homer Simpson
26 Apply
28 Table linen fabric
30 Made good on, as a loan
31 "Winnie-the-Pooh" writer
32 Before, poetically
36 Christmas drinks
37 Symbol of Americanism
38 Polymeric compound in breast implants
39 "How exciting!"
40 The Father of Geometry
42 Birth announcement for babies with blue caps
43 Chesapeake ___
45 X
46 Odds and ends for sale
47 Relating to the lower part of the upper body
48 Michael of "Caddyshack"
49 Popular computer game with geometric shapes
55 Make yawn
56 Actor Wilson
58 Davenport
60 ___ Moines, Iowa
62 That: Sp.

by Mark Feldman

30

ACROSS

1 Not reacting to pain, say
6 Playboy centerfold, e.g.
11 Col. Sanders's restaurant
14 Go round and round
15 Tennis champ Agassi
16 ". . . ___ he drove out of sight"
17 Aid for a person with a limp
19 Yang's counterpart
20 Sound from a mouse
21 Blue Ribbon beer brewer
23 Brussels ___
26 Arabian V.I.P.'s
27 River past Westminster Palace
28 Party handouts
30 "That's ___!" ("Not true!")
31 Cosmetician Adrien
32 Machine tooth
35 ___ Alamos, N.M.
36 Drug from Colombia
38 "Long ___ and far away . . ."
39 Virgil's 61
40 Long-armed ape, for short
41 Late West Virginia senator Robert
42 W.W. II admiral Chester
44 Island where many a 40-Across lives
46 Disheveled
48 Most boneheaded
49 One out of prison
50 Mick Jagger and bandmates, informally
52 ___ carte
53 1941 Orson Welles classic
58 Architect I. M. ___
59 French word before cuisine or couture
60 Respected tribe member
61 ID on an I.R.S. form
62 ___ a positive note
63 Actress Winona

DOWN

1 Opposite NNE
2 Old "Up, up and away" carrier
3 Texaco's business
4 Irritating
5 In-group
6 Senate gofers
7 Early Peruvian
8 Fargo's home: Abbr.
9 Keats's "Ode on a Grecian ___"
10 Hotel room door feature
11 Nixon's Florida home
12 Pat down, as for weapons
13 Number after a decimal in a price
18 Items in a Planters can
22 ___ Lingus
23 Play for time
24 Showy flowers
25 Creating a ruckus
26 Stereotypical Swedish man's name
28 Writer Kafka
29 Fat as ___
31 Nervous as ___
33 Fairy tale monsters
34 Whom Vladimir and Estragon were waiting for, in a Beckett play
36 War chief Black Horse's tribe
37 Copier input: Abbr.
41 In a quick and lively manner
43 Judge in the O. J. Simpson trial
44 Common shape for a dog biscuit
45 First game of the season
46 Harvests
47 Connections for car wheels
48 Egg carton count
50 Poker variety
51 Latin jazz great Puente
54 Author Fleming or McEwan
55 Put two and two together
56 Jacqueline Kennedy ___ Bouvier
57 Blunder

by Holden Baker

ACROSS

1 Toy gun shot
4 Machine that was often cloned
9 Molecular matter
13 "Don't Bring Me Down" band, for short
14 It may be "golden" in mathematics
15 Kind of shark
16 Where a cowpuncher may work
18 Sweat spot
19 School attended by James Bond . . . and Ian Fleming
20 Big bears
22 Drink made with vodka, coffee liqueur and cream
26 Equipment for Olympian Lindsey Vonn
27 Aunts, in Arles
30 "Exodus" hero
33 Grades in the mid-70s
35 "Arrivederci"
36 "Sorry if that rude word offended you"
40 Double-reed woodwind
41 Prefix with -morphism
42 "What a pleasant surprise!"
43 Letter-writing prisoner, perhaps
46 Quatre+un
48 Play whence the phrase "the most unkindest cut of all"
53 Group for young people coping with parental substance abuse
55 "Othello" villain
56 Green fruit
57 What the last words in 16-, 22-, 36- and 48-Across are
61 ___ fixe
62 "Fiddler on the Roof" milkman
63 Game cube
64 Signs of approval
65 Pictures that may be difficult to focus on
66 Word repeated in a classic "When Harry Met Sally . . ." scene

DOWN

1 Moisten, as grass
2 Animator Don
3 "Same here"
4 Like the verb "to be": Abbr.
5 Sheep's cry
6 Everest, e.g.: Abbr.
7 Selects
8 Any regular on "The View," e.g.
9 Atmosphere, as at a restaurant
10 Quentin who directed "Inglourious Basterds"
11 "I get it already!"
12 Does some lawn work
17 Sinusitis docs
21 1/7 of a Spanish week
23 Kitchen utensil brand name
24 Nothing, in Paris
25 1972 #2 hit for Bill Withers
28 Individually
29 Greenwich Village neighbor
30 Individually
31 "Streamers" playwright David
32 Exhibiting fierce determination
34 Matches, as two tapes
37 Sheriffs' sidekicks
38 Bank guarantor, for short
39 "Five Women" author Jaffe
44 Word that can follow pale, brown or cask
45 Told fibs
47 British monarch beginning in '52
49 Overseas diplomat in N.Y.C., say
50 Little Orphan Annie's dog
51 Texas A&M athlete
52 Rock's Guns N'___
53 Like, with "to"
54 Beach resort at the entrance to the Lagoon of Venice
58 Model Herzigova
59 Six-Day War land: Abbr.
60 Word with the longest entry in the O.E.D.

by Brendan Emmett Quigley

32

ACROSS

1 Path of a Hail Mary pass
4 "Remember the ___!" (cry of 1836)
9 Wranglers, e.g.
14 ___ de Janeiro
15 Pine exudation
16 Baby hooter
17 The Braves, on scoreboards
18 "Carpe diem"
20 Officer's identification
22 Family car
23 Imitate
24 Poverty
26 Burst of wind
28 Quickly satisfy one's hunger
34 "___ the land of the free . . ."
35 Spike, as the punch
36 Birth-related
38 Large number
40 Harvests
43 Owner of the bed that was too soft in "Goldilocks and the Three Bears"
44 Takes on, as workers
46 Diploma feature
48 Hosp. employee
49 Rough-and-tumble outdoor kids' game
53 London art gallery
54 Secular
55 Where you might get into hot water?
58 Passover feast
61 Motored
64 Commonplace utterance . . . or a description of 18-, 28- and 49-Across?
67 Half a dozen
68 Shake hands (on)
69 Schindler of "Schindler's List"
70 Touch on the shoulder, say
71 Breakfast, lunch and dinner
72 First-time drivers, often
73 ___-mo

DOWN

1 The "A" in U.A.E.
2 Hayworth of "Cover Girl"
3 Late 1940s to about 1990
4 Weapons depot
5 Actor ___ J. Cobb
6 Sale tag words
7 1987 Masters winner Larry
8 Fidgety
9 First impeached U.S. president
10 Mother in a flock
11 Alan of "Crimes and Misdemeanors"
12 Certain tide
13 Eye problem
19 Fully stretched
21 Talk and talk and talk
25 Ski lift
27 Squad
28 Exclamation before "darn it!"
29 Excavated item, maybe
30 What most of hail is
31 Razz
32 Regardless of the results
33 Busch Gardens locale
37 Singer k. d. ___
39 Openly grieved
41 Caress
42 Comic Mort
45 Squirrels away
47 Captains and commanders
50 Lone Star State sch.
51 Extremely popular
52 Tree with cones
55 Offer that's too good to be true, often
56 Beep, as a doctor
57 Gillette brand
59 Gaelic tongue
60 ___ over the coals
62 Medicine bottle
63 World's fair
65 Animation frame
66 ___ Bernardino Mountains

by John Dunn

ACROSS

1 Like a cool cat
4 Not the brightest bulb on the tree
8 U. of Maryland team
13 "___ seeing things?"
14 "Hollyoaks" actress ___ Atkinson
15 Bozo
16 Fuel for some trucks
18 Eating only certain things
19 With 55-Across, source of this puzzle's quote (which starts in box #38)
21 Rick's "Casablanca" love
22 Word after public or private
23 Shopping mecca
26 Danish astronomer Brahe
29 Scott in an 1857 Supreme Court case
33 Chest: Prefix
35 Touch down
37 Manning of the gridiron
38 "Au contraire!"
39 "In what way?"
40 Cast out
42 Where cranberries grow
43 In stitches
45 Calls during curtain calls
46 Wooden shoe's sound
48 How nonreading musicians play
50 Lean (on)
51 Yevtushenko's "Babi ___"
53 Abound (with)
55 See 19-Across
62 Jewish holiday in Adar
63 Insect known for conducting raids
64 "Inferno" writer
65 Wind indicators
66 Calendar unit
67 Powerful chess piece
68 Added stipulations
69 Leave slack-jawed

DOWN

1 Muslim's pilgrimage
2 Mideast leader
3 Place to fish from
4 Does some business with
5 "Don't worry about me"
6 Year the Department of Homeland Security was created
7 Visibly terrified
8 Slightly drunk
9 Trimmed to fit, say
10 Filthy ___
11 Pig's container, in a saying
12 Pig's container
14 Earth sci.
17 Some beach house supports
20 Gas in lights
23 "Morning Joe" TV channel
24 "You're such ___" (teen put-down)
25 "Unhand me!"
27 Any "Jurassic Park" dinosaur
28 "Yee-___!"
30 Chaucer pilgrim
31 It shines in España
32 Like a space cadet
34 Santa syllables
36 ___ Spiegel (German magazine)
39 Numbered rte.
41 Big name in GPS devices
44 River of Aragón
45 Zephyrs
47 It glitters but isn't gold
49 Within easy reach
52 Madison Avenue workers
54 Cupid, to the Greeks
55 Party with poi
56 Author Sarah ___ Jewett
57 Broad bean
58 Certain Fed
59 "Nothin' "
60 Be a busy beaver
61 Eye woe
62 A.S.A.P.

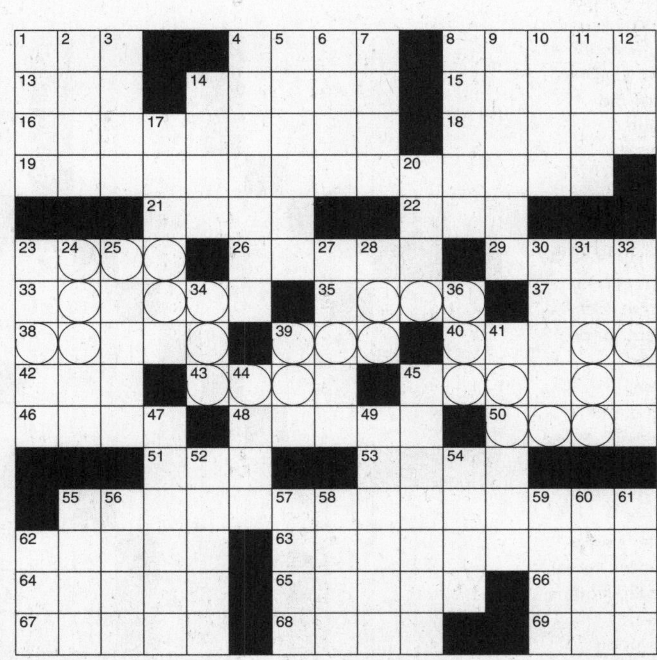

by Daniel A. Finan

34

ACROSS

1 Dog's bark
7 Nincompoop
10 Regarding, on a memo
14 ___ and 3-Down
15 "Xanadu" grp.
16 Refrigerate
17 Italian cheese that's often grated
18 Fishing pole
19 Greek god with a bow and arrow
20 Editors' marks meaning "put back in"
21 Commercial lead-in for Rooter
22 ___ and 10-Down
23 Latin "to be"
24 Disputed region between Pakistan and India
26 Office transcribers
28 Stylish again
32 Pooh's friend in "Winnie-the-Pooh"
35 Staircase aid
36 Flew high
37 Bottoms of crankcases
39 Not natural
40 Smitten
41 What may have the makings of a hero?
42 Calls from Rocky
43 Foot gear for an N.H.L.'er
44 Unfasten
46 Having a fright
48 Competent
52 ___ and 38-Down
55 Christian in fashion
56 Cloudless
57 Chorister's voice
58 Frequent, in verse
59 City north of San Francisco
60 Gin flavoring
61 Hwy.
62 ___ and 49-Down
63 Easter roasts
64 Road curve
65 Tenant

DOWN

1 Lower in rank
2 Becomes inoperable, maybe, as an old machine
3 14-Across and ___
4 Playing marbles
5 Govt. rules
6 To's opposite
7 Spray type
8 Lazy people
9 Gomorrah's sister city
10 22-Across and ___
11 Romance writer Roberts
12 Corner piece in chess
13 Besides
21 Indian princesses
24 "The Family Circus" cartoonist Bil
25 Funny in a twisted way
27 Commit a basketball infraction
29 Buffet meal carrier
30 Edit menu command
31 Tributes in verse
32 Louis XIV et Louis XVI
33 Sty sound
34 Earthen pot
36 Dieter's meal, maybe
38 52-Across and ___
39 Poetic rhythm
41 Lowers in rank
44 Snow buildups
45 Mideast confections
47 Idolize
49 62-Across and ___
50 Hanukkah treat
51 Irregularly edged
52 Hit TV show set in Korea
53 Jazz great Fitzgerald
54 Elemental unit
56 Part of an apple
59 Gridiron grp.

by Emily L. Lilly

ACROSS

1 Surmise
6 Say "Oh, that was nothing," say
11 "I ___ you one!"
14 Awaken
15 "M," "W," or "Z"
16 Small dog, for short
17 Picture in one's head
19 Barnyard male
20 Gucci of fashion
21 Face-to-face test
22 Seven-times-a-week newspaper
24 Shaving woes
26 New Orleans sandwiches, informally
27 "Do you have any jacks?" response, maybe
30 Bedding material
31 Basketballer nicknamed the Big Aristotle
32 Washer cycle
34 Nittany Lions' sch.
37 Regained one's winning status . . . or a hint to this puzzle's circled letters
41 "The buck stops here" prez
42 Speech setting
43 First, second and reverse
44 Suitcase attachment, for short
47 Justice Stephen of the Supreme Court
48 $100,000/year, e.g.
50 Rice dish
52 A-number-one
53 Flintstones' pet
54 It takes a while to tell
58 Carpenter's curved tool
59 Seabed
62 32-Down's woodlands mate
63 Carpenter's smoothing tool
64 Al ___ (like some noodles)
65 Goof
66 Madrid man
67 Faint with ecstasy

DOWN

1 "Joy of Cooking" author Rombauer
2 Holiday number
3 Supply with money
4 Native of the land known by natives as Eesti
5 Stephen of "V for Vendetta"
6 Smug look
7 Postaccident conditions
8 Indianapolis 500 track, e.g.
9 Biblical fruit
10 Use for sustenance
11 Football ploy
12 Like a sheep
13 TV awards
18 ___ Lomond
23 Grandpa on "The Simpsons"
25 Emerald ___
26 Pub order
27 One dressed in black, maybe
28 Cross to bear
29 Garden enrichment
30 Propaganda, often
32 62-Across's woodlands mate
33 Honor society letter
35 Desertlike
36 "Back in the ___"
38 Time of reckoning
39 Indian tourist city
40 Hearty entree that may be cooked in a Dutch oven
45 Beaver's work
46 Scout units
47 Gooey mass
48 Diamond alternative
49 Zeal
50 Elton John's instrument
51 Word before self or strength
53 College V.I.P.
55 "___ extra cost!"
56 Head for
57 "You said it, brother!"
60 The Indians or Browns, on a scoreboard
61 Some E.R. cases

by Ian Livengood

36

ACROSS

1 Wrestling surfaces
5 Small plateaus
10 Gets on in years
14 Pioneering razor with a pivoting head
15 Bright-eyed and bushy-tailed
16 Tedious way to learn
17 Actor Penn with two 23-Across
18 Big name in Scotch
19 Bart Simpson's brainy sister
20 Meal money in Manitoba?
23 Academy Awards
24 Show that launched Eddie Murphy and Chevy Chase, for short
25 Gangster's gun
28 Golf peg
29 Quick bite
32 Persistent, irritating critic
34 Meal money in California?
36 Unconscious state
39 Cenozoic or Mesozoic
40 Scots Gaelic
41 Meal money in Tuscany?
46 Comic's asset
47 Feudal worker
48 Tanning lotion letters
51 Spanish "that"
52 Actor Cage, familiarly
54 Daytona 500 acronym
56 Meal money in Massachusetts?
60 Was sorry about
62 The Ram
63 Benevolent and Protective Order group
64 Not much
65 Boardinghouse window sign
66 Baldwin of "30 Rock"
67 Not his
68 New Mexico county whose seat is Alamogordo
69 Actress Sedgwick of "The Closer"

DOWN

1 Georgia's bulldog or Princeton's tiger
2 "Relax, soldier!"
3 Hypnotized state
4 Yemen's capital
5 President after Jefferson
6 Home of Zeno
7 Stitched
8 Most Yemenis
9 Eerie
10 Folkie Guthrie
11 On the path to great success
12 U.F.O.'s crew
13 Word repeated in the lyric "From ___ to shining ___"
21 Villain in the title of a James Bond book
22 Ali, before he was Ali
26 Part of baseball's postseason: Abbr.
27 Rug rat
30 British W.W. II gun
31 Parsley, sage, rosemary and thyme
33 Played records at a party, say
34 Where Timbuktu is
35 Opposite of well done
36 Quote from, as a legal case
37 Elevator pioneer Elisha
38 Who owned the too-soft bed that Goldilocks tried
42 Quaint roadside stops
43 Energetically, in music
44 Che Guevara's given name
45 ". . . to buy ___ pig"
48 Mulder's partner on "The X-Files"
49 Green Bay athlete
50 Sprite alternative
53 French painter of "Le Pont de Mantes"
55 The "turf" part of "surf and turf"
57 2:1 or 3:1
58 River near the Great Pyramids
59 Wanton look
60 "Go, team!"
61 Sport-___ (vehicle)

by David Poole

ACROSS

1 Native encountered by Pizarro
5 Shakespeare, with "the"
9 D sharp equivalent
14 "Silent Night" or "Away in a Manger"
15 "By Jove!"
16 Novelist ___ Carol Oates
17 *What "S.R.O." indicates
19 Capital of more than 15 states
20 Arthritis preceder
21 Indy quick-change artists
23 Broadway singer/actress Verdon
26 Part of N.B.
27 *The Magi, e.g.
31 Pal
35 Kanga's little one
36 O'Brien's late-night predecessor and successor
37 Like wet paint
39 Helpers: Abbr.
41 "That hurts!" cries
43 "It's ___ of the times"
44 Kind of league
46 Like about half of a team's games
48 Mauna ___
49 ___ doble (Spanish dance)
50 *Sound from a palace bathroom?
53 What lines with stars at the end indicate in comics
55 Boyfriend
56 "Agreed!"
60 Stilted response to "Who's there?"
64 ___ City, S.D.
65 What the answer to each starred clue is
68 Wield, as influence
69 The "A" in A-Rod
70 Alike: Fr.
71 Response to a schoolyard denial
72 Make a fuss at a public meeting, maybe
73 Use a lasso on

DOWN

1 Skinny
2 Entre ___ (confidentially)
3 Boston cager, briefly
4 Claim
5 Prefix with hazard
6 Tempe sch.
7 Blacksmith's tool
8 Hiding the gray, say
9 VCR button
10 *Group with the 1951 hit "Tell Me Why," with "the"
11 Orpheus' instrument
12 Have ___ (lose it)
13 Thomas Hardy heroine
18 "Do you have a better idea?"
22 Flip
24 Barely make, with "out"
25 Madre's boy
27 "The Sound of Music" family name
28 One of 12 Minor Prophets of the Hebrew Bible
29 Alternatives to reds and whites
30 "Don't even think about it!"
32 Japanese verse form
33 Yens
34 Talking bird
38 Upscale London district
40 *Makeup of a double date
42 Mop
45 Shallowest of the Great Lakes
47 Sam Adams product
51 At the same level (with)
52 Writer of "The 95 Theses"
54 Supplement
56 Steamed
57 What planes do after landing
58 Whipped along
59 Role for 23-Across in "Damn Yankees"
61 Shakespearean schemer
62 [Just like that!]
63 Like some threats
66 Novelist Kesey
67 Bus. card datum

by Richard Chisholm

38

ACROSS

1 "___ hands are the devil's tools"
5 "Nonsense!"
9 Webster of Webster's dictionary
13 Do library study
14 Convention center event, for short
15 Romance or sci-fi
16 Priestly robes
17 ___ year (period of 366 days)
18 Pitchers
19 Wildflower from which the cultivated carrot originated
22 "When ___ See You Again" (1974 #2 hit)
23 AOL or MSN: Abbr.
24 Former C.I.A. chief Porter ___
26 Enzyme suffix
27 Something that is ultimately ruinous
31 Cincinnati baseball team
33 Homer Simpson exclamation
34 Nervous
35 With 37-Across, hair accessory . . . or a literal hint to 19-, 27-, 47- and 56-Across
37 See 35-Across
39 ___ point (very center)
42 Kind of sauce
43 Bank no.
47 Orange item set out by a highway crew
51 "Bali ___" ("South Pacific" song)
52 It may hit a bull's-eye
53 Nearly worthless amount
54 Region
56 Very best
60 Toboggans
61 "Drat!"
62 Taj Mahal city
63 11 ___ and spices (KFC secret ingredients)
64 German river where American and Soviet forces met in 1945
65 Bridle strap
66 "___ can you see . . . ?"
67 Marsh plant
68 German three

DOWN

1 It started in 2003 with the bombing of Baghdad
2 Comic actor Dom
3 Tagged for identification
4 1950s Ford flop
5 Lugosi of horror films
6 Plow team
7 "Cómo está usted?" language
8 [Keeping fingers crossed]
9 Incoming administration's to-do list
10 Minimal paint job
11 Nabs
12 "___ Just Not That Into You" (2009 film)
15 Hair goop
20 Suffix with refuse
21 Letters on a Coppertone bottle
25 "Once bitten, twice ___"
28 Boise's home: Abbr.
29 Lawn base
30 Aykroyd of the Blues Brothers
32 Handed a raw deal from
36 Santa helper
37 Hiss accompanier
38 Literary Rand
39 Bouquets-to-order co.
40 Magic 8 Balls, e.g.
41 Classic Porsche model
42 Fight that's less than a brawl
44 San Diego footballer
45 Some diet drinks have one
46 Kettledrums
48 Doctrine
49 Author James Fenimore
50 Before, poetically
55 Modern greeting form
57 Long-eared equine
58 Toothpaste holder
59 Hurried
60 "___ 'nuff"

by Elizabeth A. Long

ACROSS
1 Farm newborn
5 Yankees' "$275 million man," informally
9 Test proctor's command
14 Like dental surgery
15 "Good one!"
16 Blow the socks off
17 ___ mater
18 The "Y" in Y.S.L.
19 Helicopter part
20 Is ranked #1
23 Bizarre
24 Climate-change protocol city
25 Wee bit
27 Disney dwarf with glasses
30 Sign on a construction site fence
35 Lavatory door sign
37 Part of a school year: Abbr.
38 Carrots' plate-mates
39 Brief visit along the way
42 Declines to participate
44 ___ Sutra
45 Play from which the word "robot" comes
47 Civic maker
48 Dry cleaner's fluid
52 Suffix with slogan
53 Bummed out
54 Congested area, sometimes
56 Drinking binge
59 Megabucks
64 Rig out
66 Fodder holder
67 Part of an apple or the earth
68 Socially polished
69 Source of indigo dye
70 Solemnly swear
71 Whip-cracker
72 Outside of a watermelon
73 Glasgow gal

DOWN
1 Ulster, for one
2 Folkie who sang of Alice
3 Magic item of folklore
4 Toper's back-pocket item
5 "Moving on then . . ."
6 Construction fasteners
7 Forest felines
8 Arnaz of "I Love Lucy"
9 Toper's expense
10 Weezer's music genre
11 Cat in una casa
12 Shirt brand
13 Dweeby sort
21 Like a universal donor's blood
22 Tread heavily
26 Toper, slangily
27 PC storage units
28 Coming up
29 Andrew of New York politics
31 Prefix with con or classical
32 Sierra ___
33 Honor, on a diploma
34 Astronomical red giant
36 Tiffs
40 Corleone who broke Michael's heart
41 "Fee fi fo ___"
43 Rhythmic humming sound
46 "William Tell" composer
49 Ice-T or Ice Cube
50 Isaac Stern's instrument
51 Wrap around
55 L.A.'s area, for short
56 "Surely you ___"
57 Light blue
58 Island "where America's day begins"
60 Pre-1917 autocrat
61 Suddenly bright star
62 Amor's Greek counterpart
63 Trees yielding archery bow wood
65 "___ Got a Secret"

by Kristian House

40

ACROSS

1 Native Louisianan
6 Sass
9 Future's opposite
13 Make a grand speech
14 Physician's org.
15 Pinnacles
17 Appreciated
18 In good order
20 Adam and Eve's first home
21 Watch intently
22 Actor Stephen of "Michael Collins"
23 Annie Oakley, for one
26 Bandleader Shaw and others
29 Mate for 60-Down
30 Combat stress syndrome
35 Watch chains
38 Disney frame
39 Last installment of "The Godfather"
41 Cultural support org.
42 "Stop right there!"
44 Pull a bed prank on
46 Cow sound
48 Funnywoman Boosler
49 Wool gatherer
55 Thanksgiving side dish
56 Rosebush hazards
57 Make woozy
61 Bootblack's service
63 "The Taming of the ___"
64 Ankle bones
65 Title for Galahad
66 "___ bleu!"
67 Viewed
68 Tetley product
69 Set of cultural values

DOWN

1 Porter who wrote "Night and Day"
2 Saharan
3 Gyllenhaal of "Love & Other Drugs"
4 Knife, fork or spoon
5 Rorem who composed the opera "Our Town"
6 Modern surgical tool
7 Zoot-suiter's "Got it!"
8 Noah's ark groupings
9 Congregation leader
10 German exclamation
11 Wagers from those in the know
12 Shelter made of buffalo skin, maybe
16 Blacken, as a steak
19 Oom-___
21 Succeed in appearing to be
24 Lend a hand
25 Buffoon
26 Yiddish writer Sholem
27 Perlman of "Cheers"
28 "Go on . . ."
31 Prince's title: Abbr.
32 Plains Indian
33 Round fig.
34 Writers of bad checks
36 Has-___
37 Overfill
40 ___ of Wight
43 One on the Statue of Liberty is almost three feet long
45 Construction worker
47 Chooses to participate
49 The "S" in CBS: Abbr.
50 Laughs
51 Library admonition
52 Lift
53 W.W. II correspondent Pyle
54 "It's the end of ___"
58 St. Louis's Gateway ___
59 0
60 Mates for a 29-Across
62 Language suffix
63 Opposite of NNW

by Richard Chisholm

ACROSS

1 Neighbor of Kuwait
5 Sugar source
10 Ice Follies venue
14 Half of Mork's sign-off
15 Volunteer's cry
16 Arabian Peninsula sultanate
17 Governor in Austin?
19 Area that may have stained-glass windows
20 Come together
21 Card player's boo-boo
23 All the world's one, to the Bard
25 Unwelcome result of a shopping spree?
27 Chow down
28 Give kudos
30 "Black gold"
31 Sluggers' stats
33 Life stories, for short
35 Nut jobs
39 Bit of Sunday TV scheduling . . . or a hint to 17-, 25-, 50- and 59-Across
42 Aid in finding sunken ships
43 Part of a wedding cake
44 Jackson or Winslet
45 Sock hop locale
47 Galifianakis of "The Hangover"
49 Actress Farrow
50 Airport baggage handler?
54 Like half of a pair of dentures
56 Do the work of a florist or an orchestrator
57 "S O S," e.g.
58 Belly laugh
59 Sheep's accuser?
64 Cut and paste, say
65 Pungent-smelling
66 Lowdown
67 Say isn't so
68 Presidents Tyler and Taylor, for two
69 Plastic brick brand

DOWN

1 Abbr. at the end of a co. name
2 Cheerleader's cry
3 Walt Disney's specialty
4 "The Caine Mutiny" captain
5 Oven user's aid
6 Leave dumbstruck
7 Snapshots, for short
8 Cousin of an alpaca
9 Weather-affecting current
10 Place for a "Bridge Out" sign
11 Rock and Roll Hall of Fame architect
12 Like Fran Drescher's voice
13 Mournful peal
18 Have a hunch
22 Bit of equipment for a circus clown
23 Feudal drudges
24 Verboten
25 Burden of the conscience-stricken
26 Put on a pedestal
29 Attorney's org.
32 Event that may include blue films
34 Dirty campaign tactic
36 Bubbly drink
37 Protruding navel
38 Gaff, to a fisherman
40 Orator William Jennings ___
41 Rainbow shape
46 Dr. Phil's last name
48 Hip-shaking dance
50 Actor Leto of "American Psycho"
51 Chip away at
52 Choo-choo
53 Stacy who played Mike Hammer
55 Danger
57 Degs. for many profs
60 CAT scan alternative
61 A smoker might bum one
62 Trio after D
63 Kanga's baby

by Andrea Carla Michaels and Kent Clayton

42

ACROSS

1 Boeing 747s, e.g.
5 Out of bed for the day
10 Rand McNally product
13 Resting on
14 Part of the eye
15 In bed all day, maybe
16 Profits
18 Hornets' and Nuggets' org.
19 Industrial city of Germany
20 Winter precipitation
22 Gulf war missiles
25 Town dump, e.g.
28 Othello's supposed rival for Desdemona's affection
30 "Beep beep" maker
31 Commotion
32 Teacher, after exams
35 "Quickly!," on an order
39 The, grammatically
42 Musical of the Cardinals
43 Egyptian god of the underworld
44 Last in a sequence: Abbr.
45 ___ of Man
47 Actress Reynolds of "The Unsinkable Molly Brown"
49 Dodge City lawman
54 The "T" in TWA
55 German Hermann
56 Use the pink end of a pencil
58 Antlered animal
59 Emmy-winning nature series narrated by David Attenborough
65 Ginger ___
66 Grapefruit-like fruit
67 ___ as shootin'
68 Wrecker's job
69 Kick out of school
70 Shed thing hidden in 16-, 25-, 39-, 49- and 59-Across

DOWN

1 Feb. preceder
2 Summer in France
3 Tyke
4 Goes 80, say
5 Extend a subscription
6 Turner's 1986 rock autobiography
7 ___ City (Las Vegas)
8 London's locale: Abbr.
9 Former Egyptian leader with a lake named after him
10 Many a West Virginia worker
11 "The Zoo Story" playwright Edward
12 Oro y ___ (Montana's motto)
14 B&O and Short Line: Abbr.
17 Give, as homework
21 Island west of Maui
22 A lot
23 Citadel student
24 Stars and Stripes land, for short
26 Remove wool from
27 Hot
29 Baltimore baseballer
33 Bewildered
34 "Agnus ___"
36 Swim with the fishes, say
37 Bold poker bet
38 "For ___ sake!"
40 The J. and K. in J. K. Rowling: Abbr.
41 African fly pest
46 Vast treeless plain
48 Suckling site
49 Bread choice that's not white or rye
50 Mello ___ (soft drink)
51 Off-kilter
52 Actress Zellweger
53 Suave or VO5 competitor
57 From ___ Z
60 Bagel topper
61 What a guitar may be hooked up to
62 Regret
63 Gay singing syllable
64 Billy Joel's "Tell ___ About It"

by Patrick Blindauer

ACROSS

1 End of a fable
6 Place to pray
9 Game with knights
14 Hitch on the run
15 "To a . . ." poem
16 8 ½" × 14" paper size
17 Monica with two U.S. Open wins
18 Without reluctance
20 Make a legislative speech, e.g.
22 Ear doctor
23 Vote in favor
26 Go ballistic
30 Greedy person's cry before and after "all"
31 Get clean, as in rehab
32 No longer active: Abbr.
34 Catchall category
37 Popular cameras
39 Shade of green
40 Rapper's entourage
44 Choir voice
45 Be stir-crazy
49 "___ Ramsey" (1970s western)
50 "Pay to ___" (check words)
51 Where one might 20-, 26- and 45-Across?
57 Summer woe
60 ___ Jean (Marilyn, originally)
61 How the euphoric walk
62 They, in Tours
63 Bothered incessantly
64 Summer who sang "Love to Love You Baby"
65 Police dept. title
66 Performed superbly

DOWN

1 Go well together
2 Dairy case bar
3 See 11-Down
4 Mimicked
5 Anne Rice vampire
6 Propelled
7 Imposing building
8 Sturdily built
9 Advertising award
10 English king crowned in 1100
11 With 3-Down, Chinese restaurant offering
12 Mineo of film
13 On the ___ (furtively)
19 Hand moisturizer, e.g.
21 "Come again?"
24 Sign up
25 Ballplayers' representatives
26 Like state-of-the-art gadgetry
27 Get a lungful
28 Bit of gym attire
29 61, in old Rome
30 Swabbie's handful
33 General on Chinese menus
35 33 ⅓, for an LP
36 Tearful one
38 Penn of "Harold & Kumar" films
41 Olympian's no-no
42 Put in chains
43 Most weird
46 Strands during the winter, perhaps
47 Director Craven
48 Fight venues
52 More, in adspeak
53 "Letting Go" novelist Philip
54 Layered cookie
55 Neighbor of Yemen
56 9-Across ending
57 Cover with turf
58 Half of dos
59 A Bobbsey twin

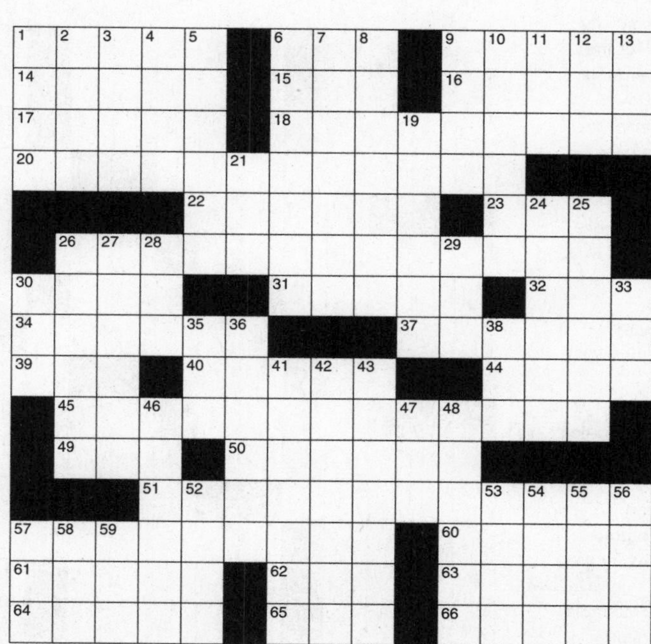

by Mark Feldman

44

ACROSS

1 Jump
5 1960s-'70s R&B singer Marilyn
10 Observe the Sabbath
14 Norway's capital
15 Thin as ___
16 "Beetle Bailey" bulldog
17 Game played with strings looped over the fingers
19 Spicy Asian cuisine
20 Shaking a leg
21 Feather pen
22 Self-description of someone who's surprised
25 Farmer-turned-conman in a 1960s sitcom
28 Not much
29 Designer Geoffrey
30 Oklahoma city named for the daughter of its first 4-Down
31 Many miles off
35 Docs' org.
36 Long time
40 Hole in one
41 Song for one
43 Electrocute, in slang
44 Former name for Congo
46 Big hauler
48 Called balls and strikes
50 Taro
54 Bosc and Bartlett
55 Move to another job, say
59 Smarting
60 What a greedy person may grab
62 The "O" in CD-ROM
63 Disney mermaid
64 Prayer starter
65 Meal on a military base
66 Ashen, as a complexion
67 Blows away

DOWN

1 ___ Ness monster
2 Biblical twin who sold his birthright
3 Cockpit readings: Abbr.
4 One who "always rings twice," in an old movie
5 Jarhead
6 Ill-tempered
7 Bum, as a cigarette
8 OPEC supply
9 Cheer for a toreador
10 Capitol feature
11 Body of values
12 Suddenly stop, as an engine
13 French fabric
18 Like Dolly the sheep
21 Sine ___ non
23 When said three times, "and so on"
24 Fawn's father
25 Many corp. hirees
26 San ___, Italian resort on the Mediterranean
27 "Physician, ___ thyself"
30 Nile snake
32 Place to buy cotton candy
33 Farming unit
34 Wetlands plant
37 Princess in L. Frank Baum books
38 Loss's opposite
39 Modern toll-paying convenience
42 Fish-eating birds
45 Event for stunt pilots
47 Quizzical utterances
48 Early computer forum
49 Pathetically small
50 ___ salts
51 Africa's Sierra ___
52 Some English nobles
53 Un+deux
56 Othello's betrayer
57 "Oh, ___ up!"
58 Nancy Drew's beau and others
60 Napkin's place
61 Savings for one's later years, for short

by Donna Hoke

ACROSS

1 Do a double-take, e.g.
6 Made a choice
11 Composition of Jack Haley's Oz character
14 God, to Muslims
15 Gaucho's plain
16 "Six Feet Under" network
17 F.A.A. supervisors?
19 Belief suffix
20 Start of a countdown
21 Jerome who composed "Ol' Man River"
22 Dolts
24 Object to online commentary?
27 Cosine's reciprocal
30 "Waiting for Lefty" playwright
31 It's walked on pirate ships
32 ". . . ___ saw Elba"
34 Awaiting scheduling, initially
37 Holiday smokes?
41 Broadcast
42 Strong desires
43 Tickle
44 Want badly, with "for"
47 Least amiable
48 Cleaned up after a spill?
52 Tilter's weapon
53 ___-Tass news agency
54 Martinique, par exemple
57 Heavenly body
58 Defamation in the Garden of Eden?
62 Fertility clinic cells
63 Potter's potions professor
64 Playing pieces in Rummikub
65 Nat Geo, for one
66 Snap course
67 Wield, as power

DOWN

1 Totally absorbed
2 Vogue competitor
3 Shepard in space
4 Pink-slip
5 "Lola" band
6 Start of grace, maybe
7 Fallback strategy
8 Subject of a cigarette rating
9 Shut down
10 Prescription measure
11 "You're right"
12 "The Wild Duck" playwright Henrik
13 Chinese restaurant request
18 Out of alignment
23 Bilko or Friday: Abbr.
24 Gershwin's "The ___ Love"
25 Windblown soil
26 Keatsian or Pindaric
27 Pet advocacy org.
28 Grades K-12
29 Allotment of one, usually, for an airline passenger
32 Make improvements to
33 Turned chicken
35 One calling the shots
36 "I'd hate to break up ___"
38 One of four on a Rolls
39 Cut jaggedly
40 Mideast potentate: Var.
45 Catchall abbr.
46 Free from anxiety
47 Font option: Abbr.
48 Burst into flower
49 Maggot or grub
50 Hardly macho
51 Totally lost
54 Pink-slip
55 Lecher's look
56 Once, old-style
59 Paternity suit evidence
60 Smallish batteries
61 Give a thumbs-down

by Alan Arbesfeld

46

ACROSS

1 Half of the Dynamic Duo
7 33 1/3, e.g., for a record: Abbr.
10 Envision
13 Stir up
14 Prefix with space
15 Word after sales or income
16 Second-stringer
18 One thing ___ time
19 Window framework
20 Milan opera house La ___
21 Rapper ___ Wayne
22 Compensation in bills and coins
25 Put a cork in
29 Mao ___-tung
30 "Great taste . . . less filling!" sloganeer
34 Still red, as a steak
38 Loosened, as a 57-Down
39 Before, poetically
40 Eskimo boat
41 Miss ___ USA
42 1986 Keanu Reeves film
44 Tip of a boot
46 Gets rigid
47 Car in the Playmates' 1958 hit "Beep Beep"
53 Suffix with rational or civil
54 Someone who gives you the willies
55 Opened one's eyes in the morning
59 Place
60 Classic TV intro . . . or a hint to the starts of 16-, 22-, 30-, 42- and 47-Across
63 Not con
64 "What's ___ for me?"
65 Magazine manager
66 Hankering
67 Banned insecticide, for short
68 Take down a peg or two

DOWN

1 Nickname for Barbara
2 Environs
3 A lot
4 A lot
5 ___ Wednesday
6 Just off the assembly line
7 Chart again
8 Church dignitary
9 Some eels
10 Like week-old bread
11 Dine at home
12 Glorify
14 Design feature over many a gate
17 Stupidhead
22 Prompted
23 Easter mo., often
24 Fish-tailed males
25 Porn
26 Fork prong
27 Merrie ___ England
28 Base of a column
31 Hawaiian garland
32 Newspaper columnist Kupcinet
33 Golf peg
35 Assists
36 Fulminate
37 Barely manages, with "out"
40 Consumer
42 Ram into from behind
43 ___ 1 (Me.-to-Fla. highway)
45 Flower often used in a 31-Down
47 A bit cold
48 Sky-blue
49 Place atop
50 Kind of badge for a Boy Scout
51 Reddish-purple bit in a salad
52 Records turning at 33 1/3 7-Across
55 Capricious desire
56 "Hold ___ your hat!"
57 Shoelace problem
58 Brontë's "Jane ___"
61 ___ Bartlet, president on, "The West Wing"
62 Poem of praise

by C. W. Stewart

ACROSS

1 Bookcase unit
6 Drill instructor's rank, often: Abbr.
9 Animal trap
14 Tool with a bubble
15 Poet who created the Ushers
16 Color variations
17 Fight card venue
18 Have payables
19 Comment to the audience
20 Distance runner's skirt?
23 Catches some rays
24 Beats it
28 Chicken, so to speak
32 Season after printemps
33 Compete
34 Military sandwich?
37 "Candid Camera" request
39 Bottom-of-letter abbr.
40 Clear wrap
42 Battle of Normandy city
43 Emitted a contented sigh
45 Outstanding crowd scene actor?
47 Sch. in Troy, N.Y.
48 Sussex suffix
50 Most robust
51 Plaything with a fulcrum
53 Defense in a snow fight
55 Valuable truck?
61 Company behind the game Battlezone
64 Hurler's asset
65 Applied 3-in-One to
66 Netflix rental
67 Juno or NetZero, for short
68 Serving a purpose
69 Antler sporters
70 Utmost in degree
71 Dry runs

DOWN

1 Verbal assault
2 Zeus' wife
3 Partner of anon
4 "Havana" actress Olin
5 Render pancake-shaped
6 Dish's runaway partner, in rhyme
7 Graduation attire
8 Abound (with)
9 Batting positions
10 Boot camp reply
11 Young Skywalker's nickname
12 "Curse you, ___ Baron!"
13 U-turn from WNW
21 Where the Styx flows
22 Believer's suffix
25 Take to the sky
26 Four-lap runners, often
27 Witnessed in the area of
28 Slings mud at
29 Cocktail hour nibble
30 Jughead's buddy
31 Stir up
32 Abba of Israel
35 Not risky
36 Mentalist Geller
38 1140, in old Rome
41 India's longest-serving P.M.
44 Works of Pepys and others
46 Visits a diner
49 Neighbor of Nor.
52 Bit of parsley
53 Leading the pack
54 Get-up-and-go
56 Genesis brother
57 Webmaster's creation
58 Yale students
59 Disappear à la Frosty
60 Fateful day for Caesar
61 Pro-___ (some tourneys)
62 Huggies wearer
63 Gardner of "Mogambo"

by Robert A. Doll

48

ACROSS

1 Painter Chagall
5 Bushy hairdo
9 Enticed
14 Pseudonym for Charles Lamb
15 Honolulu keepsakes
16 ___ Gay (W.W. II plane)
17 "Don't get too close!"
19 Police stun gun
20 Kind of energy or eclipse
21 "Wow, totally crazy!"
23 Sis or bro
25 Actress Hayworth
26 Stars of "The Breakfast Club" and "St. Elmo's Fire," collectively
31 Winter coats
35 "Mona ___"
36 Sound made when passing the sound barrier
38 What a dog walker holds on to
39 "Don't mind ___ do!"
40 Take someone's wheels from at gunpoint
42 Engineering sch. in Troy, N.Y.
43 Town square
45 Duo
46 Mideast ruler
47 Definitely past one's mental peak
49 Hiker's bag
51 Blueprint
53 Mohawk-sporting TV star of the '80s
54 Place for parsley, sage, rosemary and thyme
59 Writer Joyce Carol ___
63 Galahad's protection
64 Bulletin board fastener
66 ___ Arabia
67 Ace or deuce
68 Land of Blarney
69 Talked up
70 Chart-topping songs
71 Swing around on an axis

DOWN

1 Boot camp meal
2 Kind of saxophone
3 Mideast money
4 Variation of rummy that was a 1950s fad
5 Edmonton's prov.
6 Quite an accomplishment
7 More than well-off
8 Schindler of "Schindler's List"
9 "We can discuss this fully later"
10 Not in the know
11 Santa ___, Calif.
12 Util. bill
13 Alternative to white, as turkey meat
18 Faucet trouble
22 15%–20%, for a waiter
24 "Ali ___ and the 40 Thieves"
26 Spots of light on a radar screen
27 The "R" in N.R.A.
28 Vietnamese or Thai
29 Nasdaq listing: Abbr.
30 Old cop show starring Telly Savalas
32 Fate
33 ___ jelly
34 Dodge, as work
37 Common street name
40 Phone-screening service
41 Study hard at the last minute
44 90210, e.g.
46 Subjects of wills
48 Where to hold a telephone receiver
50 "No ___!" ("Easy!")
52 "Why, certainly!"
54 Miss America band
55 Appeal to God
56 Early morning declaration
57 Indian tea
58 Rock's Cobain
60 Showy peacock feature
61 Light brown shade
62 ___-Ball (arcade game)
65 Rx prescribers

by Ian Livengood

ACROSS

1 The old man
4 Like a pool table, ideally
9 Flights like Lindy's
14 French coin of old
15 Fail to pay, as taxes
16 Native New Zealanders
17 Yadda, yadda, yadda: Abbr.
18 "Dang it!"
19 "Primitive" feelings
20 ___ fiber
22 QB's successes
23 Dawn goddess
24 Like a bug in a rug
26 Two, for many minigolf holes
29 Postlarval
32 Burn, as a wound
34 Last Supper query
35 Quantities: Abbr.
36 Not much
37 What every answer on the perimeter of this puzzle is
40 Brit's baby buggy
41 Wings, in zoology
42 Musical featuring "Tomorrow"
43 Schoolyard snitch's words
45 Activist Chávez
46 English poet laureate Henry James ___
47 Millennium divs.
48 Exclamations of understanding
49 Reporter's question
50 Gets the best of, in slang
54 Tony's "West Side Story" love
57 Make sense
59 One in the family, informally
60 Norwegian king until A.D. 1000
61 Be dishonest with
62 Equal: Prefix
63 1/60 fluid dram
64 Guiding principle
65 Repeated machine gun sound

DOWN

1 Something good for a Boy Scout?
2 Stage opening
3 Il ___ (Mussolini)
4 "Chocolat" actress
5 Civil rights leader Medgar
6 Results may do this, in commercials
7 Summer N.Y. hrs.
8 "___ Miz"
9 Makeup mishap
10 Sculler's gear
11 Trucker's record
12 Vein contents
13 One in the family, informally
21 4:00 p.m., traditionally
22 People of Rwanda
24 Margaret Mead interviewees
25 Eggnog sprinkling
26 Rock climbers' spikes
27 "The Simpsons" voice man Hank
28 More visibly ashamed
29 Brit's "Goodbye!"
30 G.I.'s org.
31 Pontius ___
32 Comic who quipped "Weather forecast for tonight: dark"
33 Lack of experience
38 Family name in Chicago politics
39 Decorative plant holder
44 Bar mitzvah toast
48 Like a 45° or 60° angle
49 Internet café connection
50 Yemeni port
51 Black-bordered news item
52 ___ Major
53 Barfly's binge
54 Partner of baseball and apple pie
55 Induction-refusing boxing champ
56 Hightailed it
57 Key near the space bar
58 Fizzle out

by David Hanson

50

ACROSS

1 Many Eastern Europeans
6 Air passage
10 Tiff
14 "Good Will Hunting" star Matt
15 Arthur with a Queens stadium named after him
16 Bread for a gyro
17 BP gas brand
18 Wife of Jacob
19 "___ See for Miles" (song by the Who)
20 One place to follow the object named in the circled letters (reading left to right)
23 A/C stat
24 Hannibal ___, vice president under Abraham Lincoln
26 Golf peg
29 Artist whose 1999 hit "Smooth" was #1 for 12 weeks
32 These, in Tours
34 Zenith
36 Untruth
37 Something with x and y axes
39 Roughen in cold weather
40 ___ Highway (route through Whitehorse, Yukon)
43 Scottish hillside
44 Ancient Asia Minor region
46 Medical care grp.
47 Buy's opposite
48 Sleuth, in slang
49 Computer game with virtual people
53 Be sick
54 Old-fashioned paper copies
56 Carrier to Copenhagen
58 Another place to follow the object named in the circled letters
64 E-mail filter's target
66 Jacques of "Mon Oncle"
67 Governed
68 Top of the head
69 Get ___ the ground floor
70 Had a role on stage
71 Wowed
72 "___ On Down the Road" ("The Wiz" song)
73 Like mosquitoes

DOWN

1 Pierre's state: Abbr.
2 Buddhist monk
3 Love, in 51-Down
4 Words, informally
5 Haughty sorts
6 Cowgirl Evans
7 Puts to work
8 Dance related to the mambo
9 Iran's capital
10 Sales talk
11 Outdoor eating place where you might lay a blanket
12 One thing ___ time
13 Brown from the beach
21 ___ Lumpur, Malaysia
22 Slate, e.g., briefly
25 Katmandu native
26 Unspoken, as an understanding
27 Reverberated
28 Release from slavery
30 Nothing
31 Computer whizzes
33 Turtle's "home"
35 Prefix with center
38 Gridiron carriers: Abbr.
41 French friend
42 Note on a Chinese menu
45 Abbr. before a name on top of a memo
50 Immobilize
51 Madrid's land, to natives
52 Minor despot
55 Measured by a stopwatch
57 Worcestershire ___
59 Siouan people
60 WXY, on a phone
61 Sandwiches that are definitely not kosher, in brief
62 Onionlike soup ingredient
63 Spin zone?
64 Place to get a mudbath or massage
65 Furry foot

by James Tuttle

ACROSS

1 Top point
5 Thom ___ footwear
9 Barbie the doll's best friend
14 A cowboy hat has a wide one
15 Continental money
16 Dizzy
17 Something found in an old board, maybe
19 ___ Fogle, spokesman for Subway
20 Fire remnant
21 Cornerstone abbr.
22 Charge, to a physicist
23 Show-off in a show
24 Tool belt tool
26 Toothpaste tube letters
27 Measure of conductance
28 Mare's morsel
29 Triage sites, briefly
30 Big job for a housekeeper
32 It has feathers and flies
34 Little girl in 1935's "Our Little Girl"
40 Up, as the ante
41 Prefix with bus
43 Swiss river to the Rhine
46 Quart divs.
47 Gibbon, for one
50 "Batman" sound effect
51 Term of endearment for the Karate Kid
54 Speaker's place
55 Cab Calloway's signature line
56 Rowboat pair
57 Kind of party for Glenn Beck?
58 Most-played part of a 45
59 What 17-, 24-, 34- and 51-Across are
61 Transport in a western
62 Result of overexercise
63 Anything ___
64 Landlord's sign
65 Tool building
66 "The Neverending Story" author Michael

DOWN

1 Presidential first name that comes from Genesis
2 Holy wars
3 Hodgepodge
4 One skilled in CPR
5 Good Joe
6 Number after tres
7 Take for ___ (hoodwink)
8 Cambodia's Lon ___
9 Astronaut in a 1973 David Bowie hit
10 Farsi speaker
11 Obtain (from)
12 Old codger
13 Tribal V.I.P.'s
18 Polite reply from a ranch hand
22 "Come on, ___ you!"
25 St. John's ___ (herbal remedy)
31 Knight's title
32 Reply to a captain
33 Typist's speed: Abbr.
35 Record of arrests
36 Certain print, for short
37 "Put a tiger in your tank" brand
38 Drink
39 Like some decorative cookware
42 Standoff
43 Horrified
44 Blue blood, informally
45 Goodyear offering
47 Military helicopter
48 Became attentive, with "up"
49 Formerly, in olden days
52 Swamp plant
53 Doggie
59 ___ in cat
60 Get on in years

by Sharon Delorme

52

ACROSS

1 Plaster backing
5 Bigger than big
10 Wonderment
13 ___ spades (highest card in a deck)
15 Fully extended, as a ballerina
16 San Francisco's ___ Hill
17 "S.N.L." alum who co-starred in "Three Amigos!"
19 Gun enthusiast's org
20 Cheep eats?
21 Spacious
23 Westernmost of the Aleutians
24 One of two on a basketball team
26 His "Dance With My Father" won the 2003 Grammy for Song of the Year
31 Songs
32 Boxers Muhammad and Laila
33 Record co. that bought Motown in 1988
34 Social reformer Jacob
35 Take it easy
37 Thailand, once
38 Sense of self
39 Heirs, but not heiresses
40 Actress Irene
41 Traveling show of the 1970s and 2000s that originated in Cairo
45 Old geezers
46 ___ Piggy
47 Madrid museum
49 Winter headgear
53 "Now is the winter of ___ discontent . . ."
54 They're in la-la land
57 Like 1, 3, 5, 7, etc.
58 Permanently, as writing
59 Fruit that makes you pucker
60 "For ___ a jolly good fellow"
61 Names hidden in Hirschfeld sketches
62 Beaver constructions

DOWN

1 Baby sheep
2 Berry touted as a superfood
3 Guam or the U.S. Virgin Isls.
4 Sexy movie companions, maybe
5 Spoil, as milk
6 How many TV shows are now shown
7 From ___ Z
8 Neither's partner
9 Groups of four
10 Latin words before a year
11 Fish bait
12 Cyberauction site
14 Bottles of liquor
18 Post-it, e.g.
22 Canadian-born hockey great
24 Grand party
25 Computer operating system developed at Bell Labs
26 Mario's video game brother
27 Things in the wallets of many laborers
28 Sibelius's "___ Triste"
29 Barely sufficient
30 Identical
31 Voyage with Captain Kirk
35 Easy win
36 Tolkien's tree beings
37 Embodied
39 Substituted (for)
40 Gloomy
42 Odin or Osiris
43 Pirate map features
44 Put on the payroll
47 Winnie-the-___
48 Disrespectful
49 ___ St. Vincent Millay
50 Disaster relief org.
51 Partner of "to" on a gift tag
52 Nine-digit govt. IDs
55 "Gimme ___!" (start of a cheer at Iowa)
56 Yang's go-with

by Elizabeth C. Gorski

ACROSS

1 *Sermon closer
5 *Black cat, supposedly
9 *Place for a roast
13 ___ sci (coll. major)
14 Shortstop Jeter
16 The Flintstones' pet
17 Time for playoffs
19 *Tied
20 All things considered
21 Take stock of
23 Tissue injuries
24 *Times to call, in ads
25 Grid stats
26 May birthstones
30 *Storm centers
33 Fend off
34 ___ Lingus
35 Place for a nail
36 "1-Across to 63-Across"
38 When doubled, a Gabor
39 One protected by a collie, maybe
40 Like golf course greens
41 *Does some batiking
42 Signer-upper
44 Melted chocolate, e.g.
46 *Poor grades
47 Fuel container
51 Dairy Queen orders
54 Huge success
55 *Pro shop buys
56 Ob/gyn's image
58 Plugging away
59 Tab picker-upper
60 "Public diplomacy" broadcast org. until 1999
61 *Some socials
62 *Milk source
63 *"Take ___!"

DOWN

1 Horrify: Var.
2 Simpleton in "Archie" comics
3 "___ Dream" ("Lohengrin" aria)
4 Simpletons
5 Greek theaters of old
6 Fast-disappearing airline amenities
7 Gaelic tongue
8 "The Matrix" hero
9 Black Sea port
10 "___ le roi!"
11 Hydrocarbon suffixes
12 Rouen refusals
15 Cad's behavior
18 Like plow horses
22 Sealy competitor
24 Manicurist's board
26 Give the slip to
27 Unlikely to hustle
28 Brooklynese pronoun
29 Mmes., across the Pyrenees
30 Sport with lunges
31 Act that's "contagious"
32 Drink holder
33 Dreaded mosquito
36 Key
37 Hides, as from the cops
41 Apportion sparingly
43 Horace and Sappho
44 Kiddie's racer
45 Homes for squirrels
47 Jazz pianist Chick
48 Dentist's directive
49 Ephesus' region
50 Tacitly acknowledge
51 A.S.A.P., in the E.R.
52 "Our Gang" pooch
53 Princess played by Carrie Fisher
54 Ophthalmic swelling
57 Back muscle, for short

by Gary J. Whitehead

54

ACROSS

1 Order after "Ready . . . aim . . ."
5 Not cramped at all
10 Urban pollution
14 Russia's ___ Mountains
15 Protruding navel
16 California valley known for 37-Across
17 Informal gathering of musicians
19 Stuck in the freezer
20 Mensa members' stats
21 37-Across vessels
22 30-second spots, e.g.
23 One of the W's in W.W. I
24 Expressed wonder
26 1975 #1 hit for LaBelle
31 "On the Beach" author Nevil
33 "Looks ___ everything"
34 Floor cleaner
35 Send a message via cell phone
36 Dish rated in alarms
37 Cabernet or merlot
38 Lumberjack's tool
39 Red tag events
40 Clear from memory
41 Outdoor homes for endangered species, perhaps
44 More sad
45 "Ich bin ___ Berliner"
46 "Pretty Boy" of crime
48 Match a bet, in poker
50 Hit with a stun gun
53 Papers in poker pots
54 Park that's home to Yogi Bear
57 Entice
58 Samuel of the Supreme Court
59 Initial poker stake
60 Beat, barely
61 Wisconsin college or its city
62 Cubicle fixture

DOWN

1 Volcano viewable from Tokyo
2 Operation Desert Storm setting
3 Ewes' mates
4 Chicago trains
5 Nun's beads
6 Remove from power
7 Elevator pioneer Elisha
8 "O Sole ___"
9 Money in Tokyo
10 Whine tearfully
11 Nuts grown in Hawaii
12 Newspaper opinion piece
13 Gallivants, with "about"
18 Give the slip to
22 "___ reminds me . . ."
23 Light bulb unit
24 Ultimatum words
25 All: Prefix
26 Country wedged between France, Belgium and Germany
27 Gustav who composed "The Song of the Earth"
28 Astrological sign of spring
29 Mafia bigwigs
30 Olympian's blade
31 For men only
32 One more than penta-
36 Give a darn
37 Small songbird
39 Potato, informally
40 Things released from Pandora's box
42 French president's palace
43 Have confidence in
46 Blacksmith's tool
47 Deafening
48 Tie fastener
49 Kind of sax
50 The "Z" in DMZ
51 Aardvark's diet
52 Not wait until December 25, say
54 Where you might find the thematic parts of 17-, 26-, 41- and 54-Across
55 ___ Lilly and Company
56 Tiny bit

by Fred Piscop

ACROSS

1 Command to a Doberman
6 "American idol" rating
10 Crotchety sort
14 Sunshine State city
15 Place on the payroll
16 "60 Minutes" correspondent Logan
17 Spanish moray still exists
20 Broke bread
21 Art gallery site, possibly
22 Biscotti flavoring
23 Wall-to-wall measure
24 "Both Sides Now," for one
26 Polish sister showed her inexperience
33 Watch for
34 Bar opening?
35 ___ carte
36 W.W. II pinup features
37 Fleet members
39 Not much
40 Barely manage, with "out"
41 "Pet" that's a plant
42 Auto gear
43 Silver State boogie band autopsy expert
47 Stink to high heaven
48 It's pumped
49 Tale of Achilles
52 Pic
53 Parseghian of the Fighting Irish
56 Red Sox fans mourned tearlessly
60 On break, say
61 Seep
62 Deadly
63 Gets the picture
64 White-tailed ___
65 Picture holder

DOWN

1 Member of the 600 home run club
2 "Rhyme Pays" rapper
3 Batmobile "garage"
4 Super Bowl-winning Manning
5 Teen loiterer, possibly
6 Creepy 1981 Lauren Bacall film
7 ___ Cong
8 Start to fix?
9 Salon stuff
10 Holds tight
11 Jazz saxophonist Coltrane
12 God in the 49-Across
13 Corner of a diamond
18 MGM mogul Marcus
19 Maui neighbor
23 Antique shop tag
24 Sassy sort
25 Has control over
26 "Friendly" action
27 Bright-eyed and bushy-tailed
28 Japanese noodle dish
29 Eskimo boat
30 Israeli P.M. after Shamir
31 Having a pulse
32 Firefighting aid
37 Wingtip or wedge
38 Country bumpkin
39 Elvis ___ Presley
41 Doctrine
42 Leave, as kids at school
44 Gives a speech
45 Fireplace remnant
46 Algerian port
49 Sacred bird of ancient Egypt
50 Gold streak
51 Manhattan, for one
52 Clothing tag information
53 Terrier in "The Thin Man"
54 Travel aimlessly
55 Up to the task
57 Go-ahead sign
58 Female 64-Across
59 La Brea goop

by Randall J. Hartman

56

ACROSS

1 David's weapon against Goliath
6 Nose (out)
10 I.R.S. experts, you hope
14 Hawaiian veranda
15 Proximate
16 Came to earth
17 Pancake syrup icon
19 Dalai ___
20 E.R. V.I.P.'s
21 Fail to mention
22 San Francisco footballer, for short
23 Baking icon
26 French composer Claude
29 "Stretch" car, in brief
30 Abbr. at the end of a list
31 Color tones
32 ___ alai
35 Frozen vegetable icon
40 Furthermore . . .
41 "Color me impressed!"
42 Responds to a dog command
43 A.A. and A.A.A.
44 Amelia ___, title heroine in children's books
47 Spaghetti-in-a-can icon
51 Labor leader Jimmy who mysteriously disappeared
52 Hairdo for Snooki of "Jersey Shore"
53 Carrier to Oslo
56 French "her"
57 Breakfast cereal icon
60 Have on, as clothes
61 Unit of cloth or lightning
62 Japanese cartoon style
63 Concordes, briefly
64 ___-Ball (game with scores up to 100)
65 "Eek!"

DOWN

1 Grand ___ (baseball or bridge feat)
2 Heap praise on
3 Bed-and-breakfasts
4 "King" Cole's first name
5 Action figures with dog tags
6 Bad blood
7 Jupiter or Zeus
8 Pinup's leg
9 ___ of Good Feelings
10 Tricolor cat
11 Pirates may make someone walk it
12 Old-time evangelist ___ Semple McPherson
13 Ringo on drums
18 Ones dispatched by 911 calls
22 Chinese menu assurance
23 Bronze animal in New York's financial district
24 Colonel Mustard's game
25 Nothing: Fr.
26 "It's ___ vu all over again" (Yogiism)
27 School on the Thames
28 Having no need for a comb
31 "Beavis and Butt-head" laugh
32 Prison
33 Voting no
34 "___ long story"
36 ___ Linda, Calif. (Nixon's birthplace)
37 Kind of dancer at a discotheque
38 Pink, as cheeks
39 "Ah, yes"
43 Things potential homebuyers put in
44 "Jane Eyre" writer
45 No Child Left Behind dept.
46 Bear part of, as costs
47 Scolds, with "out"
48 Targets of golf greens
49 D sharp equivalent
50 Beatles' record company
53 Use tiny scissors
54 Wile E. Coyote's go-to company
55 "___ Gotta Have It" (Spike Lee film)
57 "Survivor" network
58 Thumbs-up response
59 Prefix with lateral

by Andrea Carla Michaels

ACROSS

1 "Horsefeathers!"
6 High in calories
10 ". . . three men in ___"
14 Basra native
15 Witty Bombeck
16 Situated by itself
17 Big name in orange juice
19 Sousaphone, e.g.
20 Bangladesh's capital, old-style
21 Prison "screw"
23 Rocket interceptor, for short
25 Large gem in the Smithsonian
28 Like a Jekyll/Hyde personality
30 Sign at a sellout
31 Tirades
32 Motherland, affectionately
35 ___ contendere
37 Kindly doctor's asset
42 Gives the heave-ho
43 Pre-Russia intl. economic coalition
45 Chinese menu phrase
49 Second letter after epsilon
51 "Jesus ___" (shortest Bible verse)
52 Common
56 Japanese theater
57 Like kielbasa and pierogi
58 Govt. security
60 Pause in the action
61 Artwork using both paint and collage, e.g. . . . and a hint to this puzzle's circled letters
66 Gen. Robert ___
67 A util.
68 Resort isle near Venezuela
69 Fleet fleet, once, in brief
70 Big name in root beer
71 More red, as a tomato

DOWN

1 Milne's absent-minded "Mr."
2 ___ Lanka
3 Individually crafted
4 Watery hue
5 Halloween broom-rider
6 Changes the boundaries of
7 Glass or Gershwin
8 901, in old Rome
9 Pilgrim to Mecca
10 Nissan model
11 French port near Marseille
12 Straight
13 Goat features
18 "Green" prefix
22 ___ rod (tall-stemmed plant)
23 Foofaraw
24 Tulip or lily planting
26 Che Guevara's real first name
27 Tragic end
29 Timothy Leary's turn-on
33 Plains Indians
34 Twice cinq
36 Fall behind
38 Homeowner's paper
39 Still in the crate
40 Tied, as a score
41 Defaulter's loss, informally
44 To the ___ degree
45 City near Mt. Vesuvius
46 Nonalcoholic beer brand
47 French artist who painted "The Gleaners"
48 Says "Cheese!"
50 Worshipers of Quetzalcoatl
53 "Arabian Nights" prince
54 Pull the plug on
55 Baseball's Garciaparra
59 Actress Garr or Hatcher
62 Dockworkers' org.
63 Marked, as a ballot
64 "May ___ excused?"
65 Berne's river

by Ron and Nancy Byron

58

ACROSS

1 Quantity picked by Peter Piper
5 Fellow
9 Camera lens setting
14 Worker protection agcy.
15 Snoozefest
16 Pioneering video game company
17 Rushing yards or turnovers, for short
18 Cooking in a wok, e.g.
20 Dutch bloom
22 Glance through quickly
23 ___ of luxury
24 University in Winston-Salem, N.C.
27 Act like a grandma
28 "Exodus" hero
29 ___-Magnon man
30 Ambulance sound
31 Seedy loaves
33 Blitzkriegs
37 Reinvest some funds
40 Place where borrowing is encouraged
41 Clodhoppers
44 "Three wishes" granter
47 N.Y.S.E. debut
49 "Holy smokes!"
50 Pink-slipped
51 It offers flexible support for women
55 Lines scanned by a supermarket scanner, in brief
56 Met melody
57 Set of fortune-telling cards
58 Pep
62 Period after Mardi Gras
63 Undo, as writing
64 Wee
65 Doily material
66 Treasured violin, for short
67 Aretha Franklin, the Queen of ___
68 Barely got, with "out"

DOWN

1 Like the period after 1945
2 Wide part of a river where it meets the sea
3 More like messy blackboards
4 Newswoman Couric
5 4-Down's network
6 Sizzling
7 Come to pass
8 Employee benefits
9 Old MacDonald's place
10 9-Down enclosure
11 Worker who has people in stitches?
12 Elaborately decorated
13 Perpetually dirty kid in "Peanuts"
19 In good physical shape
21 Many a G.I.
25 Toothbrush brand
26 Helicopter topper
27 Dance to Donna Summer's "Last Dance," e.g.
30 Jamaican music
32 Sphere or cube
34 Fed. electricity provider since 1933
35 Eagle's home
36 Burial chamber
38 Perjure oneself
39 Sunrise
42 As a total departure from the norm
43 Tried to kill, as a fly
44 Rain-measuring devices
45 Know-nothing's opposite
46 Drink of the gods
48 Columbus Day mo.
51 Madrid Mrs.
52 Shadings
53 Transistor, e.g.
54 Actress Berry
56 Parodied
59 Miss Teen ___ (beauty pageant)
60 Bearded African animal
61 Olive ___ (Popeye's sweetie)

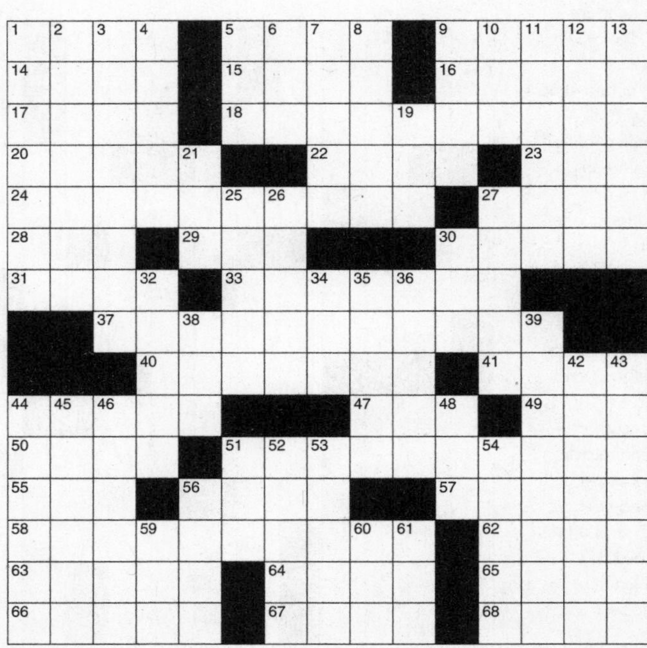

by Lynn Lempel

ACROSS

1 ___ Sea (shrinking body of water)
5 Argentine strongman Perón
9 Kern and Hammerstein's "Can't Help Lovin' ___ Man"
12 Like no-hitters
13 The Boilermakers of the N.C.A.A.
15 Slugger's stat
16 Proper way to behave in Biloxi?
18 "My lips ___ sealed"
19 Part of F.D.R.
20 Put on, as plays
22 Said no to
23 Evaluation in Eugene?
25 Lake named for an Indian tribe
26 Fiends
28 Where runs may be made
29 "Get out" key: Abbr.
30 Austria's ___ Family Singers
31 Lorillard company smokes
32 Syncopated piano piece for Seattle residents?
34 Political convention locale
38 Menial sorts
39 What the best hand may get you
42 Member of the familia
43 Dr. of children's books
44 "Take a number" place
45 Chicago balloonists' needs?
47 Freak
49 ___ d'
50 Get started
51 Six-pack set
52 Commuter trains in Boston?
56 Vietnamese New Year
57 Japanese dogs
58 Identify
59 Ernie of the P.G.A.
60 Northern French river
61 Kind of sch.

DOWN

1 Something a push-up exercises
2 Paul Revere's bandmates in 1960s–'70s music
3 Once-common pesticide component
4 Howard of "Gone With the Wind"
5 2007 Ellen Page title role
6 Gravesite sight
7 Commercial suffix with Power
8 Clinic staff
9 Never seems to end
10 Side by side
11 Adds color to, in a way
13 First woman, in Greek myth
14 This: Sp.
17 West with the autobiography "Goodness Had Nothing to Do With It"
21 Arthur in the International Tennis Hall of Fame
22 Poor mark
23 The father of songs, according to Pindar
24 Not originals
27 Said in horror, say
30 "You're going to like us.___" (1980s slogan)
31 Metric weights: Abbr.
33 Key's contents
34 Put into cartoon form
35 Put a new tag on
36 Joins up
37 Eye of ___ (witch's item)
39 Careful reading
40 Kind of religion, in song
41 Member of the familia
43 Underhanded
44 Singer Warwick
46 "___ la Douce"
48 Pilot's datum: Abbr.
50 Sirius, e.g.
53 Member of the family, for short
54 ___-Julie, Que.
55 Pro ___

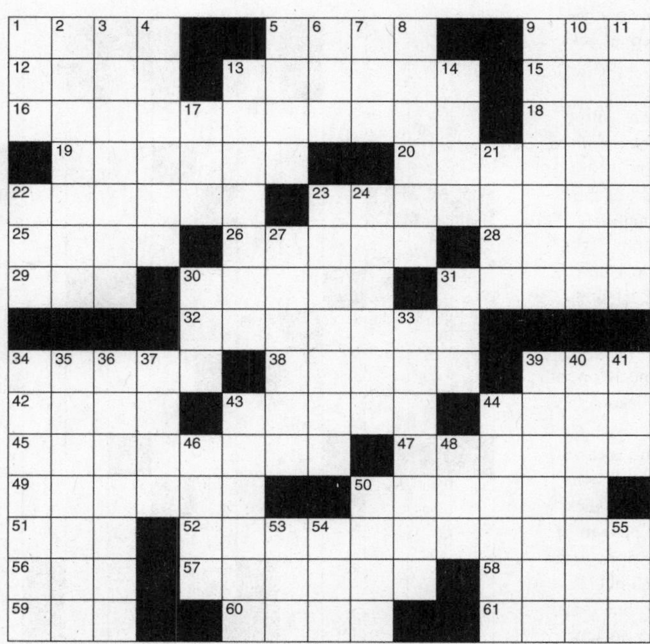

by Robert W. Harris

60

ACROSS

1 Soothing ointment
5 Big ___ (sandwich)
8 "Well done!"
13 Word after rest or residential
14 Puts frosting on
16 Take great pleasure (in)
17 "___ 62-Down" (1962 Ray Charles hit)
20 Tops worn with shorts
21 Uncooked
22 Depot: Abbr.
23 Mauna ___
24 Gets ready to shoot
25 "___ 62-Down" (1953 Eddie Fisher hit)
33 Six-sided game piece
34 Give for a while
35 More confident
36 Keep ___ on (watch)
38 Aptitude
41 First, second, third or home
42 Change, as the Constitution
44 Drubbing
46 Some milk ctns.
47 "___ 62-Down" (1989 Milli Vanilli hit)
51 "Not much longer"
52 ___ Guevara
53 Sack
56 Lennon's second mate
57 Takes one's pick
61 "___ 62-Down" 1995 Hootie & the Blowfish hit)
64 Peeling one may make a person tear up
65 Rural grain holder
66 "___, Brute?"
67 Word puzzle with pictures
68 Big name in stunt bikes
69 Faculty head

DOWN

1 Cheese in a mousetrap
2 Firecrackers' paths
3 Jacob's first wife
4 Philippine capital
5 Errata
6 Every play of Shakespeare has five of them
7 Corp. honcho
8 Reads a little here and there
9 Sun. sermon giver
10 Rara ___
11 Air outlet
12 ___ Korbut, 1972 Olympic gymnastic sensation
15 Parsley bit
18 Dweller under a bridge, in fairy tales
19 Mary had a little one
24 Fireplace log holder
25 It helps you claim a suitcase
26 City known for its Heat
27 Big name in outdoor grills
28 Sign, as a deal
29 Wheel's center
30 Baghdad native
31 Hatchlings' homes
32 Gown
37 NBC weekend skit show, for short
39 Chaney of old films
40 Carrier of a sandwich, soda and cookies, say
43 Renounces
45 California/Nevada resort lake
48 "___ Lisa"
49 Thugs
50 Made Persian or Siamese sounds
53 Socially inept sort
54 Meara of comedy
55 Smooth-talking
57 Smooth, as seas
58 Web page
59 Jazzy singer ___ James
60 Steer clear of
62 Object of affection in 17-, 25-, 47- and 61-Across
63 Penpoint

by Victor Fleming and Lynn Lempel

ACROSS

1 ___ Picchu (site of Incan ruins)
6 It's returned by a ticket-taker
10 "Arrivederci ___"
14 Standoffish
15 Topnotch
16 Designer Cassini
17 Something everybody is aware of
20 Stick with a stick
21 Nincompoop
22 Trojan War hero
23 Gun, as an engine
25 Gait faster than a walk
26 It's not very short and not very tall
32 401, in old Rome
33 "There's ___ in My Bucket" (children's song)
34 Changes course suddenly
36 Plan that changes courses
38 Expiration notices?
40 It can scratch an itch
41 Attach with needle and thread
43 Do-it-yourself relocation rental
45 Orbison who sang "Oh, Pretty Woman"
46 They may be rounded up after a crime, with "the"
49 Exam for an aspiring J.D.
50 Prefix with sphere
51 Buckeye
54 Goof up
56 Mutual fund charge
60 Cheapest choice at the pump
63 Freud's libido
64 Letter-shaped beam
65 Orange or grape soda brand
66 Peeved
67 Fries, to a burger
68 Alan or Adam of filmdom

DOWN

1 Non-PC choices?
2 Oodles
3 State it's not good to be in
4 Man, in Havana
5 Sci-fi sight
6 Noted Fifth Avenue emporium
7 Oodles
8 Numero ___
9 "Watch out now"
10 Winner of the first Nobel Prize in Physics, 1901
11 Shoppe description
12 Huge: Prefix
13 Matures
18 Like the land that includes Monument Valley
19 Sainted ninth-century pope
24 Elizabethan ___
25 Sorority members such as Ann-Margret and Laura Bush
26 "Farewell"
27 Pros and cons
28 Lose one's shirt, in business
29 Yale of Yale University
30 What the Tin Woodman sought from the Wizard of Oz
31 The Ghostbusters and the Police
32 D.J.'s collection
35 Cunning
37 Artist Henri de ___ Lautrec
39 Apartment building overseers, informally
42 Twangy-sounding
44 Comics villain ___ Luthor
47 Hawaiian verandas
48 Arrest
51 Lucky strikes?
52 Subway fare?
53 Composer Stravinsky
54 Oath of old
55 Burger order specification
57 Piggy plaint
58 Dead set against
59 Watergate figure John
61 Cleanup hitter's stat
62 "Anatomy ___ Murder"

by Paula Gamache

62

ACROSS

1 Fistfuls of money
5 "The World According to ___"
9 Mistreat
14 Baldwin of "30 Rock"
15 Polish/German border river
16 Ink for a laser printer
17 Civil rights pioneer Parks
18 Game akin to bingo
19 Mountains in Chile
20 He's famous for the words "There's a sucker born every minute"
23 "My Gal ___"
24 Mohawked actor of "The A-Team"
25 Bay window
26 Words of solidarity
31 Non-earthlings, for short
32 They: Fr.
33 Turner who led a slave rebellion
34 Flavorful citrus parts
37 Commercials
38 Carries
40 "But is it ___?"
41 Mil. command centers
42 "Cheers" setting
43 Feature of many Judd Apatow films
48 ___ New Guinea
49 Paranormal letters
50 A Gabor sister
53 1971 Gay Talese title derived from one of the Ten Commandments
56 Tarp, e.g.
57 Simon & Garfunkel's "___ Rock"
58 Mister, in Münster
59 Fortunate, old-style
60 Ruler toppled by the Bolsheviks
61 "___ expert, but . . ."
62 Alternative to Tic Tacs
63 "Auld Lang ___"
64 Compass points (seen spelled out in 20-, 26-, 43- and 53-Across)

DOWN

1 Gets bent out of shape
2 Hi from Don Ho
3 1950s-'60s TV studio
4 Read, as a U.P.C. symbol
5 Kiddie racers
6 "___ Fideles"
7 Landlord's check
8 Annual games for football's elite
9 Some old computers
10 Baby's headgear
11 Like a wave
12 Appear
13 Hosp. sites for dire cases
21 Gives off, as an odor
22 Mars : Roman ___ : Greek
27 Human cannonball catcher
28 Performed, biblically
29 Scot's refusal
30 Drunk's affliction, for short
34 Move after a zig
35 Make a wrong move
36 Pay a visit
37 Water polo and synchronized swimming
38 Home of the N.F.L.'s Buccaneers
39 Pizarro's gold
41 60 minutes
42 Money for a trip across town, say
44 Least batty
45 Water polo and synchronized swimming
46 "Yo!"
47 Does more tailoring on, as a skirt
51 Jules who pioneered in science fiction
52 --> or <--
53 Puncture
54 Having a bit of smog
55 Skinny
56 Toronto-based TV network

by Ed Sessa

ACROSS

1 Rapper Snoop ___
5 Rope material
9 Rude sort
14 "___ et mon droit" (British monarch's motto)
15 Pooch in a Jim Davis cartoon
16 Book between Daniel and Joel
17 *Reese Witherspoon's role in "Legally Blonde"
19 Spanish rains
20 Groundskeeper's supply
21 *Highest-grossing film of 1977
23 *Lakeside vacation rental
26 Browning who directed "Dracula," 1931
27 "And one more thing . . ."
28 1922 novel with a Dublin backdrop
30 Fingers, in a way
32 Syrup brand
33 *Purchase for a vacation, maybe
39 1-Down's W.W. II command
40 *Lose control of a car
42 Auction listing
43 *Personal esteem
45 Heedless
46 Gymgoer's unit
47 Neighbor of Irkutsk on a Risk board
50 "Touching" Olympic event
53 Address lapses?
56 *Emmy-winning AMC series set in the 1960s
57 *House that drains finances, slangily
59 Parishioner's place
60 Bonfire
61 What the starts of the answers to the eight starred clues are
66 Consumed
67 Like many lockets
68 Setting for an Agatha Christie mystery
69 Apply a bandage to
70 ___ Millions (lottery)
71 Sign near a stairway

DOWN

1 39-Across commander
2 Masseur's supply
3 Solidify
4 "I suppose . . ."
5 Top with a top
6 Tokyo, once
7 Central position
8 Pasta topper
9 Blacken
10 "Nonsense!"
11 Bar order, with "the"
12 Fannies
13 It may be thrown from a horse
18 Rice holders
22 "Goodbye, Luc!"
23 Diner fixtures, informally
24 Make happy
25 Snowy region of Austria
29 Hubbub
31 "Spring forward" to this: Abbr.
34 QB's statistical blemish
35 ___ scale
36 Morning device you might want to take a hammer to
37 Perez with a nasally voice
38 Patriot Allen
40 Eur. country with a king
41 Easy catch in the infield
44 Goes absolutely still
45 Port, for one
48 Cousin of a gazelle
49 Woodstock folk singer
50 Bury (in)
51 Arctic
52 Maternally related
54 Handmade sign for TV cameras
55 Avert, with "off"
58 Strong desires
62 Kind of gift
63 Quash
64 Roth of "Inglourious Basterds"
65 Solidify

by Ian Livengood

64

ACROSS

1 Out of one's gourd
5 Send somewhere else
10 Father, to a baby
14 Wilson of "Starsky & Hutch," 2004
15 ___ and kicking
16 Words after step or sleep
17 Suspicious
18 "Till next time!"
20 Nubile maidens
22 Valentine symbol
23 Rich supply of ore
24 When doubled, a Mazda catchphrase
26 "Heavyweight" of 1960s folk/pop
32 Taken ___ (surprised)
33 Gent's partner
34 What corn kernels attach to
36 Up to the job
37 Prisons
39 What catnip is to a cat
40 Citi Field player
41 Four years, for a president
42 Buoyant wood sometimes used in rafts
43 Group in a hit 2002 film with "divine secrets"
47 Animated 1998 film set in Central Park
48 Fingered, for short
49 Lex Luthor, to Superman
52 Rip open
56 Liquor-soaked cake
59 "Mares eat oats and ___ eat oats"
60 Sashimi fish
61 Flip out
62 Bridge shape
63 Grandmother, affectionately
64 Five-time world champion figure skater Carol
65 "Funny strange or funny ___?"

DOWN

1 Wedding dress, e.g.
2 Not at home
3 It may be what ails you
4 Wherever you like
5 First-class
6 Makes very, very happy
7 Conniptions
8 Actress Longoria
9 Official in a striped shirt
10 Start of the musical scale
11 Fashion style-setter Wintour
12 Fashion designer Christian
13 No. on a periodic table
19 "___ Night" (Christmas carol)
21 Take to a pawnshop
24 Ardor
25 Automaker Ransom Eli
26 Sir's counterpart
27 Westminster ___
28 Its coat of arms has a cross, but no falcon
29 Successfully diets
30 Eye: Prefix
31 Neck-to-waist area
35 Bit of wampum
37 Pull one's leg
38 Phoenix's home: Abbr.
39 Highfalutin
41 Country singer Tucker
42 ___ Rabbit
44 Kawasaki competitor
45 Gridlocks
46 One of four singing brothers of the 1950s
49 Dark black
50 California wine valley
51 Nonmusical Abba
52 Bangkok citizen
53 Nick's partner in "The Thin Man"
54 Word after Georgia or Virginia in school names
55 Job conditions agcy.
57 "Blech!"
58 ___ v. Wade

by Mike Buckley

ACROSS

1 Kitty cries
5 Architect's handiwork
9 Lots and lots
14 Indian housemaid
15 Hefty volume
16 Women's area in a palace
17 LEM maker
18 It measures less than 90°
20 Church's percentage
22 Silk-producing region of India
23 Jed Clampett's find on "The Beverly Hillbillies"
24 Stein filler
25 Say "nay" to
28 Fred's dancing sister
30 Act the pawnbroker
31 Cheapest in a line
33 Part of r.p.m.
34 Lay eyes on
38 Nautical "Stop!"
39 Milk amts.
40 Tartar sauce morsel
41 "Please?"
42 Greyhound, e.g.
43 Hoaxes
44 Cousin of an emu
46 Plumed wader
47 One who was detained, maybe
51 Kimono accessory
54 "___ on parle français"
55 Feature of many a greeting card
56 Keepers of jewels
58 Old TV antenna
61 "___ be a cold day in . . ."
62 Little green man?
63 Do some high-tech surgery on
64 Allot, with "out"
65 Some teen talk
66 Garbage hauler
67 Mouth off to

DOWN

1 Powerful ray
2 iPhone capability
3 Shrivel to nothing
4 Deposed Iranian ruler
5 Bake sale org.
6 Track down
7 Tickle pink
8 Income statement figure
9 Tribal healer
10 Pokey
11 Most common inert gas in the atmosphere
12 Places to get Reubens
13 Remove impurities from
19 Raring to go
21 Part of a meet
26 Long in the tooth
27 Cook up, so to speak
29 Tennessee Williams "streetcar"
31 Skedaddle
32 Lab eggs
33 Milk amts.
35 4 p.m. British refreshment . . . or what can be found in 18-, 25-, 47- and 58-Across and 3-Down?
36 International writers' org. with appropriate initials
37 Soph. and jr.
39 Heated exchanges
40 Biceps-strengthening exercises
42 Special Forces cap
43 Masters org.
45 In possession of
46 To a great extent
47 Turkish money
48 "Can't talk now . . . I'm expecting ___"
49 Neighbor of the fibula
50 Hayes or Newton
52 Sings out loudly
53 Cays
57 Aligns the crosshairs
59 Gridder Roethlisberger
60 Use a Singer

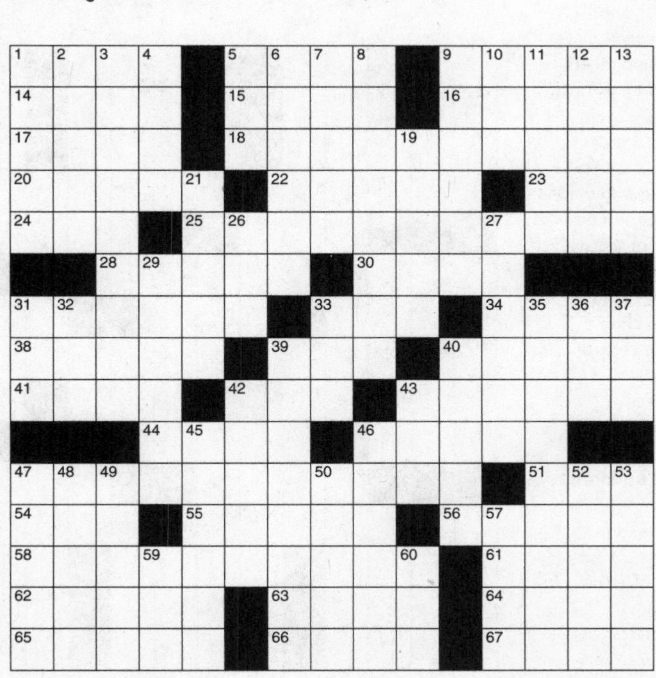

by C. W. Stewart

66

ACROSS

1 Transact business on the Internet
6 TV/radio host John
10 Turkey club?
14 Travelers alternative
15 Toss in a chip
16 Touched down
17 Tricky driving condition
18 Tax-exempt educ. groups
19 Times Roman, for one
20 Traditional use for henna
23 Tackle-to-mast rope on a ship
24 Tiny bit
25 Typist's key: Abbr.
28 Transmitter of waves
31 Train stop: Abbr.
34 Tear-gassing cause
36 Tevye's "good"
37 The Beatles' meter maid and others
39 Team in the A.F.C. South
43 Tallow sources
44 To the ___ degree
45 Trouble with a lid?
46 Time period on a financial stmt.
47 Takes a step toward biting?
51 Took a chair
52 Trap or record preceder
53 Teleflora competitor
55 Tilt-boarding
63 Techie's address starter?
64 Topic lead-in
65 Take as a given
66 The U.N.'s Kofi ___ Annan
67 Tranquilizer gun projectile
68 Two-color horse
69 Tensed
70 Terminal approximations: Abbr.
71 Towel ends?

DOWN

1 Toward sunrise
2 The "T" of TV
3 "Time to rise!" ("Up and ___!")
4 Tending to bungle things
5 Tito Jackson's sister
6 Toledo tidbit
7 Theater's ___ 'acte
8 Take the night off from partying, say
9 "The Ten Commandments" star
10 Three-country agreement of '94
11 Tons
12 Two-time All-Star Martinez
13 "The Touch of Your Hand" lyricist Harbach
21 Tears
22 Tempest game maker
25 Trying to look cultured
26 Title for Sulu on "Star Trek": Abbr.
27 Tempered, with "down"
29 Talking-___ (scoldings)
30 Track meet component
31 TDs and interceptions
32 Tucker with the #1 country hit "Here's Some Love"
33 Thing of value
35 "The Closer" airer
38 T.G.I.F. part
40 "Terminal Bliss" actress Chandler
41 Third-person ending of old
42 Thug's crime, often
48 TD Waterhouse online competitor
49 Torments
50 Treeless tract
52 Time-honored Irish cleric, for short
54 Tout ___ (straight ahead: Fr.)
55 To the extent ___
56 "Tell Mama" singer James
57 Traitor's rebuke
58 Tomás's "other"
59 Tykes
60 "This ___ what I expected"
61 TV's Nick at ___
62 "Three deuces and a four-speed" cars of old

by Paul Guttormsson

ACROSS

1 Boosts
4 Perfect balance
10 Award named after a TV network
14 Philadelphia had the first one in the U.S. (1874)
15 One hanging around a party?
16 "Do I ___?"
17 Some ballpark hits
19 -
20 One who might wear slippers
21 Prosaic
23 Provider of some outdoor entertainment
26 -
29 Broadcasters
32 John Wayne had a distinctive one
33 Palme ___ (film award)
34 Go home, maybe
35 Nick name?
36 Traffic cop's org.?
37 Group out of the mainstream
38 Allocates, with "out"
39 "Hair" composer MacDermot
40 Theologian Johann
41 Tusked animals
42 "Kitty ___" (1940 movie romance)
43 Kind of fly, briefly
44 Beginning to knock?
45 Chucked
46 "Star Wars" and "Battlestar Galactica"
47 -
49 Blue hue
50 Comic's forte
53 Painted the town red, in a way . . . or successfully completed this puzzle?
56 -
60 It might come out of a small speaker
61 Naval group
62 Not from a Scot
63 Boundary of myth
64 Liquored (up)
65 Lamb's kin

DOWN

1 Shooter named for its inventor
2 Skating venue
3 ___ bed
4 Ghost of Jacob Marley?
5 Floor specialists
6 French Literature Nobelist Gide
7 KLM alternative
8 "Lord, is ___?"
9 Grainy places to dig
10 Apprehensive
11 Youthful time
12 Nuptial starter
13 "You wanted to see me?"
18 Use a "caret and stick" approach on?
22 It's a tradition
24 I operation?
25 Spun things
26 -
27 Girl with a festive-sounding name
28 Gave a keynote, say
29 Eyeball
30 Cold cover?
31 Sugar in large crystals
35 "So cool!"
38 Quarters for quarters?
39 TMZ fodder
41 Support
42 Mattress covering
45 Old vacuum tube
48 Allen in history
49 Record label for Otis Redding
51 Musical with the song "Be Italian"
52 Really bother, with "at"
53 Dict. fill
54 Have a beef?
55 -
57 2001 World Series winner, on scoreboards
58 "Beyond Peace" author's monogram
59 "Well, I'll be!"

by David J. Kahn

68

ACROSS

1 Coach Ewbank who led the Jets to a Super Bowl championship
5 Sturdy mountain climber?
9 English derby site
14 Pac-12 team
15 Circular dance
16 Iroquoian people
17 Place for a sweater?
19 Composer Stravinsky and others
20 A Mexican might sleep under it
21 Totally wrong
22 "Peer Gynt" mother
23 La ___ Tar Pits
24 Sheets for scribbling
29 30- or 60-second spot
33 Three, in Rome
34 Mideast moguls
35 Not just mislead
36 Pocahontas's husband
38 Hogwash
39 When a right turn may be allowed
40 "You have my word on it"
41 Suitor
43 Certain fraternity man, informally
44 Antifur org.
45 Ice cream holder
47 ". . . or so ___ say"
49 "A New World Record" grp.
50 Put down
53 Beau
58 Full-bosomed
59 Fairway clubs . . . or a hint to the starts of the answers to 17-, 24- and 45-Across and 10- and 37-Down
60 "The Surrender of ___" (Diego Velázquez painting)
61 Whitaker's Oscar-winning role
62 "Zip-___-Doo-Dah"
63 Poe's middle name
64 Root beer brand
65 King with the immortal line "Who is it that can tell me who I am?"

DOWN

1 Scaredy-cat
2 Outside: Prefix
3 K–6 sch. designation
4 Entreaty to Bo-Peep
5 Earlyish teatime
6 Uncouth sort
7 Suffix with buck
8 Bump in bumper cars, maybe
9 Rat in "Ratatouille"
10 Playground lingo
11 Possible cause of school cancellation
12 Storybook character
13 Superlative adverb
18 Emma of "The Avengers"
21 Music sheet abbr.
23 Annual city-magazine theme
24 "Peanuts," for one
25 "Gladiator" star
26 Like a candle night after night, say
27 Breathing space
28 90 is a pretty high one
30 Left-hand page
31 Used the dining room
32 "Gunsmoke" setting, informally
35 Legendary siren of the Rhine
37 Fizzless drink
42 High dice rolls
45 Tie the knot
46 O.K. place?
48 Mr. Universe, e.g.
50 "Fernando" group
51 Small knot
52 Figure skater's leap
53 Succotash bean
54 "Amores" poet
55 Presage
56 Fit for service
57 River of Flanders
59 Goldfish swallowing in the 1920s, e.g.

by Elizabeth C. Gorski

ACROSS

1 Took off
5 Princess in a Nintendo game series
10 Ones trying to increase circulation, for short?
14 So-called Family City U.S.A.
15 It might have an attachment
16 One who 26-Across
17 3, 6, 11, 18, 27 . . .
20 "Caught ___!"
21 Ship's doctor, in slang
22 Joint U.S./Canada military org.
23 Journalist on a mission?
25 Jacket part
26 Bugs
28 Some chip dip, informally
30 Small, low island
31 Totally baked
32 Casting director?
34 4, 2, 4/3, 1, 4/5 . . .
40 Supports, with "up"
41 Part of a slalom run
42 Lens holder, for short
45 Setting for Genesis 2:8—25
46 Scoffed
48 Aladdin's home
50 Pop's ___ Vanilli
51 Isn't lazy, say
52 Gem
54 Alias
57 8, 1, -18, -55, -116 . . .
60 First major publisher of board games in the U.S.
61 Instruction sometimes followed by "repeat"
62 Vehicle for Calvin and Hobbes
63 Smart
64 Neuters
65 Uncle ___

DOWN

1 Classic theater name
2 Thereabouts
3 Any of the clues for 17-, 34- or 57-Across
4 Bird whose name is a Midwest school's initials
5 Complete losers
6 Improve
7 Put on
8 Uncool sorts
9 "___ right"
10 Printer brand
11 Standard of assessment
12 A language of South Africa
13 Fuddy-duddy
18 Apt name for a nun?
19 Org. that won the 1965 Nobel Peace Prize
24 Hindsights?
25 "The Wizard Of Oz" co-star
26 ___-rock
27 The time for action, often
28 Presumption, in math
29 Inhales, perhaps
32 Front for "front"
33 Brightest star in Orion
35 Belief in something bigger than oneself
36 Speaker of "Luke, when gone am I, the last of the Jedi will you be"
37 In the answers to 17-, 34- and 57- Across, it was replaced in turn by 1, 2, 3, 4, 5 . . .
38 Common French word with two accents
39 Signed as an illiterate would
42 Cause of feline friskiness
43 Show up
44 Down East native
46 Some spellings?
47 Monopoly util.
49 Ending with wilde- or harte-
50 Old-fashioned
52 Do some barbering
53 ___ salad
55 Gung-ho
56 Contributes
58 Form letters?
59 Kind of port

by Parker Lewis

70

ACROSS

1 "Big Brother" host Julie
5 Milky Way maker
9 "Oh, get off it!"
14 "The Godfather" score composer Nino
15 Riding on
16 Toothpaste brand once advertised with Bucky Beaver
17 "___ framed!"
18 Org. with Spartans and Trojans
19 Drug that treats panic attacks
20 M/C Hammer?
23 Verdi's "___ tu"
24 ___ in queen
25 Raking in
29 Closing bid?
31 Suspense novelist Hoag
33 ___ de guerre
34 Literally, "reign" in Hindi
36 Like Mendeleev's table
39 W/C Fields?
43 Former Ford minivan
44 Risk damnation
45 ___ tough spot
46 Mlle., across the Pyrenees
48 Summer camp shelter
52 Have the blahs
55 Emergency contact, often: Abbr.
57 Whichever
58 L/L Bean?
61 "Oops!"
64 Sac flies produce them
65 "___ be in England": Browning
66 Big Apple mayor before Koch
67 "Outta my way!"
68 Jockey's handful
69 "You're killin' me!"
70 Goes with
71 Brouhahas

DOWN

1 Yalta's locale
2 Stooge surname
3 List ender
4 Pelé's.org.
5 Powerful ray
6 For neither profit nor loss
7 Have a hearty laugh
8 Sci-fi travelers
9 Studio behind "Up" and "Wall-E"
10 Engender
11 Chinese dynasty name
12 Santa ___ winds
13 You might put your stamp on it
21 Comes to
22 Scottish landowners
26 Intro to Chinese?
27 Film ___
28 Yukons, e.g.
30 Hence
32 Not connected
35 Tea in Boston Harbor, once
37 Yule decoration
38 A Chaplin
39 Ragamuffin
40 Russo of film
41 "Of wrath," in a hymn title
42 Sail supports
47 Hit it big
49 Took a dip
50 Ab ___ (from the start)
51 L'eggs wares
53 Andean wool source
54 First Catholic vice president of the U.S.
56 Someone ___ (another's)
59 "An ill wind . . ." instrument
60 Director Ephron
61 Deg. held by George W. Bush
62 Tree with cones
63 Kapow!

by Michael Black

ACROSS

1 Traditional keikogi accessory
4 Apple types
9 Manic
15 One regulated by the F.E.C.
16 It's enough to take you for a ride
17 "Sleepers" co-star, 1996
18 Literary source of "Bless us and splash us, my precioussss!"
20 With force and much noise
21 Memorable ship
22 Literary inits.
24 City on the Rhône
25 Peeling potatoes, perhaps
27 Env. contents
29 Nature worshiper, of a sort
31 Onetime NASA booster
33 Pill bug, for one
35 Stop: Abbr.
36 Anticipate
38 Call, in a way
39 Part of an Asian capital's name
40 Often-cited distance between things . . . or what's hidden in this puzzle
43 Collections
46 Geom. figure
47 Epithet for the mouse in Burns's "To a Mouse"
51 Nav. leader
52 State of Grace
54 Judo move
55 Apparel
57 Jim Beam product
59 River of York
60 China ___
61 Lacto-___-vegetarian
63 Creature in Dr. Seuss's "If I Ran the Zoo"
65 From where
67 Writer featured in the memoir "Dream Catcher"
71 Reduced
72 Narnia hero
73 Center start?
74 Cool red giants
75 Himalayan legends
76 Many an old T-shirt, now

DOWN

1 Reject, with "out of"
2 "Pshaw!"
3 Source of some cubes
4 Folder, sometimes
5 With 52-Down, English-born cabaret singer
6 Hit Brit sitcom
7 Announcers
8 ___ record
9 Modern records
10 Fixed, as tiles
11 ___ and a leg
12 Notable violinist
13 1990s Mexican president Zedillo
14 Its rising signaled the flooding of the Nile in ancient Egypt
19 Cool factor
23 News deliverer
25 Ox
26 Vietnam's ___ Dinh Diem
28 Connected with
30 Free
32 "___ was saying . . ."
34 Assn.
37 Parolee, e.g.
39 Tuba
41 Period of years
42 Take in
43 Writes poorly
44 — — —
45 Most overused
48 Weary walker
49 Aegean island near Naxos
50 Farm milk provider
52 See 5-Down
53 Game stick
56 Noted test provider
58 Zhou ___
62 August 15, 1945
64 One from Germany
66 Some TV drama sites, for short
68 PC key
69 Green grp.
70 Fix

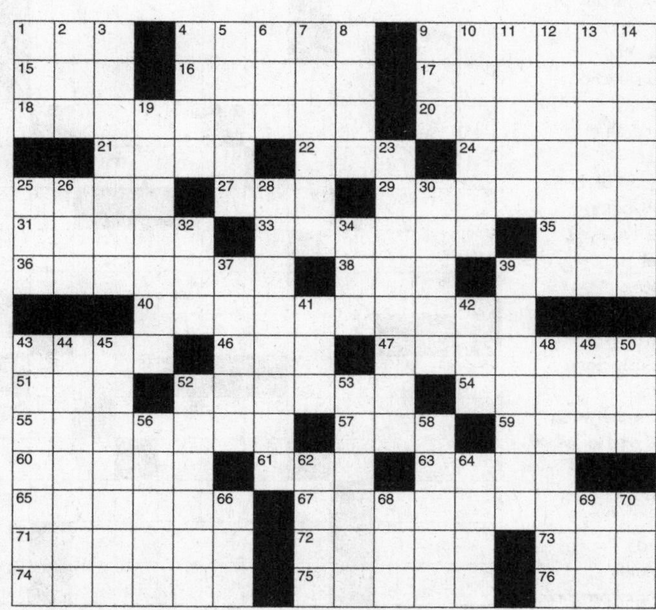

by Kevan Choset

72

ACROSS

1 Holiday time, in ads
5 Detection devices
11 One way to stand
14 Bunk bed feature
15 Fester and Vanya
16 Shipment to a smeltery
17 Physical therapist's assignment?
19 Postal worker's circuit: Abbr.
20 Gossip, to an Aussie
21 Friend of François
22 Engaged
23 The Forbidden City
24 Blackened seafood?
26 Some small power supplies
27 Facilities, informally
29 Lift up
30 La ___ Tar Pits
32 Kind of arrest
36 Castaway's day in court?
40 Enter slowly
41 Spread selection
43 Mete out
46 It may come in a blanket
48 Bionic part of the Bionic Woman
49 Lure for Popeye's sweetie?
53 ___ Kea
55 After midnight, say
56 "Go on . . ."
57 Maliciously done
58 CPR pro
59 Choosing between pounds and kilos?
61 Funny Charlotte
62 Hang back
63 Uncool
64 Georgia, once: Abbr.
65 Customary practices
66 Hydrocarbon suffixes

DOWN

1 Medical dept. room
2 Exotic dancer executed in 1917
3 Homes for drones
4 Food-stains-on-shirt sorts
5 River to the Rhine
6 Whatever amount
7 1983 Mr. T comedy
8 1836 siege site
9 Frankincense or myrrh
10 GPS heading
11 Wife of Brutus
12 iTunes search category
13 Chew on a baby toy, say
18 Thunder sound
22 Result of a '55 union merger
24 Dance around
25 Information for a oenologist
28 Reason to use Retin-A
31 Dinette spot
33 Union ___
34 Headache for a snow shoveler
35 "Give ___ thought!"
37 Johnson of "Laugh-In"
38 Like Unalaska
39 1989 movie featuring principal Joe Clark
42 Good sources of vitamin C
43 Many I.M. recipients
44 Wool-yielding pack animals
45 Runt's group
47 Auto financing org., formerly
50 Causes of ruin
51 Man's feminine side
52 Med-alert bracelet, e.g.
54 Shackle site
57 Standings column
59 Neighbor of Braz.
60 Eskimo ___

by Kelsey Blakley

ACROSS

1 See, say
6 ___ pyramid, four examples of which are seen in this puzzle
10 Real-estate abbr.
14 French affair
15 Friend of Zoe and Abby
16 "Don't you know there's ___ on?"
17 Loudly berated
19 "Say ___" (1940 hit)
20 Fanny
21 Lena who played Irina Derevko on "Alias"
22 Tech company in the Dow Jones Industrial Average
23 "Signs point to ___" (Magic 8 Ball answer)
24 Go home empty-handed, say
25 Welding bands?
26 Lepidopterist's tool
27 Whack
30 Tailors' allowances
33 1971 Tom Jones hit
35 Has no doubt about
36 Ben-___
37 Patty Hearst alias
38 Pioneer carrier
40 Harold of the Clinton White House
41 How many stupid things are done
42 Abbr. after N. or S.
43 Backsplash unit
44 Some talk on political talk shows
46 PC key
49 John who starred in Broadway's original "Carousel"
51 Break down, in a way
52 Fair
53 All at the front?
54 Conductor's place
56 Foreign farewell
57 Old Testament king
58 Shoddy stuff
59 Part of N.C.A.A.: Abbr.
60 "South Park" boy
61 Tennis great born in Serbia

DOWN

1 Fresh
2 Compère
3 Ephron and Roberts
4 Ingredient in some English puddings
5 Laundry detergent brand
6 Has a hunch
7 "Some Enchanted Evening," e.g.
8 Gulf of ___
9 Flyspeck
10 Straightforward fashion choice
11 Site of many clandestine accounts
12 Gender abbr.
13 Charlie's Angels, e.g.
18 Like some points
22 Like many a Malkovich
24 Dietary dictum for one with hypertension
25 Lou Gehrig's disease, for short
26 Reissue
27 Michael of "Superbad"
28 Falco of "Nurse Jackie"
29 Scandinavian rugs
30 Kitchenware brand
31 Presently
32 Light classical pieces
33 Clog, e.g.
34 O, symbolically
39 Otto - cinque
42 Embassy worker: Abbr.
44 City whose name sounds like a fish
45 "___ the Conqueror" (Max von Sydow film)
46 Do well
47 Zone (out)
48 Blush stoppers
49 Almond ___ (candy brand)
50 "The Pregnant Widow" author Martin
51 "King Kong" co-star, 1933
52 Heroine who says "I resisted all the way: a new thing for me"
54 Shaming sound
55 Mad people, e.g.: Abbr.

by Patrick Blindauer and Francis Heaney

74

ACROSS

1 Reindeer herder
5 Sprites, for instance
10 With 64-Across, 1963 Beach Boys hit
14 Lysol target
15 Fairy tale figure
16 Do some computer programming
17 1965 Beach Boys hit
20 "That doesn't bother me anymore"
21 Gumshoe
22 Gulf of ___
23 With 49-Across, 1965 Beach Boys hit
27 ___ Retreat (1970s–'80s New York City club)
30 Trouble
32 Mideast carrier
33 Fall guy?
34 1922 Physics Nobelist
35 It has feathers and flies
36 Egg: Prefix
37 Smitten one
40 Thrilla in Manila outcome
41 Wrestling victories
43 Prefix with -polis
44 Tend, as plants
46 "Cómo ___?"
47 Vote against
48 Dance accompanied by castanets
49 See 23-Across
51 Victim in Camus's "The Stranger," e.g.
52 Minor player, so to speak
53 Rich fabrics
57 1963 Beach Boys hit
61 "___ Ben Adhem" (English poem)
62 African capital
63 "It must've been something ___"
64 See 10-Across
65 "Let It Snow! Let It Snow! Let It Snow!" composer
66 Lotion ingredient

DOWN

1 Sets of points, mathematically
2 Man without parents
3 Kind of shirt named for a sport
4 One following general directions?
5 Packs away
6 Sen. Hatch
7 With 30- and 53-Down, 1964 Beach Boys hit
8 Thrilla in Manila winner
9 Lays on thick
10 Like some eaves in winter
11 Oslo's home: Abbr.
12 Year of Ronsard's "Odes"
13 Vote for
18 Sinatra topper
19 "You sure got me"
24 Nebraska river
25 Surveyor's stake, typically
26 Corrida combatant
27 Polite
28 Rich
29 Like
30 See 7-Down
31 Home of the Rock and Roll Hall of Fame
34 ___ Raton, Fla.
38 Ball club V.I.P.'s
39 Like some plays
42 Refuge
45 Neighbor of Montenegro
48 One of three literary sisters
50 Capital of the U.S.: Abbr.
51 Suffix with parliament
53 See 7-Down
54 Zest alternative
55 Outer: Prefix
56 ___-Ball
57 Choreographer Lubovitch
58 Native Nigerian
59 Overly
60 Didn't get used

by Peter A. Collins

ACROSS

1 It's loaded
5 Atlantic Records, e.g.
10 Blowout
14 Deprecate
15 From the start
16 It connects to the wrist
17 Eco-unfriendly coal sources
19 Auto slogan beginning in 2000
20 "Did you ___ that?"
21 Acts frugally around the holidays, say
23 Deep Blue's opponent in chess
28 One rising at dawn
29 The Gay Nineties and others
30 Idols
35 Tell
38 Hanna-Barbera output
39 Never, in Nuremberg
40 Place ___
41 "Stop avoiding responsibility!"
43 Like sandpaper, typically
44 "Vous êtes ___"
45 It's never finished, only abandoned, per Paul Valéry
46 Southern California college
48 Instruction on a box
51 Pipsqueak
52 Pro ___
53 Place to get a date
56 Secretary of state between Marshall and Dulles
60 Bogey beater
61 Looney Tunes sound
62 It may be hard to change
68 Quaint sign word
69 Accustom
70 Pacific capital
71 Part of a tennis serve
72 Prepare to go on Facebook, say
73 Pace in dressage

DOWN

1 Modern-day tech purchases
2 Like some points
3 Tie up, in a way
4 "Funny running into you here!"
5 Not so cool
6 Some
7 ___ mot
8 "Do I ___!"
9 Frets (over)
10 Paging, say
11 Standoffish
12 One who's standoffish
13 Twin gymnasts Paul and Morgan
18 ___ Tour
22 "Seems to be the case"
23 "Time's fun when you're having flies" speaker
24 Something straining credibility
25 Negotiations of 1977–79
26 Ad Council output, for short
27 Clean, in a way
31 Off
32 Traveling, maybe
33 Feinstein of the 34-Down
34 See 33-Down
36 Holders of reservations?
37 Descendant of Standard Oil
42 Like associates, on some e-mails
47 TV star who once appeared in WrestleMania
49 Much Mongolian geography
50 Some ancient scrolls
54 Filled (with)
55 Brief look inside?
56 Literally, "father"
57 Singer Green with multiple Grammys
58 Follows
59 10^{-9}: Prefix
63 Needle
64 Part of a sched.
65 Onetime name in late-night TV
66 Brand in the freezer
67 Carrot or beet

by Joel Fagliano

76

ACROSS

1 Job for a cleanup crew
5 Fasten, in a way
11 PC "brain"
14 Place for a pavilion
15 Wild child
16 Cauldron stirrer
17 Sing-along direction
20 Masago, e.g., at a sushi bar
21 Writer Chekhov
22 Team nicknamed the Black Knights
23 Obey
25 Frank with six Oscars
28 River ferried by Charon
29 Children's game
33 Direction to an alternative musical passage
36 Become fond of
37 Fertility lab stock
40 Chase scene shout
42 "___ who?"
43 Figure of many a Mayan deity
45 Before dawn, say
47 Pursue a passion
49 Spreadsheet function
53 Neuters
54 Word missing from the answers to 17-, 23-, 29-, 40-, 47- and 62-Across
56 Worthless sort
58 One of 22 in a Krugerrand
61 "Agnus ___"
62 Do as a mentor did, say
66 Home of the Tisch Sch. of the Arts
67 First-timer
68 Play ___ (enjoy some tennis)
69 Longtime mall chain
70 Times for showers
71 Modest response to kudos

DOWN

1 Some urban transit systems
2 Urge on
3 Quick
4 Turn on the waterworks
5 Knocks for a loop
6 Oxygen ___
7 Sacramento's former ___ Arena
8 Singer whose "name" was once a symbol
9 Chaney of film
10 Dyne-centimeter
11 Game with many "points"
12 Lifeline's location
13 Like a 16-Across
18 Thole insert
19 Netanyahu's successor, 1999
24 Prefix with biology
26 The constellation Ara
27 Cultured gem
29 ___ Maria (liqueur)
30 Misanthrope, e.g.
31 Balmy time in Bordeaux
32 "Frasier" role
34 Lesley of "60 Minutes"
35 Tiny bit
37 Acapulco "eye"
38 Transportation for many a rock band
39 Demographic division
41 Whiskas eater
44 Apply to
46 Fashion monogram
48 Invite, as trouble
50 Guinness superlative
51 Richard with a much-used thumb
52 Like pretzels, typically
54 Clotho and sisters
55 Game extenders: Abbr.
56 Throw a barb at
57 "And Winter Came . . ." singer
59 Isao of the Golf Hall of Fame
60 Stir up
63 Sports stat that's best when low
64 Bribe
65 ___ chi

by Jim Hilger

ACROSS

1 He played Joe Palooka in the 1934 film "Palooka"
9 Elite
15 Like the trades
16 Press agent?
17 Able to be drawn out
18 National park whose name means "the high one"
19 Bunny fancier
20 Itch
21 Like Jesus
22 Hot chocolate time, maybe
24 "Horrors!"
25 Author of the 1968 work named in the circled letters (reading clockwise)
28 Cinéma ___
30 Cartoon "Yuck!"
31 1950s political inits.
32 Perfume, in a way
35 Subject of the 1968 work
39 Source of the saying "The gods help them that help themselves"
40 Detectives look for them, briefly
41 Emulate Don Corleone
42 Castle part
44 Leader of the 35-Across
45 Archer's wife in "The Maltese Falcon"
48 Like ruckuses or roadster roofs
50 Like some poker betting
52 ___-ray
53 1950s–'60s political inits.
56 Secretaries used to make them
57 "Ciao!"
59 Will words
60 Italian scientist who lent his name to a number
61 Hauled (off)
62 Like summer school classes, often

DOWN

1 MacFarlane who created TV's "Family Guy"
2 Amount ignored in weighing
3 Org. with the ad slogan "It's not science fiction. It's what we do every day"
4 More quickly?
5 Make more presentable, as a letter
6 More twisted
7 "No way!"
8 Nevada county containing Yucca Mountain
9 Seconds
10 Loners
11 Actress Anderson
12 Related on the mother's side
13 "The Color Purple" protagonist
14 Double-cross, e.g.
21 Georgia was one once: Abbr.
22 Something new
23 Some bagel toppers
25 Steno's stat.
26 Cup ___ (hot drink, informally)
27 Neon sign, e.g.
29 Recommendation letter, maybe
31 Valued
33 High ___
34 Language from which "spunk" is derived
36 "I played already"
37 Willing to consider
38 Writer in cipher, maybe
43 Slowing down, in music: Abbr.
44 Workable if awkward solution to a computer problem
45 Like Hindi or Urdu
46 Last word in a showman's spiel
47 Let out, e.g.
49 A flower is pretty when it's in this
51 "Leave ___ that!"
53 "Episode VI" returnee
54 Meeting places
55 Noted gang leader
57 Swabbie
58 Man of tomorrow

by Matt Ginsberg and Pete Muller

78

ACROSS

1 Foe of 71-Across in Mad magazine
4 Slaps on
9 Mass seating
13 Some round components
15 "There, there"
16 Stack server
17 Genetics-or-environment debate
20 Utensil drawer compartment
21 Like guns and dump trucks, over and over
22 Brewskis
24 Shade of blue
25 "And ___ Was," 1985 Talking Heads song
28 Decathlete's implement
30 Brute
35 Discovery Channel survival show
38 "___ Theme" (1965 soundtrack tune)
39 Piedmont wine town
40 Neighbor of St. Kitts
42 Pack down
43 Wozniak or Jobs
45 Home-seeker's decision
47 Usher in
49 ___ avis
50 Bourbon and Beale: Abbr.
51 Get too much sun
53 Standing O, say
55 Chewbacca and kin
60 Saint of Ávila
64 2004 movie featuring a clash of sci-fi species
66 ___ diagram (logic illustration)
67 Wearing a disguise, informally
68 Oz creator
69 John Lennon's "Dear ___"
70 Like some rich soil
71 Foe of 1-Across in Mad magazine

DOWN

1 Went under
2 ___ B
3 Hairy legend
4 Decreases gradually
5 Off-roader, for short
6 "Evil empire" initials
7 Our 206
8 Moves furtively
9 Falafel holder
10 Israel's Olmert
11 Sported
12 Rushed
14 Some 4WD rides
18 Opts not to be discharged
19 Word before pain or treatment
23 More cagey
25 Chart-topper
26 Rush
27 Reply to a knock
29 Young migratory fish
31 Brewery lineup
32 Many Semites
33 Full range
34 Cable TV sports awards
36 South-of-the-border cheer starter
37 Washington of jazz
41 Generalship
44 Pixieish
46 Like a windmill
48 Austin Powers foe
52 Kind of question on a survey
54 Ho-hum
55 Like moiré patterns
56 Land O'Lakes product
57 "Old MacDonald" sound
58 Popular bar game
59 Adoption advocacy org.
61 Itinerary data, briefly
62 Alternative to salad
63 Camp group
65 CD-___

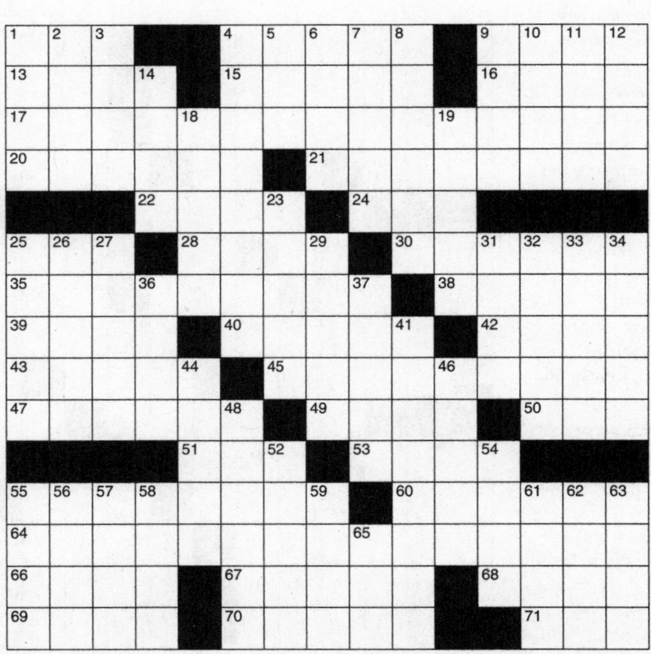

by Jeff Chen

ACROSS

1 It's better than prison
8 #1 on Bravo's all-time "100 Funniest Movies" list
15 Latitude
16 They may be grilled
17 Give back
18 Italian red
19 Country Music Mo.
20 Mine, in Milan
21 Squirreled away
22 Alphabet trio
23 X
25 Adams behind a lens
27 Good call letters for Radio Disney?
28 W.W. II attacker
30 Suffix with hotel
31 Emmy-nominated sitcom of the early 1970s
32 Lacking bargaining power, maybe
34 Waiter
35 Prominent location to build on (as suggested by this puzzle?)
37 Mathematical subgroups
40 You can't go through with it
44 Dough
45 Rear
46 Farm letters?
47 When the French toast?
48 Kind of cell in biology
50 Big name in balls
51 One on either side of the St. Gotthard Pass
52 1900s, e.g.: Abbr.
53 Where the Ringling Brothers circus began: Abbr.
55 Org. employing Ethan Hunt in film
56 "Anything but!"
58 Mount Holyoke graduates, e.g.
60 Seven-time major-league All-Star Alfonso
61 Sailing enthusiast, informally
62 Help
63 Place of learning

DOWN

1 Always going outside?
2 ___ Observatory, home of the world's largest single-aperture radio telescope
3 Has as a base
4 Subject of many lab tests
5 Biblical kingdom
6 Tiny groove
7 Publication with a 1997 headline "Drug Use Down Among Uncool Kids"
8 Zodiac symbol
9 Nothing
10 Scholar's reference abbr.
11 Start of a confession
12 Who wrote "Wealth is the product of man's capacity to think"
13 Leaves alone
14 Vacationer's help
24 Big eyes, metaphorically
26 Six Nations tribe
27 Kind of candidate who's rarely successful
29 It matures in 1 to 10 yrs.
31 Place to live
33 Org. supported by the 16th Amendment
34 End of some scores
36 Missing persons
37 Gets rid of everybody, say
38 Forecast
39 Royal rod, in Britain
41 Investigate
42 Speedy delivery
43 Place where people work for beans?
45 Hymn leader
48 Baseball general manager Billy
49 Lavender
52 Fellow
54 To so high a degree
57 Wed
59 Conductance unit

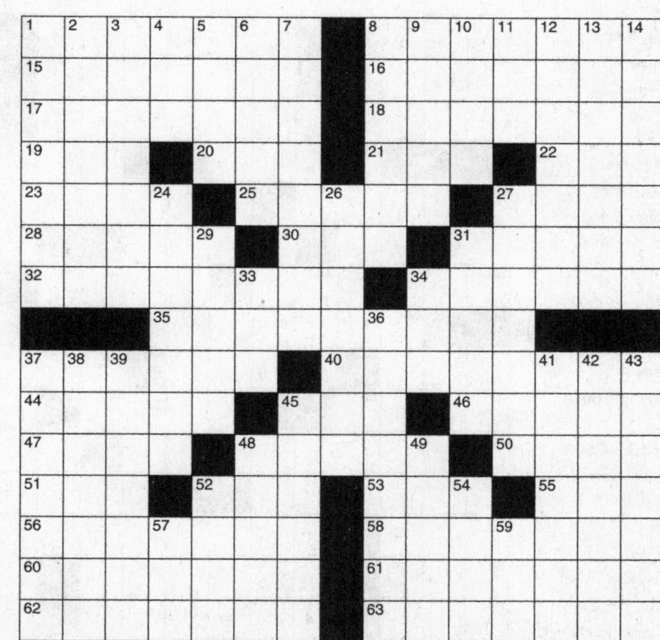

by Samuel A. Donaldson

80

ACROSS

1 Humped ox
5 Indo-European language speakers
11 Longtime Elton John label
14 "___ (So Far Away)" (1982 hit by A Flock of Seagulls)
15 Cut some more, maybe
16 "Atonement" author McEwan
17 California home of the Crystal Cathedral
19 Something that's burned
20 Morlock's counterpart in science fiction
21 It may be felt by a blackboard
23 Hums
26 California locale just south of Camp Pendleton
29 Flightless flock
30 Home ___
31 Israeli arms
32 Positive
34 Backside
37 Two out of nine?
38 California State University campus site
41 "Ere Heaven shall ___ her portals . . .": Byron
43 Guy's girl
44 Bordelaise and others
47 Traditional Christmas purchases
49 They play in front of QBs
51 Part of rock's CSNY
52 California's Sonoma County seat
55 Concise
56 Wound up
57 Shopping site
59 Ocasek of the Cars
60 Urban areas (as hinted at by the circled letters in this puzzle's grid)
66 "Naughty!"
67 Rests atop
68 "At Last" singer James
69 Urban grid: Abbr.
70 Obfuscate, in a way
71 Pringles alternative

DOWN

1 Turn one way before turning the other
2 Prohibition ___
3 Rare site during Prohibition
4 Like scuba diving
5 View from the Leaning Tower
6 Neighborhood
7 "___ out!" (shout by a 24-Down)
8 Hubbub
9 Skin care product name
10 Severe
11 Toyota Camry, e.g.
12 Collapsed
13 Ursula of "The Blue Max"
18 Trains to Wrigley
22 Sch. in Jonesboro
23 Little, in Lyon
24 See 7-Down
25 Causes of some traffic slowdowns
27 Cousins of girdles
28 Sufficient, informally
30 Thing
33 Alias
35 The Rolling Stones' "___ You"
36 ___-green
39 Puerto ___
40 Ornamental crescents
41 After a fashion
42 One who deals in rags?
45 Last of the Mohicans?
46 Sow or cow
48 Part of S.O.P.: Abbr.
50 Flintlock accessory
53 Nimble
54 Kidney secretion
55 Start of some cycles?
58 Trouble spots?
61 Japanese supercomputer maker
62 That, in Tabasco
63 Cousin ___ of 1960s TV
64 H
65 Coltrane blew it

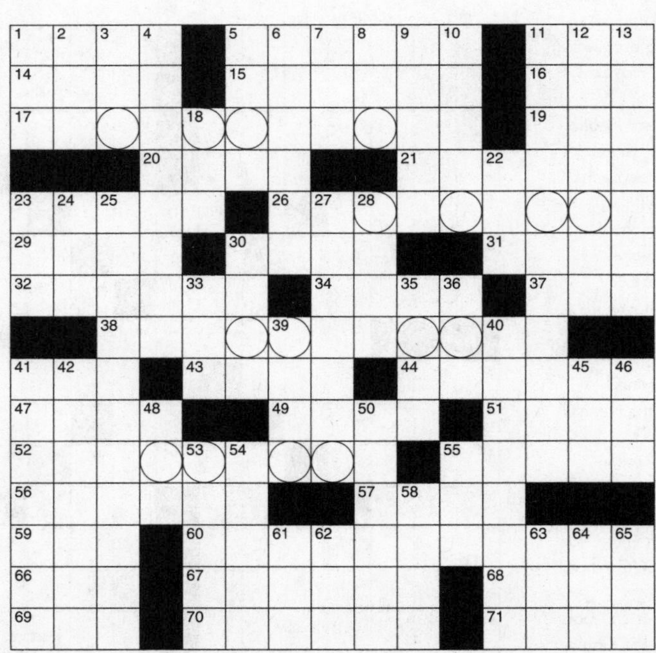

by Peter A. Collins

ACROSS

1 Vitamin C source from Southeast Asia
10 Songwriter Jimmy and Senator Jim
15 It has just 16 rules of grammar
16 Western language historically written in the Cyrillic alphabet
17 London newspaper
18 Mork's TV companion
19 Sea eagles
20 TV network since 1970
21 Bomb, e.g.
22 Alphabet trio
23 Turkey's location
27 It may be turned against you
28 Hammer's partner
29 ___ Street, main thoroughfare in "Peyton Place"
30 J.F.K. watchdog
31 Training ___
32 Jacob who wrote "How the Other Half Lives"
33 Taking one's sweet time
37 Daly of "Cagney & Lacey"
38 It's beside a sideburn
39 Muscles covering some 32-Down
40 Actress Gasteyer
41 Barrister's deg.
42 Credit figs.
44 Singer with the hit country album "Backwoods Barbie"
47 Sketch show that launched 40-Across's career, in short
50 Gist
51 It's located between two Plymouths: Abbr.
52 Scott of "Joanie Loves Chachi"
53 Mr. ___
54 "Gotcha," formally
56 Author Calvino
57 Skating venue
58 Staff up again
59 After U2, highest-grossing concert band of all time, informally

DOWN

1 Ritual in which bitter herbs are dipped
2 Three Ivans
3 "___ of sweat will save a gallon of blood": Patton
4 Fam. members
5 Lie in the sun with suntan oil
6 Wheelchair-accessible
7 No-can-do
8 Formal acknowledgment
9 "My mama done ___ me"
10 Traded beads
11 Cuban name in 2000 news
12 Win whose money, in a bygone game show?
13 Baseball commissioner starting in 1992
14 Sloppy place
23 Oven part
24 Hall-of-Famer Yastrzemski
25 30-Down, sometimes
26 Apt. parts
27 Fisherman's relation?
30 Course closer
31 It may be sandy or candy
32 See 39-Across
33 1970s sitcom catchword
34 Dog sound
35 Pop for a young person?
36 Fisherman's relation?
37 Wee bit
41 English author Edward Bulwer-___
42 Prime minister before and after Churchill
43 Coral creatures
45 Boxer Ali
46 Jon ___, at 6' 11" the tallest player in Major League Baseball history
47 Old Scratch
48 Family relation
49 Mined finds
52 String tie
53 Source of some paper pulp
54 Dah's go-with
55 Member of a D.C. nine

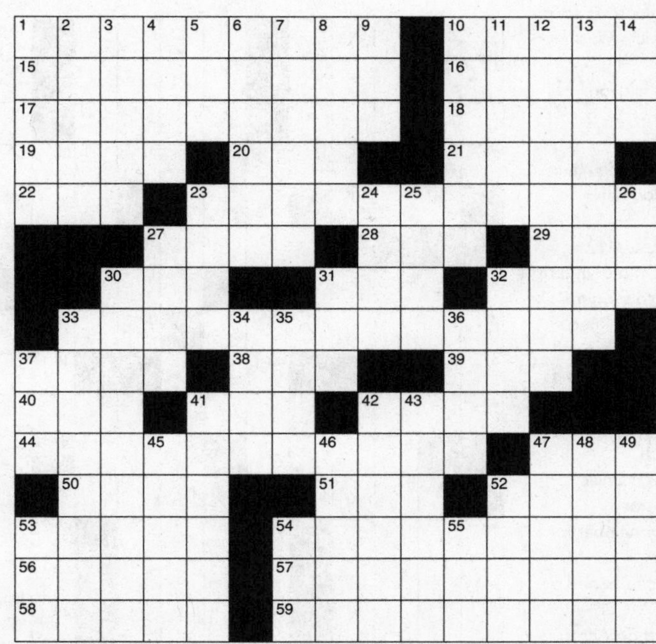

by Jeff Dubner

82

ACROSS

1 1960s "Bye!"
6 ___ de Boulogne (Paris park)
10 Web site with a "Buy It Now" option
14 Trip planner's aid
15 Way back when
16 Miser's cry
17 Angle symbol, in trigonometry
18 Mark in a margin
19 Have ___ (lose it)
20 Iodine in a barber's first-aid kit?
23 Ultimate degree
24 Passbook abbr.
25 Vamp Negri
26 Doofus given a pink slip?
31 Root used as a soap substitute
34 Balancing pro
35 Philosopher Mo-___
36 Dim bulb, so to speak
39 Hobby kit with a colony
42 Sans affiliation: Abbr.
43 Muff
45 Caffeine-laden nuts
46 One modifying goals?
51 Texas ___ M
52 One with a 6-yr. term
53 Tokyo, to shoguns
56 Cronus and Rhea's barbecue remains?
60 Official proceedings
61 Municipal laws: Abbr.
62 Like some checking accounts
63 Title in an Uncle Remus story
64 Unlucky number for Caesar?
65 Influence . . . and a hint to 20-, 26-, 46- and 56-Across
66 Anti-snakebite supplies, e.g.
67 Superheroes of comics
68 Well-versed

DOWN

1 Party spread
2 One of the Coens
3 Argus-eyed
4 Odds-and-ends category
5 Son of Isaac
6 Ordered (around)
7 Germane
8 Home of the Eyjafjallajökull volcano: Abbr.
9 Eighth-inning hurler, often
10 Many résumé submissions, these days
11 Like a New York/Los Angeles romance
12 In a bit
13 Bow wood
21 Results of most 100-yd. returns
22 You, to Yves
27 Serpent's home
28 Curative locale
29 Cornell of Cornell University
30 2012 Charlotte conventioneers: Abbr.
31 Sarah McLachlan hit
32 Bond that's often tax-free, for short
33 Rembrandt, notably
37 Player of a TV junkman
38 Hoopster Erving, to fans
40 End-of-fight letters
41 Predicted
44 "The Satanic Verses" novelist
47 Much of Libya
48 Mayo is part of it
49 Greets at the door
50 What might make molehills out of a mountain?
54 Willem of "Platoon"
55 Best
56 Spread unit
57 At one's fighting weight, say
58 Machu Picchu builder
59 Paving stone
60 Gym rat's "six-pack"

by Steve Salitan

Note: Two hints for 17- and 57-Across and 11- and 26-Down appear somewhere in this puzzle.

ACROSS

1 Easy catch
6 Site of some Galileo experiments
10 "The ___ lama, he's a priest"
14 Dutch princess who's the daughter of Queen Juliana
15 Air show sound
16 Grievous
17 [See blurb]
19 Year St. Augustine of Canterbury died
20 Org. with a targetlike mark on its flag
21 School yr. section
23 Time for a pique-nique, maybe
24 Honeybun
28 Ming jar, e.g.
30 Second bananas
31 Kind of knife
32 Bugs
33 Seventh heaven
36 N.L. West team, on scoreboards
37 Fairy tale
38 Reporter's aid
43 Best-selling PC game released in 2000
47 Hot
48 Simple ski lift
49 Learned ones
51 Analgesic
52 Scot's negative
53 Service award?
54 Upper body: Abbr.
55 Sphere
57 [See blurb]
63 Enamored (of)
64 Home for Samuel Beckett
65 Language known to native speakers as "te reo"
66 Reverse
67 Esposas: Abbr.
68 Tries

DOWN

1 Glutton
2 Bomber pilot in "Catch-22"
3 Green globule
4 German connection
5 British aristocracy
6 Claim
7 ___ exchange
8 Link in the food chain?
9 #33 on a table
10 ___ duck
11 [See blurb]
12 Baritone piece sung by Renato
13 New Orleans sight
18 Sondheim's Mrs. Lovett, e.g.
22 Range parts: Abbr.
24 Airer of hearings
25 "In ___," Nirvana album
26 [See blurb]
27 Prison staple
29 Suffix with real or surreal
34 One who says a lot in a game
35 "___ can" (campaign slogan)
39 The Depression, e.g.
40 Runners do it
41 Occasionally
42 Hopelessness
43 Wrecks
44 Puts an edge on
45 Curie, Kelvin and Fermi
46 But: Lat.
49 Major mess
50 Sorkin who wrote "The Social Network"
56 Shakespearean stir
58 La-la lead-in
59 Bath ___
60 Flapper wrapper
61 Sphere
62 French flower

by Ben Fish

84

ACROSS

1 Volcano output
4 Prospects
10 Dash
14 Person with a corner ofc., maybe
15 The Scourge of God
16 Queen in "The Lion King"
17 "The Godfather" actor
18 The 21st Amendment, e.g.
19 Sting
20 Knight ___ (former newspaper group)
22 "Falcon Crest" actress
24 Awakening
26 "How ___ Your Mother"
27 Some cons
29 It might be golden
33 Final words?
36 Dockworkers' grp.
37 Allergy-afflicted dwarf
38 Car with the numeral 9 in all its model names
39 Pro baseball level . . . or a hint to 12 answers in this puzzle
41 River across the French/German border
42 Speed skater Eric who won five gold medals at the 1980 Winter Olympics
44 Location of the quadriceps
45 Enterprise captain prior to Kirk
46 Dangerous snake
47 Raspy
49 Captain of sci-fi
51 Newborn
55 Language of Cape Town
59 Antitank artillery operator, e.g.
60 Grill
61 Jungle vines
63 It may be eaten with tikka masala
64 Itch
65 Like Jimmy Kimmel and Jimmy Fallon
66 Here, in Québec
67 ___ Turing, a founding father of computer science
68 Annual event in Los Angeles
69 Summer, in Québec

DOWN

1 Capital of Ghana
2 It's said to be salubrious
3 1953 John Wayne film
4 City or lake in northern Italy
5 Repeated step
6 The Racer's Edge
7 "___ yellow ribbon . . ."
8 Singer Morissette
9 Low bow
10 Give a right to
11 ___ de Triomphe
12 Jai ___
13 Carquest competitor
21 Make dirty . . . or clean
23 ___ Lewis with the 2008 #1 hit "Bleeding Love"
25 Doozy
28 Painter Picasso
30 He loved Lucy
31 Walton who wrote "The Compleat Angler"
32 Jane of literature
33 Producer of workplace regs.
34 Bleated
35 Footnote abbr.
37 Set apart
39 Shortstop Jeter
40 Put pressure (on)
43 Inhabitant
45 New York's ___ Station
47 Fine-tuning
48 Drunkards
50 It has its moments
52 "___ Get Your Gun"
53 Boston Harbor event precipitator
54 ___ Macmillan, classmate of Harry Potter
55 Blue-green
56 Roll up, as a flag
57 Gulf of ___, arm of the Baltic
58 Room in una casa
62 "Born on the Fourth of July" setting, familiarly

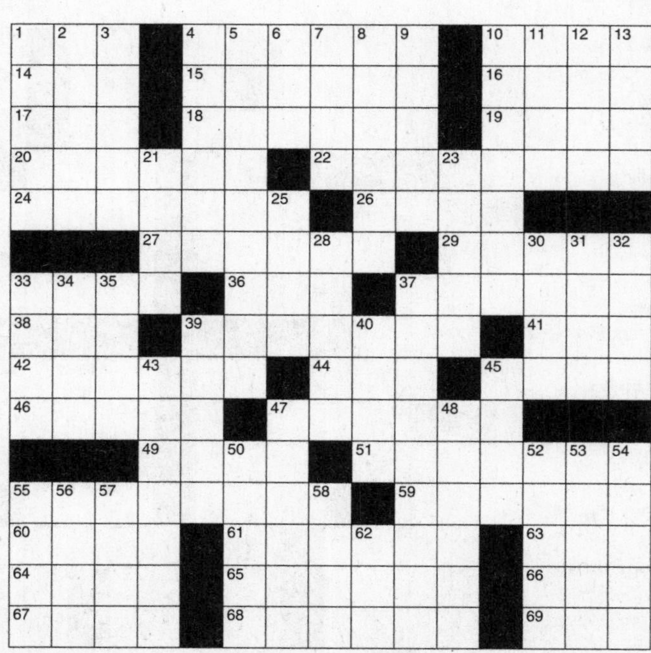

by Barry Boone

ACROSS

1 Go off course
4 Natural
10 Enjoy a pleasant situation
14 Foreman fighter
15 Symbol of Middle America
16 Fighting
17 Start of a silly underwear joke
20 Wine region of Italy
21 Extinct kin of the kiwi
22 "The Scarlet Letter" heroine
23 Joke, part 2
26 PC linkup
27 Leftovers
31 Popular bit of candy
34 Suffix with symptom
36 Final, say
37 Previously
38 Joke, part 3
41 Satisfied
42 Gordon of "Harold and Maude"
44 Small bottle
45 Wear
47 When many alarms go off
49 Good name for an investor?
50 Joke, part 4
55 Five iron
58 Browning who directed "Dracula," 1931
59 Exposed
61 End of the joke
64 Eastern nanny
65 "No way!"
66 Something not good to have on one's face
67 Sylvia who played the Queen Mother in "The Queen"
68 Fake
69 Literary inits.

DOWN

1 When tripled, et cetera
2 Elite
3 B, C or D, at a shoe store
4 Wall St. debut
5 Mad face?
6 At all
7 Geometric figures
8 Aunt, in Acapulco
9 Standard-issue item for a Secret Service agent
10 What some teens do to earn money
11 Soon
12 Render open-mouthed
13 Flier with a ground connection?
18 Farm measure
19 The second "A" of A.M.P.A.S.
24 Symbol of gentleness
25 One of the archangels
28 Sampler
29 Took advantage of
30 Major closing?
31 Maker of 31-Across
32 Fit of shaking chills
33 Child's punishment, maybe
34 Grisham's "___ to Kill"
35 Pan Am rival
39 Gradually disappear
40 Lover of brain games
43 Sinister laughs
46 Service leader
48 One who's easily duped
49 Behind on payments
51 British guns
52 Major artery
53 Country club employee
54 Leftovers
55 Corp. recruits
56 Host
57 Kingdom in "The King and I"
60 Best, but barely
62 Card game for two
63 Moroccan topper

by Alan Arbesfeld

86

ACROSS

1 "That's all right, ___" (lyric from Elvis's first single)
5 Knife
9 Flat floaters
14 Pearly gem
15 When said three times, a W.W. II cry
16 One who's called "the Merciful" and "the Compassionate"
17 Laugh uproariously
19 Brighter than bright
20 "Hee ___"
21 Like the word 16-Across
23 Dinner scraps
24 A Gershwin
25 Perspire mildly
27 Poindexter type
29 Guarantee
30 Crest alternative
32 Preferred way to proceed
35 "___ your request . . ."
36 Pay cashlessly
39 Blocks from the refrigerator
42 One of the Fitzgeralds
43 Poet who wrote "Heard melodies are sweet, but those unheard are sweeter"
47 Medieval infantry weapon
49 TV show set at William McKinley High School
50 Begin to grin
56 High point of a Swiss vacation?
57 Novelist Philip
58 Tulsan, e.g.
59 Mudroom item
60 "The Mill on the Floss" author
62 Boogie
64 Fruit related to cherry plums
65 Italian wine center
66 Change a sentence, say
67 ___ 500
68 Laura of "Rambling Rose"
69 Speeds (up)

DOWN

1 Punk rock concert activity
2 Jacket and tie, e.g.
3 It might give you a virus
4 Boxer with an allegiance to 16-Across
5 Fab Four name
6 Ancient Romans' wear
7 Dutch-speaking Caribbean isle
8 Dyed fabric
9 Sleazy paper
10 Permits
11 Recurrence of an old problem
12 Steak ___ (raw dish)
13 Business cheat
18 Keyboard key
22 Michael who starred in 39-Down
26 Small bag of chips, maybe
28 It always starts on the same day of the week as Sept.
31 Elevator background
32 Bud
33 Watch readout, for short
34 "So that's it!"
37 Longhorn's school, informally
38 Bud holder?
39 "The ___ File," 1965 film
40 Flower part
41 Jubilance
44 One way to serve pie
45 Mediterranean port
46 Disney's dwarfs and others
48 Came back
51 Eminem rap with the lyric "Guarantee I'll be the greatest thing you ever had"
52 Computer option
53 Wordless song: Abbr.
54 Admit
55 Onetime feminist cause, for short
61 Cough syrup meas.
63 La Méditerranée, e.g.

by Gary Cee

ACROSS

1 Darted
6 Grasp
12 Natl. economic stat
15 Full tilt
16 Proceeding without thinking
17 Place for clover
18 Film about how to win a MacArthur Fellowship?
21 Aoki of the P.G.A.
22 One of the 30 Dow Jones industrials
23 Ancient Anatolian land
24 Like some drugs, briefly
25 Film about a biblical serpent?
29 Winging it?
32 Conspicuously consume
33 Barq's rival
34 Trouble makers
36 Soup vegetable
38 Film about Ali/ Foreman's Rumble in the Jungle?
43 Slave
44 Goes off script
47 Word in the names of four state capitals
51 Viking king, 995-1000
54 Skin: Suffix
55 Film in which Moe, Shemp and Curly show their flexibility?
58 Lobster trap
59 Title town in a 1945 Pulitzer winner
60 "The Cat in the Hat Knows a Lot About That!" subj.
61 Mid sixth-century year
62 Film about earworms?
67 Official lang. of Ghana and Grenada
68 Judicial decision
69 Jaipur royal
70 Madrid royal
71 Vows
72 Mushroom maker, briefly

DOWN

1 Spot that's never seen
2 Figure in a Leonardo mural
3 Passage of grave importance?
4 Sound effect
5 Heavy-metal singer Snider
6 400 list-maker
7 ___ magnetism
8 Graffiti signature
9 "Say what?"
10 First N.L. 'er to hit 500 home runs
11 Unifying theme
12 Good witch
13 Didn't approve
14 Heathens
19 One that might catch a double dribble?
20 Did some garden work
26 Toni Morrison novel
27 Not kosher
28 "Anna Bolena" or "Anna Nicole"
30 Rock's ___ Fighters
31 Flanged fastener
35 Waited in line, say
37 Jason of the N.B.A.
39 Art collector's collection
40 Undesirable roll
41 Progressive Field team, on scoreboards
42 Stew container?
45 Appropriate title for this puzzle?
46 Imitation fabric
47 Second drink at a bar
48 Element in disinfectants
49 Like some country music
50 Jerry who co-founded Yahoo!
52 Become an increasing source of irritation
53 "
56 Sports no-nos, informally
57 Quit running
61 "Darn it!"
63 Like ___
64 It's very cool
65 Heat org.?
66 One piece of a two-piece

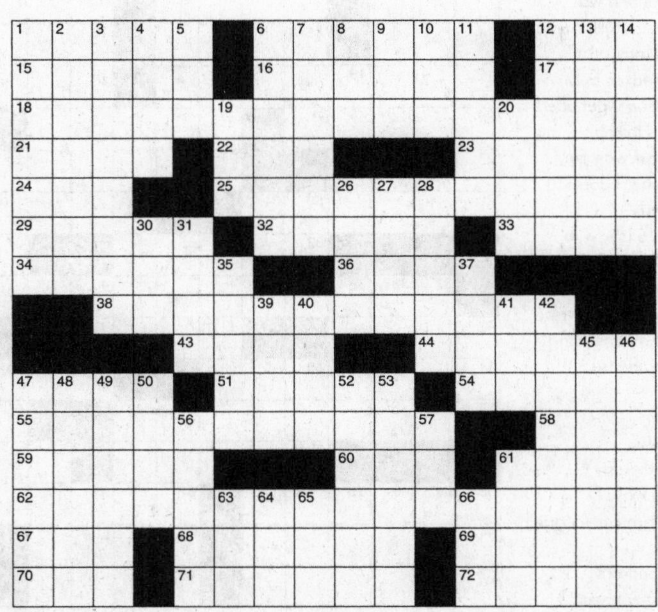

by John Farmer

88

ACROSS

1 Swiss canton
4 Good at one's job
8 Parthenon dedicatee
14 Short time to wait
15 Mast attachment
16 Brutalized
17 The cross baby was . . .
19 Places for patches
20 Brief summary
21 Book that might contain birth records
23 Homeboys
24 The cross motorist stuck at a stoplight was . . .
29 Cooks, as some vegetables
32 Doesn't give up
33 Group with revolutionary ideas
36 Author of several New Testament epistles
37 The cross man who'd been cloned was . . .
42 Pistol ___ (Oklahoma State's mascot)
43 Amassed, as debt
44 People on it get offed
47 Endless talker
52 The cross woman taking her bubble bath was . . .
55 Item in a box with seven compartments, say
56 Gettysburg general
57 Windows operating system released in 2007
58 Drift off
62 The cross aromatherapy patient was . . .
64 Lacking in knowledge
65 Exploit
66 Jimi Hendrix's "___ You Experienced?"
67 Muslim palace divisions
68 English churchyard trees
69 Naval vessel inits.

DOWN

1 Seizes unlawfully
2 Already-aired episode
3 Freezing point?
4 "Now!"
5 Object from Mars?
6 Legs and such
7 Milk carton mascot
8 Whimsical 2001 film set in Paris
9 Currency unit in the 21-Across
10 Big airport
11 "Rockaria!" band, for short
12 Just out
13 Net surfer's annoyances
18 Grp. that sends things up
22 Once-divided city
25 Stare in shock
26 Iranian coin
27 Adequately, to Li'l Abner
28 ___ modem
30 Company acquired by Verizon in 2006
31 Piteous
34 Big ___ (German W.W. I cannon)
35 What a teacher likes to hear from a pupil
37 1960s hippie event
38 James of jazz
39 Trader's option
40 Desktop item, often
41 It might make you sweat
42 21st letter
45 2001 drama whose title is taken from "Green Eggs and Ham"
46 Mounts
48 Do some political damage control
49 Guinea-___ (West African nation)
50 Lets out, maybe
51 A&E police drama set in South Florida, with "The"
53 Impart pearls of wisdom to
54 "Walk Away ___" (1966 top 10 song)
57 Ones out of service?
58 "Everybody knows that!"
59 Molecule involved in protein synthesis
60 Boston Garden legend Bobby
61 Diminutive
63 Unlovely bird sound

by Patrick Berry

ACROSS

1 Steamy places
5 "EastEnders" network
8 Toothpaste ingredient
12 Some soot
14 Fellah or fedayee
16 The Venerable ___ (old English historian)
17 Then, to Thierry
18 Insincere flattery, in slang
20 Request to an interviewee
22 "Harry and Tonto" star
23 "___, 'tis true I have gone here and there": Shak.
24 Burlesque bit
25 1980s Rowan Atkinson sitcom series set in various historical periods
28 Material you might look through
29 Every last bit
32 Items wrapped in friction tape
33 Many arcade-goers
34 Gift upon arrival, maybe
35 Winged god
36 Like zebra crossings
37 Livery delivery
38 Follow a pattern, say
39 Jimmy of "The West Wing"
40 Title role for Joe Pesci
41 House sitter?
42 Mates
43 Best Supporting Actress nominee for "Five Easy Pieces"
44 Sticks out
45 Eat in style
46 Biased
49 Pod-bearing plant
53 Started one's shift
55 Hunger enhancer, sometimes
56 Typical romance novel love interest
57 "What rotten luck!"
58 Nest-building pests
59 It's whipped to make mousse
60 Bud drinker?
61 Former life

DOWN

1 Sarcophagus lid
2 Like Death's horse
3 One of the Minor Prophets
4 Butter knife, e.g.
5 Nurslings
6 Fastener in a punched hole
7 Pink-slip
8 Famously polite Old West stagecoach robber
9 Unreactive element
10 Sedgwick in Warhol films
11 Bank
13 January department store events
15 Iconic AC/DC album with the song "You Shook Me All Night Long"
19 Filed things
21 Organic sealant
24 Bird feeder tidbits
25 Cover-up
26 Mann of rock
27 Go under
28 Volcano features
29 Unlucky in love, say
30 Country singer Rimes
31 Untainted by corruption
33 Call option?
36 Some nerve tissue
37 It's worthy of condemnation
39 Gumption
40 Woman of letters?
43 Sorento manufacturer
44 Star of 2010's "Gulliver's Travels"
45 Packed with ideas, as an essay
46 Soreness
47 Shot of liquor
48 Protracted
49 Snack
50 Novelist Jaffe
51 First-aid experts, briefly
52 Defender in a bridge column
54 Lightly apply

by Patrick Berry

90

ACROSS

1 Hanging open
6 Cousin of an ax
10 Near Eastern V.I.P.'s
14 Doesn't have a second to lose?
15 Boutique fixture
17 Exhibited perfect braking
19 Native Nebraskan
20 Followers of nus
21 "For me? You shouldn't have . . ."
22 Nicest room on a ship, probably
27 Toward the back
28 E.T.A.'s for red-eyes
29 Here, to Henri
32 Foofaraw
35 Aloe additive?
37 "Heavens to Betsy!"
38 Cashier's error, as suggested by 17-, 22-, 47- and 58-Across?
41 Henry who made a Fortune?
42 Baby taking a bow?
43 Befuddled
44 Baton Rouge sch.
45 Peace grp. since 1948
46 "___ loves me . . ."
47 Certain loaf
54 Frigidaire competitor
56 Bumbler
57 Réunion, e.g.
58 Being frugal
63 Strongly praised
64 Goose bumps-producing, maybe
65 Funnywoman Martha
66 Actress Naldi of the silents
67 Kickoff

DOWN

1 N.A.A.C.P. part: Abbr.
2 Must, slangily
3 Something to be thrown for
4 Top 40 fare
5 Medium capacity?
6 Contribute to the mix
7 Impurity
8 Eastern state?
9 That, in Tijuana
10 "___ there yet?"
11 Handy IDs in the hood?
12 Unwanted spots
13 Kind of terrier
16 Slows down traffic, say?
18 Sign by stairs, often
23 1,000-foot-deep lake that straddles a state line
24 Many miles away
25 Game with a maximum score of 180
26 Apple offering
30 Zoo keeper?
31 Noodle product?
32 Over the ___
33 Burden
34 Number of people in a room
35 Numbered thing in the Bible
36 Friendly introduction?
37 Faster's opposite
39 Bring in
40 "Yeah, right"
45 Gerald Ford's birthplace
46 Muslim mystic
48 Theodore Roosevelt, to Eleanor
49 Man of many words?
50 Press conference component, briefly
51 Arena sections
52 Carl's wife in "Up"
53 Bowling alley button
54 On ___ with (equal to)
55 Sheet mineral
59 "There is no ___ team"
60 Name placeholder in govt. records
61 Many a Fortune profilee, for short
62 "Jeopardy!" whiz Jennings

by Milo Beckman

ACROSS

1 Visibly scared out of one's wits
9 "You're ___ trouble!"
14 Alternative to a home meal
15 "___ Fall in Love" (1961 hit by the Lettermen)
16 Got comfortable with
17 1957-91 king of Norway
18 Food-stamping org.
19 Opposite of flushed
21 Dundee denial
22 Classic 1921 play set partly in a factory
25 Atlanta-based cable channel
26 In ___ (undisturbed)
27 Helps for autobiographers
31 Make available
33 Spooky sound
34 For two
36 Up
37 Befuddle
38 Having spirit?
40 Olympic entrant: Abbr.
41 "A Passage to India" woman
43 Cut back
44 Contest in which the rules must be followed to the letter?
45 1990 title role for Gérard Depardieu
47 Fictional character who says "I wear the chain I forged in life"
49 Caesar's "these"
50 Tuna type
52 On the other hand
53 Ritual garment
54 X-File subj.
55 One of the Castros
59 Cubbies, e.g.
61 Tibetan terrier
66 Altoids alternative
67 "Most certainly!"
68 Stage direction
69 1984 film whose soundtrack had a #1 hit with the same title

DOWN

1 Brake parts
2 Slightly
3 Italy's ___ Islands
4 Certain M.D.
5 Senesce
6 Lay turf on
7 Self: Prefix
8 Result of a boom and bust, maybe
9 Lucky lottery player's cry
10 Senator's org.
11 Toy collectible of the late '90s
12 Enamors
13 Cash in one's chips
14 Glace, after thawing
20 Fed. bureau
23 Jazz fan, probably
24 The scarlet letter
25 Something of earth-shaking concern?
26 Part of a band's performance
27 Tiny possibility
28 Who wrote "It's not that I'm afraid to die, I just don't want to be there when it happens"
29 "Life Itself: A Memoir" autobiographer, 2011
30 Start another tour
32 Make by interlacing
35 Additional, in ads
39 Mysterious: Var.
42 Fond du ___, Wis.
46 Buffoon
48 Major discount brokerage
51 Trinity member
54 Cold war inits.
56 Copycat
57 Plays for a fool
58 City near Ben-Gurion Airport
60 Artery: Abbr.
62 New Test. book
63 The Sun Devils, for short
64 Auntie, to Dad
65 Word with black, red or white

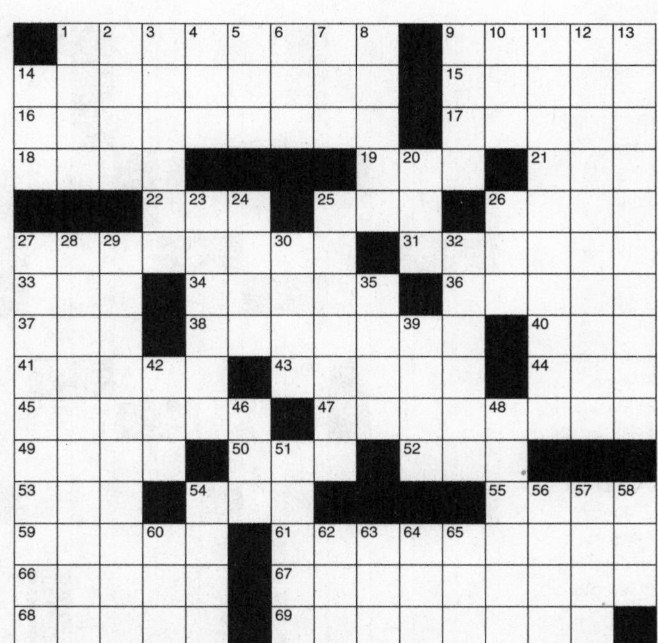

by Kurt Mueller

92

ACROSS

1 Astronomer Sagan
5 Final preceder
9 Like E.T.'s voice
14 Sounder of the tuning note at the start of an orchestra rehearsal
15 Gillette ___ II
16 Apple communication tool
17 See 37-Across
19 Palace employee
20 Appeal
21 "Aren't you special!"
22 Caleb who wrote "The Alienist"
23 See 37-Across
28 Provider of a jawbone to Samson
29 G.I. address
30 Traffic caution
31 "Stat!"
34 Clingy wrap
36 London's ___ Gardens
37 Grammatical infelicity . . . or what 17-, 23-, 48- or 60- Across is?
41 Part of R.S.V.P.
42 Runaways
43 Linear, briefly
44 "___ tu" (Verdi aria)
45 Foot soldiers: Abbr.
46 TV extraterrestrial
48 See 37-Across
54 Neck of the woods
55 Crones
56 A hand
58 Where the brain resides, slangily
60 See 37-Across
62 "Ask me anything"
63 Part of Georgia is in it
64 Sound
65 "___ Doone," 1869 historical romance
66 Alpine capital
67 Food safety org.

DOWN

1 Some prison furnishings
2 Circa
3 Official state sport of Wyoming
4 Wahine wear
5 Bar lineup
6 Weasley family owl, in Harry Potter books
7 ___ Picchu (Inca site)
8 Put away
9 Pasta variety
10 Honda division
11 Shiny suit fabric
12 Score to aim for
13 Stock page abbr.
18 Part of R.S.V.P.
22 Hearings channel
24 Big ___ (nickname of baseball's David Ortiz)
25 "We'll always have ___" (line from "Casablanca")
26 Student in 25-Down
27 Planted
31 It's a plus
32 Vice president Agnew
33 Pricey belt material
34 Smokeless tobacco
35 At the back of a boat
38 Ambitious track bet
39 Ancient Aegean region
40 Elegantly dressed bloke
46 Crocheted item
47 Simpson girl
49 1970s–'90s film company
50 "Along ___ lines . . ."
51 P.L.O.'s Arafat
52 Goodbyes
53 Cede
57 Actress de Matteo of "The Sopranos"
58 Communication syst. for the hearing-impaired
59 However, for short
60 Bar bill
61 Fifth of seven: Abbr.

by Barry Franklin and Sara Kaplan

ACROSS

1 Certain lamp goo
5 Home
10 Subject of an exhaustive E.P.A. study?
14 Give ___ up
15 Thoroughly enjoy
16 Monarch moniker, for short
17 Part of an equine pedigree
18 California's Santa ___ University
19 Cemetery sights
20 Nearly impossible target, literally
23 Apt name for a crime boss
24 Gist
25 One who's enraptured, say, literally
31 Ship navigation hazard
33 Detected
34 Equatorial land
35 Promenade
37 Weenie
40 Caboose
41 "It must be ___ news day"
43 Some jeans
45 Young ___
46 Inadvertently destructive sort, literally
50 Mardi follower
51 Five pairs
52 Something rapidly deteriorating goes to it, literally
59 A good one is cracked
60 "Bye-bye, mon ami"
61 Something that's just for starters?
62 "The Lord of the Rings," e.g.
63 Set the volume of to zero
64 "Chocolat" actress Olin
65 Weasel relatives
66 Chimpersonators?
67 Purpose of many a doctor's visit

DOWN

1 Pirate's punishment
2 Inter ___
3 First part of an I.P. address?
4 A chair usually has one
5 Rose
6 Treadless
7 Like faces, typically
8 Bread
9 Cleared
10 One without a title
11 Chicago exchange, informally, with "the"
12 Porcine protest
13 Division units, for short
21 Ages upon ages
22 Job to do
25 Stringed instruments
26 Wood used in Voldemort's wand
27 Sound at a funeral
28 Top
29 Film private
30 They may ring or have rings
31 Jobs plan, once
32 Convert, in a way
36 Certain beer bottle
38 Sushi staple
39 Intimates
42 ___ of the state
44 2000 World Series locale
47 Grand ___ Island
48 Depleted
49 Marked down
52 Neighbors of the Navajo
53 Similar
54 Having less fat
55 Uninviting look
56 Building toy brand
57 Italian mount
58 ___ U.S.A.
59 Scout's brother

by Parker Lewis

94

ACROSS

1 Sting figure
5 Car dealer's starting point: Abbr.
9 Old Buckeye State service station name
14 Chewy candy treat
15 Old buffalo hunters of the Great Plains
16 Work that gives the illusion of movement
17 Needing no invitation
19 Safety ___
20 Like a successful marathoner?
22 Late-night beverages
23 1960s teach-in grp.
24 Bit of crying
27 Same: Prefix
28 Helsinki hoosegow?
32 Himalayas, e.g.: Abbr.
34 "___ me my Highland lassie, O": Burns
35 Pulitzer nominee for the novels "Black Water" and "Blonde"
36 Accommodating person? . . . or a hint to 20-, 28-, 48- and 57-Across
40 Bat cave deposit
43 It's part of the gene pool
44 Intentions
48 Call of a siren?
52 Chess champion Mikhail
53 It may be green or black
54 Seek damages
55 Warm and comfy
57 Jaded ale drinker's question?
61 Pied-à-___
63 Like many a whisper
64 Rugged rocks
65 Pro's foe
66 Some readouts, briefly
67 Not realized
68 For fear that
69 They may be announced en route: Abbr.

DOWN

1 Darken
2 Most downcast
3 French city associated with lace
4 Gianni's grandmother
5 Lesser-known astrology symbol
6 Missing women?
7 Massage deeply
8 Longtime Democratic House leader
9 Tapless tap-dancing
10 Mayberry moppet
11 Construction worker
12 Org. with auditors
13 Giant legend
18 Little slapfest
21 Takes too much, briefly
25 Alternative to I, you, he or she
26 Gives the nod to
29 Suffix with peace
30 Food and shelter
31 Home in a Mitchell novel
33 ___ Fein
37 Registering the most on the applause-o-meter
38 Music producer Brian
39 Women's businesswear
40 Prime meridian std.
41 Slangy reversal
42 Chemical agent for climate change
45 "You're on!"
46 Title woman in a Harry Belafonte song
47 Duplicity
49 Many a rosary carrier
50 Good-humored
51 Prod
56 Like an acrobat
58 Prod
59 Non-P.C. suffix
60 They're taken in high sch.
61 Home of the Horned Frogs: Abbr.
62 Directional suffix

by Paula Gamache

ACROSS

1 Snowmen and snowwomen?
6 Analogy words
10 Fraternity characters
14 Word akin to "-ish"
15 "Absolut nicht!"
16 River to the Arctic Ocean
17 Get an A, say
18 Vulnerable parts
20 Lago
22 Half of a 1955 merger, for short
24 "Alea iacta ___": Julius Caesar
25 Poet Elinor
26 Ion
31 Wind up
32 "If I were king of the forest . . ." singer
33 Gave pills, e.g.
35 Iams, say
42 It might hold you back
43 "Such is life"
44 Med. unit
47 Lamb's place
51 "In bad company," per Ambrose Bierce
53 Boxcar
54 Ones getting base pay
55 Feature replaced in four clues in this puzzle
60 Locale for some diving
61 Touches
64 "My Life" autobiographer, 1975
65 Clip
66 Trouble
67 The Ponte Vecchio spans it
68 Approximately
69 Cicely of "Roots"

DOWN

1 Dollar coin figure before Susan B. Anthony, familiarly
2 "Ain't gonna happen!"
3 Strip
4 Dome light?
5 One may be smooth
6 A part of, as a gang
7 Comprehended
8 Mexican kin
9 Cleaning a mess in a mess, maybe
10 Roman writer who originated the phrase "with a grain of salt"
11 Beyond reason?
12 Fills, as black squares
13 Like many windows
19 "Compromise is the best and cheapest ___" (saying attributed to Robert Louis Stevenson)
21 PC key
22 Roping target
23 Myth ending
27 Things picked out of the earth
28 Take in
29 Passport info
30 Picking up things?
34 Call
36 Spring break locale, casually
37 Order member
38 They may do write-ups, for short
39 Hard-to-clean floor covers
40 Big name in luxury hotels
41 "___ Declassified School Survival Guide"
44 City on Commencement Bay
45 Assassin
46 Comes calling unexpectedly
48 Experienced with
49 Gradually slowing, in mus.
50 Still around
52 "Explosive" roller coaster at Six Flags Great Adventure
56 Mythical ship with a speaking oak beam
57 Angle iron
58 Hawaiian handouts
59 Where Al Yankovic bought a "Dukes of Hazzard" ashtray, in song
62 "The way"
63 Depot: Abbr.

by Tim Croce

96

ACROSS

1 The two together
5 In fighting trim
8 Sparks's state
14 Quick as a wink
16 For all, as a restroom
17 Online university staff?
18 Trig function
19 Anthem contraction
20 Phone no.
22 Body designs, informally
23 What Nashville sunbathers acquire?
27 One to hang with
28 Special attention, for short
29 Golf ball's position
30 "Not on ___!"
32 Hasty escape
34 Ballplayer with a 40-Down logo
39 Sign prohibiting sunshades?
43 At attention
44 Sgt. or cpl.
45 Like many fast-food orders
46 Bailed-out insurance co.
49 Local govt. unit
51 Make public
52 Salon jobs from apprentice stylists?
57 Zinging remark
58 Coffee, slangily
59 Nest egg letters
60 Where to find a piece of Turkey
62 "Stop that!" . . . and a hint to the answers to 17-, 23-, 39- and 52-Across
67 Chips away at
68 Seinfeld's eccentric relative
69 Many a Little League rooter
70 "Go team!"
71 Sunbathers catch them

DOWN

1 Coal holder
2 Indivisible
3 Demolitionist's aid
4 Biker's invitation to a friend
5 Former Big Apple mayor La Guardia
6 Global currency org.
7 Lab jobs
8 Atomic centers
9 Brian of ambient music
10 Scenic view
11 Like most Turks
12 Body shop jobs
13 Graph lines
15 1545–63 council site
21 Moray, e.g.
23 Drum accompanying a fife
24 École attendee
25 Emotionally damage
26 Blue-green hue
27 Plexiglas piece
31 Muscle spasm
33 AOL alternative
35 W. C. Fields persona
36 Bar closing time, perhaps
37 Philbin of live TV
38 "P.U.!" inducer
40 See 34-Across
41 "Hamlet" has five
42 Fastball in the dirt, say
47 Kiddingly
48 Prefix with thermal
50 Jeopardy
52 Michelle's predecessor as first lady
53 Goof
54 "Humble" home
55 Come back
56 Zagat, to restaurants
57 Microwave sound
61 Porker's pad
63 Old-time actress Merkel
64 Suffix with pay or plug
65 Driver's one-eighty
66 How-___ (handy books)

by Tracy Gray

ACROSS

1 Office device appropriate for this puzzle?
7 Await
11 Rte. suggester
14 Setting for many a fairy tale
15 Assistant played by Charles Bronson in "House of Wax"
16 Drama set in Las Vegas
17 Command agreement
18 "That's of little importance"
20 Out of service?: Abbr.
21 Road hazards
23 Fence builder's starting point
24 Small doses may come in them
26 "Charlotte's Web" girl
27 One half of an old comedy duo
28 Like the Paris Opera
31 Airport need
34 Substitute
37 I.R.S. 1040 line item
38 They might give each other French kisses
39 Way to get around something
40 No longer interested in
41 Undecided: Abbr.
42 Album half
43 Space under a desk
44 End of a perfect Sunday drive?
46 Grill
48 Impulse path
49 33-Down's group, with "the"
53 Kitchen tool
55 Physicist Bohr
56 Jim Beam product
57 Like some patches
59 1940s British P.M.
61 Times in classifieds
62 Game played on a world map
63 Quick outing for Tiger Woods . . . or what this completed puzzle contains
64 Violin cutouts
65 What a peeper uses to peep
66 Can't stand

DOWN

1 Game item usually seen upside-down
2 Check writer
3 Is of ___ (helps)
4 Some Windows systems
5 The Cutty Sark, for one
6 Lifesavers, say
7 Features of homemade cameras
8 Big ones can impede progress
9 Montréal or Québec
10 Window dressing
11 Feigns ignorance
12 Play ___ (perform some songs)
13 Seal's opening?
19 Conflicted
22 Photography aid
25 Portable info-storing devices
26 Below-ground sanctuary
29 Almond or pecan
30 Batting helmet feature
31 Filthy place
32 Prefix with valent
33 See 49-Across
35 Pre-schoolers?
36 Light-blocking
39 Part of a home security system?
40 French eleven
42 Ones who sleep soundly?
43 Alley behind a bar on TV?
45 They're drafted for service
47 Higher ground
49 Topographical feature formed by underground erosion
50 1957 hit for the Bobbettes
51 Parts of masks
52 "Thou ___ I have more flesh than another man": Falstaff
53 Role for which Marion Cotillard won a 2007 Best Actress Oscar
54 Vest feature
55 Like a quidnunc
58 Feature of many a ballroom dance
60 "We Know Drama" channel

by Mike Nothnagel

98

ACROSS

1 The old man
5 Bare minimum
10 Arias, e.g.
14 "Thirteen" actress ___ Rachel Wood
15 Ob/gyn test
16 Eliot Ness and cohorts
17 "anyone lived in a pretty how town" poet
19 Manassas fighters
20 Modular, as a home
21 Author better known as Saki
23 Fakes, as figures
26 Whopper topper
27 "Star Trek" director, 2009
30 "The Thrill Is Gone" bluesman
31 "Bad, bad" Brown of song
32 Banking nos.
34 Cameo gem
35 Juice box go-with
36 Big Indian
40 Animals in a Western herd
41 Neighbor of Chad
42 Big name in mail order
46 "The Monkey's Paw" author
48 Heroine in Bizet's "The Pearl Fishers"
49 Not real
50 Creator of Eeyore
52 One of a winter pair
56 Some med. scans
57 2007 A.L. Cy Young winner
60 Years, in Rome
61 "___ dead!" (worried teen's words)
62 Srs.' lobby
63 Cookbook instruction
64 Grid play starters
65 ___' Pea

DOWN

1 Slightest sound
2 No longer disturbed by
3 Eight minutes/mile in a marathon is a good one
4 Ornamental tobacco holder
5 Letter resembling an inverted "V"
6 ___ Group ("big four" record co.)
7 One of Heart's Wilson sisters
8 Heaved sounds
9 Brit's "Baloney!"
10 "The Elements of Style" co-author
11 Subtitle of 1978's "Damien"
12 Former Cavalier James
13 How Broadway characters may break out
18 TV host Povich
22 Crowds around
24 Hurdles for M.B.A. hopefuls
25 Third-party accounts
27 "Selena" star, familiarly
28 Aniston, in tabloids
29 Suffix with vision
30 "Incidentally," to texters
33 Eager kids' query to parents
35 Ugly as ___
36 Ravioli fillings
37 Back in time
38 Brother of W.
39 "___ Poetica"
40 Jezebel's god
41 Gymnast Comaneci
42 Andean wool sources
43 Found out, British-style
44 Fountain of Youth site, it's said
45 "L'___ d' Amore" (Donizetti opera)
47 747 and Airbus A380, as jets go
49 Praline nut
51 CBS military drama
53 Warming trend
54 Limerick's land
55 Target of a rabbit punch
58 Wee, to Burns
59 Cleopatra biter

by Samuel A. Donaldson

ACROSS

1 French clerics
6 President after Tyler
10 Medicinal amts.
14 General's cry
15 This and that
16 Stimulate
17 Game maker starting in 1972
18 Actress Carrie and others
19 Like wetlands
20 *Antimicrobial bit in mouthwashes [90 degrees]
22 *Like wizards' caps [90 degrees]
24 ___ volente (God willing)
25 Really thin person
27 Tornado
30 Judgment
32 Food thickener
34 Undivided
35 #1 hit by the Byrds . . . or directions for reading the answers to this puzzle's starred clues (always clockwise as indicated)
38 Mai ___ (drinks)
41 Wine: Prefix
42 "Comin' ___!"
43 *Apollo 11 and 12 [180 degrees]
48 Given the nod
49 Dance at a Jewish wedding
50 Showing signs of disuse
54 Iranian city of 1.2+ million
56 Masculine side
58 Insurance plan, for short
59 *Marriage, say [270 degrees]
61 *Specification in a burger order, maybe [270 degrees]
63 Attorney General Holder
65 Endure
67 Dessert cake
68 [I'm kidding!]
69 Nobelist Wiesel
70 Dipsomaniac
71 Jumpy
72 LP or 45
73 Biblical dry measures

DOWN

1 "She's the Man" actress Bynes
2 Washes
3 Longest river in Texas
4 Off-white shade
5 Tibetan dog
6 Kind of scheme
7 West Coast brew, for short
8 Place
9 Dweller in Pristina
10 Like many TV movies: Abbr.
11 Public mention
12 Candy that comes in more than a dozen flavors
13 Farm structure
21 Short person?
23 N.F.L. coach Jim
26 St. Louis's arch, symbolically
28 "Just you wait, ___ 'iggins . . ."
29 TV warrior princess
31 Formal/informal response to "Who's there?"
33 Ben ___, "Treasure Island" pirate
36 "The Big Sleep" film genre
37 Shooters
38 General ___ chicken
39 Egyptian cross
40 Treating, in a way, as table salt
44 Bygone sovereign
45 Three sheets to the wind
46 Of little ___ use
47 Should
51 Five-time Olympic gold-medal swimmer
52 One overacting
53 Catnappers
55 Tumultuous
57 Old pyramid builder
60 District of Colombia?
62 Camera feature
63 Animal often seen with a bell around its neck
64 Clear (of)
66 Family girl

by Andrew Zhou

100

ACROSS

1 Home, slangily
5 Rio Grande city
11 In the manner of
14 Rhein tributary
15 Food storage area
16 Mick Jagger's title
17 Signs of elation → marathon segments
19 Liberal arts maj.
20 Prefix with skeleton
21 Italy's side, once
22 Melt ingredient
23 Put down
25 Sign of trouble → commercial writers
27 Greedy sort
28 Certain offshoot
31 Lech of Poland's Solidarity
32 Beehive State Indians
34 "Born from jets" automaker
36 Watch readouts, for short
37 Pigtail → cause for a siren
40 Hydrotherapy sites
42 Squandered, as a lead
43 Courtroom attention-getter
47 Like some phone minutes
49 Furry sci-fi creature
51 That, in Tijuana
52 Toaster food → dazzling designs
54 Smoothly, on a score
56 Spanish counterpart of a mlle.
57 "Dies ___"
60 Rotund Wolfe
61 Ore suffix
62 Fireplace part → fall color
65 TV spot, often
66 Katharine Hepburn's foursome
67 États-___
68 What a farmer in Del. works on?
69 Surgeon's probe
70 Bog product

DOWN

1 Locomotive part
2 Cheesy dish
3 First millennium B.C., roughly
4 Worrier's handful
5 Chi-town rails
6 Holy man in an Ogden Nash verse
7 ___ fixe
8 Forgo the script
9 Plaything for two
10 Places for scrubs, for short
11 Like an alias
12 Disney's Nala, for one
13 Deep secrets
18 Performs
22 El Greco's city
23 Satyajit Ray's "The ___ Trilogy"
24 First name in '50s TV comedy
26 Painter of dreamscapes
29 Prepare for a marathon, say, with "up"
30 Set aside
33 Cascade Range peak
35 Make stout
38 On the ocean blue
39 A.F.B. truant
40 Showed contempt for something
41 Soldier's shelter
44 The start of time
45 Where Skype was invented
46 Wild scene
47 Positive aspect
48 Having the least vermouth
50 Ranges of knowledge
53 Comics character with a wrist radio
55 Fancy duds
58 Asia's ___ Sea
59 To be, to Brigitte
62 Jolly sounds
63 Prez who said "If you can't stand the heat, get out of the kitchen"
64 Ballpark fig.

by Robert W. Harris

101

ACROSS

1 Fighter in the "Iliad"
5 Excellence
10 Similarly round
15 Sumptuousness
16 Onetime name at the Taj Mahal
17 Apt
18 OPEC dignitary, maybe
19 It might be run in a hospital
20 Annoyance, in British slang
21 Microsoft debut of 2001
22 Common result of high humidity
23 Located
24 Infrequent blood type, informally
26 Like some doors
28 Keeps going
33 Modern sum?
36 Stone work
39 Blue hues
40 Drank heavily
43 What this puzzle is, orthographically
46 Spanish ___
47 Head of the class, in slang
48 Dressing tool
49 1990 autobiography subtitled "Baseball, the Wall and Me"
50 "Hold on . . . what's going on here?!"
53 Basketball's Isiah Thomas, to fans
55 Suitable for teen audiences
58 Gets set
61 Some child-care center sites, for short
66 Plug
68 Prepare for battle
69 Like the Addams Family
70 ___ Croft, Angelina Jolie role
71 Optimistic
72 Hall-of-Famer Michael of the Dallas Cowboys
73 "Semper Fidelis" grp.
74 Model Cheryl
75 Judges
76 Longest-lived first lady

DOWN

1 "A Clockwork Orange" lead role
2 Extra-large
3 Hypothetical fundamental particle
4 Persepolis king
5 Put out
6 "If I ___ . . ."
7 Sitarist Shankar
8 Don Juan's mother
9 "Me" follower
10 "Lawrence of Arabia" city
11 Sweetening
12 Mediterranean harvest
13 It's about 90 yards of a football field
14 Eliminated from a boxing match, in a way
25 Sentry
27 "St. Matthew Passion" composer, for short
29 Loudly voice one's objections
30 Male sheep, in Britain
31 Noted Finnish chair designer
32 "___ little silhouetto . . ." ("Bohemian Rhapsody" lyric)
34 Locale of a much-visited mausoleum
35 Flagon contents, perhaps
36 Presidential inits.
37 Alecto, Megaera or Tisiphone
38 Hindu god of desire
41 ___ pursuit
42 Part of Korea, for short
44 Brilliant
45 Manhandle
51 Geezer's cry to a young 'un
52 Tech-savvy school grp.
54 Awards show with a Best Play category, with "the"
56 Stage
57 "Bugs"
58 Witticism
59 Distant leader?
60 Crescent shape
62 Abraded
63 Coastal feature
64 Actor Tamiroff
65 Thesaurus contents: Abbr.
67 W.W. II group

by Peter Wentz

102

Note: When this puzzle is done, read the eight circled letters clockwise, starting with square #24, to identify this puzzle's theme.

ACROSS

1 Crept (along)
7 Word with Orange or Peach
11 Car that was the subject of a 1964 top 10 hit
14 Sesame seed-based sauce
15 Eye area
16 Put out
17 Passes
18 #2
20 Mid 12th-century year
21 Hosp. areas
23 Cantankerous
24 ___ Valley
26 At the home of, to Henri
27 Hoist
29 Infomercial host Gibbons
33 Co-star of Hanks in "Forrest Gump"
35 Puts away
37 Cambodia's Lon ___
38 Carry on
39 Singer Studdard who won the second season of "American Idol"
41 Sunroof or moonroof alternative
42 What rings reveal about a tree
43 Funeral fire
44 "___ Be Stupid" (1985 Weird Al Yankovic album)
46 Performer dubbed "The Great Dane"
48 Like a next-door neighbor's lawn, or so it seems
50 Just sitting around
52 Tool
55 W.W. II battle cry
58 Qxe5, e.g., in chess
59 Way in Québec
60 #5
62 Kind of kick
64 Fish-fowl nexus
65 Old space-launched rocket
66 Still on the shelf
67 Envoy's bldg.
68 Gazpacho, e.g.
69 Team with a big B on its helmets

DOWN

1 Twosomes
2 Folk singer Griffith
3 #3
4 Hawaiian Punch alternative
5 Lures
6 #4
7 Tampa Bay gridders, for short
8 Lacto-___ vegetarian
9 Laura Bush's maiden name
10 Symbol of victory
11 Andy with the #1 hit "Shadow Dancing"
12 "Lou Grant" paper, with "the"
13 Give a thumbs-up
19 It may be hedged
22 Mozart's "___ donna a quindici anni"
25 Tennis's Nastase
26 Grammy-winning Winans
28 Italian waterway
30 #1
31 ___ suit
32 Mighty Dog rival
33 Q-tip, e.g.
34 "I am not what I am" speaker
36 #6
40 Exhort
41 Dos follower
43 Nitpicking types
45 Dish alternative
47 City with the Great Sphinx
49 Prefix with hazard
51 Certain printing process, briefly
53 "September 1, 1939" poet
54 Does some yardwork
55 Ruin
56 Orbit site
57 Workers' rights agcy.
58 Letters on a car sticker
61 Letters from a debtor
63 Aspen or Tahoe

by Allan E. Parrish

ACROSS

1 The Divine, in 23-Across
4 "M*A*S*H" co-star
8 Get started
14 Woman's name that means "messenger of God"
16 Simple hydrocarbon
17 *Omaha-born human rights activist
18 Mauled
19 Pick ___ (quibble)
20 Supérieur et Érié
22 Baum princess
23 Ligurian capital
25 Having harmony
28 Suffix with ball
29 Physics unit
30 Tee follower
32 1955 Platters hit
34 Plunk preceder
35 Follows
36 *Today's kids, demographically speaking
38 Plessy v. ___ (landmark Supreme Court decision)
40 Gate opener for Apollo
41 Afternoon services
42 Drew Barrymore hosted this show at age 7: Abbr.
43 Est., e.g., once
46 Approximately 946 of these make a qt.
47 Bouquet : pheasants :: covey : ___
49 Volkswagen model
51 Hockey's Phil, to fans
53 Hubbub
55 "Dianetics" author ___ Hubbard
56 How some gym instructors stand
59 *Brand with the challenge to lose one inch from your waist in two weeks
61 Many a campaign fund-raiser
62 Sweet wine
63 It goes in front of a coal tender
64 Hayes portrayer in "The Mod Squad," 1999
65 Number of tiles per Scrabble set for the letter at the end of the answer to each starred clue

DOWN

1 Split or crack
2 More asinine
3 Viewing with elevator eyes
4 ___-pitch
5 It may be good or free
6 Con
7 Mexican silver center
8 Trick
9 Chiwere-speaking tribe
10 "And ___ the field the road runs by": Tennyson
11 Courtroom cry
12 Feeling gloomy, say
13 Lockjaw
15 ___-1 ("Ghostbusters" vehicle)
21 Part of a pig
24 *"What Do You Do With a B.A. in English?" musical
26 ___ régime
27 *Performer born James Todd Smith
31 Mocedades hit subtitled "Touch the Wind"
33 Urges
34 Gunpowder holders
35 Japanese surname follower
36 Comprehending
37 Latin lover's bouquet, maybe
38 Where the N.S.A. is headquartered
39 Some wallet material
42 Blunder
43 Prefix with cumulus
44 Like some kisses
45 Irk
48 "Hello ___" (Todd Rundgren hit)
50 Director Kazan
52 Bygone science/sci-fi magazine
54 Sued party in a legal case: Abbr.
57 Michael Jackson's first #1 solo hit
58 Calif. neighbor
60 Hosp. units

by Bill Thompson

104

ACROSS

1 With 66-Across, subject of this puzzle, born 12/1/1935
6 "Maude" star Arthur
9 With 64-Across, 1-/66-Across movie of 2005
14 "If memory serves . . ."
16 Dress in the Forum
17 . . . of 1987
18 Some tomatoes
19 Faux pas
21 Winter hrs. in St. Louis
22 . . . of 1990
26 ___ exchange
27 It's high on the pH scale
28 Silents actor Novarro
29 . . . of 1979
31 Asian nurse
32 Dorothy's state: Abbr.
33 "Too bad!"
34 . . . of 1971
36 . . . of 1973
40 Be up
41 Mayo is in it
42 ___ land
43 . . . of 1977
47 Par ___
48 Part of l'été
49 A mean Amin
50 . . . of 1983
51 Nelson Mandela's org.
52 Shaded passageway
55 Verdi's very
57 . . . of 1978
62 Close, in verse
63 Feverishness
64 See 9-Across
65 Raiders make them, informally
66 See 1-Across

DOWN

1 Something played out in a theater
2 Spanish she-bear
3 Geometric suffix
4 Demoisturized, in commercial names
5 Palace workers
6 Flock sounds
7 Heavenly
8 Hall-of-Famer Walter who was a Dodger manager for 23 years
9 No. on a car
10 ___ Z
11 Male with whiskers
12 Top-level
13 Get a move on
15 Early fifth-century year
20 Surround with a glow
22 Sheik's mount
23 Spiritual guide
24 One-named 1970s–'80s supermodel
25 Live together
27 Vitamin involved in cell metabolism
29 "Keep them coming, Juan!"
30 Amazement
32 TV's ___ Lee
35 Scot's not
36 Show announced by Don Pardo for 30+ years, for short
37 Construction worker's lunch container
38 H. G. Wells people
39 Phoned
41 Neatened, in a way
43 Certain travel guide
44 "Stop! You've got it all wrong!"
45 Centers
46 Unmoored
47 Hank with voices on "The Simpsons"
52 Left side
53 Places where the Daily Racing Form is read, in brief
54 Celtic sea god
56 Get bronze
58 Excellent, slangily
59 Lube (up)
60 Way: Abbr.
61 Dict. listing

by Caleb Madison

ACROSS

1 Orient
8 Orient
15 Ace
16 Ace
17 Lower in stature
18 Lower in stature
19 Part of B.C.E.
20 Shakes
22 Runnin' ___, 1944 N.C.A.A. basketball champs
23 Party favorites?
24 Onetime sponsor of Richard Petty and Mario Andretti
26 Uses a needle
29 Dummy
31 Epitome of simplicity
34 I, for one
38 I, for one
40 Understanding
41 Understanding
42 Tire
43 Tire
44 Tax form datum: Abbr.
45 Major sight in the sky?
47 Ballet bend
48 East end?
49 Sweater woes
53 Raw side?
56 Sway
57 "Nonsense!"
60 Loose
63 Loose
65 Mean
66 Mean
67 Bristles
68 Bristles

DOWN

1 What some things do in the sun
2 Profess
3 Latvian capital
4 Elephant's-___ (plant)
5 Whatever
6 "Me too!"
7 Lock
8 They're good for crying out loud
9 Serpent tail?
10 Good companion for an ace in Vegas
11 Burn through
12 Pit-___
13 Lug
14 Old English letters
21 J.F.K. posting
23 Ed of Hollywood
24 Froth
25 Lure
26 Gushes
27 Coastal fliers
28 Odin, to the Germans
30 Lulu
31 Old Russian co-op
32 Religion with an apostrophe in its name
33 River through Glasgow
35 "___ Own," 1989 #2 hit by Bobby Brown
36 Possible response to a driving mistake
37 Trawlers' gear
39 Brothers of the Wild West
46 ___ result
48 Vessels by basins
50 Lake bordered by Malawi, Mozambique and Tanzania
51 Moving
52 ___ body (cell part)
53 Denigrate, in English slang, with "off"
54 In the flesh
55 Aid's partner
56 Something that's fun on the coast?
57 Person under the Union Jack
58 Fuji rival
59 Startled cries
61 Winning Super Bowl XXXIV player
62 Turkish title
64 Response: Abbr.

by Joe Krozel

106

ACROSS

1 Shade of green
5 Workplace watchdog, for short
9 "That ___ my question"
14 Each
15 Mrs. Frisby's charges in "The Secret of NIMH"
16 See 26-Across
17 Home of Eastern Michigan University
19 Rodeo rope
20 Harry Belafonte's specialty
22 "___ natural"
25 U.N. workers' grp.
26 One may be lit on a 16-Across
27 Veer off track
29 Pole, for one
31 It might precede a collection: Abbr.
32 Guns' partner
33 Rapper parodied by Weird Al Yankovic in "Amish Paradise"
35 1979 film with Capt. Willard and Col. Kurtz
40 Universally known
41 "Idylls of the King" lady
43 Motocross racer, for short
46 Skating maneuver
47 P.F.C.'s punishment
49 Some prayer clothing
51 My ___, Vietnam
52 ___-wolf
53 Undercover operatives . . . or what are hiding in 17-, 20-, 35- and 58-Across?
57 Onetime TWA competitor
58 Leaf-eating insect scourge
62 Hundredth: Prefix
63 Gray ___
64 Tot's injury
65 Couldn't stand
66 Garden divisions
67 Post-baby boomer group, for short

DOWN

1 Homer Simpson's middle name
2 iPad download, in brief
3 First of a pair of lists
4 Awesome
5 How some medications are taken
6 Big name in Japanese electronics
7 U.R.L. start
8 Sale condition
9 35-Across, for one
10 North Pacific islander
11 Immobility
12 Longtime local
13 Finder of missing persons
18 Cubs' place
21 Most toilet seats
22 Turkish title
23 Result of trauma, maybe
24 Pack (down)
28 Bark
29 Russian space program started in the 1960s
30 Takes the top (off)
33 Medical condition treated by thrombolysis
34 Lacking width and depth, for short
36 Screening aid
37 Something that can't be missed
38 Burden
39 ___ child (pregnant)
42 Hair salon stock
43 In and of itself
44 Title location in a Hemingway novel
45 Like rooms to rent
47 Where Manhattan is
48 Unfortunate circumstance
50 Correspond
51 Cartoon stinker
54 Food thickener
55 Greek deli specialty
56 Urban woe
59 Be short
60 Cookie holder
61 Do voodoo on

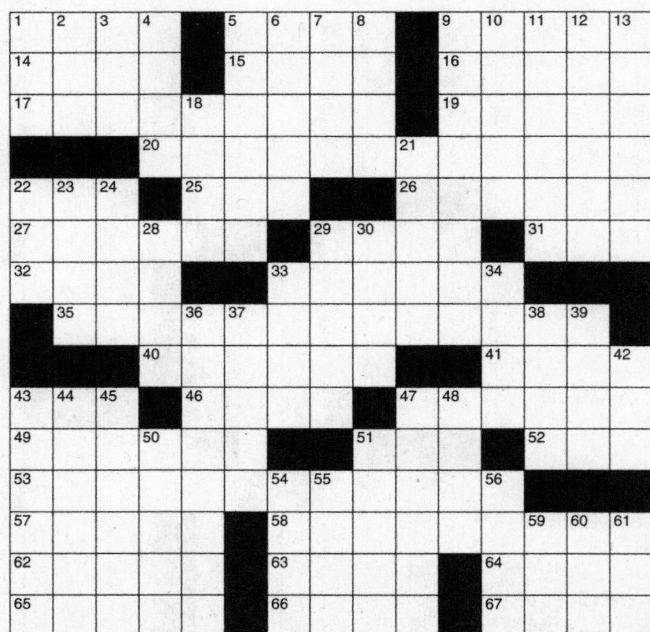

by Mike Nothnagel

ACROSS

1 Opposite of race
5 Pyramid schemes, e.g.
10 Its scores are used in selecting Natl. Merit Scholars
14 For all grades
15 Shanty
16 Prefix with -pod
17 Comical Martha
18 Actor Hirsch of "Into the Wild"
19 See 44-Down
20 Five Jacksons
22 *Dramatically expose
24 *Home near a shore
26 Prevaricate
27 Patron saint of Norway
28 They're shown in a beauty pageant
32 Madam
35 Just out
37 Where to find eBay and Google
38 Govt. watchdog since 1970
39 Miller products?
41 Big Ten sch.
42 Co. bought by Verizon
43 One leading a cheer, perhaps
44 1998 Roberto Clemente Award winner
45 Like a vampire's victims
47 Classification for some popular Spanish music
48 Push
49 Mount Whitney's range
51 Et ___
53 'Fore
54 *Massachusetts college
59 *1975 Southern rock hit stereotypically requested at concerts
61 Words mouthed to a camera
62 Pro team?
63 Beef type
65 Tropical vegetable also known as elephant's-ear
66 "I ___ dead!"
67 Part of 41-Across
68 Short race, briefly
69 Paula of TV news
70 Whom Raskolnikov confesses his crime to in "Crime and Punishment"
71 Word that can combine with the ends of the answers to the six starred clues

DOWN

1 Stool, perhaps
2 Southwest plain
3 Words to a kidder
4 Fresca, e.g.
5 Maroon 5's "___ Will Be Loved"
6 Dos that are don'ts?
7 St. Teresa's place
8 Youngest Hall-of-Famer (at age 22) to hit 100 home runs
9 Whole bunch
10 Baked entrees
11 *Porch feature
12 Lots
13 Nerf ball, e.g.
21 Sinuous swimmer
23 Pueblo pots
25 Outlaw's accessory
29 Late Soviet diplomat Dobrynin
30 Italian poet who was the subject of a Goethe play and a Donizetti opera
31 ___ car
32 Turkeys
33 PC character set
34 *Hillbillies' put-down
36 Baylor's home
40 Kantian concern
43 Oberon of "Wuthering Heights"
44 With 19-Across, U.S.C.'s marching band
46 Checks the fit of
50 Literally, "way of the gods"
52 I, to Wilhelm I
55 Silent film accompaniment
56 Certain rial spender
57 More peeved
58 Word that can combine with the starts of the answers to the six starred clues
59 Org. criticized in "When the Levees Broke"
60 See 64-Down
62 Bosox legend
64 With 60-Down, big Chilean export

by Byron Walden and Caleb Madison

108

ACROSS

1 Friends and neighbors
5 Bend one's elbow, e.g.
9 Cornered
14 Start of an incantation
15 Wash up
16 "On the Beach" author
17 Hard-boiled crime genre
18 Aesir ruler
19 Perfect Sleeper maker
20 Athlete who has pigged out on snacks at a bar?
23 Interstate-championing prez
24 Strippers' tips, often
25 Explosive of old
28 Special treatment, for short
29 "___ geht's?" (German "How are you?")
30 ___ pro nobis
31 Chief heckler?
36 Skewer
37 Place for a Dumpster
38 Juan's "what"
39 Lavender, for one
40 Pesky arachnid
41 Skydiver's amended plans?
43 Troop-entertaining grp.
44 Cara ___ (Italian term of endearment)
45 Performer yukking it up
46 Friend from afar
48 Tickled
50 Indy letters
53 Insulation from jokes?
56 Rodeo ride
58 Astronomy's ___ cloud
59 Brand for woofers, but not tweeters?
60 Cultural prefix
61 Purple shade
62 Sound from a steeple
63 Core belief
64 Critic's unit
65 Primordial stuff

DOWN

1 Japanese writing system
2 Old Apple laptop
3 Brief moment
4 "Listen!," old-style
5 Walk with jerky motions
6 Chili server
7 Escapees from Pandora's box
8 Alien: Prefix
9 Take on
10 Angle symbol, in trigonometry
11 Explode like a puffball
12 "Boston Legal" fig.
13 Truly, in the Bible
21 Unwise undertaking
22 Brand once advertised with the jingle "We wear short shorts . . ."
26 Circular gasket
27 Barista's offering
28 Back into a corner
29 Boo-hoo
31 Copier malfunction
32 Beethoven dedicatee
33 "Rocket Man" rocker
34 Pastel hue
35 Scat syllable
36 Bernie Madoff's hedge fund, e.g.
39 Parasol's offering
41 Leave high and dry
42 Say "Hey, batter batter batter" and such
44 Mr. Met, for one
47 Tubular pasta
48 Mosaic artist's material
49 Spanish poet García ___
50 Fifth-century canonized pope
51 Birthstone for many Scorpios
52 Working stiff
54 The old man
55 Banjo accessory
56 Double or nothing, e.g.
57 Tpke., e.g.

by John Lampkin

ACROSS

1 "Caro nome," for one
5 Gov. Faubus in Arkansas history
10 Black
14 Bryn ___
15 Unsuspecting
16 Second to ___
17 *"I don't know yet"
20 Comment put in by Putin, perhaps
21 Ballet headliners
22 Decide to take, with "for"
24 *1968 #2 hit heard in "Easy Rider"
27 Grp. at home on the range?
28 To ___ (just so)
29 English fashionista Bartley
33 Air or ami preceder
34 Biblical verb with "thou"
36 Aligns
37 "Yo te ___"
38 Ill-fated . . . or a hint for answering the six starred clues
40 Hit Jerry Bruckheimer TV drama
41 Scorch
43 Boozer
44 Sportage maker
45 Applies
47 They may be boxed
49 Over there
50 *1924 Isham Jones/Gus Kahn song
52 Interview part: Abbr.
53 Hollywood's Anderson and Reed
56 Diamond on a record player
58 *"No way!"
63 Character in "Beowulf"
64 Alternative to hash browns
65 Through
66 People mover since 1853
67 Vintner's need
68 What a rake may do

DOWN

1 Tsp. or tbsp.
2 When repeated, excited
3 *Memorable movie quote of 1932
4 Like many a gallerygoer
5 Length in years of a lenient sentence, maybe
6 Head of the Egyptian god Amun
7 Through
8 Arthur Miller play "___ From the Bridge"
9 Soup variety
10 Person with special access
11 Good name for someone born on Dec. 25
12 What might give a physical reaction?
13 Wishes
18 Old WB sitcom
19 Substance in a chemistry experiment
22 In a position to steal
23 Blend before using
25 Vaquero's rope
26 Snug, as in bed
30 *Like someone who's had a narrow escape
31 Wound
32 Chinese, e.g.
35 Sweet wine of Hungary
38 Irk
39 Certain English poetry scholar
42 Feels a loss
46 Hirsute
48 Took to court
51 "That's ___ subject"
53 Fire starter?
54 Follower of juillet
55 San Francisco's public transit system, with "the"
57 Favorite
59 ___ Maria
60 Pawn jumpers: Abbr.
61 Formerly
62 [Mumble, mumble]

by Charles Deber

110

ACROSS

1 *Cry at the start of a vote
6 Tree in California
10 Soulful Redding
14 Duane ___ (New York City pharmacy chain)
15 Land west of the Pacific
16 "This is terrible!"
17 Greased
18 "Believe" singer, 1999
19 Liberals, with "the"
20 *"Soon enough, my friend"
22 Big mess
24 "Bien ___!"
25 Former "S.N.L." comic Gasteyer
26 French theologian who wrote "Sic et Non"
28 Jean Sibelius, for one
29 Seat of Albany County, Wyo.
30 Biggie ___ (rapper a k a Notorious B.I.G.)
33 Bennett of "What's My Line?"
34 "Am ___ risk?"
35 Women's rights pioneer Elizabeth ___ Stanton
36 *As a package
37 Old man: Ger.
38 Here, in Juárez
39 Bomber type
41 More agile
43 Relinquish, as arms
45 Move from site to site?
46 Hall of TV fame
47 Oslo Accords party, for short
48 One way to sway
51 Many a Justin Bieber fan
52 *Completely imagined
54 Restaurateur Toots
55 Kirk's foe in a "Star Trek" sequel
57 Lofty dwelling
58 Unadulterated
59 Alveoli site
60 "I love you," in a telenovela
61 Sacred chests
62 Tense
63 Poker phrase . . . or what's needed to complete the answers to the six starred clues

DOWN

1 Aristophanes comedy, with "The"
2 Alphabetic pentad
3 Bravery
4 Took too much
5 Common North American hawk
6 Iconic chomper
7 New York stadium eponym
8 Taradiddle
9 Classic candy with nougat
10 "How lu-u-uxurious!"
11 *Top-rated TV series of 1971–76
12 Madden
13 Lush
21 Quaint lodgings
23 Brand of 45-Down balls
26 Direction at sea
27 Block
28 Pass muster
30 Where "Otello" premiered, with "La"
31 General played by Fonda (in 1976), Peck (1977) and Olivier (1982)
32 *To be expected
33 MSNBC competitor
36 Vintner's prefix
37 Terrier's sound
39 Exemplar of dryness
40 Glimmer
41 U.S.S. Enterprise helmsman
42 How some wages are calculated
44 Popular tractors
45 See 23-Down
48 Untamed
49 Sam who directed "Drag Me to Hell"
50 Classic theater
52 Masculine side
53 Cad
54 Where the robed are rubbed
56 Movie for which Patricia Neal won Best Actress

by Michael Sharp

ACROSS

1 "___ time"
4 Originator of the phrase "rosy-fingered dawn"
9 Last picture in an alphabet book
14 Lay
15 Adult
16 Ducks, in "Peter and the Wolf" productions
17 What to use to spell 30-Down, according to George Bernard Shaw, reputedly, Part 1
20 Shout into a canyon
21 Still
22 Notorious 1999 computer virus
25 Conservative philosophy in Britain
28 Actress Lupino and others
29 They're usually white or brown
31 Letters from a mathematician
32 Books often read on Saturday
34 One of the five counties of Hawaii
36 Part 2
40 Beginning of a saying about evil
41 Object of Andy's affection in "The 40-Year-Old Virgin"
42 Flight board abbr.
43 Workplace for a 23-Down
44 Goals
48 Intro
52 Lion's home
54 Like some eyes and soup
56 Prefix with -pathy
57 Part 3
61 Zero, in slang
62 Lips
63 Nod, perhaps
64 Noisome noise
65 The Tower, e.g.
66 Flight board abbr.

DOWN

1 Panama and Suez
2 Snickered
3 Designer McCartney
4 Alternative to Ring Dings
5 A little peculiar
6 Spoil
7 They may be deal breakers
8 Opposite of invoices
9 One fighting urban sprawl, say
10 Black
11 Shop
12 Like some gas: Abbr.
13 Memento from an old flame?
18 Shine
19 Grp. with the platinum album "Out of the Blue"
23 Worker on a 43-Across
24 Lab gel
26 Reggae/dancehall artist ___ Paul
27 Century-starting year
30 "Fish"
33 Tic-tac-toe win
34 Ring results, for short
35 One of the Five Colleges
36 Abbr. on an old map of the West
37 Shout at the top of a roller coaster
38 Who'll "talk 'til his voice is hoarse," in a 1960s sitcom
39 Good radio station for a bride?
40 Simpleton
43 Find (out)
45 Spot
46 Fade
47 High
49 "Peace out"
50 Of service
51 High-___
53 A goner
55 Jedi with a big forehead
57 Big inits. on cable
58 Old Chinese dynasty
59 Boss: Abbr.
60 Prefix with conservative

by Oliver Hill and Eliza Bagg

112

ACROSS

1 Jettisoned compartment
4 Update, in a way
10 Noise in a comic book gunfight
14 Expert
15 Key of "The James Bond Theme"
16 Bathe
17 Big ___
18 Margarita alternatives
20 Spanish for "the meadows"
22 Mexican bloom
23 Like telemarketing headsets
24 Bit of a climb
26 They're caught in Chicago
27 What a cheeky one's cheek might get
29 Screen role for Skippy the dog
31 Pit-___
34 Cook Island carving
36 Card game of Spanish origin
40 Salsa verde ingredients
43 Barrio outsider
44 At 30° W 30° N, e.g.
45 Lock part
46 Goals against, e.g.
48 "What ___ be done?"
50 Certain Protestant: Abbr.
53 Golfer Aoki
55 Reason for an evacuation
59 Baja buddies
61 Like traditional Mexican music
63 Procrastinating words south of the border
65 Castor ___ (old comic strip character)
66 Subj. involving cells
67 Be altruistic
68 Mustachioed "Simpsons" character
69 Kournikova of tennis
70 They might be knee-jerk reactions
71 Carbohydrate suffix

DOWN

1 "Tortilla Flat" character
2 Jersey Shore county, appropriately
3 None too swift
4 Officially annul
5 Go from home to home?
6 One of a 15th-century trio
7 "With the jawbone of ___ . . ."
8 Comfy footwear, briefly
9 Slowly disappears
10 Bor-r-ring
11 Soup kitchen server
12 Use
13 Tijuana tables
19 One turned off for takeoff
21 Virgins of ancient Rome
25 Island capital of 2.6 million
28 It requires one who's blind with a bat
30 Two-handled vase
31 1977 double-platinum album by Steely Dan
32 Sweeping shot
33 Medit. land
35 Flattens, for short
37 Arthur of "The Golden Girls"
38 $200 Monopoly properties: Abbr.
39 Gift in "The Gift"
41 Crone's concoction
42 White House ceremony site
47 Syrian presidential family
49 Helping for the very hungry, maybe
50 "La ___"
51 At full speed
52 Evergreen with edible nuts
54 Psi follower
56 Cheap, in adspeak
57 "But of course"
58 Mark used four times in this puzzle's solution
60 Pricey event
62 Yucatán years
64 Soak (up)

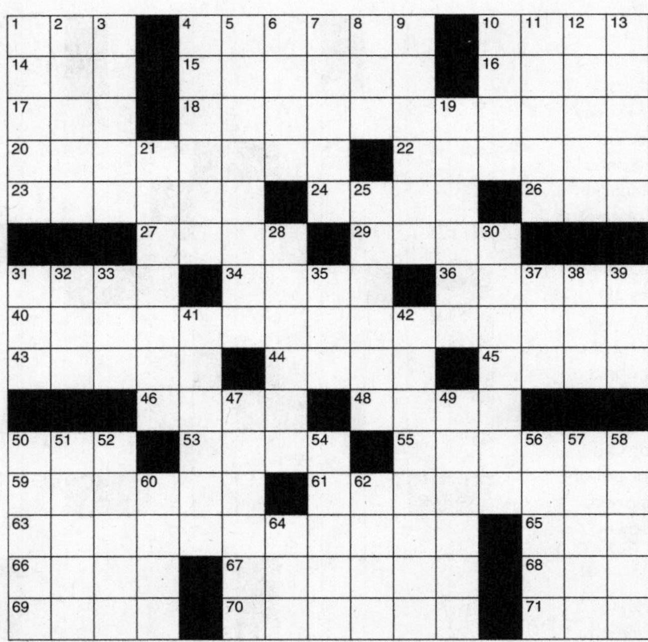

by Patrick Merrell

ACROSS

1 Dull shade
4 Road caution
7 Place for a hammer
12 One in on the founding of a company
14 -
16 -
17 River of York
18 Record label of the Beatles' "Ain't She Sweet"
19 Spy sent by Moses into Canaan
20 Production site chief
21 -
22 -
23 Wonder of note
25 Yes ___
27 One getting a bouquet?
28 -
29 -
32 Makes fun of
35 Profess
36 It flows near the Piazzale Michelangelo
37 Workplace where there are many openings
38 -
39 -
40 Sorento and Sedona
41 "Our Gang" approval
42 Plentiful
43 Song played at the school dance in "Back to the Future"
44 -
45 -
46 Kind of year: Abbr.
47 Chinese for "black dragon"
50 Officially
52 -
54 -
56 Schubert's "Eine kleine Trauermusik," e.g.
57 1996 Gwyneth Paltrow title role
58 River in a 1957 hit film
59 Warning to intruders
60 -
61 -
62 Young fish that has migrated from the Sargasso Sea
63 Rubble maker, for short
64 Some Windows systems

DOWN

1 Rent-___
2 Synagogues
3 Attacks
4 Cholesterol medication
5 Helper's offer
6 Sea menace
7 Certain pie toppers
8 Big bug
9 Fit
10 Thomas Moore's "___ Ask the Hour"
11 Eye, to poets
13 Some passport applicants
15 It's all the same
24 Something that's stamped
26 Green
28 Town on Lake Geneva opposite Lausanne, Switzerland
29 Too: Fr.
30 Hydroxyl compound
31 Setting for "Coriolanus"
32 One may be running over time
33 Headquarters for Polynesian Airlines
34 Schnapps flavor
35 Legal cases?
36 Judo maneuvers
39 Highlander
41 Song words accompanying "Sherrie" and "Susanna"
44 Nervous laugh
45 Enter an Ivy League school, maybe
46 Many a French business partner
47 "The Suze ___ Show"
48 Kind of situation
49 Award
50 Half-wit
51 Airing
53 Pre-___ (take the place of)
55 Pad
56 Ft. Myers-to-Orlando dir.

by Joe Krozel

114

ACROSS

1 Renowned family of Italian history
7 Thom ___ shoes
11 ___-a-Mania, candy collectors' convention since 1991
14 Coral islands
15 Island of exile
16 Hew
17 Opening line from a TV show that debuted on 1/5/61
20 Ideal ending?
21 Buttinsky
22 "Smart" guys
23 Subject of a hotel policy
24 Pumpkinhead
25 With 43-Across, line spoken by the show's star
33 High-tech surveillance acronym
34 "Rama ___ Ding Dong" (1961 hit)
35 Org. in the health care debate
36 Pens sold in 10-packs
37 Canine complaints
39 ___-a-brac
40 ___Kosh B'Gosh
41 Phileas ___, fictional circumnavigator
42 Part of a "Macbeth" trio
43 See 25-Across
47 It was "lost" in 1981's top-grossing movie
48 "The Lord of the Rings" tree creatures
49 Wing it
52 Of the lower small intestine
54 "Fee, fi, fo, ___"
57 Familiar title for the star of the show
60 Hit the jackpot
61 Furrow-producing
62 Former space shuttle commander Collins
63 Pained cries
64 Pilots' announcements, for short
65 Pilots

DOWN

1 When repeated, a food fish
2 Summers in la cité
3 Definitely no genius
4 Indisposed
5 Suitable sites for suits
6 Really digs
7 Office reminder
8 "Good" rate
9 Sit-up muscles
10 "Rocky and Bullwinkle" villainess
11 Skin
12 Big cheese
13 Jazz duo in London?
18 ___ pit (rock concert area)
19 Ultimate word in an ultimatum
23 Neighbors of 9-Down
24 Bill dispensers
25 Like cannibalism, e.g.
26 "Wouldn't that be nice"
27 Chuck Yeager's breakthrough
28 "Send me"
29 Dance like the Hines Brothers
30 Poker Flat creator Bret
31 Friends, in Florence
32 Luxury craft
37 Fergie's duchy
38 Object of a spring hunt
39 Bridle parts
41 Prohibited
42 "Be careful!"
44 ___ accompli
45 Holden Caulfield, for one
46 Since way back when
49 "A one and ___"
50 Indian Ocean vessel
51 Monocle part
52 Chain founded in Sweden
53 Logo image for "The Rocky Horror Picture Show"
54 Unattached
55 Lead-in for friendly
56 Department store department
58 Tennis judge's call
59 "Bravo!"

by Mr. Ed Sessa

ACROSS

1 Thirsty toddler's request
5 Hurl curse words at?
9 With 65-Across, go against the group . . . or what the circled squares literally do in the answers to the starred clues
14 Reply suggesting "perhaps"
15 Big name in PCs
16 Sister of the Biography Channel
17 *Average national earnings
20 Let it all out?
21 Mont. neighbor
22 "Hooked on Classics" record company
23 Era of ___ (period in Notre Dame football history)
24 One who works in feet and meters
25 Chamber workers: Abbr.
26 *Capital ENE of Jerusalem
30 Olympic gymnast Paul or Morgan
31 Something for pairs to enter?
32 Screw up
37 Organ donation site
39 Genre for the Spice Girls and Oasis
41 "Slow and steady wins the race," e.g.
42 Poker game memento, maybe
43 Turn around
44 *Symbol above a 5
48 Danish kroner, topologically speaking
52 Not look so good?
53 Partner of 40-Down, traffic-wise
54 Nervous as ___
55 Pole position holder?
56 Use a portion of, as one song in another
59 *Easter basket treat
62 Ex-governor Spitzer
63 Jerk
64 Race assignment
65 See 9-Across
66 Spotted
67 Ciudad del ___ (second-largest city in Paraguay)

DOWN

1 Exhaust, with "out"
2 Green card, in brief
3 Medieval close-combat weapon
4 Bart Simpson catchphrase
5 Mock
6 French "present"
7 Make some connections
8 Saw right through?
9 Shut out
10 Sets up, as pool balls
11 Short online message
12 Pro pitchers
13 Falls (over)
18 Actor Rickman of the Harry Potter films
19 Bit
24 Bill bloater
26 "Excuse me . . ."
27 Lunch spread, often
28 Qtr. starter
29 Application letters
33 "No sweat . . ."
34 Some soup ingredients
35 QB Flutie
36 Place the first bet
38 2006 Winter Olympics backdrop
39 Orange Free State settler
40 Partner of 53-Across, traffic-wise
42 Penguin's locale
45 Ca, Co or Cu
46 Some races
47 Get out of the cold?
48 Circus chairperson?
49 Florida's ___ National Forest
50 ___ to go
51 "There, there"
56 Before you know it
57 Time to give up?
58 Thin blade
60 Cleveland ___, O.
61 Caustic soda

by Mike Nothnagel

116

ACROSS

1 Poorly developed, as an idea
7 Clear of dishes
10 50%
14 Milton Berle's longtime sponsor
15 Actress ___ Alicia
16 ___-Dixie Stores
17 Spoil, as a parade
18 "Stat!"
19 "___ homo"
20 Tony winner Hagen
21 Joule fraction
23 "Misty" composer Garner
25 The second "T" in TNT
28 Vitamin label fig.
29 Rock's ___ Lonely Boys
30 Sunken ships
31 Unmoved
33 Anka's "___ Beso"
34 Port on the eastern Mediterranean
35 Go ___ length
36 Q's point value in Scrabble
37 Coffee additive
38 Bikini part
41 Draws back
42 Big Apple enforcement org.
46 Improviser's asset
47 Artist Matisse
48 Tahitian-style wraparound skirt
50 Dam-building org.
51 Western treaty grp.
52 Most dismal
54 Worker in a cage
56 Pickup truck feature
57 Book before Esth.
58 Joy Adamson's lioness
59 Way of the East
61 "As if!"
64 Marsh growth
65 Year-end helper
66 "Time After Time" singer Cyndi
67 Four hours on the job, perhaps
68 Cool, in slang
69 Opening 30 minutes of football

DOWN

1 Deceptive remark
2 Barely defeat
3 With respect to a graph line, e.g.
4 Toto's state: Abbr.
5 Prefix with system
6 "Singin' in the Rain" director Stanley
7 Prank cigar sound
8 Game with Draw 2 cards
9 How a magician's assistant might appear
10 Person in the hole
11 Lake Michigan explorer Jean ___
12 Box in
13 Wrestling hold
22 Puts a new finish on
24 Risqué
26 Kiev's land: Abbr.
27 Suffix with Sudan
28 Like some inns or hot dog stands
32 Cartridge filler
37 Hardly enthusiastic
38 Wife, colloquially
39 In a tangled mess
40 Amu Darya's outlet
41 Do some blacksmith's work on
42 "Wait Wait . . . Don't Tell Me!" airer
43 Shaggy animal in a herd
44 Marriage contracts, briefly
45 Provisional Mormon state
49 Jacob Riis subjects, with "the"
53 Moe parodied him in some W.W. II–era Three Stooges shorts
55 Tramp's love
56 Broadway hit, slangily
60 Pub offering
62 Yes, in Yokohama
63 Big ___, Calif.

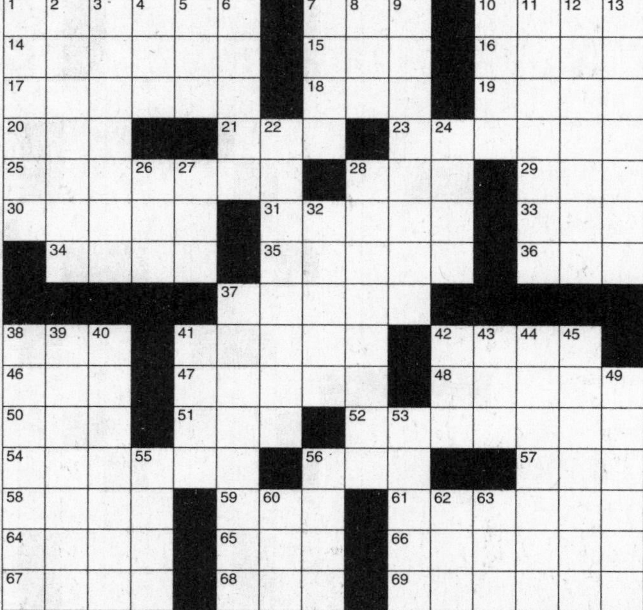

by Jim Hilger

ACROSS

1 Bunk
5 Turkish honorific
9 Jean-Luc Godard's "Une ___ Mariée"
14 Words said with a nod
15 They're seen from a porch
17 1944 mystery play by Agatha Christie
19 1950s White House name
20 Fashion designer Tahari
21 Spouse in 2009 headlines
26 Rookie
27 Nickname of Schumann's Symphony No. 3
30 Miles Davis jazz number
33 Stick around a barroom
35 Billy Joel's "___ Extremes"
36 Certain Buddhist
37 Something that may be on a house
40 Playbill item
41 Fund
43 N.Y.C. subway inits.
44 Vassal
45 Some snowmobiles
48 Division politique
50 Who said "I put up my thumb and it blotted out the planet Earth"
55 Teeming (with)
56 Pegasus appeared in this company's logo
57 Takes things a bit too far
63 Yellowish dessert
64 Dregs
65 Is conservative in blackjack, say
66 ___ before (no later than)
67 Members of a former union: Abbr.

DOWN

1 "I want it, and I want it now!"
2 Norm
3 1938 Physics Nobelist
4 Was a tributary for
5 Source of about half the world's diamonds: Abbr.
6 Miracle-___
7 Practiced
8 Horn
9 Carte blanche
10 Long time
11 "Voulez-vous coucher avec ___ ce soir?" (1975 lyric)
12 Mid-century year
13 Oxford-to-London dir.
16 ___-high boots
18 Choosing-up word
22 Shamu or Keiko
23 Sauce thickener
24 School subj.
25 Weeper of Thebes
28 Rouse
29 Place for a shoe
30 Awful "Dancing With the Stars" scores
31 Blockhead
32 No ___ sight
34 Golf course planting
37 They're helpful for long shots
38 Tabloid couple
39 Vittles
42 Something Ben Jonson wrote to himself
44 Boardwalk activities
46 Tony ___, 1964 A.L. Rookie of the Year
47 ___ Field (where the Mariners play)
49 "Don't throw bouquets ___"
51 Screened again
52 Annual spring ceremony, with "the"
53 Montana, once
54 Emmy winner Sharon
57 Literary monogram
58 Bran choice
59 Bygone Spanish queen
60 Opinion
61 Ref's decision
62 Part of H.R.H.

by Elizabeth C. Gorski

118

ACROSS

1 Old Testament verb
6 Locale for a lashing
10 Ann's advice-giving sister
14 Prom rentals
15 Locale
16 Hip bones
17 Leave slack-jawed
18 Part of the house where one might check Google messages?
20 Number of trades Jack is a master of
21 Enero through diciembre
22 Some winners on a Fox talent show
23 Cry for help on an F.B.I. cruise?
27 Punkie
28 Puts down, as the red carpet
31 Reach a concord
34 Carbohydrate suffix
35 Stage that includes a cocoon
36 Grazing site
37 Beaver Cleaver expletive . . . or what you might need to be to answer 18-, 23-, 51- and 60-Across?
41 Pepper's rank: Abbr.
42 Wee bit
44 AOL rival
45 Substitute for
47 Dory's affliction in "Finding Nemo"
49 Half of a McDonald's logo
51 Guess as to how the thong came to exist?
56 Like a prefall Humpty Dumpty
58 Pale pub potable
59 Gen. Robert ___
60 Where Neil Armstrong might store his gear?
63 Part of basketball practice
64 Latvia's capital
65 Kegger locale
66 Coke, to Pepsi
67 Basketball All-Star Nick Van ___
68 Lubricates
69 Kangaroo babies

DOWN

1 Some teen talk
2 Bleachers sign
3 Appliance brand
4 Sore throat soother
5 Lao-___
6 Word with babe or bar
7 Knight's gear
8 Deep blue
9 Mai ___
10 Certain plane delivery
11 Rambo's drive
12 H.S. science class
13 Candied dish
19 Teller of tales
21 One of Frank's exes
24 A thousand bucks
25 Political family name
26 "The ___ Love"
29 Org. for Michelle Wie
30 Info on college applications
31 Alan who was born Alphonso D'Abruzzo
32 Lysol target
33 Meteorologist's tool
34 Admit, with "up"
38 Mideast ruler
39 "NYPD Blue" actor Morales
40 Actor Galifianakis of "The Hangover"
43 Inhuman
46 "Toodle-oo!"
48 Leave in
49 Shoelace tips
50 U.S. 1, for one: Abbr.
52 Like Bob Dylan's voice
53 Green shade
54 Bit of electrical work
55 Hollers
56 "Fee fi fo fum" sayer
57 Kind of engine
61 Corp. V.I.P.
62 N.L. West team, on scoreboards
63 Onetime Sixers great

by Kristian House

ACROSS

1 Ancient gathering place
6 ID card issuer
9 Drink whose name means "little water"
14 Subatomic particle
15 "Rocky ___"
16 Mesmerizing designs
17 Jai alai catcher
18 Fool
19 Insinuate
20 With 54-Across, opposite of 18-Across
23 Male swan
24 Chinese for "water"
25 Launches
26 Part of a preconception?
28 It's breath-taking
30 To be, to Benicio
31 Tea option
33 Putting one's foot in one's mouth, e.g.
35 Opposite of 32-Down
40 Odysseus saw him as a shade in the underworld
41 Gulliver in Lilliput, e.g.
43 Mythical monster
45 First option
48 Ancient Greek vessel
49 Nickname for baseball's Leo Durocher
51 End
53 Fish tale, essentially
54 See 20-Across
57 Onetime Facebook president Parker and others
58 It may be taken at a gun range
59 Stumped, after "up"
61 "All the King's Men" woman
62 Big camping inits.
63 Send, as to a specialist
64 Vertical
65 NBC fixture since '75
66 Prefix with sound

DOWN

1 2 letters
2 Reviews
3 Veal shank dish in un ristorante
4 March org.?
5 Writer Nin
6 Obsolescent alternative to broadband
7 Opposite of 58-Across
8 Woodworking class holder
9 Ostensible backdrop of the 2003 roman à clef "The Devil Wears Prada"
10 Many a Handel work
11 Kind of case
12 Bowl for mixing wine and water in ancient Greece
13 Court figs.
21 "Oh, I see"
22 Worthless matter
23 Cape ___
27 World-famous institution in Rochester, Minn.
29 Ring holder . . . or receiver?
32 Much
34 Flying hazard
36 Painter Fra Filippo ___
37 Instant messaging pioneer
38 "Carmina Burana" composer
39 Mastermind
42 XXX part
43 "This can't be good"
44 Newly fashioned
46 Like a body temperature of 98.6°
47 Org. that rates members of Congress on their liberalism
49 Thé cup, maybe
50 Feature of many a ring
52 Centipede maker
55 Neiman Marcus competitor
56 L.A.-to-Jacksonville rte.
60 Time on earth

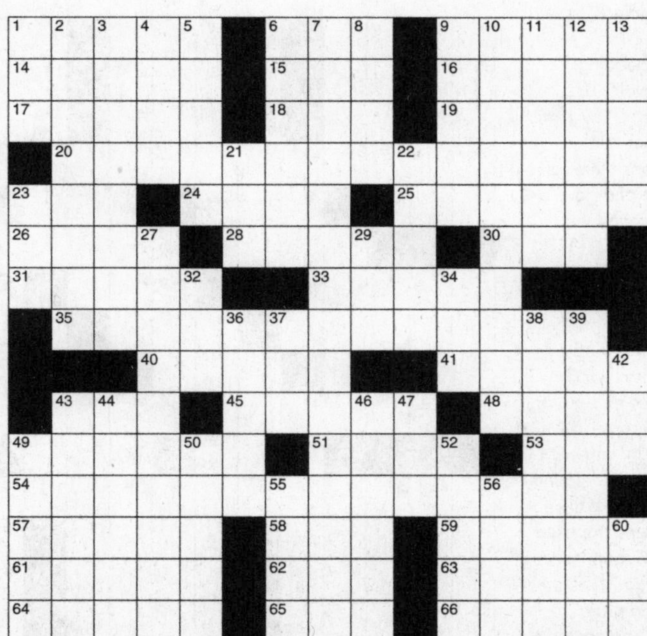

by Michael Shteyman

120

ACROSS

1 With 65-Across, the starts of 20-, 26-, 43- and 51-Across taken together
5 Scopes Trial org.
9 Place for scrubs
14 Start of an incantation
15 "Double" facial feature
16 Normandy beach
17 Assault or battery
18 "Please?"
19 React to mold, perhaps
20 Alien abductions, e.g.
23 Command to a plow horse
24 It's fairly insensitive to shock, fortunately
25 Houston-to-K.C. direction
26 "All kidding aside . . ."
32 Menu heading
35 "Au Revoir, ___ Enfants" (1987 film)
36 ___-chef
37 Backspace through
38 Get-up-and-go
39 Ring around the collar, say
40 Chamonix setting
41 Season box holder, e.g.
42 Like a par 5 hole vis-à-vis a par 3
43 Unwelcome sign for a sales rep
46 "Aladdin" prince
47 "Open wide" sound
48 Center of a ball?
51 Magazine opposed to the Cuban trade embargo
57 Old and gray
58 Signs, as a contract
59 Lena of "Chocolat"
60 Composer Bruckner
61 Astringent fruit
62 Word with cut or exchange
63 Dry out, informally
64 Salon acquisitions
65 See 1-Across

DOWN

1 "Why, of course!"
2 Jungle menace
3 You might wait for it at a stoplight
4 "Fiddlesticks!"
5 Dialect coaches teach them
6 Monastery music
7 "The Mod Squad" role
8 Shop steward, briefly
9 World's third-largest island
10 Release
11 Mane area
12 Mother of Chaz Bono
13 Brinker of children's lit
21 Exercise on the keys
22 Aussie colleges
26 Low man at the Met
27 Nicholas Gage best seller
28 On drugs
29 Something to break into
30 Race in a chute
31 River in a 1914 battle
32 Rapper Combs a.k.a. Diddy
33 Alice's chronicler
34 Swimmers do them
38 Conscientious objector
39 "Tiny Bubbles" singer
41 Adidas competitor
42 Is a go-between
44 Adam's apple site
45 Add later
48 ___ Lama
49 Magazine jobs
50 Dice, slangily
51 2000 election scrap
52 Skye of "Say Anything . . ."
53 Intl. commerce pact replaced by the W.T.O.
54 Suffix with buck
55 "To Live and Die ___"
56 What's expected

by David Murchie

ACROSS

1 Deliberate
5 Rice with three rings
10 Prepare to sing an anthem
14 Not out of the running
15 One of a literary trio
16 Part of I.M.F.: Abbr.
17 Mean, illegal wrestling hold?
19 Dog command
20 Like poorly cleaned glasses
21 One with a yard stick?
23 Certain pipe joint
24 Musical syllable singing system
27 "Dune" director
29 Moore in entertainment news
31 Hip-hop's ___ Fiasco
33 Granting that, briefly
34 Standard tobacco wad?
38 "___ take arms against . . ."
41 "That really hurts!"
42 In ___ (actual)
43 Woo President Arthur?
46 Pillager, maybe
47 Go bad
48 Piles
51 Where Panasonic and Sanyo are headquartered
53 It's billed as "The Place for Politics"
56 Clichéd cry
58 Stylish
60 Noted earthquake locale
62 Satisfy
63 Fat fool?
66 Landlocked land of Africa
67 Coke is used for this
68 "Salus populi suprema lex ___" (Missouri's motto)
69 Speechless
70 Clinton defense secretary William
71 Copy cats

DOWN

1 Thick
2 One way to stand
3 "Yes ___!"
4 Kitchen extension?
5 Onetime tabloid nickname
6 Kind of alcohol
7 Euripides character?
8 Seoul soldier
9 River that begins in Nord
10 Perilous
11 How metric units are divided
12 Stiffens, in a way
13 Screen swinger Ron
18 P.L.O.'s Arafat
22 "Family Ties" son
25 Blooms
26 Q5 and Q7
28 N.H.L. star nicknamed "Mr. Hockey"
30 El Cid foe
32 One with stressing work?
35 Tickle Me Elmo manufacturer
36 Yawn-inducing
37 Michael of "Superbad"
38 ___ Rios (Jamaican resort)
39 "The Sleeping Gypsy" painter
40 Lunch counter order
44 Bolshevik target
45 Multivolume ref., usually
49 Leaf through
50 Appear that way
52 ___ Bell, witch who was a fellow student of Harry Potter at Hogwarts
54 Celt or Cav
55 In the worst way
57 [Bam!]
59 Shortening used in recipes
61 "Don't you forget about me"
62 "Yum!"
64 U.S.P.S. abbr.
65 Contraction that sounds like a conjunction

by Patrick Blindauer

122

ACROSS

1 Remain
5 Feeling down
9 See 47-Down
13 ___ Anderson, Super Bowl XXV M.V.P.
15 Kentucky senator Paul
16 15-Across and allies: Abbr.
17 Start of an old Army recruiting line
18 "After the maid cleans out the ___ ___ going to polish the fireplace doors"
20 Zombies might be on it
22 Org. for 9-Down
23 Caste member
24 "The note accompanying the ___ ___ that all money should go to charity"
28 Relax
29 Sorority letters
30 Take ___ (lose one)
33 Accept a contract
34 Long-legged waders
36 "The reporter heard the New York ___ ___ his coach"
41 "___ Nacht" (Christmas carol)
42 One-quarter of "Whose woods these are I think I know"
43 Club for knights
44 Latin 101 verb
45 Alone, on the stage
49 "At the organic market, the price of _____ from moderate to ridiculous"
53 Penny collector
55 John, to Paul, George or Ringo
56 Young salmon
57 "The teacher found that ___ ___-a-longs helped her pupils remember their ABCs"
61 Rocky ridge
62 Tex-Mex fare
63 "___ that cute?!"
64 "___ to you!"
65 Whizzed
66 Hwys.
67 Lith. and Lat., once

DOWN

1 Tennis player, at times
2 Loose
3 Turns over, as an engine
4 Fight with
5 Part of a two-piece suit?
6 ___ Cruces
7 Doffs one's lid
8 Plant swelling
9 Members of the 22-Across
10 Went over again
11 Welcoming customers
12 "Hey there!"
14 Blind component
19 Rode the pine
21 Happen
25 Graybearded sort
26 Stirring time?
27 Make
31 Suffix with magnet
32 Old Dungeons & Dragons co.
33 Weekly NBC staple, for short
34 Glue brand
35 Flap one's gums
36 Suffix with magnet
37 End of the line, say: Abbr.
38 Center of Good & Plenty candy
39 Tiger, e.g., informally
40 Lip
44 Self-promoter
45 Sounds from barracks, maybe
46 Lascivious lookers
47 With 9-Across, post office mail slot . . . or a hint to this puzzle's theme
48 Evaluate
50 Class with many functions: Abbr.
51 Response to a general question?
52 Asian nanny
53 Sticks (out)
54 P.D.Q.
58 Bobblehead movement
59 Houston-to-Chicago dir.
60 Some muscle cars

by Peter A. Collins

ACROSS

1 ---
6 Does yard work
10 Longest river entirely in Switzerland
14 Deuce follower
15 ---
16 Summer cooler
17 ---
18 Held up
19 Slaughter who dashed home to win the 1946 World Series
20 Kind of cheese
21 Food orders sometimes prepared in toaster ovens
22 Excellence as a virtue, to ancient Greeks
23 Advice for solving this puzzle, part 1
25 Kaput
27 "Just Say I Love ___" (hit of 1950)
28 Fouls
32 There is a "super" one every four yrs.
35 Business TV newsman Ron
37 Roll's partner
38 Advice, part 2
41 ---
42 Set right
43 Broadcast
44 1980s hairstyle with a long strand in the back
46 Baseball's Cobb and others
48 Goes for the bronze?
49 End of the advice
53 ---
56 Go quickly
58 Earl of ___ (Sir Anthony Eden)
59 ---
60 Scraps
61 Failed spectacularly
62 ---
63 Fancy
64 "#@&%!," e.g.
65 ---
66 Dispatch
67 Perfume ingredient

DOWN

1 Official traditionally seen in a black hat
2 First name in W.W. II infamy
3 Service site for some veterans
4 Harem guard, typically
5 Marie or Jeanne: Abbr.
6 Minnesota lake ___ Lacs
7 One ___ (baseball variant)
8 Dish-washing aid
9 Call . . . or call on
10 ---
11 Crack
12 Source
13 In addition
21 Like the poem "Tam o' Shanter"
22 Org. for Joe Namath
24 Hawaiian handouts
26 Exhibitionist
28 C.F.O.'s concern
29 Bambini
30 Return to sender?
31 Twist
32 Cake part
33 "Choice" agcy.
34 Discharge
36 Left-handed
39 "A pity"
40 Frightful river to cross
45 King who gained international prominence in 1922
47 ---
49 Rank
50 Unmistakable
51 Static
52 Break in, say
53 Eastern holy men's titles
54 Do programming work
55 Wilson of "Shanghai Noon"
57 Volcano whose eruption was described by Virgil
60 Band-Aid removal comments
61 Von Richthofen, for one

by Matt Ginsberg

124

ACROSS

1 Grant for a movie?
5 Painter's preparation
10 Make lace
13 Succulent plant
14 Richard nominated for seven Oscars
15 Writer Umberto
16 *Cracker feature
18 1930s org. with a blue eagle logo
19 When repeated, a dance
20 Discourage
21 Pimply
23 How a hangover sufferer might feel
25 Scottish hillside
26 Was in charge
27 Springfield family name
30 Essential oil
33 *Union, e.g.
35 "There ___ 'I' in 'team'"
36 Some salamanders
37 Otologist's focus
38 Bethlehem ___
39 Onetime hair-removal name
40 *It's bad when it knifes
41 Much-advertised exercise program
42 Containing many items, as a bill
44 Actor Kilmer
45 "That is correct"
46 Certain tuna . . . or what this puzzle's 10 starred clues do
51 Emulated a wolf
53 "The Threepenny Opera" composer
54 Got the gold
55 Fraternity letter
56 *Flap
59 Na+, e.g.
60 Nasdaq company with an asterisk in its name
61 Pitcher Hershiser
62 Image on the back of a dollar bill
63 Wee
64 Optimal

DOWN

1 Cry after "Here!"
2 It may accompany waves on a Hawaiian beach
3 Palace-related
4 Word of affirmation
5 CNN's "Sanjay ___ MD"
6 Was off base
7 Make a mistake preparing James Bond's martini
8 "Sending out an ___" (repeated Police lyric)
9 Physical feature of Britain's Lord Nelson
10 *Daniel's home
11 One of a thousand in a Jane Smiley title
12 *Natter, e.g.
14 Dalmatian or Pomeranian
17 Cow features
22 *Start of the name
24 *Necessitator
25 1988 Tom Hanks film
27 Bollywood costume
28 First-class aisle seat on most planes
29 ___ contendere
30 Start of many dates
31 Abound
32 *Black
33 Airfare add-ons
34 Flight
38 Rice, for many
40 Go a-courting?
43 Bad thing to be over
44 Suffix in many place names
46 Four-door, often
47 Kind of pool or ride
48 Alert
49 Drinks in red-and-white cans
50 Genuflected
51 *Distant relative of Monterey
52 Seafarer's greeting
53 Finish line marker
57 66, e.g.: Abbr.
58 Male swan

by Victor Barocas

ACROSS

1 "Mr. ___" (1983 film)
4 "Them's fightin' words!"
10 Buddy
13 Buddy
14 Easy
15 Glazier's frame
16 Big name in women's fashion
18 New York's ___ Field
19 Inner: Prefix
20 Supreme Court justice who was formerly a U.S. solicitor general
22 Reason to keep moving
24 ___ Melodies
25 Make a long story even shorter?
26 Tongs, e.g.
28 Accented part of a poetic foot
29 Bluff
30 Bit of gymwear
31 Host of an Emmy-winning PBS series
34 Bump
37 Fuel sources
38 2010 Olympic ice dancing gold medalist ___ Virtue
42 Starve
44 Like some prunes and faces
45 Subjects of the first 10 Amendments
46 Volleyball players, at times
47 Star of TV's "8 Simple Rules"
50 Turkish coin
51 Sacred symbol of ancient Egypt
52 Author who co-wrote the screenplay for the Beatles' "Yellow Submarine"
54 Part of the New Haven landscape
55 Shakespearean term of address
56 Detroit-to-Toronto dir.
57 New York city where Ogden Nash was born
58 One-act Strauss opera
59 Children's writer Asquith

DOWN

1 European wine
2 Patricia who wrote "Woe Is I"
3 Students with personal guides
4 "___ Man Answers" (1962 Bobby Darin/ Sandra Dee film)
5 Stand the heat
6 Teatro alla ___
7 Send, in a way
8 Cumming of "Nicholas Nickleby"
9 Changing of labels
10 Georges Simenon detective Jules
11 He said "I just put my feet in the air and move them around"
12 Something full of interesting characters?
15 Line of cliffs
17 Like most Icelanders
21 Persevered
23 "Tsk!"
26 Brave deed of yore
27 Formations at the mouths of some streams
29 Motorist's woe
32 Give another look
33 Sting source
34 Less smooth
35 With cordiality
36 "The Entertainer" musical genre
39 Oscar-winning actor who played Napoleon, Mussolini and W. C. Fields
40 Red hot chili pepper
41 Magazine department
43 Benjamin Franklin's "The Morals of ___"
44 "The Taking of ___ One Two Three"
46 Prefix with iliac
48 A cabaletta is a short one
49 See 53-Down
53 Pronoun for a 49-Down

by Derek Bowman

126

ACROSS

1 Anoint with sacred oil, old-style
6 Cause of a scar
10 Physics Nobelist Victor who discovered cosmic radiation
14 Painter Magritte and others
15 Where the Storting parliament sits
16 Heaps
17 "Twenty-One"
19 Colorado feeder
20 First American magazine to excerpt "Moby-Dick"
21 Wink, e.g.
23 Son of Saddam
24 2100
27 Awards four stars, say
29 Party planner, for short?
30 In no other place
31 Tennis shoes, informally
33 ___ de mer
35 21
40 Hall-of-Fame QB Dawson
41 32-card game
44 Setup for a switch
48 Fighter in gray
50 Georgia's capital, in slang
51 "21 ___"
54 Suffix with psych-
55 1950s tennis champion Gibson
56 "Great" Catherine, for one
58 Former Italian P.M. Aldo
59 Twenty-ones
62 ___ Lysacek, 2010 Olympic figure skating gold medalist
63 One of the Three B's
64 Allan-___, Robin Hood companion
65 Alcoholic beverage often served warm
66 Where there are "many ways to have a good time," in a 1978 hit
67 Took back the top spot

DOWN

1 King ___ court
2 Resident of one of only seven states with no income tax
3 Made an impression on?
4 1984, e.g.
5 Salinger girl
6 Rumors and such
7 Parliament residue
8 Pavement warning
9 "In what way?"
10 Bargain
11 "Sense and Sensibility" sister
12 Bond film "Quantum of ___"
13 Follow closely
18 It follows directions
22 Freud's "I"
25 Oscar hopeful
26 Style
28 Take to the slopes
32 Wiig gig, for short
34 Big: Abbr.
36 Steve ___, 1990s teammate of Michael Jordan
37 30-Across, in Mexico
38 Product pitched by Michael Jordan
39 Blue
42 What stars do
43 Boxed in
44 Watchmaker with the first U.S. TV commercial, 1941
45 Acela Express operator
46 "There's an app for that" device
47 Mao ___-tung
49 The Stylistics' "___ By Golly, Wow"
51 "Bond, ___ Bond"
52 Housecat
53 "For shame!"
57 Slightly open
60 Flight
61 Duke's athletic org.

by Michael Barnhart

ACROSS

1 "Huh . . . ?!"
4 Fleet
10 Muscle car feature
14 What this would be to Caesar?
15 Jaded response to a movie suggestion
16 Comb container
17 Wanted poster abbr.
18 *Photogenic athlete from Cincinnati?
20 Ceremonial presentation
22 *Cozy rooms for playing?
23 Tax collector, e.g.
26 Drifts (off)
27 "You must be joking . . ."
29 Food made from fermented beans
31 "___ hope?"
32 Drafted, with "up"
34 Company concerned with automobile history
38 Spring
40 Opposite of 33-Down
42 Bob, e.g.
43 Indian city now known as Chennai
45 Mount
47 NPR's Shapiro
48 Days before
50 Yaps
52 Actress Blanchett
54 What dirt may come out in
56 *Social gathering for auction participants?
58 Drags
61 *Diatribes from captured criminals?
64 Stadium cheer
65 Bank holding
66 Get into a habit?
67 Andy's dinosaur in "Toy Story"
68 Shade of green
69 "I'm impressed"
70 See 28-Down

DOWN

1 Pow!
2 Shout before a snap
3 *Commercial for a private school?
4 Henry Clay's historic Kentucky estate
5 "The End of the Affair" actor, 1999
6 Playing pieces
7 "Start . . . now!"
8 Neutralize, as a bomb
9 Mr. ___, radioactive enemy of Captain Marvel
10 "Hello, I Love You" band, 1968
11 Shopworn
12 Kitchen window sites?
13 Walkers, in brief
19 Organization that sponsors an annual Mind Games competition
21 Let go
24 Halloween costume, maybe
25 Cutesy, in London
27 Like Type B personalities
28 With 70-Across, vitamin bottle phrase
30 Winter fishing tool
33 What's broken out of the answers to the starred clues?
35 *Expose oneself to a former U.S. president?
36 Prefix with -naut
37 Marked, as a questionnaire box
39 Much of Nickelodeon's target audience
41 Reference
44 States
46 Passed
49 Caterer's supply
51 The Wildcats of the N.C.A.A.
52 ___ cabinet
53 1948 Best Actor nominee for "Johnny Belinda"
55 Gift from the Wizard of Oz that's really a clock
56 Lip ___
57 Classic Army bomber plane
59 Pet peeve?
60 Hot
62 San Francisco's ___ Hill
63 Not yet determined: Abbr.

by Mike Nothnagel

128

ACROSS

1 Audibly in shock
6 Rack item
9 Can't stomach
14 State-run revenue source
15 1945 flag-raising site, briefly
16 Arledge who pioneered Monday night football
17 Grammy winner James and others
18 Horror film star Chaney
19 Widely known
20 Big Bopper hit
23 [as printed]
24 Common gout site
25 Title for Paul McCartney
26 Actor McShane of "Deadwood"
29 Barrier with a diamond pattern
33 Thurman of film
34 Baseballer-turned-spy Berg
35 Unaccompanied
36 Place to get a bucket of balls
39 In a funk
40 Like some paper and coats
41 "Understood"
42 Sock-in-the-gut reaction
43 Mauna ___
44 Group overseeing Notre Dame Cathedral
49 H.M.S. part
50 Just fine
51 California town name starter
52 Rock's ___ Rose
54 Remote possibility . . . or a hint to 20-, 29- and 44-Across
58 Yawl's pair
60 "No dice!"
61 Weighed down
62 Russian pancakes
63 First Liston/Clay fight result, in brief
64 Republican-turned-Democrat Specter
65 It's a plus
66 Anthem contraction
67 Like a neglected lawn

DOWN

1 Smart guys?
2 Notre Dame's architectural style
3 Tack on
4 Satirist Freberg
5 When racehorses are at the gate
6 Jewish campus group
7 M.P.'s quarry
8 Press secretary under George W. Bush
9 Kennel outburst
10 Old U.K. carrier
11 Follow a signal to
12 Admit ___
13 Badly chafed
21 Inner Hebrides isle
22 ___ button (Facebook icon)
27 Oxy 5 target
28 ___-to-know basis
30 Boring tool
31 "Bye for now!"
32 ___ González affair of 2000
36 Rolling in it
37 1975 Wimbledon winner
38 Phobic disorder, e.g.
39 Check out
40 Ordinance aimed at pet owners
42 Shouts of surprise
43 Ray who built McDonald's into a giant
45 Watch a kitty
46 Limb-bending muscle
47 Thing to snuff
48 Go over
53 1974 title role for Dustin Hoffman
55 ___ Reader (alternative magazine)
56 Flood barrier
57 Rhine feeder
58 Wharton deg.
59 Capp and Capone

by Barry C. Silk

ACROSS

1 Zapper's casualty
5 Rodgers and Hart's "___ to Be Unhappy"
9 Malapropos
14 Event starting at 2 a.m., maybe
15 Shankar who played at the Concert for Bangladesh, 1971
16 Newswoman O'Donnell
17 Pass over
18 Blood-related
19 Lit
20 End of a 1978 new-wave album title
22 Beat
23 Mark up
24 Embalming chemical
25 Single at the beginning?
26 Italian bitters
30 QE2's domain: Abbr.
31 Low jack?
33 Met's 1969 World Series rival
35 Fashion rule for the liberated . . . or one of four arrangements found literally in this puzzle
39 Other half
40 The "20" in "Drop and give me 20!"
43 Lötschberg Tunnel locale
46 Body of water named for an English explorer
49 Dithery, with "up"
50 "The ___ o' the Green" (old Irish ballad)
52 "Really!"
54 God of the south wind
55 Elvis instrument now in the Country Music Hall of Fame
58 Muscovite prince known as "Moneybag"
59 Instrument for Johann Jacob Bach
60 Shellac
61 Word on a lens cap
62 Hereabout
63 House of ___ (European princely dynasty)
64 Cleaning, as if for military inspection
65 Recess sites, at times
66 Storied loch

DOWN

1 Big, now
2 "Give me an example"
3 F.A.A. center
4 Vampire ___ (fanged fish)
5 Tops
6 It may be skimmed over
7 Tel ___
8 Natural history museum exhibit, for short
9 Shortly
10 Apartment ad come-on
11 Afghanistan's national airline
12 Quote by rote
13 "___ never know"
21 Abbr. for those who didn't make the list
24 Ferry's front
27 ___ vivendi
28 Imperative in an automated telephone message
29 Buenos ___
32 Directory listings: Abbr.
34 Bud's place
36 Rebellion
37 XII, maybe
38 Run through
41 Brown strip
42 Balls at balls?
43 Overhang
44 10th-century pope interred at St. Peter's Basilica
45 New York governor before Spitzer
47 Ducks for cover?
48 Guido Reni painting "Cleopatra With the ___"
51 Ramble
53 Dilate
55 Sound heard at the end of "Bohemian Rhapsody"
56 Not rock the boat
57 Gardener's bagful

by Gary Cee

130

ACROSS

1 Only patron on "Cheers" to appear in all 275 episodes
5 Honshu metropolis
10 Sound
14 Manitoba native
15 Needing nourishment
16 Over, in Oberammergau
17 "Taxi Driver" tagline?
20 Org. in a 1955 merger
21 Super Bowl XLV M.V.P. Rodgers
22 The Minutemen of the 1-Down
23 Buy-now-pay-later arrangement: Abbr.
24 Cavaliers, on scoreboards
25 "Back to the Future" tagline?
31 Tapenade ingredient
32 Actor/composer Novello
33 Truckload
35 Cat's tongue?
36 Bailiwicks
38 Dreyfus defender
39 Band of geishas?
40 Lipinski leap
41 Have a cow
42 "Titanic" tagline?
46 Archaic
47 Bumps hard
48 Like the Aramco oil company
51 Teem
53 Geller with a spoon-bending act
56 "Return of the Jedi" tagline?
59 Pitcher-turned-sportscaster Hershiser
60 Grammatically dissect
61 Marlon's "On the Waterfront" director
62 Striped swimmer
63 Worked at home?
64 Dix halved

DOWN

1 March Madness org.
2 "Carmina Burana" composer
3 Down-to-earth
4 Cousteau's milieu
5 Power failure
6 Sawed logs, so to speak
7 Big do
8 Gung-ho
9 Naval V.I.P.: Abbr.
10 G.M. brand discontinued in 2010
11 "Dancing Queen" group
12 Dregs
13 Slips up
18 Inscription on a Wonderland cake
19 Swiss who pioneered in graph theory
23 Bxe5 or 0-0-0, in chess
24 Corp. money execs
25 What an accused perpetrator needs
26 Palindromic car name
27 Triangular traffic sign
28 They travel down fallopian tubes
29 Bikini, for one
30 Figure out
31 Spanish eye
34 "No way, laddie!"
36 Fired
37 "Michael Collins" actor
38 Microwaves
40 Ignore the cue cards, say
41 Short stop?
43 Mountain airs
44 Purpose of an ode
45 Like most runs, in baseball
48 Person who uses a sleeve for a napkin, say
49 Je ne sais quoi
50 Strings at luaus
51 E-mail from a Nigerian prince, probably
52 Cincinnati sitcom station
53 Aptly named fruit
54 It may hold your horses
55 Mesopotamia, today
57 Kwik-E-Mart owner on "The Simpsons"
58 I.B.M. competitor

by David Poole

ACROSS

1 Historic U.S. place in the shape of a five-pointed star
12 Present time?: Abbr.
15 Russet Burbank, e.g.
16 Leader of leaders?
17 Tryst spot
18 Outfit's biggest suit
19 What might send Rover right over?
20 Directly
21 Is catlike
23 Newbery Medal-winning author Lowry
25 Has a seamy job?
28 Rush
29 Bright
31 Scaling challenge
33 Cicero's servant and secretary
34 Red Man rival
36 First #1 Billboard hit by an Australian artist (1972)
38 Hospital gown go-with
40 Small yarn?
43 Occurrences between springs
46 Fishing spot
47 Strike authorizer
49 Camaro options
51 Campus home for mice
53 Area near Manhattan's Union Square
55 First name in mysteries
56 Eponymous Greek island
58 Festive cry
60 Tobacco holder
61 NASA fine?
62 Natal setting
66 Single opening?
67 Handler of intelligence agents
68 Kickback site?
69 Researcher's audiotapes and such

DOWN

1 Campus stress source
2 Nose-noticeable
3 Canary
4 & 5 What iconoclasts break
6 79, say
7 Students might clean up in it
8 The Lorraine Campaign was part of it: Abbr.
9 Red rival, briefly
10 GPS choices: Abbr.
11 Whites' counterparts
12 Give a passionate recital
13 The Doors' record label
14 Seal, as a deal
22 Current
24 Frequent catch on TV's "Deadliest Catch"
26 E-mail, say
27 "Move your mind" sloganeer
30 Half a fathom
32 Old pulp fiction hero
35 ___ of Judah
37 N.Y.C.'s PBS station
39 Persian for "place of"
40 Express approval
41 Expression of approval
42 Wallet material
44 Classical Greek temple feature
45 Old-fashioned film editor
48 "What a girl" lead-in, in an Eddie Cantor hit
50 Based on the number six
52 Hershey's alternative
54 King surnamed Tryggvason
57 Rocket
59 Pair of buffalo?
63 Stars represent its constituents
64 Letterhead abbr.
65 Slowing, in mus.

by Barry C. Silk

132

ACROSS

1 Wants, with "to"
8 It may be held in battle
15 1977 Jacqueline Bisset movie
16 Literary critic Broyard
17 Acted unfairly
19 Aluminum foil alternatives?
20 Quite
21 Liability-limiting words
22 Natl. Humor Month
23 One in Germany
25 Slough
27 One may be called in court
29 Holiday time
31 It might go for big bucks
32 Equestrian's command
33 Bit of evidence in court
35 Concertedly
37 21st-century epidemic concern
40 Flibbertigibbety
42 Hymn words before "beyond all praising"
43 Get hush money from, for instance
46 It's "not master in its own house," said Freud
47 Family: Abbr.
49 Stop-press order?
51 Kind of 6-Down
53 Lord's domain
55 It once stretched from France to Russia: Abbr.
56 Shakespearean words following "Speak, hands, for me!"
57 "___ well"
59 ___ rage
61 "Not to my recollection"
64 Scholar
65 "The Morning Show Murders" novelist
66 Bleach component
67 "Happy" sorts

DOWN

1 Deep down
2 U.P.S. customer
3 Easter character
4 "___ delighted!"
5 Candy brand
6 One that swims with a current?
7 Cuddle, in a way
8 Broadway smash whose poster image consisted of just two eyes
9 Like some nursing
10 ___ Bo
11 Being tried
12 Registers surprise, say
13 National Book Award-winning novelist named after Emerson
14 "Hmmm . . ."
18 Never
24 Motor add-ons?
26 Patron saint of carvers
28 Biblical endings
30 Prefix with -phile
34 Bad way to go
36 Refuse at a mill
38 Name abandoned for Rochester
39 Skirt
40 Ruses
41 "Understood"
44 Dine at another's house
45 Some deals
48 Took out
50 Maintain
52 TV detective Peter and others
54 One spared in a sacrifice
58 Superman's mother
60 Blue-roofed chain
62 It's declared after the last hit, for short
63 Grp. in 1974 news

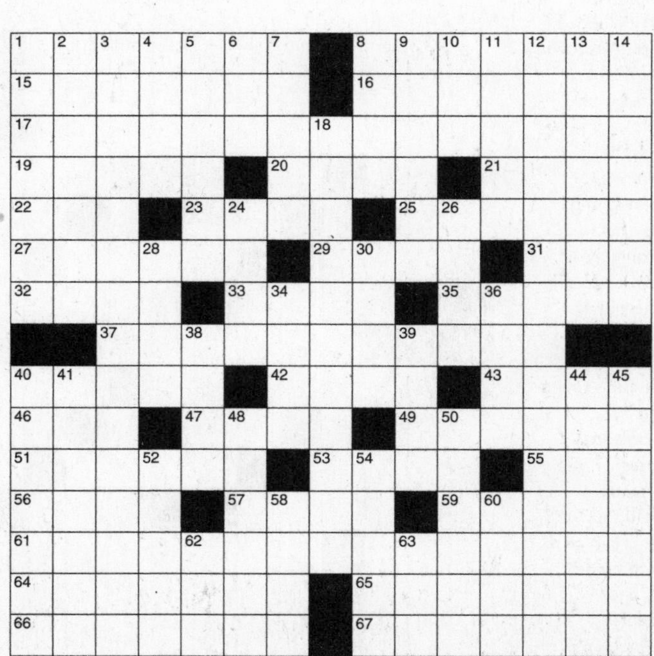

by Joe Krozel

ACROSS

1 Officers
6 Award show category
11 In haste
14 Derided
16 It might help you catch your breath
17 Kind of pickup
18 "St. Martin and the Beggar" painter
19 Tenth Commandment subject
20 "Just this time . . ."
21 Upbraided
22 Lascivious sorts
24 Beans and others
25 Go on
26 Having more bites, say
28 Word from a waiter
29 Language with no word for "hello"
32 Sloven
35 Enthusiast
36 One wiping out
39 Pitt athlete
41 Mercurial
43 Former
44 Subject of the Fujita scale
45 British dish with an American version called a Hot Brown
46 Polka relative
47 Fathers, of a sort
48 Lachrymose
49 Attacked
50 What the cogent make

DOWN

1 Summary
2 Need replenishing
3 Silverish
4 "My" girl in a 1979 hit
5 Knee cap?
6 Coins for Cicero
7 College student's request
8 Judge
9 Varmints, in a classic cartoon line
10 Extra
12 Big name in wafers
13 Creator of "The Simpsons"
14 Blubber
15 Having a hard time connecting?
23 Missouri metro
27 It may come down after a win
28 Native to a certain region
29 Like some spirits
30 It's typed with the left pinkie
31 Check
32 Echoes
33 "That makes 50-Across"
34 Lie in the sun
35 Start of a Christmas refrain
37 :-(
38 Equestrians
39 It may be screened
40 Softens in water, in a way
42 Thicket of trees

by Julian Lim

134

ACROSS

1 Lit
6 Up to one's old tricks
15 Trigger-happy sound?
16 Propositions
17 In a main location?
18 Like newly available products
19 Take care of the spread
20 Winnebago relative
21 New Mexican, e.g.
22 It's raw
23 "That's it"
25 "Singin' in the Rain" co-director
26 Unlike aristos
28 Allspice and clove's family
30 Ki ___ (legendary founder of Korea)
31 City representatives?
32 Letters in some church names
33 Walk-___
35 Pastoral prophet
36 It worked from a prompt
38 Allowing peeking, perhaps
42 Viroid composition
44 Offensive time?
45 Splendid
46 See 62-Down
49 Like old AM radio
51 AM or FM specification
52 Make a measure
54 Clear wrongs
56 Jacques Cousteau, e.g.
57 Am or Fm stat
58 Sci-fi writer Frederik
59 Go all the way through
61 Fifth in a series of seven old comedy films
63 Her temple was adorned with cows' horns
64 Extravagant way to live
65 Set up
66 View on a clear night
67 Gets down to the ground?

DOWN

1 One you don't want to have a crush on you
2 Order to curtail public bussing
3 Not block out
4 Arch type
5 Slip site
6 MoMA and Epcot, e.g.
7 Mind-numbingly exhausted
8 "That made no sense to me"
9 "SCTV" segment?
10 Polymer finish?
11 "You couldn't be more wrong!"
12 Install in an office
13 Its logo features two eighth notes
14 Zip
24 Yardbirds hit of 1965
25 Place for a retreat
27 Red giant, once?
29 Clay target?
34 9–5, e.g.
37 It's concerned with ports
39 Follower of Arlo Guthrie at Woodstock
40 Come out with
41 Duck, emu, etc.
43 Baby beef?
46 Finds on a bed
47 Digging something
48 Godzilla creator Tomoyuki ___
50 They call their native language "te reo"
53 Many a software company employee
55 Comforter material
58 Like tailgated drivers, often
60 Red giant in Cetus
62 With 46-Across, prehistoric animal preserver

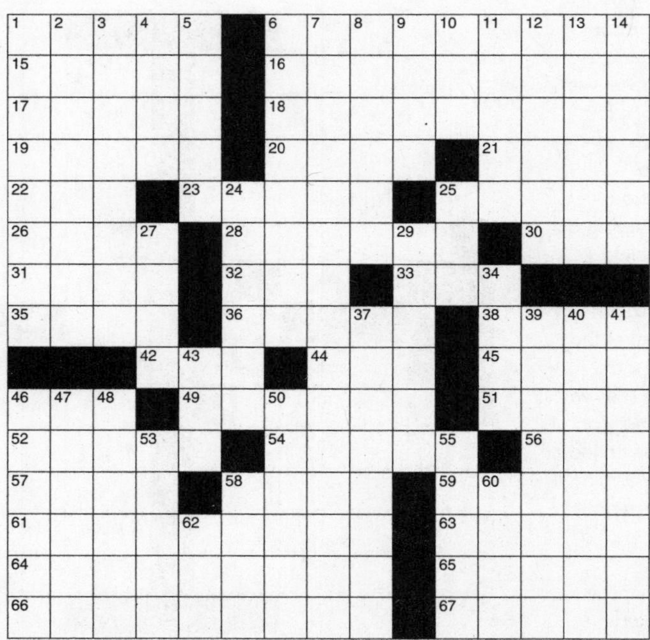

by Tim Croce

ACROSS

1 Actual title of the 1979 #1 hit known as "The Piña Colada Song"
7 "Family Guy" mayor, or the actor providing his voice
15 Dump truck filler
16 Deliver
17 Shameless yes-man
18 1984 film starring Tom Selleck as a jewel thief
19 Front covers
20 Fashion magazines, e.g.
21 Trespasses
22 Higgins's pupil in elocution
23 Abbr. rarely seen at the start of a sentence
24 One rudely put out?
25 Satellite community?
28 Small brawl
33 Removes from a spool
34 Ignoring copyrights, say
35 "In the Night Kitchen" author
36 Lady famous for piemaking
37 Cash in
39 Vegas hotel that hosts the World Series of Poker
40 Nighttime assignment, often
44 "Star Trek: First Contact" villains, with "the"
46 Girl's name meaning "messenger of God"
47 Second run
49 Foot-stomping music
50 Unfazed by
51 Top-quality
52 DVD box set purchase
53 Wild West show headgear
54 Place to sit, ironically

DOWN

1 "___ in Berlin" (1960 live album)
2 Mineral used as chalk by tailors
3 One born on Christmas Day
4 Enlargement
5 Unskilled laborers
6 Newton-meter fractions
7 No more
8 Kind of box for input
9 Moral theory that doesn't allow for shades of gray
10 Old-fashioned letter opener
11 You might keep a watch on it
12 Weird Al Yankovic's first Billboard hit
13 What tuning forks are made of
14 Clipped
22 Sleep, in British slang
23 Skinny-legged trotters
24 Had one do through persuasion
26 Outlaw Kelly of Australian legend
27 Like Lincoln before his presidency
29 1950s–'70s senator Ervin
30 Added to the soup, say
31 Pressed one's suit?
32 Return a call?
34 Little game, perhaps
36 Falling rocks
38 Company behind the 1960s yo-yo craze
40 Fishing hooks
41 Dark
42 Mesoamerican plant
43 Ran into again
44 Hemmed in
45 "No good ___ plot can be sensible . . .": W. H. Auden
47 Former Wisconsin senator Feingold
48 Dispose of

by Patrick Berry

136

ACROSS

1 Indian home
6 Store
15 Gloucester and Kent, in "King Lear"
16 1822 Walter Scott novel about Capt. Clement Cleveland
17 Its calling code is +39
18 President Harding's Laddie Boy and others
19 Elvis's and Mariah's record number of weeks at Billboard's #1
21 Big mouth
22 Carmen Sandiego cover-up?
23 8 on the Beaufort scale
24 Until June 25, 2011, its first three digits had geographical significance: Abbr.
25 "Tempest" Golden Globe nominee Julia
26 Purple
27 Lived in King James's era?
29 "Jason Lives," e.g.
30 Notes in passing?
33 Like the word "its," often
34 Crows
35 Ice cream case selections
36 Take what one oughtn't
37 Weapon that comes in easy-to-carry and hard-to-carry varieties
38 Lacuna
41 Snarling, say
42 Ursi maritimi
45 Place that shows placing and showing: Abbr.
46 Miami or Amsterdam, for example
47 Uniform shade
49 "Let's ___ there"
50 Something one might be forced to wear at work
51 Top
52 Deal incentive
53 Some of them are flukes

DOWN

1 Withdrawals that may incur substantial penalties?
2 Tom Mix vehicles
3 Second Commandment word
4 Wrench handle?
5 "It's Gonna Be Me" band of 2000
6 Emergency directive?
7 Become sparse
8 From above
9 Blown
10 Mask
11 Constellation between Scorpius and Triangulum Australe
12 Supercenters, e.g.
13 More than gnawed at
14 Celebratory chant at Chicago's Grant Park on 11/4/08
20 Basketball long shots
23 Mavens
26 In a bad place?
27 Sweet, to Scipio
28 Dating
29 Sebastián ___ (president of Chile beginning in 2010)
30 Reprimands
31 Gary Cooper played one in "Man of the West"
32 Certain ATV
33 Dickens character whose first name is Wilkins
35 Blonde picked up at a bar?
37 "We feel your pain" sloganeer
38 Ankle covering
39 Kind of eraser
40 "Hearts and minds" activities, in military slang
42 Luke's mother in "Star Wars"
43 Already
44 Tightwads' prefix
46 Exploit
48 Capital of Victoria

by Byron Walden

ACROSS

1 Like a snap
9 With 46-Down, strike zones
15 Kind of stew
16 Role Enrico Caruso was preparing for when he died
17 Eye openers?
18 He said "I never think I have finished a nude until I think I could pinch it"
19 Glossy scarf fabrics
20 Japanese mat
21 Well and good finish?
22 Like Hollywood
24 Landing place
26 Yardbird
27 "Here's Johnny!" memoirist
31 Line in the sand?
35 Give a hand
36 Think that just maybe one can
37 Put down in writing
39 Deep orangish hue
40 Take in
41 One code-named Renegade by the Secret Service
43 Hundred Years' War leader
46 Colonial group
50 A destroyer may be in one
51 "Forget I said that"
54 Like pupils that are too small
55 Big, purple Hanna-Barbera character
56 Take stock?
57 Go mano a mano
58 Discharges
59 Romulus and Remus, to Rhea Silvia

DOWN

1 1956 movie monster
2 What some dictators end up in
3 What may hold a world of information?
4 Good earth
5 Inside opening?
6 Like many ports
7 "Absolutely!"
8 "Absolutely!"
9 Rich dessert
10 Elite soldiers
11 Dollar store?
12 Show poor sportsmanship about, say
13 Waste
14 Like Life Savers
23 Cowboys compete in it: Abbr.
24 Tiny amount
25 Aid in gaining an edge
27 Start of the 16th century
28 "1984" activity
29 Played
30 Turns off
32 Very early 2-Down
33 Hardly seen at the Forum?
34 Sign of assent
38 E.R. status
39 "Goodbye, Columbus" co-star, 1969
42 Intelligent
43 ___ Oliver, a k a the Naked Chef
44 Certain foot specialist
45 Trivia quiz fodder
46 See 9-Across
47 Just ducky
48 Court gimme
49 Correction corrections
52 Language spoken on Pandora
53 Not settled

by Brendan Emmett Quigley

138

ACROSS

1 It may be seen in a 3-Down picture
10 Times up?
15 Like bending over backward
16 Lowest deck on a ship
17 Feign concurrence
18 Words of concurrence
19 Bit of consolation
20 Google rival
21 Scriveners
22 Yesterday, to Yvette
24 "Gomer Pyle, U.S.M.C." star
26 Their lines have ties: Abbr.
27 It's taken while waiting
29 "Le Roi d'Ys" composer
30 Lumpkin
31 Bible supporter, often
33 One may be suckered
35 Hedonist's opposite
39 Unwanted tail?
40 Black-and-white
42 W.W. II agcy.
43 Bottom of the ocean?
44 Group sharing a coat of arms
46 Feeds on the farm, maybe
50 Offensive time?
51 City that lost its "tallest building" distinction in 2007
53 Not apart, in scores
54 Club alternative
56 ID figures
58 ID issuer
59 Match
60 "Let's roll!"
62 Long
63 Very close game, e.g.
64 Bloody Sunday march site
65 Like some skiing and swimming

DOWN

1 "The tenth Muse," per Plato
2 Oblong temptation
3 Beyond suggestive
4 Far from forward
5 Quatrain scheme
6 Author of "America by Heart"
7 Missing a key?
8 Dope
9 Lines coming from the heart, briefly?
10 Gardeners' aids
11 One letting off steam
12 1970s music genre
13 What the Faroe Islands were granted in 1948
14 Frumpy loner, stereotypically
21 "Now!"
23 Undo
25 Accented cries
28 Out of practice?: Abbr.
30 Line forgetter's substitute
32 Magick worker
34 It causes lights to go out
35 Camels' resting places
36 Sponge alternative
37 Kind of awareness
38 Title locale in a 1998 Notorious B.I.G. hit
41 The Notorious B.I.G., e.g.
45 Tabloid nickname
47 Ripley's love
48 Pound
49 Very bad
51 Singer ___ Marie
52 Fireplace
55 Shoulder
57 Displays disconsolation
60 Like Beethoven's Sixth
61 Black-throated ___

by Ashton Anderson

ACROSS

1 Sensitive information is often shared on it
16 Thing rolled in a classroom
17 Continue cordially despite differences
18 Cousin of a canvasback
19 Scapola or clavicola
20 It gets lapped a lot
21 Potential mouth choker
23 Agricultural Hall of Fame locale: Abbr.
24 Certain X or O
25 It includes an analytical reasoning sect.
27 ___-80 (old computer)
29 Nascar Hall of Fame locale: Abbr.
32 A good defense may result in it, briefly
34 A wee bit
36 1968 title role for Vanessa Redgrave
40 "Thinking . . ."
41 Chihuahua assent
42 Idyllic place
43 ___ suspension (ear drops)
44 "And that sort of thing": Abbr.
46 Evidence of some growth
49 One-third of nove
51 "Configuration" artist
53 Enrich
55 Not as experienced
57 Earth as an organism
59 Place for a rip
61 Like real danger
64 Toiletries and such
65 Feature of many a residential neighborhood

DOWN

1 Ingenious
2 Ball's lack
3 Continental pass provider
4 Common flashlight fillers
5 South Korea's Roh ___ Woo
6 Cartoon busman Mann
7 Small business site
8 Gives a passing acknowledgment
9 Piquant sandwich base
10 "Time ___ . . ."
11 Firing result
12 Kandahar cash
13 Dust-laden winds
14 Soprano player Robert
15 Hook accompanier
22 Hit lightly
26 Painful struggle
28 Look bad?
30 Put down
31 Movie heroine Norma ___ Webster
33 Dumas hero
35 Some cashless commerce
36 Prefix with -meric
37 Get on the bottom?
38 Seemingly
39 Cut
45 Protect
47 Six-Day War figure
48 Attic locale
50 Owl in Harry Potter tales
52 Brought (in), as music
54 He met Charon in the underworld
55 Return request: Abbr.
56 A, Jay or Ray
58 Boxer rebellion cries?
60 ___ Mary's (L.A. college)
62 Black bird
63 Young pond dweller

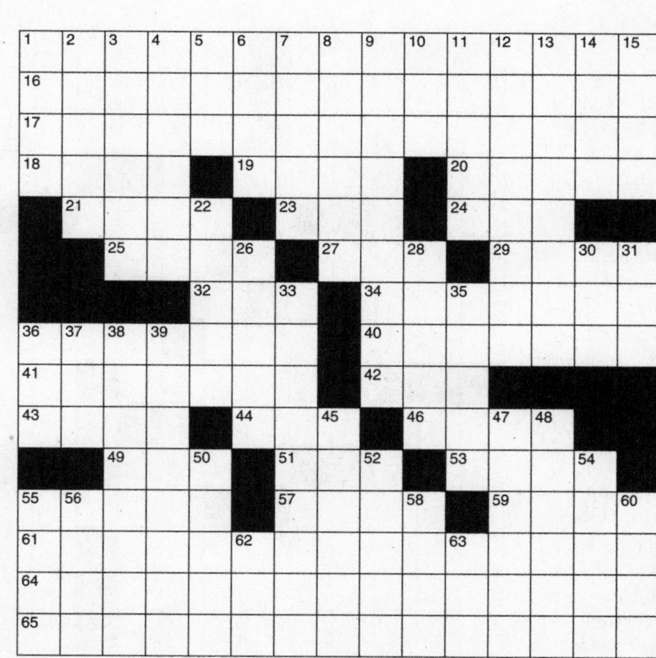

by Tim Croce

140

ACROSS

1 "Star Wars" villain
6 Broken thing in "Gimme a break"
15 Perform "All of Me," say
16 Performing perfectly
17 Chili container
18 Pirate's implement
19 Sapporo's home
21 Nobel-winning economist James
22 "Would you look at that!"
23 Inventor of the battery in 1800
26 Extinct wingless bird
27 Birth city of Mother Teresa
30 It's acquired in the sun
33 A little too quiet, perhaps
34 Gruff rejoinder
35 Brewmaster's science
37 Term for some morning deejays
41 Having been tainted, as a drink
43 United hub
44 Noted role for 46-Down
47 Many domes
48 Great Society inits.
49 ___ Park
51 "That's awful!"
52 "David ___," Edward Noyes Westcott novel
55 Ninnies
58 It stirs things up
61 About to happen
62 Gathering place for animals
63 Glandular opening?
64 They're thrown over the shoulder
65 Ready for another play

DOWN

1 Former 'N Sync vocalist and judge on "America's Best Dance Crew"
2 Pointer for a computer user
3 Bibliolater
4 Dark quaff
5 "Tonight My Love, Tonight" singer
6 Little fella
7 Absorb
8 Sliver
9 Former org. for Azerbaijani president Heydar Aliyev
10 Poisonous lily
11 Moved with force
12 Cleanser with the logo of a chick emerging from an egg
13 Photographer who once collaborated with Capote
14 Brushed up on
20 "___ changed"
24 Excited state
25 U.K. highway connecting London and Dover
28 Ninth successor of St. Peter
29 Beef product
31 Screamingly funny
32 Part of a mudslide, maybe
34 "The Tinker's Wedding" playwright
36 Japanese capture after Pearl Harbor
38 Projects, in a good way
39 "Grey's Anatomy" actor
40 Chink in the armor
42 Relatives
44 Fashion strip?
45 "The ___ Diaries" (2007 best seller)
46 Actor Pat
47 Sponge
50 They're added in some infrastructure upgrades
53 Conference USA sch.
54 "The Sands of ___" (Arthur C. Clarke's first science fiction novel)
56 Window coating?
57 German fantasy writer Michael
59 Article in hip-hop
60 Org. against doping

by Peter Wentz

141

ACROSS

1 Starting point for a ferry ride to Alcatraz
16 Ways to avoid traffic jams
17 Many people can make this claim
18 See 55-Down
19 It's less than premium: Abbr.
20 Drilling type: Abbr.
21 Be unable to get the rest?
28 Battling something, say
29 Mock
30 North American singers with raspy notes
39 Bozo's suggestion
40 As a hobby
41 Not overseas
42 "That so?" reply
43 Beggar's receptacle
44 Result of prolonged worry
51 "Aloha nui ___" (warm greeting in Waikiki)
52 From ___ B
53 Going, going, going
62 Appalachian, e.g.
63 1953 hit for Mitch Miller

DOWN

1 Side
2 "Any volunteers?" reply
3 Some wild parties
4 Attendees of 3-Down
5 Unscripted utterances
6 Makeup of some strands
7 Large-scale
8 When some retire
9 Snow on les Alpes
10 Sign of a good show
11 Like some hands and hearts
12 Czech religious reformer Jan
13 Carry ___
14 Tend to again, as an injured joint
15 Shooting setting
22 Cause to pull over
23 "Imagine that!"
24 Mr. Cub and others
25 More together
26 One may take your heart
27 Run
30 Things traveling on sound waves?
31 Ear part
32 Quit lying
33 Ice cream shop request
34 Plains homes: Var.
35 "Away! you are ___": Shak.
36 Head of design
37 Cancel
38 Saint-___ (Delibes contemporary)
45 Dissolve out
46 Tough question
47 It's not a long shot
48 Local theaters
49 Anatomical aqueducts
50 "___ Alice" (1971 antidrug book)
53 Home of Sun Devil Stadium, for short
54 Stopping-off point: Abbr.
55 With 18-Across, no-goodnik
56 Santa ___
57 Service address
58 Opening for birds?
59 Last article of the U.S. Constitution
60 Dijon toasting time?
61 Roads with train tracks: Abbr.

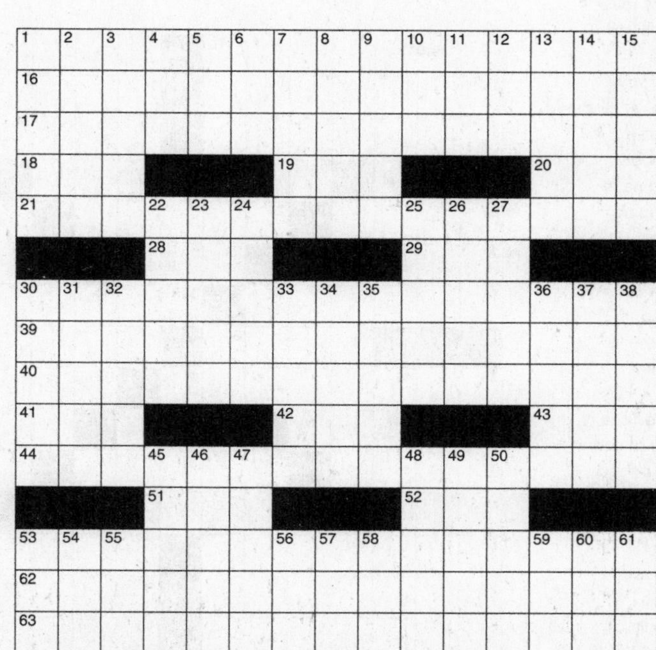

by Joe Krozel

142

ACROSS

1 Only song on Rolling Stone's "500 Greatest Songs of All Time" list that is not sung in English
8 Midweek
15 Unitedly
16 See
17 Humor
18 Goes back and forth, in a way
19 Bread pudding ingredient
20 Subject on a wanted poster
22 NPR's Shapiro
23 "A God in Ruins" novelist
25 Man of steel?
26 Gridiron cues
27 Reduces
29 Country music's ___ Brown Band
30 Line up
31 Shady, say
33 Frequently disputed court call?
35 Map abbr.
37 First name in auto racing
38 Transfer
42 Concedes
46 Island near Ayr
47 It ended in 1947
49 Welcome to paradise?
50 Tower
51 Charybdis, e.g.
53 Source of some highly prized 19-Acrosses
54 1940s–'60s world leader
55 Where one's head is
57 Robitaille of the N.H.L.
58 #1 in sports
60 Northern air
62 Sometimes-banned work
63 State of anarchy
64 Misters abroad
65 Setting of many plots

DOWN

1 Some boots
2 Name on the highest award of the American Society of Plant Taxonomists
3 Diamond handler?
4 Had
5 Keyboardist Saunders who played with the Grateful Dead
6 Mongolian for "hero"
7 "A Perfect Peace" novelist
8 Drink in a mug
9 Wolf pack member
10 U.S.M.C. E-8
11 Tuning device
12 "Stop Whining, Start Living" author
13 Turned away
14 "That is clear"
21 Boarder's aid
24 Rising time, for some
26 Writer on whose work Woody Allen's "Sleeper" is loosely based
28 Setting for a set
30 Basilica de San Vicente setting
32 Home of Pyramid Lake: Abbr.
34 Christian ___
36 Balustraded locales, often
38 Honors
39 Major export of Brazil and Australia
40 Marketing giant with a portmanteau name
41 Bust
43 "Hot!"
44 "Poetry makes nothing happen" writer
45 It's unfortunate
48 2002 horror sequel
51 Many an heiress
52 Lure
55 Bergman's last role
56 Response to the '08 financial crisis
59 Pou ___ (vantage point)
61 Void: Fr.

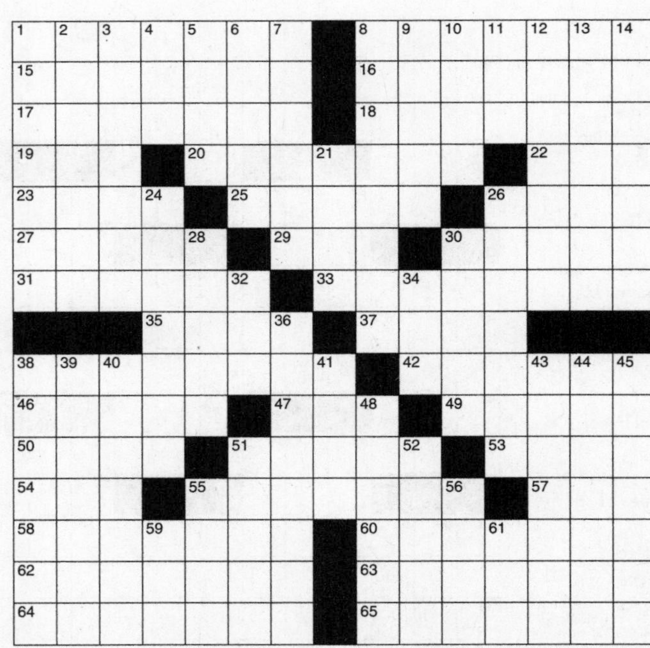

by David Quarfoot

ACROSS

1 Reduce to bare bones
10 "Hey you!"
15 1990 Clint Eastwood cop film
16 Studio sign
17 Likely to take chances
18 Figure on a bridge score sheet
19 Money competitor
20 Was up to date, with "out"?
21 They may work for both sides
22 Pitlik who directed "Barney Miller" and "Mr. Belvedere"
24 Toledo-to-Columbus dir.
26 Shut (up)
27 Reaction of thirsty people
31 Firm
33 Wallace who wrote "Angle of Repose"
34 Stolen
35 Old "One mission. Yours." sloganeer
36 Miss ___
37 Worse than awful
41 Blowout
46 Small night creatures
47 Reckless smuggler of sci-fi
48 Area close to a hockey net
49 Abbr. before "Co." in some company names
51 Suffer from the heat
52 Having less coverage
54 Go down again, so to speak
58 Frost relative
59 "Get ___ on!"
60 "Generally speaking . . ."
62 Hit the bottom of?
63 Spread quickly over the Internet
64 Laments
65 Put one's feet up in neighborly fashion

DOWN

1 Series
2 Become sparse
3 Change one's image, in a way?
4 Needle
5 ___ wheelie
6 Actress Diana
7 "Enough already . . . relax!"
8 Blushes, say
9 Has trouble getting started
10 Piles of chips, say
11 Stir-fry vegetable
12 Pronounced
13 Matte finish?
14 Met on the down-low
23 Certain meas. of economy
25 Kings prophet
28 Getting dragged along
29 Minnesota home of Martin Luther College
30 Semiterrestrial bug-catchers
32 Sap
37 Alice Cooper's appropriately titled theme song for "Friday the 13th Part VI"
38 Morse who sang "Cow-Cow Boogie"
39 "From my perspective . . ."
40 Much less than that
42 Australian state: Abbr.
43 "Is it worth the chance?"
44 Criminal
45 Recovered
50 Explorer John Cabot's birthplace
53 Some M&M's
55 "I'm busy then"
56 Eye part
57 Powers (up)
61 Big swing

by Joe DiPietro

144

ACROSS

1 Singer/songwriter Scialfa
6 ___ student
9 Banjo accessory
14 Cause for some spatial relationships?
17 Debut at the 1979 Frankfurt Auto Show
18 It can heat up Roquefort
19 Smooth
20 One with nothing to hide
21 Wallop
23 Last movement of a sonata
25 Like bath beads, typically
28 Show one's stamped hand, perhaps
32 Can't take a bit
33 Bear essentials?
35 Relatives of the Iowa
36 They're in the vicinity: Abbr.
37 Sartre's "Les Jeux Sont ___"
38 Box office need
39 Got things down
40 Damn
41 Like 14-Across
42 Tool handle strengthener
44 Member of a very early union?
46 Titan after whom one of the oceans is named
48 Silver checker
49 Some time
52 Choice job
54 Lid around a loch
57 Suffered serious consequences
60 Groups aiming for good returns
61 Smoking and heavy drinking
62 Security demands
63 They go with uppers

DOWN

1 Surface
2 Over and over
3 One spending a long time in the bathroom?
4 Drug in a sci-fi novel series
5 What swallows swallow
6 Suits often hold them
7 Landscaping aid
8 Like some balances
9 Memphis hospital, familiarly
10 Like sashes
11 Indian flatbread
12 Some marching bands
13 Math is part of it: Abbr.
15 Benefiting from Vivarin
16 It's shown on TV monitors at many airports
22 Tips, often
24 Is a spellbinder
25 Bundle of a sort
26 51-Down division
27 Alexandria is in it
29 Coming down hard
30 Net sales
31 Spur part
34 Tulipe relative
37 Maximum
38 Numerical prefix
40 Pirate's appurtenance
41 Grandfathers, e.g.
43 Speakeasy scourge
45 Blow
47 "The primary factor in a successful attack," per Lord Mountbatten
49 Capital near Faleolo International Airport
50 "The Joy Luck Club" director, 1993
51 Busy place
53 Magnifier
55 Lofty place
56 Hoarder's problem
58 "I think you overshared," briefly
59 Locomobile competitor

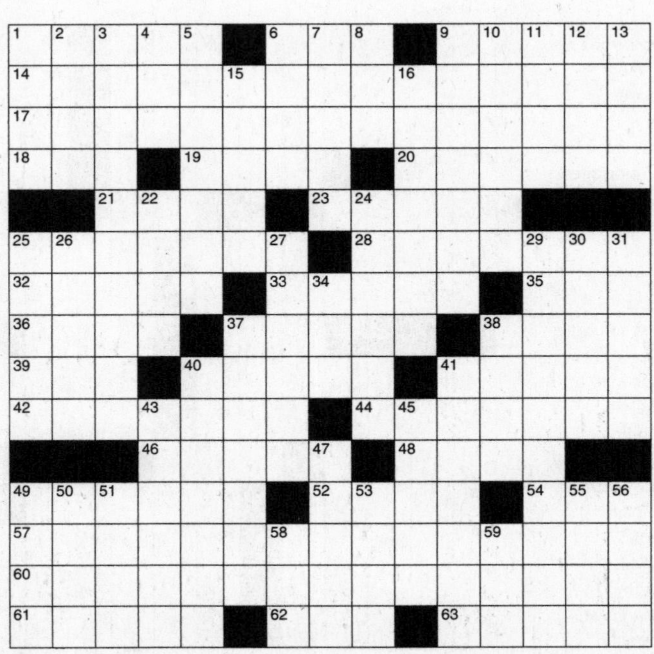

by Peter A. Collins

ACROSS

1 It has rock bands
6 Pooh-pooh
14 ___-toothed
15 Informal show of approval?
16 Stroll
17 Factor affecting Google search results
18 Juicer detritus
19 Modern proofs-of-purchase, for short
20 Takes for a ride
21 Many gamblers have them
23 Self-help book
24 Gaston who wrote "The Phantom of the Opera"
25 Include as an extra
28 ___ Lady (decades-old commercial creation)
29 Movie credits, usually
31 Collision sound
34 "Dominus illuminatio ___" (Oxford University's motto)
35 Validate
36 "___ Como Va" (1971 hit)
37 It makes a lot of connections
38 Give a slant to
39 Follower's response
40 In many cases
41 Worries
43 Last report on the evening news, typically
46 Deny
48 Give a good rubdown
49 Blue shade
51 Providers of directions
53 Admitted
55 The Temptations' "Since ___ My Baby"
56 Leisure
57 Spitting mad
58 Something a drunkard is liable to hit
59 Turns brown quickly

DOWN

1 Before all else
2 Series ender, sometimes
3 1969 #1 album for 11 weeks
4 Betrays, in a way
5 1974 lyric repeated after "Como una promesa"
6 Plea from the self-conscious
7 One looking for a deal?
8 Some blockers
9 Old Tokyo
10 Diamond substitute
11 Grant
12 7-Down, for one
13 Many a sculpture
15 Like some Olympic races
22 Not counting
23 Multitude
24 Asian spiritual guide
26 One who's gone but not forgotten
27 Muscles strengthened by squats
30 Put on a scale
31 Music style derived from samba and jazz
32 Agreement from one's mate?
33 Big competition
35 Aficionado
39 Phrase used to 46-Across
40 Proposals
42 Forgers' tools
43 He famously asked "Why didn't you burn the tapes?"
44 Vinegar quality
45 Attachments to pronator quadratus muscles
47 Botanical balm
49 Object frequently painted by Degas
50 Grand
52 Some govt. issuances: Abbr.
54 Employer of many a 7-Down

by Mike Nothnagel

146

ACROSS

1 Bit of miner's gear
9 Go for first
15 Take pains
16 Where it's at
17 Upbeat
18 Much of Micronesia
19 Use a Zen garden
21 Gloating cry
22 Disallowed FedEx destination
25 ___ Aarnio, innovative furniture designer
26 Put on cloud nine
27 Spacewalks and moonwalks, briefly
28 Put back in order?
29 Direction for a boxer
30 Tip for a writer
31 Creator of many 38-Across
35 Response to "Thanks so much"
37 Once-common urban skyline sights
38 Many 31-Across characters
40 Free
41 See 42-Across
42 With 41-Across, discuss
43 Kellogg's brand
44 Wrigley sticks?
46 Characteristic governor
47 Bakers' dozen, maybe?
48 Mars, e.g.
49 Title for Wallis Simpson
51 Opening for the wrist or the back?
53 Attend the lectures of
57 Curve-cutting line
58 She played Jane in "Fun With Dick and Jane," 2005
59 Where traditional bloomers gather
60 Aim for

DOWN

1 Cool, once
2 "Warszawa" instrumentalist
3 Much e-mail
4 Martian moon
5 Glove material
6 Like noisy fans
7 Place to witness a big scene?
8 What a bar mitzvah recently was
9 "Apology" author
10 Drills that can bore
11 Conscious beginning?
12 Bum rap
13 Astronaut Ochoa
14 Fix, as ribs?
20 Nude showers?
22 Kind of code
23 Like ones that are fleeced
24 Bum rap?
26 Aye-aye relative?
28 Certain
29 Sean Connery and Roger Moore, e.g.
31 End it with suddenly
32 Be mephitic
33 Associate (with)
34 Kind of PC command
36 Certain crosses
39 Ice-T or Ice Cube persona
43 Plane, e.g.
44 Nova preceder
45 Composer nominated for an Oscar for "Blues in the Night"
46 Lavatory label
47 Circular windows
49 Make more efficient
50 "___ at the pane": Robert Browning
52 Mate
54 ___-eyed
55 Fictional creature whose name is Old English for "giant"
56 Museu do Índio site

by Jeremy Horwitz

ACROSS

1 Many viviparous births
8 Where many beads are formed
13 Pretty good result for a golf round
14 Without incident
15 Coyote, say, to a Western rancher
16 Subject of the 2001 book subtitled "The Shock of the Century"
17 Stumble
18 Like many resorts
20 Expression of praise
21 Clouds
23 Toppers popular with jazzmen
25 1958 Pulitzer-winning novelist and family
26 His character had the signature line "Book 'em, Danno"
27 Territory on a Risk board
28 Like stools and many benches
29 Event for many a dashing young man
31 Having been overexposed to the sun, maybe
32 Unrefined sort
36 Officially starts work
37 "Nature's lay idiot, I taught thee to love" penner
38 Sea food
39 Points of view?
40 "Chariots of Fire" co-star Charleson
41 Doesn't go away
43 Thing to drive off of
44 Choices for snaps
46 Like some Internet searches
48 ___ monkey
49 Least desirably
50 Sounds from a 3-Down
51 They're far from stars

DOWN

1 Slight show of affection
2 Going ballistic
3 One producing 50-Across
4 Petty recording
5 Boots
6 "___ Most Wanted" ("best-of" compilation of a popular TV cop show)
7 Miss hitting a piñata?: Abbr.
8 Bauhaus artist and teacher
9 "___ I had heard of Lucy Gray": Wordsworth
10 "La Loge" and "La Grenouillère"
11 Skipped over
12 General George at Gettysburg
14 Performed brilliantly
16 Warehouse workers
19 Job for some wall fixers
22 Deuterium has one
24 London letter getter
26 Twenties
28 Wheelie supporter
30 Daredevilish
31 Muleta material
33 Four years as governor, say
34 Like most apartments
35 Minds
36 Danes featured in films
37 Renounce
38 Little digit?
39 Prefix with type
42 Israel's first U.N. delegate
45 Orthodontist's concern
47 Mauna ___

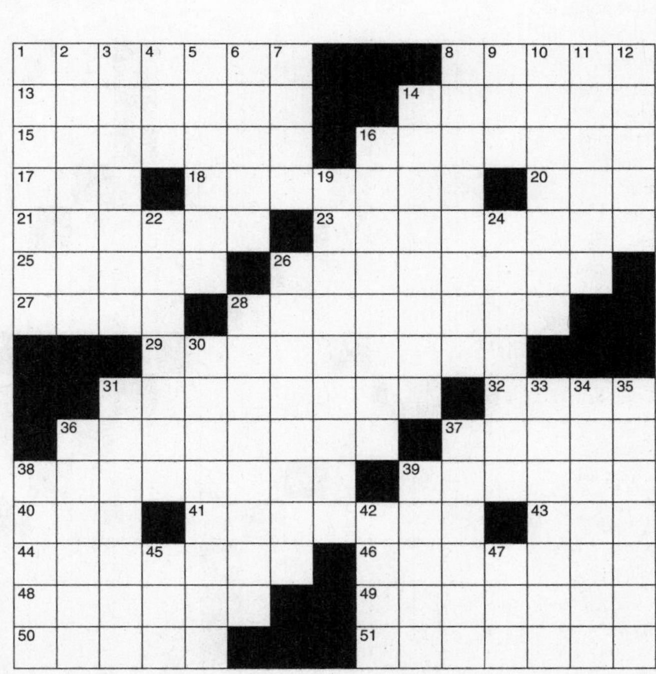

by Joe Krozel

148

ACROSS

1 Subject of search engine optimization
9 Changing place
15 It may involve the colon
16 Investment option, informally
17 Right part of a map
18 Portmanteau wear
19 Arsenal decommissioned in 2005
20 "The Play About the Baby" playwright
22 Ease
23 Volunteer's offer
25 City of the Altiplano
27 Abandon
28 Certain adjustments
30 Flying Dutchman captain of film
32 Fictional character whose first name is Kentaro
34 One vertex of the Summer Triangle
35 Big name in confectioneries
36 "Delightful!"
38 E-5: Abbr.
39 My country's follower?
42 Ignition trouble
44 Library spot
46 Way to see the big picture?
50 Kind of card
51 French singles
52 Foil alternative
54 Spiced quaffs
55 North Atlantic catch
57 ___-Obama Proliferation and Threat Reduction Initiative (2007 law)
59 Footnote abbr.
60 Rung
62 Time for Conan, informally
64 He played Mandela on TV's "Mandela"
65 Joins, redundantly
66 Movie genre named for a food staple
67 Starbucks offering

DOWN

1 "Step aside, I'll help"
2 Bit of green in a wallet
3 Side in an epic battle
4 Letters for college-bound students
5 Annual romance writer's award
6 Place ___
7 "I'm impressed!"
8 Bit of in-line skating gear
9 Price abbr.
10 Canadian singer with three #1 Billboard hits
11 Growing concern for a surgeon, informally?
12 Transportation to Sugar Hill, in a 1941 song
13 Get to
14 They're positive
21 Collection sites, of a sort
24 Romantic introduction?
26 Company behind the popular social network games FarmVille and CityVille
29 Commercial prefix since the 1950s
31 "Romeo Must Die" actor, 2000
33 Bounces
37 Good
39 Where some write checks
40 "Bingo!"
41 Censor's target
42 Free
43 Anarchy
45 Atlanta's ___ Center
46 Angry lover's dismissal
47 Beverage nickname, with "the"
48 Product of Bordeaux
49 Olympics site that introduced snowboarding
53 Smart
56 Bucks and bucks
58 Casting need
61 Hospital grp.
63 Kind of card

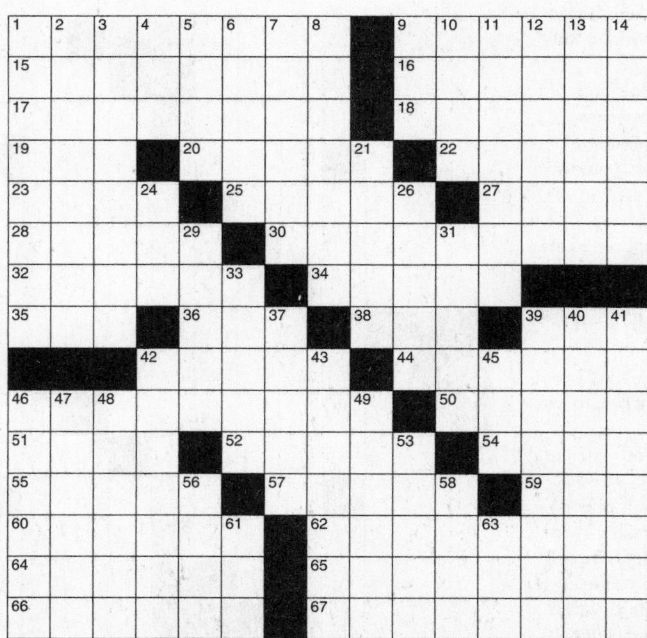

by David Quarfoot

149

ACROSS

1 Brainchild of 57-Across
5 1998 Sarah McLachlan hit
9 1972 Bill Withers hit
14 Some documentary workers
16 Film studio spearheaded by 57-Across
17 Brainchild of 57-Across
18 Parade V.I.P.
19 Post-PC ___
20 Thimbleful
21 Finest example
23 Focus of some prep work
25 Ulan-___ (Siberian capital)
26 Slogan associated with 57-Across
32 Flatterer
33 Bitmap images
34 Tyler of "The Lord of the Rings"
35 Hole punchers
36 Huffs
38 Singer Simone
39 Head
40 Like some Arabians
41 Reacted to an unveiling, say
42 Frequent description of 57-Across
46 Wheeler Peak locale: Abbr.
47 Many an early computer user
48 "Doonesbury" cartoonist
52 Anderson who directed "Rushmore"
53 ___ drive
56 Cover again, as terrain?
57 This puzzle's subject
60 Company co-founded by 57-Across
61 Rocket parts
62 Prepared to be shot
63 E-mail heading: Abbr.
64 Company founded by 57-Across

DOWN

1 "Have a Little Faith ___" (1930 hit)
2 Onetime host of "The Tonight Show"
3 One seeking to catch some rays?
4 Soft & ___
5 "Sic 'em!"
6 Thingamajig
7 Return letters?
8 ___ Stadium, sports venue since 1997
9 They're positive
10 Junior watcher
11 Site of some unveilings
12 Term of address for a lady
13 "Symphony in Black" artist
15 "Friends, Romans, countrymen, lend me your ears" speaker
22 Patisserie offerings
23 YouTube content, for short
24 One of many from 57-Across
26 "Prelude ___" (1942 Frank Capra film)
27 Split, in a way
28 Tailor's concern
29 Root of diplomacy
30 Good diving scores
31 Show stopper?
32 Baby powder ingredient
36 Hindu god often depicted meditating
37 All Saints' Day mo.
38 Mitchum's genre
40 Got into hot water?
41 "Hold on"
43 Speedy Gonzales shout
44 Film in which the Marx Brothers join the gold rush
45 Gridiron group
48 Golfer's concern
49 Unwanted collection
50 Ones who might cry foul?
51 "From knowledge, sea power" org.
53 Tract
54 Mountain climber
55 Cheater's whisper
58 Tater ___
59 Pianist Nakamatsu

by Kevin G. Der

150

ACROSS

1 Accessories for some suits
16 It's often popped on a shoulder
17 Assassinated leader called "the Liberator"
18 Part of many a chain
19 Blow off
20 Go off
21 Largest city in Nordrhein-Westfalen
22 Like many dyed eggs
24 They may be networked
25 Supermarket chain
26 Predecessor of Pope Hilarius
28 It's often enough
32 Kind of memory
34 Permanent, in a way
37 Unquestioning adherents
40 Stigma
41 ___ nitrite
42 Its minimum score is 60, briefly
43 End of the lion
45 ___ Lingus
46 Old political inits.
48 Quality of the queen's jewels?
50 Set, as the sun
54 Opposite of "Happily . . ."
56 Quarter-millennium year
57 Singer called "The Jezebel of Jazz"
58 Jails
62 Shows oneself
63 Responded to some rapping

DOWN

1 Certain fabric worker's work
2 Richard ___, 2002 Pulitzer winner for the novel "Empire Falls"
3 Ever
4 Existentialist Kierkegaard
5 Kind of request in Burns's "To a Mouse"
6 ___-pros
7 Grandpa player in "Look Who's Talking," 1989
8 Like some clothing ensembles
9 Savanna grazer
10 Big brand of writing instruments
11 The Taurus replaced it
12 "Xena: Warrior Princess" role
13 Parts of some pay-as-you-go plans?
14 "Giant Brain" of the 1940s
15 Sounds like a broken record
22 Sound investment
23 21-Across refusal
27 Cleaning the mess?
28 Stamps, say
29 With 50-Down, fair
30 Ones holding wraps in restaurants
31 "Dream-Children" author, 1822
33 What's caught during a tumble?
35 Long reign, e.g.
36 Reason for a late shift?: Abbr.
38 Plant in the pea family
39 "___ Pastore" (Mozart opera)
44 Like some vertebrae
46 Hayek of Hollywood
47 Hoops Hall-of-Famer Jerry
49 Where it's at
50 See 29-Down
51 Fictional Sicilian town in a 1944 novel
52 Member of a crack team?
53 Bandleader with the hit "Three Little Fishies"
55 Twist
59 From Bakersfield to L.A., say
60 Kind of power
61 "Forgot About ___" (2000 Grammy-winning rap)

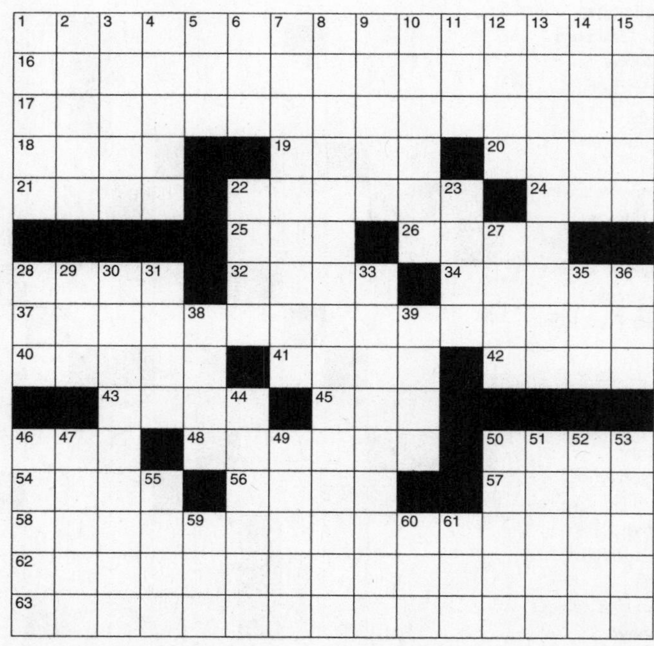

by Tim Croce

ACROSS

1 Bologna is in it
7 Look out for, say
11 Pilot's point?
14 Player of Duke Santos in "Ocean's Eleven," 1960
16 What may come between two friends?
17 Co-writer and star of "Bridesmaids"
18 Part of the former U.A.R.: Abbr.
19 Blocks of history
20 One concerned with blocking
22 More reasonable
24 Caucus call
25 Sports org.
26 Coal-rich valley
28 "Are you up for it?"
32 One helping with filing, for short
35 Momentary disruption
37 "Gotcha"
38 Where to see the writing on the wall?
41 A. J. who wrote "The Citadel"
42 Will of "Jeremiah Johnson"
43 Lou Gehrig's disease, for short
44 Abnormally small
46 Little middle?
48 Terre Haute sch.
49 Cousin of the cassowary
51 Messing around on TV?
55 Melodious birdsong, maybe
59 Composer Khachaturian
60 Peabody Museum patron, perhaps
61 Wind instrument?
63 Abbr. after several examples
64 Playwright who became a president
65 Big hits, for short
66 Artist whose moniker is the pronunciation of his initials
67 Vice president from Tennessee

DOWN

1 Official in the Clinton White House
2 ___ nullius (no man's land)
3 Like about 25% of legal U.S. immigrants
4 Gals across the pond
5 N.Y.C. subway inits.
6 Father of Harmonia, in myth
7 Distributor of Nutrilite vitamins
8 Sandy shades
9 City on Presque Isle Bay
10 ___ party
11 It "isn't what it used to be," said Simone Signoret
12 So to speak
13 William ___, 1990s attorney general
15 One side of the Detroit River
21 Part of U.S.C.: Abbr.
23 Hopper
27 Exclusively
29 New worker
30 Dear
31 "Vous ___ ici"
32 Ozone destroyers, for short
33 Liking
34 Sound system?
36 Env. alternative
39 Lassitude
40 1968 Julie Christie movie set in San Francisco
45 Extract the essence of by boiling
47 Cartoon villain who sails the Black Barnacle
50 Filmmaker Louis
52 Applause accompanier
53 More bloody, so to speak
54 Big
55 Easily imposed upon
56 Mass gathering place
57 Tour de France setting?
58 Source of venanzite
62 The Stars may play the Blues in it, briefly

by Caleb Madison and J.A.S.A. Class

152

ACROSS

1 Bibelot
11 Overweening
15 It really sucks
16 1997 Home Run Derby champion Martinez
17 One-way flights?
18 Not again
19 1973 Nobel Peace Prize decliner Le Duc ___
20 Singular
21 Has to repeat, maybe
22 Get the best of
24 Rodin's thinker?
25 Germany's University of Duisburg-___
26 Wore
28 Like depleted uranium
30 Lao-___
31 House party?
33 One who's got no hope
35 Frito-Lay product
39 Sets at ease
40 Island state in a 1964 merger
42 Explorer's need
43 Places for cutters, for short
44 Star
46 Try to bite
50 What a mail carrier might use in self-defense?
52 ___ Nordegren, ex-wife of Tiger Woods
54 They're counted at meals: Abbr.
55 Growls
56 Cousin of a cutter
58 Nasdaq listing: Abbr.
59 Minotaur, e.g.
60 "You said it!"
62 Formally appeals
63 Malady that typically worsens in the spring
64 You need only scrape the surface to get it
65 1940 cartoon in which Woody Woodpecker debuted

DOWN

1 Beef producer?
2 Home of Daniel Webster College
3 "Brrr!"
4 Reviewer of books
5 Letter before lima in the NATO phonetic alphabet
6 Dog topper
7 Cleared
8 Decided not to run
9 Went without control
10 Gold meas.
11 Sides of some ancient temples
12 Tend
13 Steely-gazed pointer
14 Flips
21 Consumes
23 Funny George
27 Classifieds, e.g.
29 Whiz
32 Gray area?
34 "It's ___!"
35 Leon ___, McKinley's assassin
36 Vituperation
37 Catches up
38 They do better when they close early
41 Chile ___ (Mexican dish)
45 Superhuman, in a way
47 Afghani tongue
48 Language family including Mongolian
49 "You shouldn't have"
51 Waveform maximum
53 Unacceptable
57 Chops in a kitchen
60 "Don't ___"
61 When repeated, hero of children's lit

by Joon Pahk

ACROSS

1 "King Kong" co-star, 2005
10 Magazine subtitled "The Horse Owner's Resource"
15 Son or daughter, usually
16 Aachen appetizer
17 Fictional king with an enormous appetite
18 "Passion" actress, 1919
19 It had "three deuces and a four-speed and a 389," in song
20 Yachting event
22 Thousandth of a yen
23 Has a yen
25 Showy
26 One hanging around the house
27 Napoleon biographer Ludwig
28 Maker of a small purchase, sarcastically
30 Buttonwood
32 Bakery gizmos
33 Fire
34 Writer Jaffe
36 Like some antes
39 Arboriculturist
43 "The Fearless Vampire Killers" actress
46 First name in design
47 More than plenty
48 Claptrap
49 Turkish province or its capital
50 Some income: Abbr.
51 Unfair
53 Opened
54 "Dilemma" rapper
56 Superlatively stout
58 Newsman Roger
59 Fiancée, say
60 Popularity
61 Operation in 1998 news

DOWN

1 Shakes
2 All the things you are
3 Prolonged
4 It's tapped
5 Chutzpah
6 Propositional phrase?
7 Cry to an obedient dog, maybe
8 Heart
9 African livestock pens
10 Feudal worker
11 Lab. neighbor
12 Better model
13 Opposite the current
14 Some fishing boats
21 It's often put on backward
24 Bakery gizmos
26 Protected
28 Campy wear
29 A single, in Stuttgart
31 "Love ___" (1964 hit)
34 Contributions to them are not tax-deductible
35 It may have a lead part
36 "Memed My Hawk" director and star, 1984
37 Cell assignment: Abbr.
38 What a toddler might pull
39 What a scammer might pull
40 Brewed bit
41 Former Mexican president Zedillo
42 Drivers' duty
44 Its members may be seen traveling: Abbr.
45 Sluggish
49 ___ nothing
51 1944 Pulitzer correspondent
52 "Look ___!"
55 N.Y.C. school
57 N.Y.C. subway

by David Bunker

154

ACROSS

1 Treaty signer with Ger. in 1939
5 Horse of a sort
9 Eddie Fisher's "Oh! My ___"
13 Campaign/election analyst ___ Silver
14 Oven brand
15 Resting, say
16 Nickname since 1999
17 Exceedingly hard to see
18 Really small amount
19 Stage-sharing speaker
21 Oxen might be put in it
23 Find contest's meta-answer by reading ___ of these clues
25 Tenth Commandment word
26 Heraldic drawing
27 Incline
29 Seven ___ (Civil War battle site)
31 Workers who play?
34 Enclosing fence
35 Equipped for a ride, perhaps
36 Kite part
37 Saddler's aid
38 Goes across
39 Role for Young
40 Insults playfully
41 Diminutive battery size
42 Solvers must ___ in the grids to determine the grids' proper order
49 Rat Island natives
50 Expenses for globetrotters
51 Anarchy
52 Drunken jag
54 Islander's need, maybe
55 Not mad
56 Outer parts
57 Real-time
58 Day on old calendars
59 Exterior area
60 Ruptured couple

DOWN

1 Suitable's opposite
2 "Princess" in its Hebrew translation
3 Evade while being questioned
4 Label anew
5 Lay up
6 Activist/singer Bonnie
7 Former Texas governor Richards
8 Assaulted, in a way
9 Muralists' needs
10 One that might be humble
11 Ustinov of "Topkapi"
12 Second or sixth in a series
14 Lighted
20 Elevate
22 Accepters of deposits
24 Driving divisions
27 Évian, for one
28 Regulation
29 Astronomical appearance
30 Nonneutral particle
31 "Death of Sardanapalus" painter Eugène
32 Hit that begins a one-two
33 It's what's up
35 Strip since 1961 that's printed in black and white
36 Causing only minor irritation, say
38 Raw beef fat
39 Oliver Twist, e.g.
40 Seat cushions?
41 Spread
42 Iranian tongue
43 Narrative set in the Bronze Age
44 Genre film director Sergio
45 Worth more to collectors, say
46 Output
47 Run along
48 Democratic senator Kefauver
53 Shepherd's pie tidbit

by Patrick Berry

ACROSS

1 Theory related to eugenics
16 What good competitors may give one
17 Part of many confessions
18 Old Testament book before Neh.
19 Some services
20 Composer of "1/1," "1/2," "2/1" and "2/2"
21 Some HDTVs
23 Noodle
24 Guidebook listings for the budget-conscious
32 Gossips
33 Winter cry in New York
34 Riddle
36 Like some cross-dressers
38 Stoker who wrote "Dracula"
39 "Hooked on Classics" company
41 "That's the spot"
42 Pacific, perhaps
49 Here, in Juárez
50 Fictional maker of earthquake pills and elephant bullets
53 Feature of the ideal path
54 Some I.T. experts

DOWN

1 More prudent, say
2 "The People and Its Leaders" muralist
3 Tangy pie fruit
4 Amsterdam-based financial giant
5 Pitch ___
6 It means nothing
7 De Matteo of "The Sopranos"
8 Note passers?
9 Korean War leader
10 Filling yarn
11 "Look at me, ___ helpless . . ." (first words of "Misty")
12 What may come before so much?
13 How Ginger Rogers danced
14 Taken for
15 "Discobolus" sculptor
22 New York's ___ Building, designed by Mies van der Rohe
23 Crazy way to go?
25 Jerry in the Basketball Hall of Fame
26 Polo and others
27 Go out with ___
28 Some Parisian income
29 Walter ___, two-time winner of golf's U.S. Open
30 Echo, e.g.
31 Short
34 Some rodeo bulls
35 Doesn't lay off
36 Actress Ullman
37 Boil down
38 Some idols
40 Heat divisions
42 Part of a Molière work
43 Abram of "This Old House"
44 Oh so
45 Res ___ loquitur
46 "How's it ___?"
47 ___ Minor
48 Like some monuments: Abbr.
51 Wilfred Owen poem "Dulce et Decorum ___"
52 Scotland's longest river

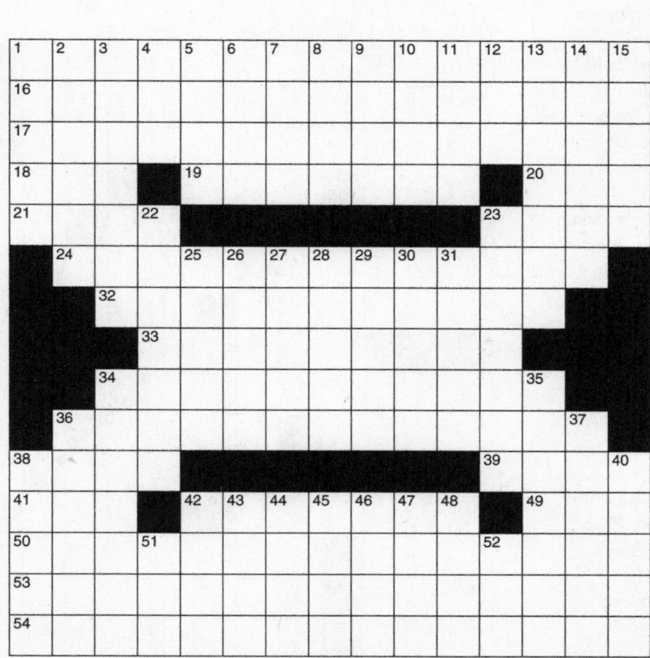

by Tim Croce

156

ACROSS

1 Coffee shop, often
12 "Sid the Science Kid" network
15 Stops being infantile
16 Pianist Stein
17 Producer of shooting stars
18 Ado Annie, e.g.
19 Pentagon-to-Lincoln Memorial dir.
20 Aid in relieving xerostomia
21 Breaks up
23 Bullish declaration
25 What has made some people miss the mark?
28 Pungent dressing
29 Barely visible art collection?
31 Polynesian port, when doubled
33 Game player's concern
34 Stopped being infantile
36 Part of the Buchanan High faculty
38 Certain preserved strips
40 Shape preserver, of a sort
43 Not so stuffy
47 Banks with many spreads
48 Pack of lifesavers?
50 With 1-Down, good thing to have for a tornado
51 Does some piece work
53 "Mottke the Thief" novelist, 1935
55 Music critic's concern
56 Scored very quickly?
58 It holds the line
60 British big shot
61 Love
62 Its title character is Manrico
66 Contact info spec.
67 March locale
68 Clinton was its first gov.
69 Attachable bulletin

DOWN

1 See 50-Across
2 "Ditto"
3 Base in Anne Arundel County: Abbr.
4 Metaphor middle
5 "Wayne's World 2" actor James
6 How orchestra members enter
7 Band
8 Subj. of the Privacy Act of 1974
9 Holder of notes
10 Look like a sleaze
11 Mrs. Mulder on "The X-Files"
12 Gorges
13 It has many tangible points
14 Having more four-letter words
22 Fink
24 Pop trio with the 1964 hit "Bread and Butter," with "the"
26 Aircraft propellers without moving parts
27 Damsel distresser
30 Cake makeup for a feeder
32 Southern side
35 Old man of Orléans
37 Ado Annie, e.g.
39 Damage-assessing grp.
40 King with revolting subjects
41 Like citric acid and lactic acid
42 Points
44 Resolve
45 Land above the Rio Bravo
46 Cousin of kvass
49 Splits for cooking, as fish
52 Mushroom supporter
54 Shack
57 Wang Lung's wife, in literature
59 Playground provocation
63 Italian TV channel
64 Some kind of nerve?
65 Rattle holder

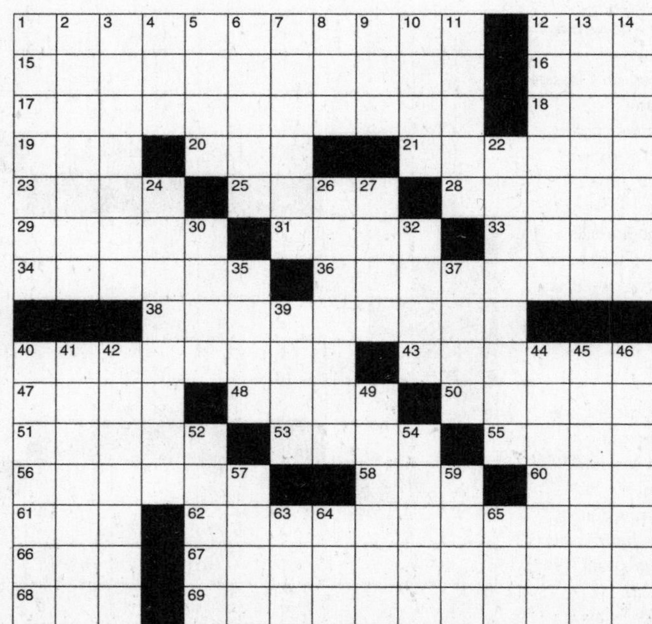

by Barry C. Silk

ACROSS

1 Leave the pad, say
9 Rustle up some food
15 ___ Brewster, beleaguered nephew in "Arsenic and Old Lace"
16 Grammy-winning 1996 Beck album
17 How some legal conversations are held
18 Newly christen
19 Touch up
20 African migrators
22 "The Amazing Race" network
23 Born earlier
24 Neeson of "Taken"
25 Decision
26 Some distillery products
27 Lunchtime queueing spot
28 Metaphorical crowd
29 Dodges, as an obligation
32 Gets bent out of shape
35 Shirt or skirt
36 R&B "drinking song" covered by Ray Charles
38 Shoots in the foot, say
39 Yarn unit
40 Buddyroo
44 "You've got a deal!"
45 OS X runners
46 What a cookie cutter cuts
47 Large amount
48 What stars might indicate
49 Foul ball's landing spot, often
50 The DC-10 was one
52 While
54 "Gone With the Wind" actor Howard
55 1994 sci-fi film about an alien artifact
56 Controversial one-act play by Mamet
57 Visited a vacation house, maybe

DOWN

1 Bach's "Mass in ___"
2 Unfrequented
3 Establishment with children's quarters?
4 Leading ladies?
5 Proctor's need
6 Sign
7 "___-de-Lance" (debut of Nero Wolfe)
8 Warning on a box
9 Discussion venue
10 High-flown tributes
11 1990s cartoon dog
12 Without sides, you might say
13 Take the risk of
14 Marching order
21 Shooters on the boards?
24 Symbol above the comma on a keyboard
25 Amount scarcely worth arguing over
27 Confounded
28 Ruptured
30 Ninth-largest body known to orbit the sun
31 La Jolla's ___ Institute for Biological Studies
32 Doctor in Hugh Lofting tales
33 Lovestruck
34 Doctrine associated with Betty Friedan
37 Contemptible fool
41 Craft store?
42 Bit of new info
43 Blundered, with "up"
45 Out of the game, in chess
46 One tracked by radar
48 Curb
49 Close with a bang
51 2001 album featuring "Love Don't Cost a Thing"
53 ___ Redman, hero of Stephen King's "The Stand"

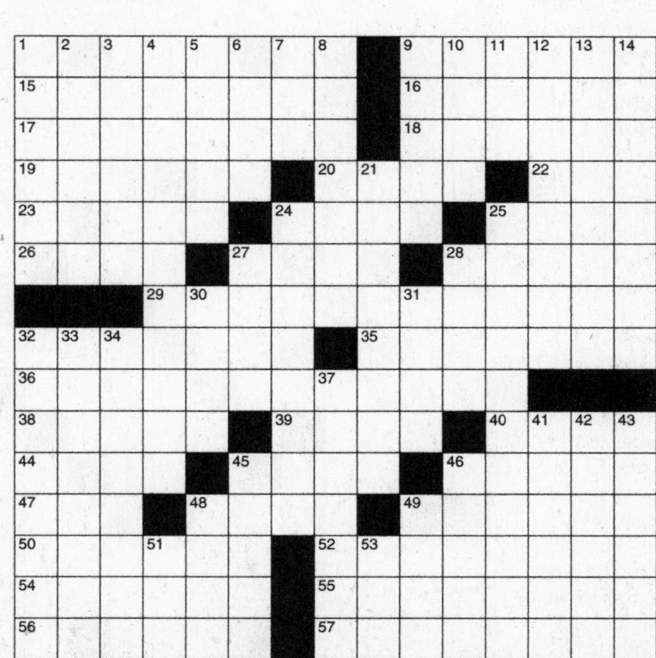

by Patrick Berry

158

ACROSS

1 First name in eroticism
6 Confab
9 Queen ___ (Maryland county)
14 Relative of a bobolink
17 Friendly
18 Minor despot
19 It has a crosspiece for a head
20 One in a Biergarten?
21 Title role for Omar Sharif or Benicio Del Toro
23 "Ulysses" star, 1967
26 Like some outlets
28 One is often said to be dead
30 Not notched
31 Plays with masks
32 Gets out in the open
33 Current event around Christmas?
35 With 39-Across, street fair fare
37 19th dynasty's founder
38 Take
39 See 35-Across
40 Composition of some stars
41 Symposium offering: Abbr.
42 Commuter's annoyance
44 Popular tech news site
45 Massachusetts town near the New Hampshire border
47 Like some survey boxes
48 1970s radical grp.
49 Frittata alternative
51 Options for building torpedoes
55 1930 Laurel and Hardy film
58 What a lessee often gets back less of
59 Gives a "Yoo-hoo!" on Facebook
60 Vous, over the Rhine
61 Part of a beehive

DOWN

1 "Take ___" (1994 Madonna hit)
2 Family nickname
3 Creator of much suspense
4 Biased, in a way
5 Kinsman of Jesus
6 Visa offering
7 Man's name that spells another man's name backward
8 Like losers
9 Half of a sci-fi name
10 TV producer's concern
11 1960s–'70s foe
12 Wahoo, for one
13 22-Down, in Dijon
15 It was last inhabited in 2000
16 15-Down went around one
22 Matching pair designation
24 Wee: Var.
25 Apply chrism to
26 Tony's boss on "Who's the Boss?"
27 Armstrong blew it
28 Specialty
29 Obviously not happy
32 KO connection maker
34 KO connection?
36 2004–06 Haitian P.M.
37 Shoulder holder
39 French key
43 Wields
44 Hullabaloo
46 Glassware ovens
48 Was quiescent
50 Bank of China Tower designer
52 The 4th of November?
53 Sister of Nephthys
54 Former high fliers
55 Possible cause of paralysis
56 Liberal leader?
57 Memo opener

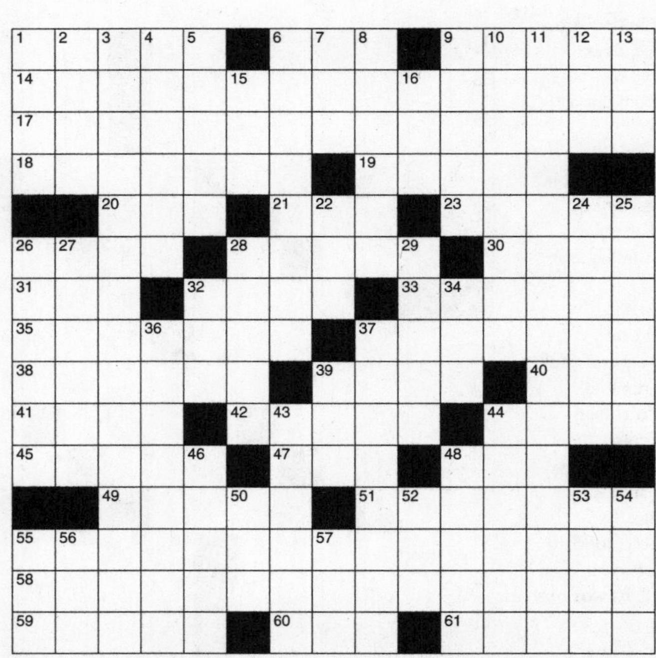

by Kurt Mueller

ACROSS

1 ___ scan
4 Media inits. since 1927
7 Music genre of the Mighty Mighty Bosstones
10 Solid rock center?
13 It's shown on a topographical map
15 Disheveled
17 Family members
18 Parents, e.g.
19 Prefix with -matic
20 Google search object
22 First name in auto racing
23 Cousin ___
24 "Well done!"
25 Actress Merrill
26 Bygone espionage org.
28 Biology div.
30 Cry of repugnance
31 Morales of "Gun Hill Road"
32 Hot spot
33 First name in auto racing
35 Philadelphia landmark
36 Denigrates, in British slang
37 Over
38 Reverse
39 Things gotten with a credit card, often
40 Get beat
41 Atlanta sch. with 30,000+ students
42 Publication that clicks with readers?
43 "Star Trek" extra: Abbr.
44 Carrie Chapman ___, founder of the League of Women Voters
45 Buttocks
46 1974 Gould/ Sutherland spoof
48 W.W. II rationing org.
49 Norse equivalent of Mars
50 Death on the Nile cause?
51 Female charmer of myth
55 Montana neighbor
59 Rockefeller Center is built in it
60 More rich, as soil
61 Meeting
62 Breaks

DOWN

1 Year the first Rose Bowl was played
2 1940 Crosby/Lamour/ Hope comedy
3 Irregularly
4 It might make you jump
5 Rotary Club members
6 Outlawing
7 Medical bigwigs
8 Place for a pad
9 Wanted letters?
10 Carnegie Hall debut of 1928, with "An"
11 Building safety feature
12 Befuddled
14 Familia member
16 Wipes out
21 It's not a dream
27 Recuse oneself from, say
29 Some services
31 Layer of green eggs
34 "Concentration" pronoun
44 Flat ones are not good
47 Wrangles (with)
52 Glamour types, for short
53 Gift on a string
54 Prefix with car
56 ___ cit. (footnote abbr.)
57 Dickensian cry
58 Record label inits.

by Alex Vratsanos

160

ACROSS

1 Musical great whose grave went unmarked for nearly 150 years
7 Bombing, e.g.
15 Pôrto ___, Brazil
16 One whose crush was caped
17 Frank
18 Player of the evil Blofeld in "Never Say Never Again"
19 Make more efficient
21 All-inclusive
22 All targets
23 Troubled
24 Pulitzer-winning sports reporter Berkow
27 Sight-seeing need in Spain?
28 What a weaver may be guilty of, briefly
29 Inner city, e.g.
35 Words of betrayal
36 Cheese ___
37 Eat
39 495
42 It's cut and dried
43 One often seen in drag
44 Dir. from Gramercy Park to Central Park
45 Stage part
48 One side in a 1960s civil war
51 Record producer Talmy
52 People who see what you're saying?
56 Didn't approve
58 Some dishwashers
59 Prescription proviso
60 Herald
61 Quaint introduction
62 Picks up

DOWN

1 Awesome parts of a Museum of Natural History display
2 Cut
3 See 24-Down
4 Georgia's ___ Scott College
5 Tyra Banks, vis-à-vis "America's Next Top Model"
6 Lead-in to some royal names
7 All-Star Dark of the 1950s Giants
8 Masked scavengers
9 Sticker on a plate
10 "Inglourious Basterds" org.
11 Boxing class
12 Relatives of arroyos
13 Part of an ignitron
14 Keep from drying out
20 2005 Emmy winner for "ER"
23 17-Across supporter
24 With 3-Down, Bud product
25 Coll. elective
26 Broadway acronym
28 The "me" in "nothing can stop me now," in a 1962 #1 hit
30 Place for some car fluid
31 Shocker, perhaps
32 Al-___ (one of the names of God in Islam)
33 Grass roots development?
34 Form of "John"
38 Good looker?
40 Form of "John"
41 North Platte feeder
45 Name of father-and-son world leaders
46 Period
47 Palacio resident
48 Junkyard dog, probably
49 They may help people tune out conversations
50 Turkish city or province
52 California wine locale
53 Many a Lockheed Martin employee: Abbr.
54 Pavement pounder
55 ID theft targets
57 Video game letters

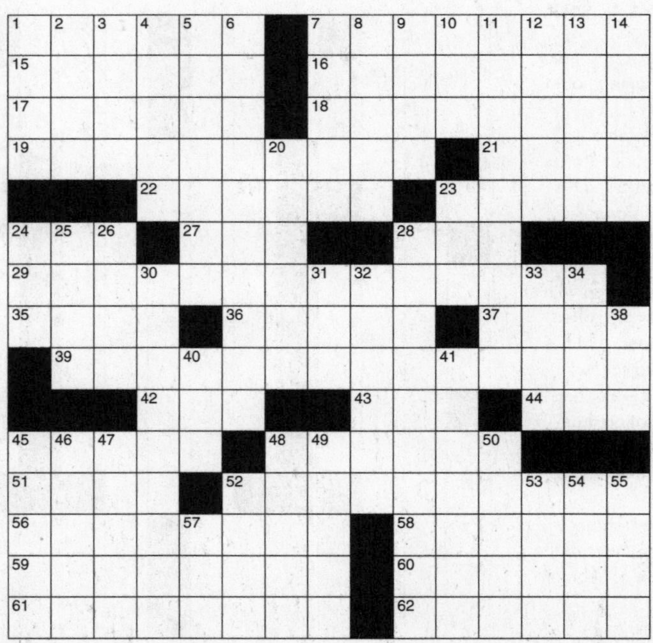

by Barry C. Silk

ACROSS

1 ___ hole
7 Early film star who wore lipstick in the shape of a heart
15 Severe sales restriction, informally
16 Plunge
17 City that's home to Parliament Hill
18 Has a service break?
19 Reqmt. for giving someone the third degree?
20 Some compact light sources
22 Try to fit a square peg in a round hole, e.g.
23 With 8-Down, takes a lot of shots, say
24 Non-union?
25 Suggest for the future
26 ________ B (first step)
27 Sweltered
28 ___ Farm, setting for a George Orwell story
29 Member of a campaign staff
31 National Wear Red Day mo.
32 Came out of a hole, say
33 Continues, as a band
37 Its first two vols. covered 43-Across
38 Top-level commands, collectively
39 Hard to discern
42 Pin in a hole
43 See 37-Across
44 "Dinner's ___"
45 Measures of volume
46 House of prayer
47 Spirited response?
48 Runs up
49 Farm shelter
50 "Uh-huh"
52 Iberian city that lends its name to a variety of wine
54 It's not useful in a long shot situation
55 Food writer Nigella
56 Extremely touching?
57 Noted TV twins

DOWN

1 "You played well"
2 Maryland's historic ___ Creek
3 Litter pickup place?
4 South's declaration, perhaps
5 Mint
6 Like rulers
7 Toronto landmark
8 See 23-Across
9 Solicited
10 Actor Roger
11 Things that pop up annoyingly
12 Crunch
13 Go too far
14 One in an outfit
21 Approved, as a contract
25 Subject of a 1980s surrogacy case
27 Produce
28 Not accidental
30 Coin with a hole in it
31 Goes it alone
33 Worker with street smarts?
34 Fish whose male carries the eggs
35 Starting point?
36 Bundles of bound quarks
38 Something from which something else is taken away
39 As an example
40 "Star Wars" name
41 Brew
42 "Way to be, man!"
45 [Bo-o-o-oring!]
46 Junk vehicles
48 Peculiar: Prefix
51 In addition
53 Bud

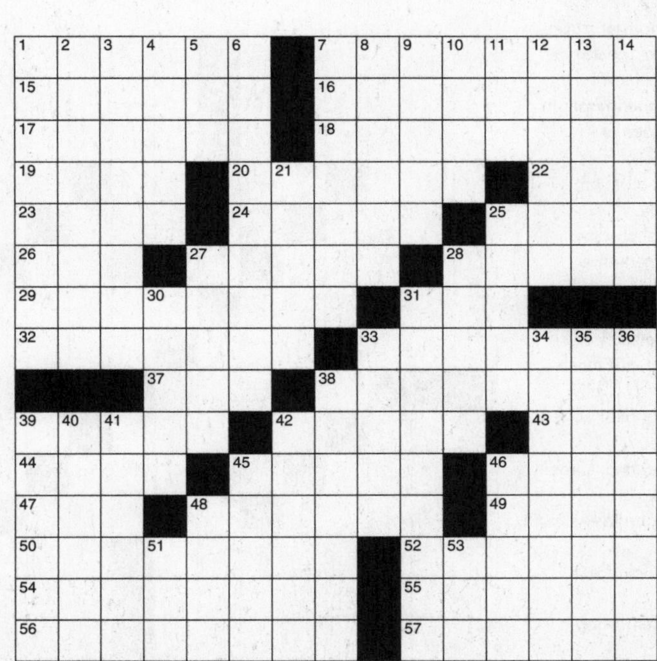

by Mike Nothnagel

162

ACROSS

1 Baseball All-Star's nickname . . . or a popular food product
7 Music that may make you get down
15 Crazy Horse, e.g.
16 Kooky
17 Physically show elation
18 U.S. Civil War starting point
19 Financial report: Abbr.
20 Coming up on the hour
22 Old Chicago Outfit frontman
23 Go for
25 Actor Rogen and others
27 Register indicator
28 Like monster trucks or their spectators
30 Hardly inclined
32 Commuting options
33 Macaque or marmoset
35 Many a benefit tourney
37 Axel alternative
39 Argumentative
43 Cause of a rash reaction?
45 Reel revolution
46 Settings for much stitching, briefly
49 Capital near Lake Titicaca
51 Capital near Green Peter Lake
52 NOW head?: Abbr.
54 Buns may cover them
56 Cheese portion
57 Bolt
59 John's neighbor
61 Oslo Accords grp.
62 Treats served toasted and buttered
64 Triple-platinum 1982 album with the #1 hit "Africa"
66 One drawing many blanks
67 Rodin worked in it
68 Past paranoia producer
69 At that place

DOWN

1 Wear after a serious spill
2 Signature song of Peter Allen
3 Delightful
4 Lt. col.'s inferior
5 Put down
6 Aviary supply
7 Feature of many a Jeep
8 Producer of simple chords
9 Woe while getting clean
10 Floor
11 Like some resistance
12 Vex
13 Fictional woodcutter's daughter
14 Character traits?
21 "Regnava ___ silenzio" (Donizetti aria)
24 Flip response?
26 Bore
29 Dadaist Hausmann
31 They may appear over icons
34 "___ of Her Own" (Clark Gable film)
36 Western scenery
38 One with a notably hard bed
40 Wheel-powering reservoir
41 Put on a pedestal
42 Cover-up unlikely to fool anyone
44 "Got it?"
46 G.M. system with a "Virtual Advisor"
47 Poinciana feature
48 42-Down unit
50 Part of an English wizard's spell?
53 Doctors with spirits
55 Reserve for future use
58 Like 60-Down: Abbr.
60 Zodiaco animal
63 Rondo producer
65 Host

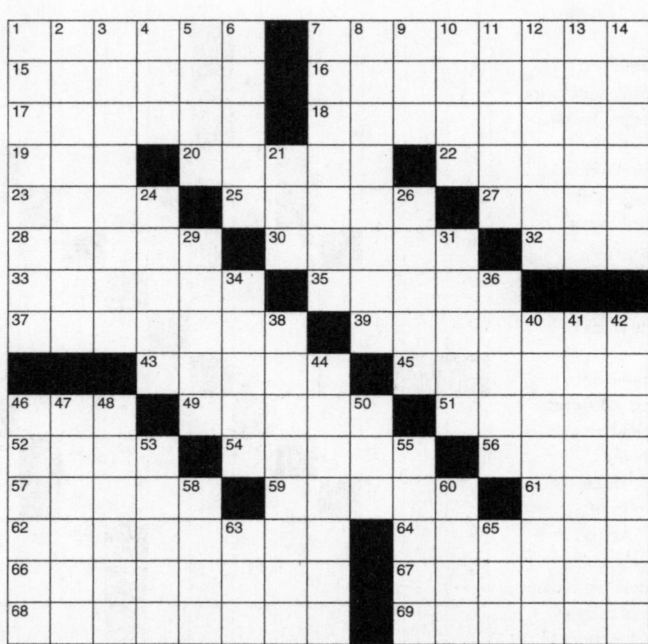

by Brad Wilber

ACROSS

1 One "standing by the ocean's roar," in a 1963 song
11 Fall times: Abbr.
15 Newton alternative
16 "The Battle Hymn of the Republic" lyricist
17 Traveler's check
18 It might cross 1st, 2nd and 3rd
19 What's gained after taking off: Abbr.
20 Most fetching
22 Letters of discharge?
23 Trough's opposite
25 No slowpoke
27 Division indicator
30 Ross Perot's birthplace
32 Ancient resident of Mexico's Cholula
34 Choir practice?
35 Chronological threshold
36 Backwash creator
38 Put away
39 It's often in a sling
41 Was present
44 Fruit-ripening gas
46 Crassus defeated him
48 Like jugs
49 TheraFlu alternative
50 Nürnberg or Neu-Ulm
52 Stock page abbr.
53 Monotonous beating sound
55 Expert on plays
58 Piece of cake?
60 "Don't mention it"
63 División del día
64 Birth of a notion?
65 "Idylls of the King" figure
66 Quartzite and such

DOWN

1 1997–99 N.L. strikeout leader
2 Russia's ___ Airlines
3 Robbed, old-style
4 Scarecrow, to Batman
5 External: Prefix
6 Early car company co-founder
7 Lose one's shirt
8 1960s R&B backup group, with "the"
9 Chafe
10 1983 #1 hit for David Bowie
11 Omega, to a physicist
12 Aid for not losing one's shirt
13 Like some fighters
14 Civic rival
21 Not scattershot
23 Midwest setting: Abbr.
24 Slot car controller
26 With 45-Down, unisex topper
27 Abbr. in many Québec addresses
28 Preparation that makes folks hot?
29 Grandson of Catherine the Great
31 Top of many a timepiece
33 Maze full of dead ends?
37 Sport, for short
40 Jarrett of Nascar
42 Old N.Y.C. elevated operator
43 Bunny collector?
45 See 26-Down
46 Means of splitting stalks?
47 Hard to stir
51 Periods of prayer?
54 Pioneering woman lawyer Bradwell
55 Make unusable
56 Contemporary of Ngaio
57 Some badge flashers
59 "Outstanding, man!"
61 Put-on
62 "The Big C" airer, briefly

by Barry C. Silk

164

ACROSS

1 Calisthenics for show-offs
12 Plaintive cry
15 Saturn, for one
16 Diminutive Spanish name suffix
17 European neolithic monument
18 Lawyer's thing
19 Doctors
20 Least
22 Pablo Neruda's "___ to Common Things"
23 ___ tie
24 Go after
25 Bit of centurion gear
27 G.E. unit: Abbr.
28 Something a father may hear
32 Play at recess
34 Coal holder
36 British form of 33-Down
37 Hint
39 Widows' allowances
40 Many a character on "The Big Bang Theory"
41 Web site with the subheading "Merchant Services"
43 Overthrew, e.g.
45 Samosa ingredients
46 Some fishing gear
50 Import/export business concern
52 Air traveling over snow?
53 Actor Somerhalder of "Lost"
54 Rental for many an apartment dweller
56 Freon initials
57 Like critics
58 "Animal Farm" locale
59 Kitschy stuffed toys

DOWN

1 Red cocktail, for short
2 Played some dulcet tones
3 Square things
4 Isn't settled
5 U. V.I.P.
6 Supermarket lines, for short
7 Loafer, e.g.
8 Five Norwegian kings
9 Exposes
10 Trophy, of sorts
11 Firewood measure
12 Kind of wheel
13 Took something in at night?
14 They may take you in at night
21 Back to back
23 Engage in a bachelor party activity
25 Zen Buddhists, e.g.
26 Hamilton and Hunt
28 Study making sound judgments?
29 Rapid transit?
30 It's just not normal
31 Penned in
33 See 36-Across
35 Frenzied
38 Sign meaning "Let this be our little secret"
42 Footnote word in Latin
44 Shows at an expo
46 P.M. before Sharon
47 Stand and deliver?
48 Menace in the air, maybe
49 Moves along tirelessly?
51 Middle management?
52 Didi of "Grease" and "Grease 2"
55 Word accompanying "Much," "Little" and "Late" in a 1978 #1 hit

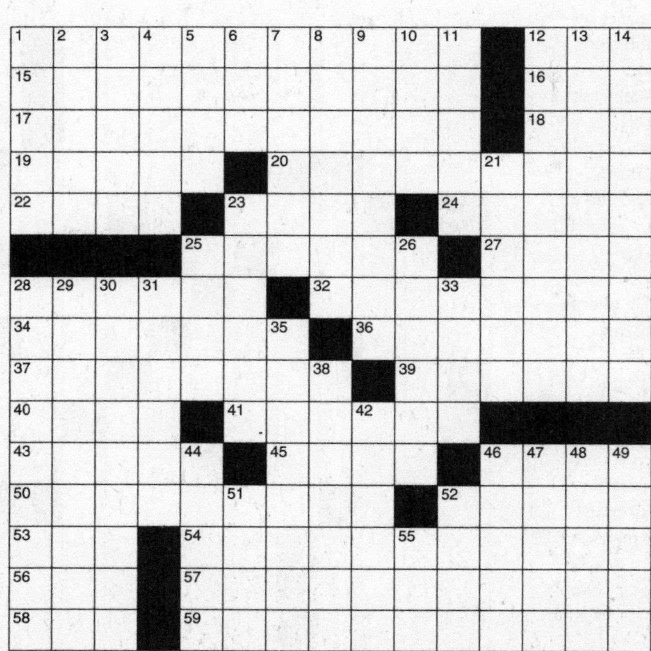

by Mark Diehl

ACROSS

1 Locals make them often
6 Pic
10 ___ pros. (court record abbr.)
13 Actress Roberts
14 Bridge unit
15 Nixon pal Rebozo
16 It's high when it's red
17 Stage part
18 At sea
19 1980s–'90s women's magazine
20 Rockies rangers
21 Períodos de 52 semanas
22 "Moses" novelist
23 Setting for a roaster
24 Massage locale
25 Start a scrap
27 Enjoyed a British tradition
29 Lemon on a baseball field
30 Tops at the dinner table?
31 Heat sources
34 Barbers
35 Legislation station?
37 Done to ___
38 Did as suggested in a Gershwin musical?
39 Relatives of 20-Across
43 Spring times
44 One who might have an original imitation
46 Heavyweights face off in it
47 Crab Key villain of book and film
48 Ciliary body setting
49 Locale shrouded in mystery?
50 Bodily channel
51 Basis
52 Joined
53 Digging for dirt?
54 Succotash bit
55 Place for a small flag
56 Some racecars
57 Police dept. figure
58 Ones being shot at

DOWN

1 Compound used in wartime
2 "A Writer's Life" autobiographer, 2006
3 Like Sartre's "No Exit"
4 Win offset by losses
5 Their scores may be on transcripts
6 Colonial stinger
7 Old Greek coins
8 Gets on the phone, say
9 They're often lying in beds
10 Kind of ward
11 Superseded
12 Doesn't challenge
15 A state symbol of Maryland
23 Neither nails it nor blows it
24 In one's cups
26 Trig symbols
28 Dispossession
31 Very hot
32 Deep-fried mouthful
33 Transparency
36 Not excise
37 Tour guide?
40 Grand tour setting
41 2009 Grammy winner for "Relapse"
42 Miss America host after Bert Parks
45 Salon jobs
48 Aptly named hybrid
49 Something to weave

by Victor Fleming

166

ACROSS

1 Word that keeps the same meaning if "cap-" is added at the front
5 Group whose 1968 album "Time Peace" was #1
15 They burn
16 Could still have gotten
17 Some people with sports M.B.A.'s: Abbr.
18 Subject of 1987 Congressional hearings
19 N.Y.C. neighborhood
20 Pharaoh's head?
21 Bibliophile's suffix
22 Mayo setting: Abbr.
23 Charlemagne, e.g.: Abbr.
24 Back
30 Coach Mike of the 1994 Stanley Cup-winning Rangers
31 ___ Poly, school nickname
32 What-___
35 Platinum-group element
37 Delete from copy
39 Basketball Hall-of-Famer Holman
40 "Come ___?" (Italian greeting)
41 Yelena ___, Soviet dissident and wife of Andrei Sakharov
42 Flooring option
45 Short lines at checkout?
48 Diminutive suffix
49 Costume party costume
50 Tiny, valuable beads
55 Wide-headed fastener
56 "Shhh!"
57 Classic football rival of Notre Dame: Abbr.
58 Hero whose statue appears in front of Chicago's Tribune Tower
59 Not an orig.
60 Expressionless
61 Like some friends

DOWN

1 Oscar-winning actor with the autobiography "Halfway Through the Door"
2 Time past
3 Give the business
4 ___ Blue (old kerosene brand)
5 "Insane!"
6 African capital of 1.5+ million
7 Fess Parker's TV co-star
8 Objurgation
9 "East River" novelist, 1946
10 Place to put a tap
11 Hustles
12 "___ Zoo," 1967 hit
13 Super Bowl XIV competitor, for short
14 Forever ___
25 Share of responsibility
26 Mrs. Gorbachev
27 Number in a pack?
28 No-good
29 "The Sacred Wood" writer
32 Highly seismic area off the Greek coast
33 Tank-to-carburetor conduits
34 Graffiti, e.g.
36 Whole world in one's hands?
38 Basic cable inits.
43 It can follow two hips
44 One may be dominant
45 On drugs
46 Bee's landing place
47 Item of sports equipment worn on the wrist
51 Three of these make an O
52 Free TV spots, for short
53 Start of a children's rhyme
54 Long
55 Gang land

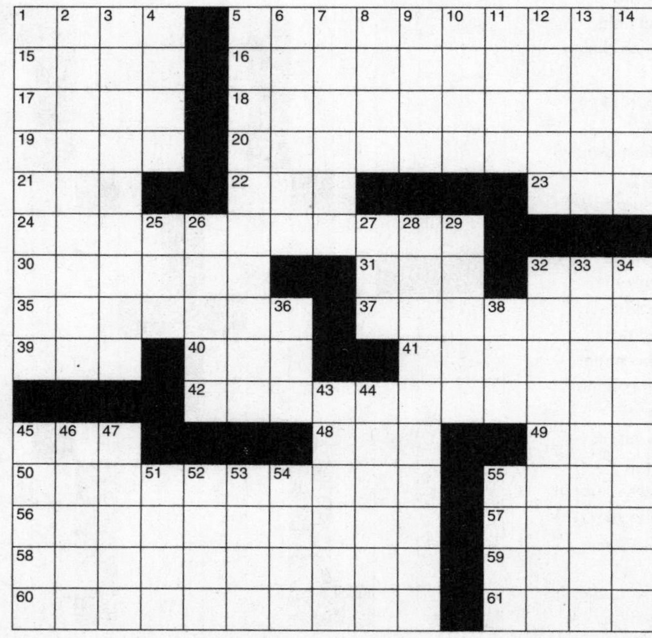

by Joe DiPietro

ACROSS

1 Showed great discomfort
8 Turkey tots?
14 Lamont Library locale
15 Like some expense reimbursements
16 1968 Rock Hudson action film
18 They can make waves
19 It's out of bounds
20 H.M.O. personnel
21 Grow together
22 One way to be in love
24 "Dressing Rich" author Feldon
25 Heartbeat
26 Sights in an intensive care unit
27 "___ of Roses" (1995 adult contemporary album)
28 Green Monster's squad
29 One on board an outboard
30 1940 Tyrone Power adventure film, with "The"
32 Strongly realistic
34 Dweller along the Skunk River
35 1935 Pulitzer-winning biography
36 Take over
37 Many a prof
40 "Aida" chorus subject
41 Where Hausa and Djerma are spoken
42 Adonis' undoing
43 Sitter's charge, maybe
44 Big bank investment?
45 "She's Got You" singer, 1962
46 1937 Ronald Colman adventure film, with "The"
50 Political tactic
51 Thing under a tumbler
52 Transplants
53 Without any gas?

DOWN

1 Egg beaters
2 County south of Milwaukee
3 Peaceful
4 Show case?
5 They have crowns
6 Big time
7 It's been banned in the U.S. since 1972
8 Wise leader?
9 Italian side dish
10 Ulan-___, Russia
11 Book
12 Like a clover leaf
13 Atom ___
15 Crawl spaces?
17 Telephone dialer?
22 Like some perfume
23 "Bug ___" (1999 Destiny's Child hit)
24 Wise up
26 Calorie-rich dessert
27 Ingredient in artificial gems
28 Katharine Lee ___, writer of "America the Beautiful"
29 Garden shelter
30 Revolutionary War groups
31 Neighborhood
32 Vise
33 What things may be held in
36 Conrad who wrote "Ushant," 1952
37 ___ shoes (ballet wear)
38 "Ezio" composer
39 Gray
41 Young hijos
42 Smile upon
44 Darer's cry
45 Powerful person
47 Tampa-to-Ft. Myers dir.
48 Time of much raking: Abbr.
49 One to counter

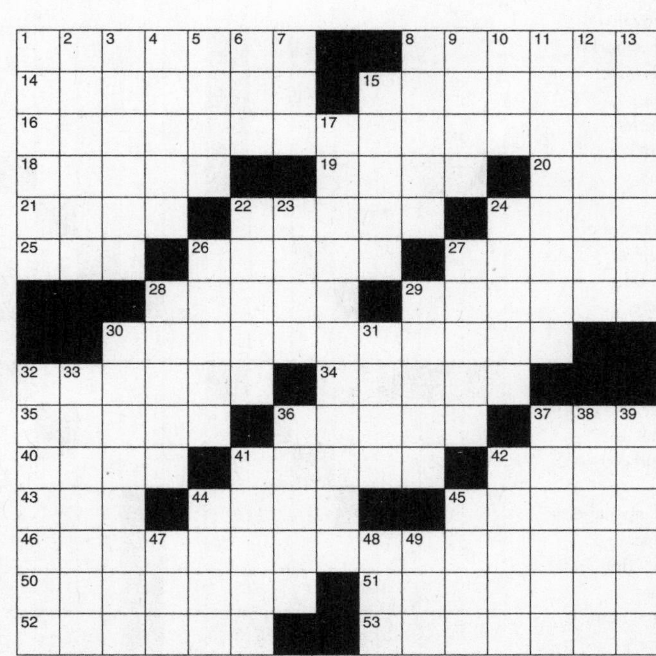

by Gary Steinmehl

168

ACROSS

1 Reaction from one who has a bone to pick?
7 Duel action
15 Confusion
16 Working class's antithesis
17 Game with tricks
18 Literally, "small wheel"
19 Word on a scale
20 Old dirk
21 Tony winner Caldwell
22 High-class affliction?
25 Patent-Motorwagen inventor
26 Historic institution near Slough
27 Buzzes
28 "Check it out!"
29 Poll fig.
30 Nabokov novel
31 Casual remarks?
32 Show in which many pots disappear?
38 Took back, as words
39 Ticked
40 Moose Drool or Trout Slayer
41 Send a Dear John letter
44 Like some eyes
45 Turtle's eye, often
46 See 33-Down
47 Bouncer in a sports stadium?
49 Bond girl player Green
50 District in southern Kazakhstan
51 Ryan of "Star Trek: Voyager"
52 Mediterranean appetizer
54 Novelist Diamant and others
57 It uses 20 different end rhymes for "ore"
58 Aging establishment
59 Float maker
60 Felt

DOWN

1 Something to be struck with
2 Ping-Pong or dancing, for short
3 Harmony spoiler
4 "Quickest way to Harlem," in song
5 Back in
6 Like some chickens
7 Defeated contestant in a face-off
8 Male doll
9 Turns sharply
10 TV segment
11 N.F.L. cornerback ___ Bly
12 Alternatives to Triscuits
13 Show opener
14 Allergy symptom
22 Deux into quatorze
23 Do some impressive work?
24 "Gotcha"
25 Chowderhead
28 Deprive of vitality
30 British leader in the Seven Years' War
31 Features of some bear traps
33 Cost to get out of 46-Across
34 Dinar earner
35 Something intended to move fast
36 "Old China" essayist
37 Like many offs.
41 Red-cards, say
42 Adjective-less language
43 Got on the horn
44 Kite, often
45 Iconic building?
47 Unlike chickens
48 Kids' rhyme starter
50 Setting of Mozart's only clarinet concerto: Abbr.
53 Neighbor of Scorpius
55 Is for you?
56 Folk rock singer Straw

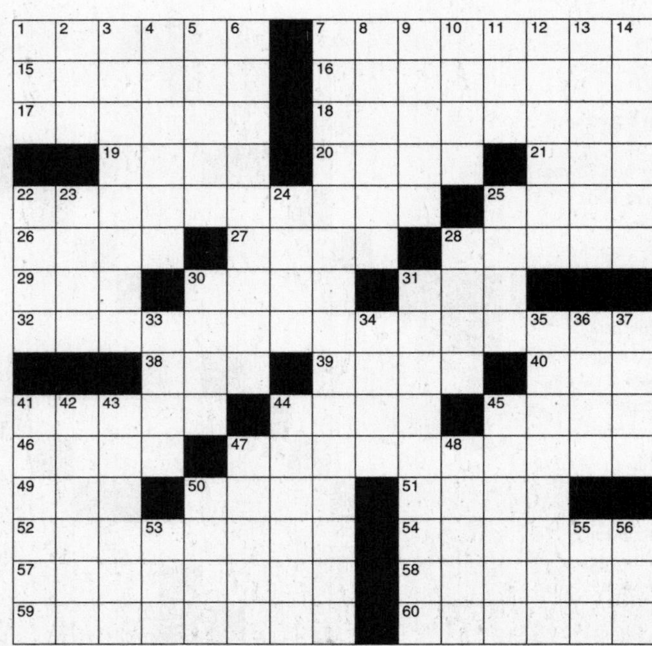

by Xan Vongsathorn

ACROSS

1 German superhighway connecting the Ruhr with Berlin
5 Where the Beatles opened their 1965 North American tour
9 Mountain climber?
13 Sleuth's quest
14 Hang loose
15 Our genus
16 Like some communication
18 Shady group?
19 Going ___
20 Weight or freight
21 Road hog?
23 Computer action of last resort
25 Definitely not a company man?
26 Endangered Arctic presence
27 Cabbageheads
29 How a toddler eats
31 Knit alternative
32 Out
35 Spade, e.g., for short
36 1959 Broadway hit with the song "All I Need Is the Girl"
37 Rolling stone?
38 "The powerful scent of real clean" sloganeer
40 They're set in place settings
42 Edible clam
46 Put right?
47 What snake oil is, supposedly
48 Chucked out
49 Pointed encouragement
50 Largest labor union in the U.S.
51 "___ quote . . ."
52 Game time?
55 Angel Cheryl
56 Elizabethan barmaid
57 What some hearts are made of
58 Or ___
59 Ambassador of old autodom
60 Home of a Big 12 school

DOWN

1 Service centers?
2 Home on the range
3 Shipyard worker fired in 1976
4 Lyricist's offering
5 Young hog
6 Back
7 2010 title role for Denzel Washington
8 13-, 20-, 49- and 57-Across, commonly?
9 Where Persia defeated Sparta in 480 B.C.
10 Bungle
11 Evaluators of current events?
12 Positive
14 Walking the dog and others
17 Found a job for
22 Tentacle
24 They won't wait, in a phrase
25 Tom of "Animal House"
27 They're put on many cars
28 Rocky, really
30 It may help you make big strides
32 W.H.O. concern
33 Reasoned
34 Oxymoronic chances
36 Haitian currency
38 Define clearly
39 Game played with a dotted ball
41 Get it
43 Victorian taxi
44 Soccer cheer
45 Secretive group?
47 Beach souvenir
48 It may be tied up in farmwork
49 Washington, Grant and others: Abbr.
53 Snow ___
54 Ottoman officer

by Matt Ginsberg

170

ACROSS

1 Capital NE of the Gulf of Trieste
10 Housemate in Steinbeck's "Tortilla Flat"
15 With nothing on
16 Outfit
17 Fiery rhetoric
18 "You're nothing but a pack of cards!" speaker
19 Becomes fixed
20 File stuff
22 Sparkle
23 With 3-Down, collectively
24 Fringe group?
26 Easter egg design
30 Spell
32 Stop running
33 Victoria's "Dallas" role
35 Some shirt pocket problems
37 Presbyterian-founded Michigan college
38 Stir
40 Puma rival
41 Mrs. Dalloway in "Mrs. Dalloway"
43 Treasure
45 Get down
46 Kitchen mishap
48 Not flowery
49 Dress down like a sailor?
51 Co. with many keywords
53 Wrong
54 Wind sounds
56 Monarchy since the 1740s
60 Collection of 24 books
62 Russian famously played by an Egyptian
64 Superhighway service site
65 Like many former friends
66 "Days of Our Lives" town
67 It may have you in an awkward position

DOWN

1 Culture development sites
2 De ___ (by law)
3 See 23-Across
4 Smashing sounds
5 Some capts.-to-be
6 Old Isle of Wight settlers
7 Invisible enticements
8 New Mexican?
9 Red flag's purpose
10 Ed supporter
11 "Cafe Terrace at Night" setting
12 Hit the roof
13 Settings
14 "Let me in," facetiously
21 One noted for ingenuity
23 American leader?
25 GPS data: Abbr.
26 "Avatar" craft
27 Home of Whitman College
28 Neither here nor there
29 Can
31 Like some pools
34 Sting in 1980 headlines
36 Brie alternative
39 It has color-coded sections
42 Its highest mtn. is Meron
44 Card letters
47 Birthplace of Günter Grass
50 Floor
52 Tony-winning Tessie
55 Joan followed him at Woodstock
56 Like olives
57 ___ Hari
58 Dating service data
59 Signs an agreement?
61 Stop from running
63 Letterhead abbr.

by Doug Peterson

ACROSS

1 Dealers' dreads
6 Clothes hangers?
15 Plant whose roots are used as detergent
16 Something you can bank on
17 Tart flavor
18 Totally assured, as victory
19 Two-time U.S. Women's Open winner
21 ___ date
22 Like swift streams
23 People who have been 45-Downed
26 Air-gulping swimmer
27 Went wild
28 What flounder flounder in
29 Grp. knocked in "Sicko"
30 Needle point?: Abbr.
31 Alternative title of "Mack the Knife"
33 & 36 "Babes in Arms" tune that's apt for this puzzle
37 Sodium ___ (cleansers)
38 Like some people resisting arrest
39 It might accompany a bar line
40 N.Y.C.'s Washington ___
41 "___ date"
42 Stuck, in a way
47 Kitties
48 99 times out of 100
49 Spot for a tot
54 Stethoscope inventor Laënnec and others
55 Early 19th-century engineering marvel
56 Bill Bradley, once
57 Where cells are of little use
58 Friends and such

DOWN

1 Inventor of logarithms
2 Dualistic Egyptian deity
3 "All right, dude!"
4 Superb
5 What a motto encapsulates
6 Dupes in some mailboxes
7 Part of AIM
8 Part of many an AIM chat
9 P.G.A. Tour Rookie of the Year two years before Woods
10 Femme canonisée: Abbr.
11 Fancy shooters
12 One who surrenders
13 MSG component
14 Apart
20 Tennis's Goolagong
23 Being reserved
24 They may be incubating
25 Accents
32 Like Bach's second violin concerto
33 Author of "Chasing the Dream: My Lifelong Journey to the World Series"
34 Aeschylus trilogy
35 Dogged
37 Appeared on screen, in a way
43 Rich of old films
44 Like some tattooed characters
45 Give a seat to
46 Anchors' places
50 Dupes in some mailboxes
51 Chance
52 Dweller near Central Park's Strawberry Fields
53 Kind of flour

by Elizabeth C. Gorski

172

ACROSS

1 Abbr. for change
4 One who's just arrived in Mexico?
8 "I got ___"
14 Possible result of high temperature
16 Setting of muchas islas
17 What Tito shows, in opera
18 Recipient's reply
19 Daughter of Alexander VI
21 These, on Ibiza
22 What an aspiring model may read
23 One with star power?: Abbr.
24 Comic with the 1955 album "At Sunset"
25 Open
26 ___-robe (Calais closet)
27 Didn't just ask
28 Ancient amulet inscription
30 19th-century, say
31 Doctored account
32 Bread source
33 Nigerian language
36 "Emma" studio
38 Kodak film used in surveillance
39 Under control
42 Quinceañera treat
43 "___ goes!"
44 Country whose name is occasionally used as an exclamation?
45 Time, to Freud
46 Eddy site
47 What a Yankee is unlikely to have
50 Bit of beachwear
51 Projection creator
53 Sitcom witch
54 Element between polonium and radon on the periodic table
55 They go in and out
56 Wreck-checking org.
57 Matt Dillon title role of 1982

DOWN

1 Flu-fighting org.
2 Blabs, blabs, blabs
3 Did some digging around
4 Backwoods sibs
5 Stern article
6 Thrilling hoops shot
7 One may attach something
8 "This should ___!"
9 A third of veinticuatro
10 Riot control agent
11 One in the closet
12 One way to respond
13 Register message
15 [Brrr!]
20 "The die is cast," to Caesar
21 Boston Garden nickname
25 Midway point?
26 Tittle-tattle
29 Love letters?
31 Hamper part
33 Affirmation of seriousness
34 Military band piece
35 Draft team
36 Tiger Balm ingredient
37 Best bud
38 Security problem
39 Scraps
40 Aggregate
41 Foot-washing ceremony
45 Some Greek sisters
46 1983 Joel Schumacher film
48 Storied slacker
49 Analog oscilloscope parts: Abbr.
52 Playmate for Spot

by Paula Gamache

ACROSS

1 Progress too slowly
4 Joe Btfsplk's creator
8 Effective salesman
14 Tavern
16 Micro wave?
17 Popular name for tolnaftate
18 Things holding up the works?
19 Image that stays with you
20 Traffic reporter, you might say
22 TV show whose opening music is the Who's "Who Are You"
23 Where Alfred Krupp was born
24 Frequent flier
25 What an only child lacks
26 Lump in one's throat?
28 "The Cryptogram" playwright, 1995
29 Noisy vehicles
32 Meeting in which one person is anxious to leave
33 Staples of old police work
34 PayPal transactions, e.g.
35 Lock
36 Welsh word in a Pennsylvania college name
37 Held back
38 "I Just Can't Wait to Be King" singer
43 Subj. of Stansfield Turner's "Burn Before Reading"
44 Attain success
45 A term may end with one
46 Full-blown
48 Declutter
50 Malicious sort
51 Aids in breaking shells
52 Arthur who wrote "The Symbolist Movement in Literature"
53 Part of the American Greetings logo
54 1950 film noir

DOWN

1 Milky drink
2 Cover
3 Bathroom door sign
4 Natural skin moisturizer
5 Caddy, e.g.
6 Clairvoyance and such
7 Means of getting the lead out
8 Ecclesiastical council's formulation
9 Embroidery expert
10 Black ___
11 Lab stock
12 Analyst who leaked the Pentagon Papers
13 Puts up a fight
15 Word on Harry Powell's left fingers in "The Night of the Hunter"
21 Common glow-in-the-dark item
24 Liquid dispensers in laboratories
25 "Vexations" composer
27 Mouse lookalike
28 Canadian singer with a 1995 album that went 16x platinum
29 Language that reads the same backward and forward
30 ___ Man, commercial symbol since the 1950s
31 Dumbarton ___ Conference (1944 meeting that laid the groundwork for the U.N.)
32 Three-time N.B.A. Coach of the Year
33 Monitor toppers
37 High-strung items?
39 Slush Puppie alternative
40 Like horses
41 Comic strip bully
42 Series opener
44 Leave destitute
45 Unimpressive attire
47 1969 bed-in participant
49 Roman I

by Patrick Berry

174

ACROSS

1 Aid in deep diving
12 One might use Peter Pan, in brief
15 "Casino" Golden Globe winner
16 Sch. with a 60-foot "Praying Hands" sculpture
17 Proverbially newsworthy item
18 Designer of Alabama's Civil Rights Memorial
19 It displays an array of spikes: Abbr.
20 Trunk attachment
21 Basic drive
23 Take on
25 Marine muncher on mangrove leaves
26 Explosion producer
27 Smashes
28 Heroine of Inge's "Picnic"
31 1986 Indy 500 winner
32 Poule's counterpart
33 Sparkle
34 Opposite of frumpish
35 Actor awarded a Distinguished Flying Cross in W.W. II
36 On-target
37 Deltoid ligament attachment point
38 French frost
39 Old Rory Calhoun TV western
41 Disney character prone to spoonerisms
42 Period about a decade before the 34-Down
43 Person in a pool
46 "Saving Fish From Drowning" novelist
47 Fist pumper's cry
48 Spider, Snoopy or Intrepid: Abbr.
50 Football Hall-of-Famer Huff
51 Artwork depicted in Dalí's "The Hallucinogenic Toreador"
54 "Last Train to London" grp.
55 Financial option upon leaving a job
56 Father's alma mater: Abbr.
57 Tag with a message, often

DOWN

1 Woman in all four "Twilight" novels
2 R&B's ___ Khan
3 Pays dearly for one's crimes
4 Astronomical discovery
5 Stain
6 Good way to arrive
7 1972 Bill Withers hit
8 Wreck checker: Abbr.
9 U.S.N. and U.S.A.F. div.
10 Ship with devastating cargo
11 Queenly
12 Like some platforms
13 Engagement party?
14 Queenly
22 "Ridiculous!"
24 Plus or minus, say
25 Israel Philharmonic maestro
27 Après-midi follows it
28 Places to display cuts
29 First mate?
30 Intergenerational MTV reality show
31 Home to Mohammed V University
34 When William Safire worked at the White House
35 One may be Protestant
37 Shalom Meir Tower locale
38 Entered rehab, e.g.
40 Three-day holiday
41 Not just dangerous
43 Inebriate
44 Rival of Yastrzemski for 1960s A.L. batting titles
45 Filled anew, as a flat
47 Chess master Averbakh
49 Hog's desire
52 Book editor Talese
53 CO, e.g.: Abbr.

by Brad Wilber

ACROSS

1 Not an ideal answer to "Do these jeans make me look fat?"
4 Chief
8 Something to unscrew on an auto
14 Feu fighter
15 Uncommon, in ancient Rome
16 Land of Papá Noel
17 N N N
18 Carols, often
20 Mr. Hilarious
22 Chair: Abbr.
23 Nonverbal congratulations
24 Scrooge player of film
29 It has 3,750 "steps of penitence"
30 Intimate
33 Down
34 Bird, e.g., once
37 Comment upon receiving a large bill
38 Polar opposites?
42 "___ doing . . ."
43 Cold capital
44 Pique condition?
46 Saw
48 Entered cautiously
51 Time before the present day?
54 Palindromic girl's name
57 With 67-Across, sacred symbol to Zeus
58 TV's Anderson
59 Song of 1859 . . . or what the five circled letters represent?
64 It's taken to calm down
66 It takes place on board a ship at sea in "The Tempest"
67 See 57-Across
68 Be a certain way?
69 Bit of candy
70 Start of something
71 Brief subject

DOWN

1 Game ___
2 Its capital is Nouakchott
3 Score keeper?
4 Inverse trig function
5 Exclamation heard 12 times in Lady Gaga's "Bad Romance"
6 Word on a vin bottle
7 Head of cattle?
8 The Iron Horse of baseball
9 Silvery-gray
10 19-Down employee
11 Rough it, say
12 Lady whom Don Giovanni tries to seduce
13 Over
19 Employer of 10-Downs: Abbr.
21 "___ don't know"
24 Fr. title
25 Per
26 Misinform, maybe
27 #10 on a table
28 Seamstress's aid
31 Chance
32 "Dirty Rotten Scoundrels" setting
35 Lily, in Lille
36 Flat sign
39 Car-racing org.
40 Van follower
41 Tramp
45 Chemical suffix
47 Blue
49 Like many winter roads
50 Peruvian pronoun
52 Ziering of "90210"
53 Burlesque bits
54 Bob Cratchit to Scrooge, e.g.: Abbr.
55 Part of a boast
56 Smart ___
60 Three-in-one M.D.
61 Class-conscious grp.?
62 Princeton Review subj.
63 Part of a snicker
65 Fresh

by Jay Kaskel and Daniel Kantor

176

ACROSS

1 "The Twentieth Century" producer
8 Point
15 Knock noise
16 Spring
17 How some pranks are done
18 1970s "first mother"
19 Santa ___
21 Security Council veto
22 Makeup of some burgers
23 Stunning
28 Put away
30 Get stuck
33 Off-white shade
34 Sight from the top of the Leaning Tower
35 Out-and-out
36 Santa ___
39 Isn't straight
40 Certain party, in headlines
41 Members of an ancient empire
42 Golf scorecard abbr.
43 Part of the planning for many a surprise birthday party
44 Happy cohort?
45 Company with an I.P.O. in both 1992 and 2009
46 Point
48 Santa ___
56 Stir up
57 Schmaltz
58 Builds a foundation, say
59 Bridge topic
60 Lab procedure
61 Some game show questions

DOWN

1 Big snapper, informally
2 Actor who played the villain in 2009's "Star Trek"
3 Doctor's directive
4 Zip
5 Endnote abbr.
6 Big blender maker
7 Old office worker
8 Place for a ham
9 E.P.A. measurement
10 Tap
11 Fine furniture feature
12 Water carrier
13 Slightly
14 Wiseman who directed "Live Free or Die Hard"
20 Wife of Perseus
23 How distant stars shine
24 Go around
25 Thinks about nothing, with "out"
26 Tennessee's state flower
27 Former U.S. capital: Abbr.
29 Heavy load
30 Oomph
31 "I Love Lucy" executive producer
32 Embarrassing
34 City north of Des Moines
35 Stamp sheet
37 Fawns over
38 Corrosion-resistant plating
43 Circumvolve
44 "Perfection under fire" product
45 Imply
47 Certain chamber piece
48 Uninformative attribution: Abbr.
49 Granada girl
50 Doctor's directive
51 Turner and others
52 Chins or jaws
53 Opponent of the Patriot Act, for short
54 Give a hand?
55 They have all the answers
56 Foot up

by Stanley Newman

ACROSS

1 One likely to die on the road?
7 What something may go down to
14 Foster girl
15 Poster girl
16 Debunked?
17 Response to great news
18 Big tin exporter: Abbr.
19 Beat badly
21 Battle joiner's choice
22 Kind of replication
23 Sticks up for, maybe?
25 Serbian city where Constantine the Great was born
26 Org. with towers
27 Luzón, e.g.
28 Thingamajig
31 Film in which Eddie Murphy voices the dragon Mushu
33 Lit
35 Be revolting
40 Homes within nations
41 San Francisco's Museo ___ Americano
42 Red giants in the night sky
45 Procure
47 Big hit
48 Cross character
49 Not dormant
51 As
52 Ice legend's family
54 Head start?
56 It's often hung illegally
57 "The Humbugs of the World" author, 1865
60 Be coerced
62 Relationship in the 2009 film "I Love You, Man"
63 1974 hit with Spanish lyrics
64 "Got it"
65 The Allman Brothers Band, e.g.

DOWN

1 Creator of TV's "Alias"
2 Blimp navigator
3 Boxer who wrote "Reach!"
4 Switch sides?
5 Some county fair contest entries
6 Folks getting into dirt
7 Bait
8 Bucks, e.g.
9 Rock's Brian
10 Freaks (out)
11 Not going anywhere
12 Carrier of drum cases, maybe
13 First in line, say
15 Over and over
20 Like M&M's
24 Sacrifice fly?
27 Cartoonist, at times
29 64-Across, to a cat
30 Debugger?
32 Court proceedings
34 Freak
36 Self, in a Latin phrase
37 Many users follow its directions
38 "Gentille" one of song
39 Problem for one who's trapped
42 Visit
43 "The Transcendence of the Ego" writer
44 Some muscle cars
46 ___ National Park
50 It may stick to your ribs
53 Language related to Finnish
55 Dummy on a greyhound track
58 Coll. peer leaders
59 Uptown's dir. in N.Y.C.
61 Really try

by Caleb Madison

178

ACROSS

1 Star of India, once
5 Concert spectacles
15 29-year Knesset member
16 "Prêt-à-Porter" actress
17 Material for a suit?
18 Convention fighter
19 Ring bearer
21 "Roots" name
22 It's free in Paris
23 Hazardous obstruction
25 Humidifier output
26 It often gets fed
27 Where the biblical lost tribes were held captive
30 N.Y.P.D. descriptor
32 Cry to get 40-Across
37 What Taft, Hoover and Carter each had
39 Gave a face-lift
40 People with saving accounts?
42 "Rock Me ___" (1984 hit)
43 One worthy of emulation
45 Simon & Schuster's parent
46 Opposite of 4-Down
50 Tunnel creator
51 Leaving lines
53 Order in a rush order
55 Barn dance accessory
57 Onetime Chevy Blazer competitor
59 Mythological trickster who was punished by being held to a rock
60 Steamroller?
61 Peck, e.g.
62 What loaded people have
63 Strings used in payroll depts.

DOWN

1 Take, finally
2 Native
3 Far from frilly
4 Opposite of 46-Across
5 Spot of seclusion
6 Racks up
7 Dingbats
8 Dug in, with "down"
9 What stops swings, briefly
10 Give the heave-ho
11 Area where blood vessels enter an organ
12 Sur citizen
13 Bridge openers
14 Rip into
20 Make stand on end, as hair
24 "That's it!"
28 Course
29 Pad
31 "That sorta thing"
33 Pumpkin
34 People are not 35-Down after these occur
35 See 34-Down
36 Publicists' preparations
38 Hit from the 1983 platinum album "Kilroy Was Here"
41 Sultan who captured Jerusalem in 1187
44 Palais des Nations setting
46 Not worthless
47 Yanks' foes
48 Drawn-out chemical
49 It may cut things close
52 Educational ideal
54 Arizona county or its seat
56 Bouncing baby
58 Kind of chip

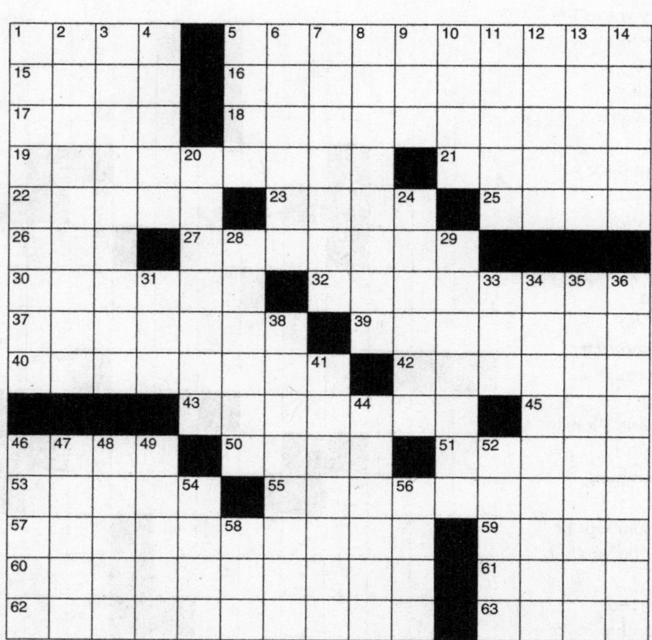

by Mark Diehl

179

ACROSS

1 Rome's ___ Choir
8 Didn't go out
15 Iron-deficient?
16 Subject of 2002 Senate authorization
17 Unstable
18 Going by
19 Glycerides, e.g.
20 Actress Mazar of HBO's "Entourage"
21 Prefix with biology
22 Complaint
23 Fine-tuning
25 Gambler's opening?
26 Person with dreads
27 Bust
31 Privy to the gag
33 Source of the line "Midway upon the road of our life I found myself within a dark wood . . ."
35 Brief online messages
36 Apply with force
37 Saber rattlers
39 Place name in 1960s TV
40 Dom Pedro's ill-fated wife
41 It's probably played first
43 P.M. counterpart
45 Loud horn
47 Stayed out?
48 Palindromic girl
51 Departure info?
52 Match venues
53 Seeks
55 Better, as cuts of meat
56 Bit of change in Cuba
57 Source of heat
58 Bulk up
59 Bristles

DOWN

1 Pressure, metaphorically
2 Overseas fabric spun from flax
3 Prime seating area at sporting events, maybe
4 Censured
5 French department or a river that runs through it
6 Pulls in
7 Ice cream eponym
8 Carriage part?
9 Indus outlet
10 Hard-to-miss shot
11 Command ctrs.
12 Boo-boo
13 ___ cat
14 Consequently
20 Mohawk and others
23 Lid
24 It's known as "the Prairies" in Canada
26 Transcends
28 Robber's target
29 Unbroken
30 Get into
32 Toshiba competitor
34 Zipper hider
35 Owner of Capitol Records and Parlophone
38 Spade mashie
39 Cooler
42 Point
44 Acted rudely, in a way
46 Diet
47 Lay up
48 Indirect lines
49 Puccini's "O Mimi, tu più non torni," e.g.
50 ___ mundi
52 Actor Andrew of 1990s TV
54 Poker legend Ungar
55 Ty Cobb and Willie Mays, positionally: Abbr.

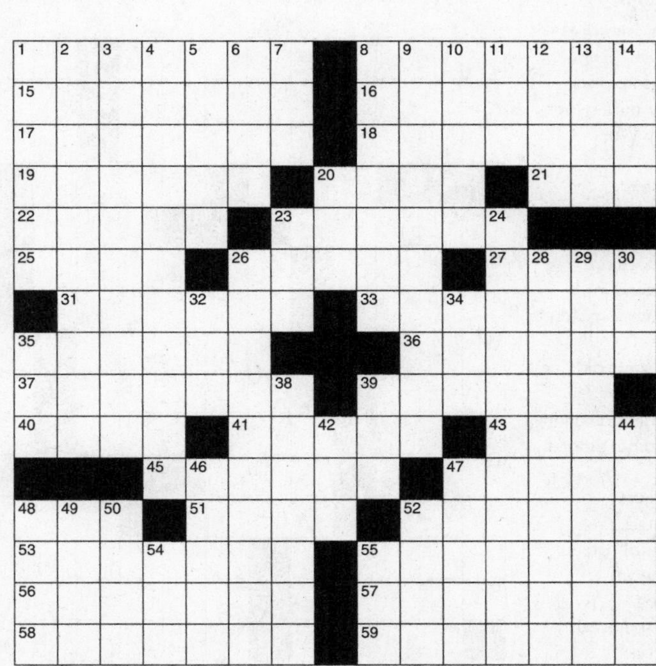

by Joe DiPietro

180

ACROSS

1 Balderdash
10 1981 best seller set in Castle Rock, Me.
14 Midwest city in the middle of the I-70/I-71/I-75 triangle
15 Satisfy
17 "Shoot!"
18 Neuter
19 Operculum
20 Result of some heavy lifting
22 Dashboard Confessional's genre
23 It lost to "Born Free" for Best Song of 1966
26 What a plus sign may indicate
27 Grammy-nominated film composer Brion
28 Minderbinder of "Catch-22"
29 Woodstock artist
32 Red state
33 Israel's foreign minister during the Six-Day War
34 Prime
35 Golfe setting
36 See 52-Across
37 "Hamlet" composer
38 What bugs are often found in
39 Some academicians: Abbr.
40 It's the same old story
41 Transfusion amount
42 Thing to get pinned on
43 Rally figure
44 Internet ___
45 "Rockaria!" grp.
46 Jazz piece?
47 Bothered
48 Site of some '60s tours
49 "Get ___ Up" (John Mellencamp hit)
51 Long way to go?
52 With 36-Across, school gathering equipment
54 Swiftly written?
59 Like spots in which nails are often used
60 1902 Kentucky Derby winner that was named after a fictional character
61 Central Asia's Tien ___ Mountains
62 RadioShack stock

DOWN

1 Second-century year
2 Post-retirement occurrence
3 Suffix with railway
4 A ton
5 Bush or Cheney, once
6 Square-___ (prim)
7 "Of course!"
8 Pound of Turkey?
9 Highest mountain in Australia
10 Virtuosic improvisation
11 Explorer or Navigator, briefly
12 He pitched a no-hitter in 1999
13 Over
16 No longer charged
21 Place for a hanging piece
23 Its first word is "Congress"
24 They're not technical
25 Result of good middle management?
29 ___ buckle (eye surgery procedure)
30 Doesn't get any higher than
31 Tears into
38 Hitch
40 Calvin's baby sitter in "Calvin and Hobbes"
47 Measure associated with Leyden jars
50 Many an opening event
51 All right
53 "Huh?"
55 Shoe add-on
56 Fashion designer Posen
57 Buckskin source
58 "Porte ___ Lilas" (Oscar-nominated 1957 film)

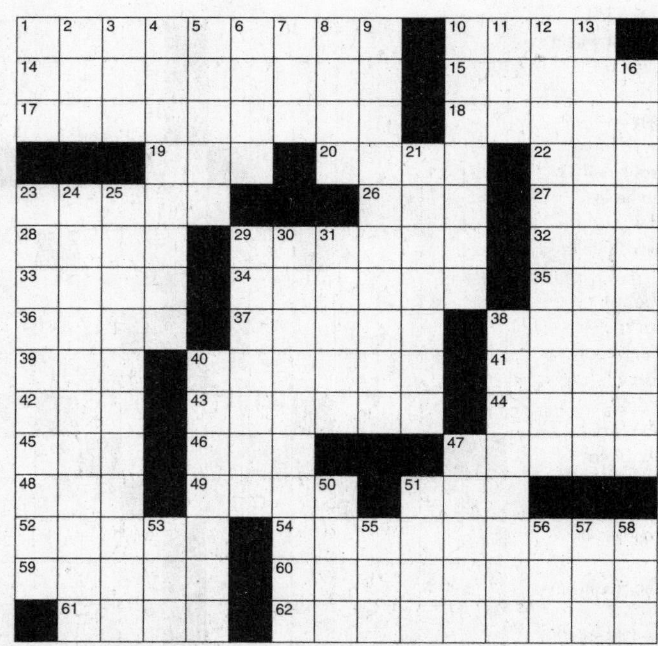

by Will Nediger

ACROSS

1 It's now called "Periodicals"
16 Uppity
17 Dangerous thing?
18 Muchacho
19 Cross letters
20 Pandemonium
21 Blu-ray relative
22 Interject
25 Part of a farm harrow
27 Go out with
28 "The Poverty of Philosophy" author
30 Peaty places
32 Hot
35 Blueprint feature
37 Ward of Hollywood
38 Hotel waiters?
40 Genealogist's study
42 Robotic rock group popular in the 1980s
44 Frosty's relative
46 Cost of living?
48 Kind of bean
49 Std.
50 Auburn competitors
52 Survey check-off
53 Ace
54 "That's nasty!"
57 Time starter
59 R.I.P. part
60 Navigator's aid
65 Broad appeal
66 Union of 1284

DOWN

1 Jerks
2 Spiced up
3 One who knows the value of a dollar
4 Not had by
5 Pocket
6 Cable alternative
7 1969 biopic starring 10-Down
8 Taylor of "The Haunting"
9 Means
10 Star of 7-Down
11 Fez wearer
12 Calendar abbr.
13 Mex. neighbor
14 "This ___ joke!"
15 Big name in construction
22 Quantity: Abbr.
23 Zip
24 Overnight sensation
26 Violinist/ bandleader ___ Light
29 Base line
31 Green energy source
33 Pack rat
34 Bust finds
36 Argue (for)
39 Island along Cuillin Sound
41 Overlooks
43 100 centesimi
45 Musical instrument inventor Adolphe
47 Bird on a Kellogg's cereal box
51 Burn
54 "Good Luck, Miss Wyckoff" novelist
55 Normandy city
56 ___ fu
58 "All Fool's Day" writer
59 Chute opener?
61 ___ el Amarna, Egypt
62 Author Beattie
63 Former Ford
64 Small gull

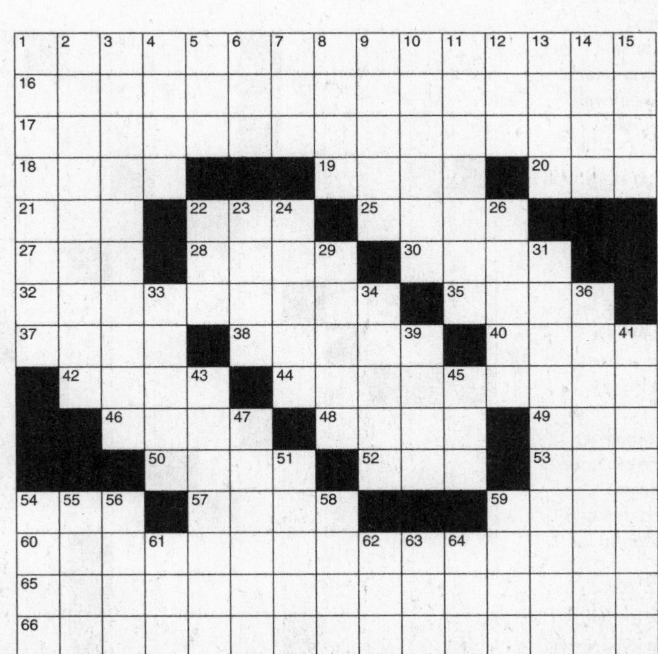

by Martin Ashwood-Smith

182

ACROSS

1 Notes' counterparts
6 They have soles
10 "What are you waiting for?!"
14 It's like -like
15 Growing part of the economy
17 Good thing to end a close race with
18 "Whatever"
19 Deviled
21 Nuprin alternative
22 Plant toxic to sheep and goats
23 Stable stock
24 "Frost at Midnight" poet
27 Like a fig
28 Cabell who was the 1978 N.L. at-bats leader
29 Byzantine weaving output
31 Place to litter
32 Arizona national monument with Pueblo ruins
33 Office of Small Business Utilization agcy.
36 One way to be married
37 Churn
38 Not release, as bad news
41 Item of current technology?
43 Knot
45 LSD and others
46 They have major bifurcations
47 Grilling demand
49 Rifle shot, so to speak
51 Kol ___ (Yom Kippur prayer)
53 No wear for waifs
54 "___ in a sentence"
55 Bribes
56 Discrimination fighter: Abbr.
57 Plastic surgery may change it

DOWN

1 Flat, e.g.: Abbr.
2 Sports-themed restaurant chain
3 Rat out
4 They have retractable heads
5 Passer and blocker's teammate
6 Santos rookie of 1956
7 Eating stuff
8 Food is often tossed in it
9 Bad mark
10 They take years to end
11 Very wise one
12 1954 Patti Page hit, whose title is sung three times before "Please, don't go"
13 Minute
16 Bit of bunny slope gear
20 Out of action
22 Nailed
23 Memorable J.F.K. arrival
25 Smart
26 Priority Inbox offerer
30 Overhead shooter
32 Idle people may scour them
33 "That just might work!"
34 Cruise option
35 They're often tapped
36 Eater seater, sometimes
37 Like a 23-Down
38 Crown covers
39 Port on the Panay Gulf
40 Appear
42 Countdown term
44 Paranormal, say
47 Chevy model
48 Fam. tree member
50 Organ finale?
52 Côte d'Ivoire's rainy season

by Barry C. Silk

ACROSS

1 Aflac ad figure, facetiously
11 Omegas represent them
15 She played Appassionata von Climax in Broadway's "Li'l Abner"
16 Janus-faced
17 Chinchillas and boas, e.g.
18 Words before expert or fool
19 "The Gene Krupa Story" title role player
20 Pamplona pronoun
21 Bygone N.Y.C. punk club
22 Handles
24 Literary inits.
26 Chocolate ___
27 Ace pitcher's reward?
30 Epoch when bats first appeared
32 Starbucks offering
36 Homebuyer's "bargain"
38 Quiche ingrédients
40 "___ Ferienreisen" (Strauss polka)
41 Cool
42 Result of a permanent failure?
45 Basis of growth
46 Jockey wear
47 Ones concerned with custody
49 Put down a can?
50 Telecom techies
52 Profanable
57 "___ on the Line" (Thomas the Tank Engine story)
59 Residencia
62 Bit of a grind
63 Byron poem
64 Outrageous
66 Clarifying words
67 Bad blood
68 Totally not happening
69 Make a spectacle of oneself, say

DOWN

1 Watch things
2 User of a 58-Down
3 When a quick snap may happen
4 Bush and Jackson
5 Writer known as Old Possum, and his family
6 Lib. arts major
7 Suck in
8 They're hung across roads
9 ___ Optics (telescope maker)
10 Laura Bush biographer Ronald
11 Like some poetry
12 Crow
13 Iron's preceder on the periodic table
14 Acted like a baby, in a way
23 Palooka
25 Introductory course?
28 Many an interrogee
29 Radiate
31 Navy equivalents of S.F.C.'s
32 High-fat dish with greens
33 Sit on the bench
34 Assembly places
35 "___ Should Ever Leave You" (Tom Jones song)
37 High-tech transmission
39 Trustworthy
43 Motion approval
44 "That's what I'm talkin' about!"
48 Bag in a trunk
51 Make last, maybe
53 Crayfish claw
54 Wankel engine part
55 Jagged
56 Secretaries' charges: Abbr.
58 Item used by a 2-Down
60 One of Swoosie's co-stars on "Sisters"
61 Shoulder-to-shoulder
65 They often hang around sports bars

by Pete Mitchell

184

ACROSS

1 Papers and such
10 Many people surf on them
15 When trading ceases
16 A point is a division of one
17 Feature of many tires
18 Big name in coverage
19 Firm acceptances?
20 Blast source
22 Delivered piece: Abbr.
23 Develop ruts, say
24 Bit of aid
25 With 43-Down, storied Bronx station house
26 Count
27 Like Russ., once
28 Eames lounge chair feature
30 Gather
32 "Die Fledermaus" maid
33 She's no naïf
38 By surprise
39 What's now in Mexico?
40 "In My Own Words" missionary
42 Suffix with ethyl
43 Basic travel path
47 Apt to snap
48 Stick with it
50 Chicken's lack
51 Cove's cousin
52 13 religious heads
53 Gothenburg's river
54 One wished long life, overseas
56 Sound bite in bytes?
58 With no break
59 It's left during a digression
60 Physics Nobelist Stern and others
61 Used wastefully

DOWN

1 Advance man?
2 Invitation information
3 Kind of ester
4 Ally of New York City
5 Hockey game highlight, for many
6 Is refluent
7 Gold finish?
8 Regular's request
9 Glenn Miller's real first name
10 Declaration of determination
11 Murray of silents
12 Gallery fixture?
13 Singer Blu with the 2001 hit "Hit 'Em Up Style (Oops!)"
14 Taken 38-Across
21 They may develop ruts: Abbr.
24 He was declared dead in absentia in 1982
25 Spot follower, perhaps
27 ___ Mountain (Pennsylvania ski resort)
29 Thirsty tot's request
30 Tattooist's supply
31 Neighbor of Loire and Ain
33 Undoing
34 Like good pointers
35 Court on the court
36 ___-deucey
37 "___ thou and peace may meet": Shelley
41 Get saggy, say
43 See 25-Across
44 Name provider
45 Flight status
46 Sounded the alarm?
49 Compost ingredients
50 Opposite of industry
52 Tupperware stock
53 Guinness measure
55 "Walking on Thin Ice" singer
57 División del mes

by Victor Fleming

ACROSS

1 Run in two places at once
10 Savannah growth
15 Nut's suggestion
16 Home of Creighton University
17 Station finder
18 Iron Age people
19 Mythical mortal who helped raise Dionysus
20 Aye's opposite, poetically
21 Used the name
22 See 49-Down
24 Out of top form
26 1925 Literature Nobelist
27 Cartoon series
29 Middle of summer?
31 Frog-eating bird
32 Tangle
33 Temperature, e.g.
36 Herpetologist's supply
38 Some island dwellers
41 French for "clog"
45 Washington Irving hero, informally
46 Father, e.g.: Abbr.
47 Vigil locale
48 What some veterans recall
50 Japanese brew
53 Burst
54 X'd
56 More than surprise
58 What you may do when you're beat
59 Sunbathing spot
60 Bob Fosse specialty
62 Not rounded
63 Minor restrictions
64 Two-bit
65 Dead duck's cry

DOWN

1 Doesn't blow dough
2 Like much oil
3 One often seen with her child
4 Magazine holder
5 Lord ___ (overseer of Scottish heraldry)
6 Press releases?
7 Literally, "to God"
8 Brands . . . or carrier of brands
9 ___ vez (Mexican "maybe")
10 Take place
11 Forecaster's concerns
12 Dish topped with crushed peanuts and lime
13 Ball of wax
14 Romp
21 Longtime Rolling Stones bassist
23 Trim, in a way
25 Parisian thinkers?
28 Like the Bay of Rainbows
30 Washing machine sound
33 Glasses for a scientist
34 It creeps up
35 Upper-class?
37 Small change
38 Like rice in some cereal treats
39 On-demand flier
40 One of 300 at Thermopylae
42 Stretches between Ryder Cups
43 Plays without a break
44 Nautical danger
47 Thing often heard in short order?
49 With 22-Across, genius's asset
51 It may become a cliché
52 "Animal House" figure
55 President after Auriol
57 Better papers?
60 Hook connection point
61 "Just ___" ("Hold on")

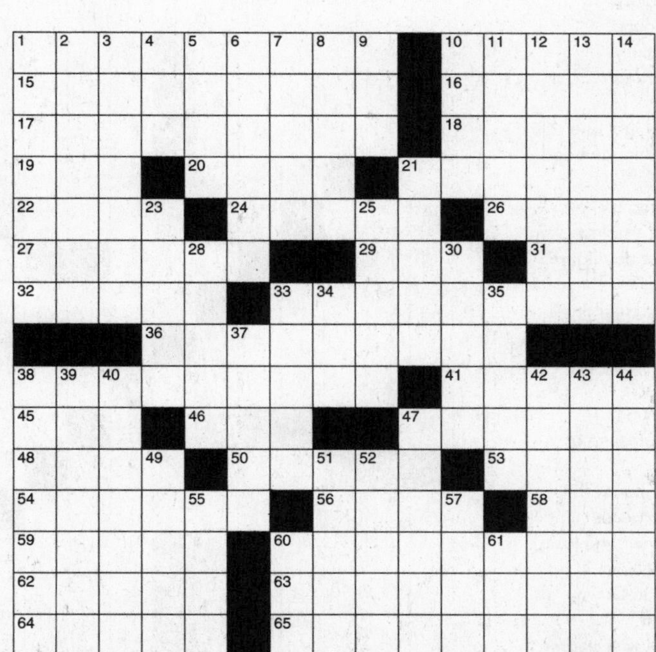

by Kevin G. Der

186

ACROSS

1 Eric ___, Google C.E.O. beginning in 2001
8 Period between Shaban and Shawwal
15 "It doesn't matter . . . anyone's fine"
16 Home of Nascar's longest oval
17 It may be free or attached
18 Title for Columbus, in the Indies
19 Start of some picture books
20 They can make people break up
22 More than un peu
24 Rags
25 Firth class?
27 Soapmaking compound, chemically
28 Make clean . . . or dirty
32 Expect that one will
34 Something handed down
37 Turn into a chestnut
39 Keeps cruising
40 Present day figure in Paris?
42 Cheap cigar, in slang
43 They have maridos: Abbr.
44 Glass part
46 One kneeling at work
47 More than ruffles
50 Sheep genus
51 A runner who loses may still win it
56 With 36-Down, cocked
57 Works with steam?
58 Smallish ballpark, in slang
60 Clues from 7-Down
61 Lazuline
62 Camphor and such
63 Aids in preparing spots?

DOWN

1 Much of New York's Garment District, once
2 Upscale wedding reception amenity
3 Wild West show?
4 TV diner employer of 9-Down
5 English poet/composer Gurney
6 Checkout choice
7 TV host with a star on Canada's Walk of Fame
8 Sends
9 See 4-Down
10 Some big trucks
11 He had righteous blood, per Matthew 23:35
12 Say "You can't do that!" to, say
13 The love of Juan's life?
14 Passage blockers
21 County with the resort town Red River
23 Volume measures
26 Floor
28 Texas city near the Coahuila border
29 Like the equation "x = x + 1"
30 Case the joint
31 Staples of jazz music
33 Big creature in un zoológico
35 Aye's counterpart
36 See 56-Across
38 Freshwater plant also called wild celery
41 Actor Schreiber
45 Emmy-winning reality show host of 2008, '09 and '10
47 Not from around here
48 Inlay option
49 Driven supporter
51 Trough's opposite
52 D-Day invasion river
53 A Webmaster may approve it
54 Aircraft in 1960 headlines
55 Mononymous four-time Grammy winner
59 Volume measures: Abbr.

by Ned White

ACROSS

1 Unbeatable mark
6 Ne plus ultra
10 "Squawk Box" airer
14 Ship out
16 Ring event after exchanging rings
17 Affectionate utterance
18 Sharing
19 Sustenance for a fatigued person?
20 Name in old German duchies
21 Like many Scandinavians
22 Event at which reporters rub elbows?
24 One in an affair
28 Still no more
29 Parisian possessive
30 Like "10," but not "9"
32 Puncher's nickname
33 Life ___
34 Boss's address?
36 Chance to meet
38 "Fusses" is a form of it
39 It's not a very big story
41 Heavenly radio source
42 Like a Scottish young 'un
43 Asteroid belt orbiter
45 Harvester maker
46 Potentially paintable
49 Encrypt?
50 Stagger
51 Sister co. of Applebee's
55 Impoverish
56 E-tail detail
58 Poem referencing "the darker brother"
59 Modicum
60 Volunteer's place: Abbr.
61 It may change your perspective
62 Backing

DOWN

1 Tap-on-the shoulder alternative
2 Paneling material
3 Old Fords
4 Mountain West team
5 Oldies syllable
6 It may include destroyers
7 Nice thing to do peacefully
8 Beast to beware
9 It starts in Mar. in D.C.
10 Its flag is red, white and blue
11 Plain and simple
12 Award won by Henry Fonda
13 Where suckers lure people?
15 Relative of Manx
21 Cold response?
22 Member of an extensive empire of the seventh century B.C.
23 Play matchmaker for
24 Maker of one's own rules
25 Under-the-wire
26 Chemistry
27 Slight
31 Direct
33 Noxious
35 Like a nudnik
37 As one entered the world
40 Keeper of the rings
43 Many a stray
44 Leg-building set
47 Joint part
48 Knot, say
51 Dictator's start
52 Watergate-era White House chief of staff
53 Westin alternative
54 Ringtoss equipment
56 Connection letters
57 Grant grp.

by Ashton Anderson

188

ACROSS

1 Food that makes a crunch
11 Means to ease withdrawals
15 Some Navy personnel
16 Eats
17 Potential offices
18 Cry with a swelled chest
19 Things sometimes seen on shoulders
20 Stay current (with)
22 Took the place of
25 Final
26 Future alums: Abbr.
27 Not just check out
29 Allan who directed "Sands of Iwo Jima"
31 Corn-filled state
34 Mineral in the form of quartz or flint
36 South-central U.S. city named for a woman in English literature
37 Common St. Tropez sight
39 Jade
40 About half of all dates
42 Actress who played Endora on TV's "Bewitched"
44 New varsity team member, maybe: Abbr.
45 Provokes
46 ___ 21, Intl. Day of Peace
47 4×4, e.g.
49 Icing tool
53 Operations are performed in it
56 Barbers shave them
57 Band whose self-titled 1982 album was #1 for nine weeks
58 Dramatic piano effects
61 Dot-___
62 "I'll be finished in a minute"
63 Sack starter
64 Cocktail attire

DOWN

1 They can be made with adobes
2 Shred
3 Provoked
4 Moved to the top, perhaps
5 A boulevard in Memphis is named for him
6 Saw attachment?
7 Company quota
8 Confusedly
9 Things that may be worn by someone sleeping with the fishes
10 Earliest stage
11 Book that begins in Jerusalem
12 "Not so!"
13 Nowadays, with "the"
14 Pulls the switch?
21 Many academics, for short
23 Choice word?
24 Ohio town where "there's a happiness" in an old Glenn Miller song
28 Red wear for Speedy Gonzales
30 Holds off
31 N.T. book
32 Run of TV's "My So-Called Life"
33 Korean-made sedan since 2001
35 Struck
38 Piehole
41 Nickname for a noted L.S.U. grad
43 Issue
46 X
48 Draw a little at a time?
50 Common prom coifs
51 West African currency
52 Zebra kin
54 Door fixture
55 Alcopop brand
59 The Old ___
60 Old atlas letters

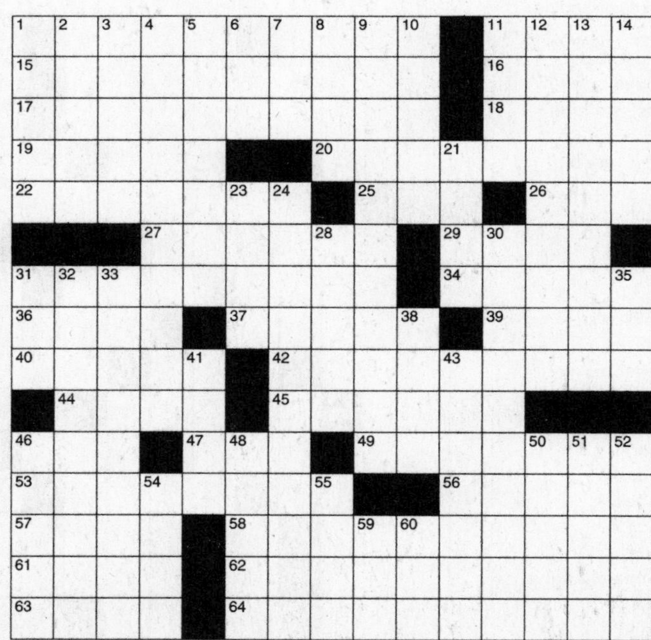

by Mark Diehl

ACROSS

1 Loser to Al Pacino for Best Actor of 1992
11 Simple folks don't put them on
15 Where pitchers are often placed
16 Get in a hold
17 Paparazzi targets
18 Scratch
19 Two out of twenty?
20 Wheels
21 "Let's Cook It Right" author Davis
23 "She ___ Dian's wit": Romeo
25 Cutting back
26 Sunshine State athletes
29 "Antigonae" opera composer
30 Honest ___ (drink brand)
31 Form a clandestine union?
32 Focused (on)
33 Référendum vote
34 They're often broken after being reached
35 Group seen in late-night hours?
36 Wildly positive
37 Onetime communications giant
38 Pesäpallo is their national sport
39 He broke Gehrig's 70-year all-time hits record
40 Like a series finale?
41 TV persona giving prank interviews
42 They're not allowed to travel
43 Service stripe sites
45 Protein-rich seed
46 Second hand
47 Creation on the sixth day
48 Oscar-winning screenwriter Tally and others
52 Title character of 1920s Broadway
53 Navel base?
56 Flooring option
57 Its newspaper is the Nugget
58 24-Down, in Dijon
59 Old Hollywood's method of promoting talent

DOWN

1 Squad leader: Abbr.
2 Something that's related
3 Fashion designer Saab
4 They offer lots of food that people won't eat
5 Cold war inits.
6 Causes to stand
7 Singer Jones
8 Cannon sound
9 First responder, for short
10 Cause of global panic in 1957
11 Pled
12 Like much Renaissance art
13 Renewed, in a way
14 Deal-closing aids
22 Crackers
24 Add up to
25 Onetime meringue-filled treats
26 Work out
27 Some
28 Not be a rebel
29 Taking credit?
32 Actor O'Hare of "Milk"
35 Wing parts
36 Sails events?
38 Top pick, informally
39 Big name in late-night
42 Dances with one person after another?
44 They often have pistol grips
45 Not so 22-Down
47 Remembered one?
49 "The even mead, that ___ brought sweetly forth . . .": "Henry V"
50 Hockey player's "dangle"
51 Rich layer
54 Bushwa
55 Minnesota city with Vermilion Community College

by Adam Cohen

190

ACROSS

1 Urban playground barb
11 ___ Cervin (11-Down, to French speakers)
15 All-purpose putdown
16 Keystone's place
17 Region with the highest concentration of national parks in the U.S.
19 "Don't forget about me"
20 "The best of animals," in a classic children's book
21 Curly rider?
22 Work's antithesis, briefly
23 "Football Night in America" host
27 It develops before your eyes
32 Like 21-Across's behavior
33 What runs ruin
34 Set of sheets
35 They're prepared for breaks
36 The redbud is one of its symbols: Abbr.
37 Try demonstrating that one can
39 Buttinsky
40 Fifth-century capital of the Visigoths
41 It's dangerous to do on the road
42 Bearded ___
43 What some A.L.'ers play for
44 1961 film scripted by Arthur Miller
49 Capping
53 They're the cutest in the world, per a hit song
55 Handful, maybe
56 "Ooh, aren't you special!"
57 Composition of some hedgerows
58 Education supporters

DOWN

1 Geneva-based org.
2 "I know that one!"
3 Father or son
4 Excitable one
5 Nick, say
6 Poplar trees
7 Foster child in '60s TV commercials
8 Some growlers, in Granada
9 Didn't surrender
10 "Out of the Silence" novelist Cox
11 It was first conquered in 1865
12 Its outsides are ornately embossed
13 Org. with a Hall of Champions
14 Fall's end
18 Variety
21 Leopard runner
23 100 points
24 Almost at the hour
25 Result of bill-passing
26 Features of many quiz shows
27 What a copier will often do
28 Seeing right through
29 Some police dept. personnel
30 It may have a single palm
31 Sugar
33 Spread things?
35 High-tech "guts"
38 Interior decorator's concern
39 27-Acrosses, slangily
41 Key phrase
43 Cousin of an avocet
44 Tastee-Freez alternative
45 Fabulous slacker
46 Pigtailed mothers?
47 Not rest easy
48 Visiting the Getty, e.g.
49 "Another Pyramid" musical
50 Honeycomb alternative
51 Quaint, quaintly
52 Some TV spots, briefly
54 Piece of the 'hood

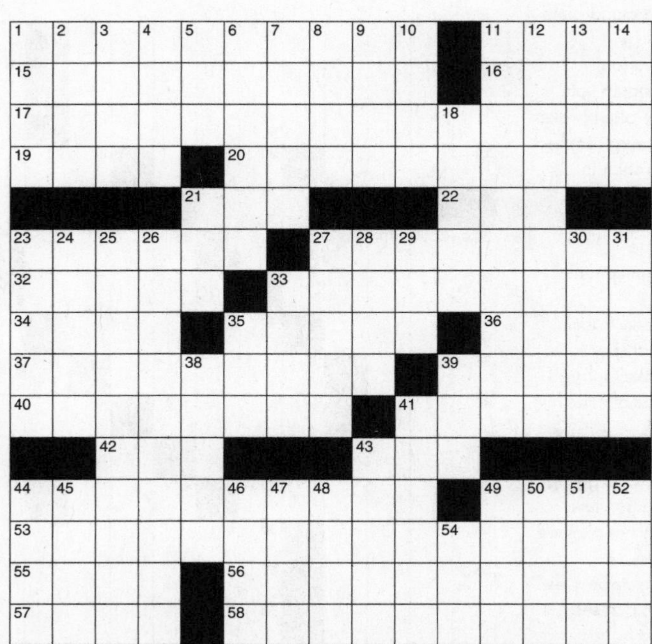

by Joel Fagliano

ACROSS

1 Crossbar supporter
9 2009 "Survivor" setting
14 Attempt
16 Like wearing socks on your hands
17 "Be that as it may . . ."
18 Four-time presidential candidate
19 "Isn't that so?," to Rousseau
20 Roman leader?
21 Sci-fi beeper
22 Old doctor's supply
24 Milquetoast of old comics
28 Stop order?
29 Return a letter, say
32 Venezuela's ___ Margarita
33 2008 greatest hits album that includes the song "Proud Mary"
34 Palindromic name high on the Forbes billionaires list
35 Indicator of second thoughts
36 Statement of resignation
37 Peevish
39 Knife injury
40 Touch screen toucher
41 Certifies
43 They support TV viewers
48 Take temporarily
49 Creator of strange worlds
53 Unseen "Mork & Mindy" character
54 Totals
55 Common praenomen among Roman emperors
56 Bright school member
57 Blank ___
58 Considers beneath one's notice

DOWN

1 African soccer powerhouse popularly known as the Black Stars
2 Gun show?
3 Stop order?
4 Slower than adagio
5 Bird in a Sean O'Casey title
6 Baddie in Perrault's tales
7 It may be found in a dish
8 "Toodles"
9 Expose to flame
10 Disorderly sort?
11 Got a move on
12 Like early life
13 Balloon, e.g.
15 Early radio transmitter
23 1974 Billboard hit with Spanish lyrics
25 Run interference for, e.g.
26 Game animal?
27 Evasive answer
29 Involving both sides
30 1997 animated film set in Russia
31 Quits gambling
33 More than a quarter of native Filipinos, ethnically
38 "The Mambo Kings" co-star
42 Somehow know
44 Mixer maker
45 Handmade things?
46 Word in Kansas' motto
47 Fur source
50 ___ Research Center (NASA lab in Silicon Valley)
51 It comes before one
52 Make less sharp, maybe

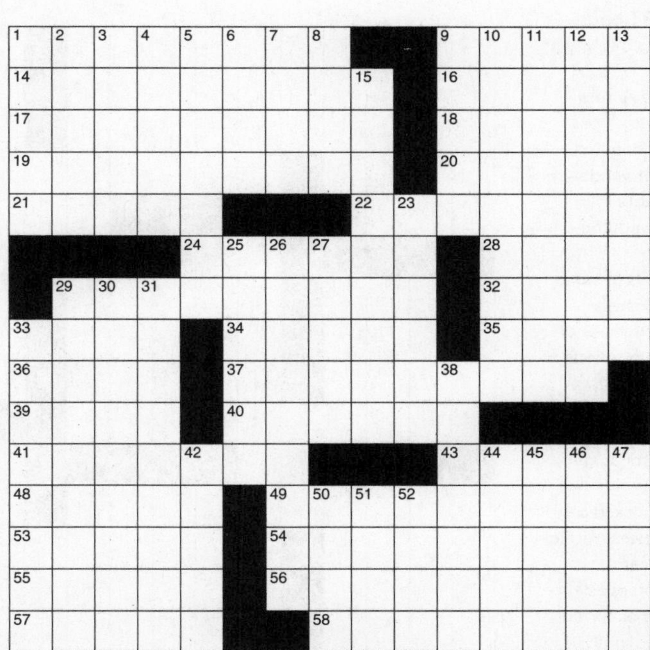

by Patrick Berry

192

ACROSS

1 Like a message in a bottle
11 What makes cats happy?
15 Needed to relax and unwind, say
16 Parisian possessive
17 Get in on the ground floor, perhaps?
18 Palma's place
19 "Wielding ___ Sword" (Piers Anthony novel)
20 Classic novel with biblical parallels
22 Old
23 Some office equipment
24 Flake
31 Language with 44 consonants
35 Kind of tart
36 With 37-Across, express freely, with "to"
37 See 36-Across
38 Not free
39 Unlike one
40 Aisle or window, e.g.: Abbr.
41 Do a wedding, maybe
42 Contents of some farm bushels
43 Eliminate lines of communication?
45 Shut up
46 Sam Adams alternative
50 Wear for some guards
57 Not knocked off
58 Controversial color enhancer
59 Reunion question
61 Source of current information?
62 Allows an adequate period
63 They've split
64 Many a police officer must pass one

DOWN

1 Key starter?
2 City of a Thousand Minarets
3 Tidying tool
4 "Billy the Exterminator" network
5 Drafting org.
6 Paper quantity
7 Some ancient halls
8 They're good stds. to follow
9 Santa drawer
10 Surprises
11 "Death in the Desert" writer, 1930
12 Opposite of much
13 Bus schedule specification
14 Utah's ___ Canyon
21 Grp. caring about airing
24 "Wannabe" hitmakers
25 Kind of code
26 Penetrating
27 Spade work?
28 Hissy-prone missy
29 Present opener?
30 Composition of some wads
31 "Seinfeld" designation
32 One may win a heart
33 Fresh
34 "I should have guessed as much"
44 Led
46 1980 A.L. M.V.P.
47 Takeoff point for many a flight
48 "The Colbys" co-star
49 Driving danger
50 Mass gathering place
51 Oil source
52 Pool or carpool concern
53 Shuffled things
54 Baseball's Minaya
55 "Le ___," Picasso painting of his sleeping mistress
56 Some Eur. ladies
60 First degs.

by Tim Croce

ACROSS

1 Spice mix used in Indian cuisine
7 "Far out!"
14 Pasqueflower, e.g.
16 Shade of green
17 Conditions
18 Proved to be quite a poser?
19 16th-century assembly
21 Winner of a famous 1938 rematch
22 Colonial captives
27 Becomes cracked
32 Brooklyn neighborhood
33 Construct
34 Kansas City university
35 Plot line
37 1988 animated action film set in 2019 Tokyo
38 "The Newlywed Game" contestants
39 Attractive
41 36-Down's locale
42 Site of Napoleon I's coronation
43 "Raging Bull" co-star
44 Detractors' comment concerning 19-Across?
53 Convert to pounds?
54 One who's withdrawn
55 Enormous statues
56 Say "Hallelujah!"
57 Short-___
58 Choice in bottled water

DOWN

1 Canvas holder
2 Lit. collection
3 Drought-stricken
4 In
5 1970s pinup name
6 "___ Ashes"
7 High priest in "Aida"
8 Swears
9 Dummy
10 Champagne bucket
11 0 on the Beaufort scale
12 Vitamin C providers, maybe
13 City near Ben-Gurion Airport
15 Member of the U.N. since 1991 and the E.U. since 2004
20 As far from the heart as possible
22 Roguish sort
23 Montreal suburb
24 Novelist Brookner
25 Jeeves, for one
26 Indulge in character assassination?
27 Washington Irving character
28 Followed a trail, maybe
29 Gut reaction?
30 Adar festival
31 Opportunity for privacy
36 Bench, for example
40 Mourned
42 Calypso, e.g.
43 Entourage
44 Architect ___ Ming Pei
45 Account
46 Liqueur flavor
47 Weapon for 21-Across
48 North American peninsula
49 Screen figure
50 Bankruptcy
51 Retro style
52 Discovered
53 Alternatives to Pepsis

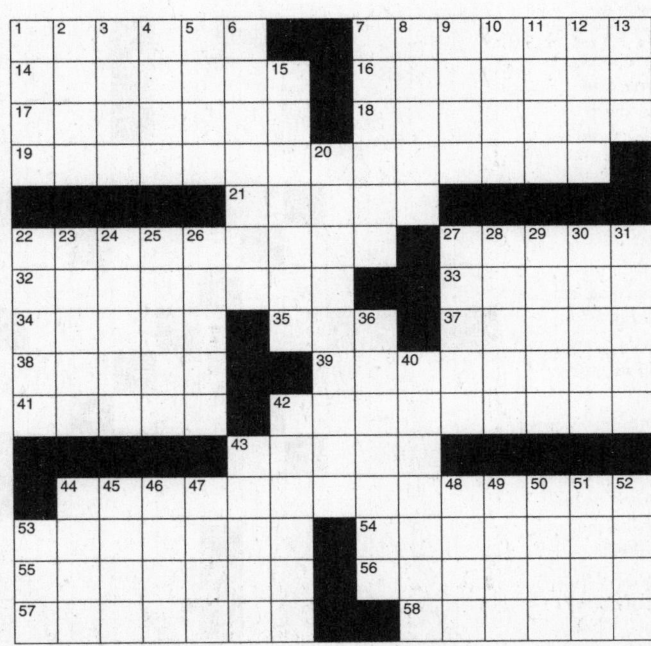

by Henry Hook

194

ACROSS

1 Glamorous, high-profile pair
9 Group worshiping at a teocalli
15 Make airtight, in a way
16 Shut in
17 Light pop
18 Remove some strips from
19 Ham preserver?
20 Red flag for the I.R.S.
22 Some deer
24 Olympus rival
25 Big Red rivals
26 Goofballs
28 Italian possessive adjective
29 Gregor's sister in "The Metamorphosis"
30 Lager brand
32 Band with the 1985 #1 hit " Broken Wings".
34 California river
36 Not too sharp
37 Shoot for the stars
42 Amphibious W.W. II vehicle
47 Decorating do-overs, for short
48 Pal
50 Longtime classical music label
51 Class with many makeup exams? Abbr.
52 Avifauna
54 Routing aid: Abbr.
55 "She's as headstrong as an allegory on the banks of Nile" speaker
58 Documentarian Burns
59 Potpourri collection
60 Ex
62 Many a homeowner
63 Having a flush
64 "The Diary of Anne Frank" Oscar nominee
65 Optician's offer

DOWN

1 "Amen, bro!"
2 Spot for a spot
3 Set for driving
4 Needing no script
5 Ace's setting: Abbr.
6 Like some laws
7 Big dippers
8 Perfectly happy state
9 Maker of the ZDX crossover
10 Man-to-man alternative
11 Is close to failure
12 Fringe holder
13 Certain red ore
14 One-named fictional detective
21 Wishes one can get on a PC?
23 Inveterate brown-bagger
27 Bird-dogs
29 Curt command
31 Country with a tree on its flag: Abbr.
33 Italian possessive adjective
35 Hydra's neighbor
37 Crush
38 He played Laszlo in "Casablanca"
39 All anxious
40 Two, say
41 Opening for firing
43 Melodic bit
44 Exhausting thing to run
45 Intermittently
46 Accept as valid
49 Competitive lumberjack
52 Cub reporter of comics
53 Like some outfields
56 Chrysler Building architect William Van ___
57 Indication of a dud
61 ___-di-dah

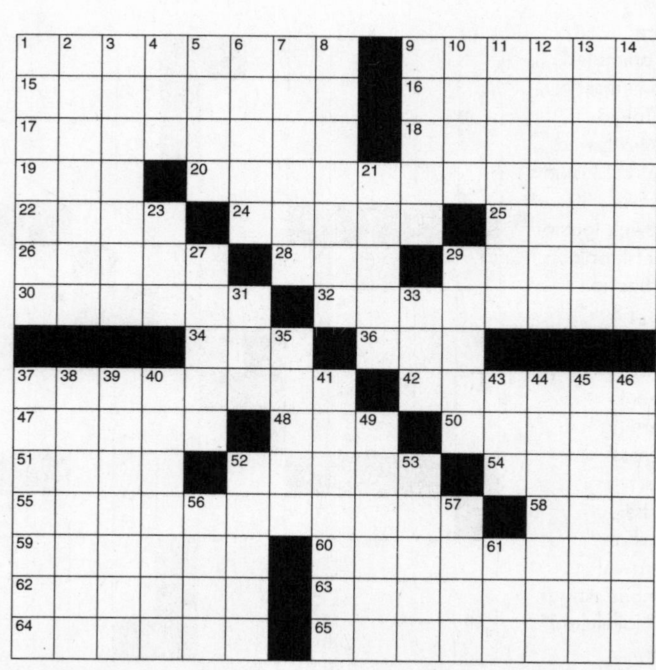

by Bob Peoples

ACROSS

1 Certain contracts
16 Procrastinator's comment
17 Last of Nordhoff and Hall's "Bounty Trilogy"
18 East Germany and such
19 Infant follower?
20 Source of collectible deposits
21 "Please?"
23 What may be put on before spelling?
29 Prefaced
30 One of Frank's four wives
31 Book before Phil.
32 ___ times
33 Turn down
34 Get off the mark?
36 Philanthropist/art collector ___ Broad
37 "Fabien ___ Franchi" (Oscar Wilde poem)
38 ColorQube maker
39 Port terminal?
43 They may hold many pks.
44 Unknown name
45 Latin pronoun
46 Term popularized by Jesse Jackson
55 Much that has to get done
56 City on the Niagara Escarpment
57 Strain to see, in a way

DOWN

1 Uses a 39-Across
2 #3 hit from the 1997 album "Surfacing"
3 He followed Dole in the Senate
4 Pregnant
5 Casanova
6 Have ___ on (track the activities of)
7 "The Facts of Life" actress Jewell
8 It may be stabilized
9 Further
10 Wonder-working biblical figure
11 Buddy
12 Bond girl player in "The Man With the Golden Gun"
13 Smart
14 Point of eating?
15 Regular things: Abbr.
21 They're straddled in pits
22 Contribute
23 Film fish
24 Brown's group
25 Depth finder?
26 "La Cage aux Folles" Tony winner
27 Lhasa ___ (supposed good luck bringers)
28 "___ Factor" (TV talent show)
29 MGM co-founder
34 Clips
35 Go for
40 Make part of the manuscript
41 Lose momentum
42 Rough roof
45 Intervening, in law
46 Music to masseurs' ears
47 Needing to get keyed up?
48 See 52-Down
49 Hand-passing time
50 A dozen mesi
51 "Turnin ___" (2009 Keri Hilson hit)
52 One loved in 48-Down
53 Play to ___
54 Traditionalists' opposite, briefly

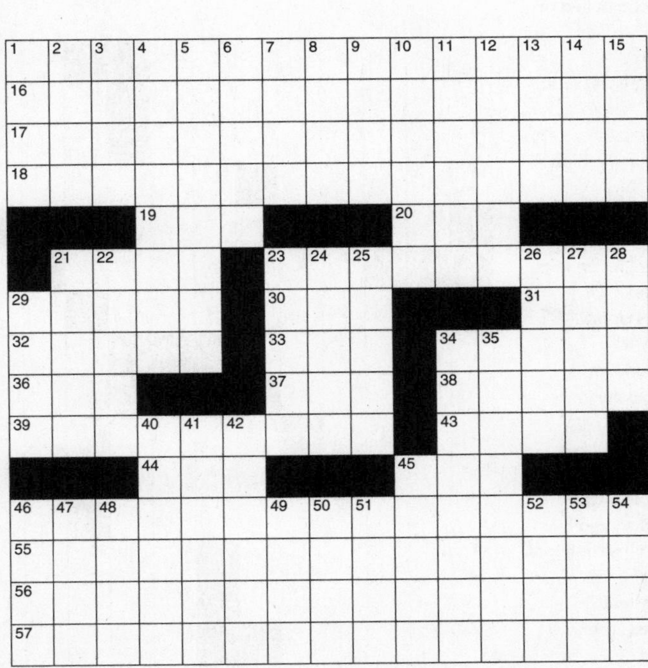

by Joe Krozel

196

ACROSS

1 Drawing room gathering
9 Yankee star who batted left and threw right
14 Went off on
15 Channel between mainland England and the Isle of Wight, with "the"
16 Place to stretch one's legs
17 Leg supports
18 It has two bridges in India
19 Homeostatic
21 Head-tail connection
22 Fathers, in the Bible
23 Jack-a-dandy
24 More often than not
26 Neil Diamond's "September ___"
27 It may be pulled on a field
30 Abided
31 Missing links, so to speak
32 Euphemizes
33 Figure in the high 60s
34 Things rolled over by cars
37 "___ of life, an imp of fame; / Of parents good . . .": "Henry V"
38 Like many an unsuccessful politician
39 It's perfect
40 Secret places
41 Title in Topkapi
44 Capital served by Faleolo International Airport
46 "A transient madness," per Horace
48 Audits, with "on"
49 Term of endearment
51 Getting ready, with "up"
52 Subway line
53 Piece of schoolwork
54 See 40-Down

DOWN

1 They're open on Saturdays
2 Took to the clink
3 Hook up with
4 Poorly explained
5 Specialty oven
6 Upset
7 Real-life opera composer who's a title character in a Rimsky-Korsakov opera
8 Arm of the British military
9 Churns
10 "Valentine's Day" co-star, 2010
11 Buttress
12 Trapped
13 Slope
15 Only one bears the name of a U.S. president
20 E.U. member
22 Place for a dance
25 Images on windows of une cathédrale: Abbr.
26 Area where Dalí, Monet, Picasso and van Gogh all painted
27 Sipped
28 McDonald's offerings
29 Black gemstones
30 Stand at a ceremony
32 Hugo's Thénardier and others: Abbr.
34 Word: Suffix
35 Toppled
36 Senator supporter
38 Rue Morgue murderer
40 Hit TV series featuring 54-Across
42 Goggles
43 Mushroom grower, for short?
45 Land shared by Iraq and Iran
46 Tapestry thread
47 Lots of laughs
50 Touchdown stat

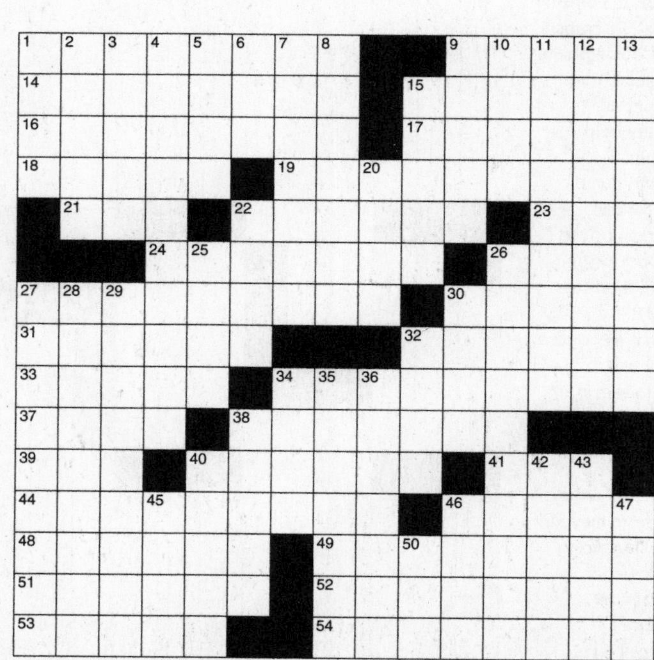

by Randolph Ross

197

ACROSS
1 Cosmonaut's craft
6 Runner, of a sort
15 Eat up
16 Suggestions
17 Signal withdrawal
19 Cabinet dept. since 1965
20 Range rovers
21 Mailing courtesy, briefly
22 Second-rate
25 Cows
27 Bulls, e.g.
28 Designer's deg.
29 Fields in which 6-Acrosses are found
38 Much to do
39 Concentration for an English major
40 Close
41 Glamour types, for short
42 Super ___ (1990s video game console)
43 Game keeper
47 Tipped off
51 Colorado's ___ Mountain
52 Food quality
54 Verdi's "___ giardin del bello"
56 They may keep you up
60 Outlines
61 Long-distance commuter's home, maybe
62 Pretty good poker hand
63 Superman, for one

DOWN
1 What the narrator "threw up" in "The Night Before Christmas"
2 Baseball's Lefty
3 "Seriously?"
4 Columbarium object
5 Letter in the Globe and Mail
6 Ben of Ben & Jerry's
7 Parry
8 Square type
9 Hooks, of a sort
10 Onetime owner of Sheraton Hotels
11 Backs
12 Close, poetically
13 One likely to get men's attention
14 Children's author Eleanor
18 Egyptian expanse
23 Etiolate
24 Made a comeback
26 High-tech auto device
28 Hallowed
29 ___ Pinto (Texas county or its seat)
30 Lena of "Havana"
31 French novelist Pierre
32 Bulblike bases of stems
33 Daughter in "The Cherry Orchard"
34 Cain, e.g.
35 Shaving alternative
36 "Lemme ___!"
37 Legis. period
43 Sailor's stopper
44 Russian alternative
45 Bartlett, notably
46 Slimming cut
47 Part of a stage
48 Good earth
49 Boredom
50 Raison follower
53 Tom T. Hall's "Mama Bake ___"
55 Novel ID
57 Daniel ___ Kim of "Lost"
58 Main
59 Rock's ___ Rose

by Martin Ashwood-Smith

198

ACROSS

1 Kind of beam
6 It's generated for high-quality pictures
15 What many are forced to live in
16 Lifelong friend of Truman Capote
17 Crazy, in rap slang
18 "Lay it on me"
19 Like signs
21 All the time
22 Court area
23 Some extended arguments
25 It may be extended
26 Follower of Mao
27 Still
28 King of Tartary in "Turandot"
30 Begins brawling
32 Bathing resort on the Lahn River
33 Issachar's uncle
34 Rosencrantz or Guildenstern
35 Tags
38 Brake-slamming result
42 Exercise done while pedaling
43 Nickname for a Manhattan jail, with "the"
44 Kind of virus
45 Results of big hits?
46 Meadowsweet
48 Hierarchy part
49 Scorecard data
51 Stance of impatience
53 Stirring up more trouble
55 Like some blocked passages
56 Aroma
57 Bounteous
58 Sports Illustrated's 2010 Sportsman of the Year
59 Chemistry Nobelist Hoffmann

DOWN

1 Battle of the Nations site, 1813
2 Frontman on the 2008 rock album "Chinese Democracy"
3 "The Colbert Report" ends with one
4 Drop in speech
5 Painter of the "Crucifixion of St. Peter" in the Vatican
6 Words of recognition
7 Its three strings are plucked with a bachi
8 Accessory popularized by Louis XIV
9 Marquand title character
10 Sects' appeal?: Abbr.
11 City next to Fullerton
12 Poem set "in the ghoul-haunted woodland of Weir"
13 Like games without win-win outcomes
14 They only scrape the surface
20 Court baskets
24 Cheering section
27 Places for runners
29 Yearly dozen
31 Progeny
32 Kid's repetitive plea?
34 Lands around mansions
35 Tiger's successor, computerwise
36 Lee who advised Reagan and Bush
37 Reason to hire a coach
38 Small, furry-tailed hibernators
39 Big name in weight-loss supplements
40 It's solid yellow
41 Like many ex-cons
43 Capital whose central plaza is Skanderbeg Square
47 One going off on somebody?
48 Words from un innamorato
50 Throw below, say
52 Lumber feature
54 43-Down's place: Abbr.

by Joon Pahk

ACROSS

1 Carpaccio base, maybe
8 Rite aide
15 "I haven't a care in the world"
16 He succeeded to the Chrysanthemum Throne in 1989
17 Certain committee member
18 Surveys, usually with negative responses
19 Music genre
21 Barbados, e.g.
22 Worms cries
25 Ulysses S. Grant was its eighth pres.
26 Refuted
28 State sch. in Kingston
29 Severely rebukes
31 What mown lawns do
33 Wheelchair attachments
36 Home of Hampshire College
38 Part of an ancient procession
39 Pressured
41 Get rid of
42 Dolphin, e.g.
44 Organizational figure
45 Strapping
47 Jules Verne harpooner ___ Land
48 Singer Vannelli of 1970s-'80s pop
49 "___ mouse!"
50 Flightless bird
52 Standard with the lyric "Ain't these tears in my eyes tellin' you?"
55 Smooth
59 Beady-eyed and sneaky
60 Criminal types
61 Was irritated and made some noise about it?
62 Semiannual event

DOWN

1 Some linemen: Abbr.
2 What may be coming after you
3 Not ruddy
4 23-Down caramel desserts
5 "Must've been something ___"
6 When there's nothing doing
7 City known as Salisbury until 1982
8 Farm delivery
9 Accomplish by economy, with "out"
10 You: Ger.
11 Games that go into overtime, say
12 United States divider
13 ". . . ___ told by an idiot": Macbeth
14 "Got it"
20 Rancor
22 Like something you've heard?
23 See 4-Down
24 Wasted
26 Home to more than 5 1/2 million Arabs
27 Kind of pass
29 Ethnic cuisine
30 ___ Crighton Trophy (Canada's Heisman-like award)
32 Like wind and solar energy
34 Wheel alignment
35 Pope with a Nov. 10 feast day
37 Gob
40 Pretty ballerina in an Abba song
43 Respite from dependents and everyone else
45 Some circus performers
46 Bring back to full strength, as a staff
48 Guardian spirits
50 Papyrus, e.g.
51 Some soft white blocks
53 La ___ (Hollywood nickname)
54 Marilyn Monroe played one in "Some Like It Hot"
56 Suffix with bass
57 Operation Mail Call grp.
58 B.O. buys

by Patrick Merrell

200

ACROSS

1 Lead follower
7 They make vehicles very volatile
15 Item removed before showering
16 "See!"
17 Locations for many pipes
18 Where many people fall asleep at the wheel
19 Pablo Neruda's "___ to Opposites"
20 2, 4, 6, 8, 10 . . . , e.g.
22 Naval inits.
23 Reason to wear earplugs
24 Underweight delivery, maybe
25 "Lemme ___!"
27 Resin used in varnishes
29 Spout
32 Keeps in order
34 Away, in a way
36 Heads off
37 Borderline fare?
38 Strategy game with disks
40 Unwilling to stay in line
41 Shot
42 Used a knight stick on?
44 It can be bought without money
45 Big ball
46 Rockling, e.g.
47 See 48-Down
50 Whence Romeo
52 Basilica di San Nicola locale
53 Cookware item with low sides
55 Carmine's cousin
57 It's between 90 and 100
58 1951 title role for Mario Lanza
59 To a very great degree
60 Shake

DOWN

1 Distinguished oneself
2 Act like the master of
3 2003 Grammy winner for "A Mighty Wind"
4 Dress ___ (look like)
5 It may be hung on a board
6 BP competitor
7 It's white and wispy
8 Depleted
9 Optimistic
10 They're listed near clubs
11 Shows no moderation, briefly
12 One often dispelled
13 Business owner's delight
14 More than noshes
21 Geologic succession
26 Plowing problem
27 Item next to a phone
28 Pitch setter
29 Spirit of the Caribbean
30 In yet a greater way
31 Something to paste in
33 Abbr. associated with certain shortcuts
35 Tollbooth site
39 Burning up
40 Certain disciplinarian
43 Matchmaker's output?
47 ___ palm
48 With 47-Across, it stopped flying to New York in 1979
49 Prepares for dragging
50 Bea Arthur's "Mame" role
51 Thing pulled up in a bank: Abbr.
52 Stripped
54 Bounce
56 "Knots Landing" actress ___ Park Lincoln

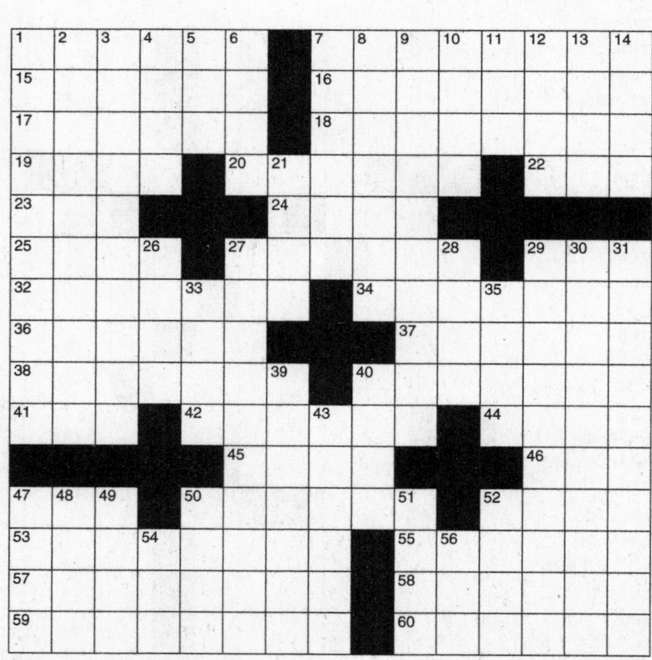

by Joe DiPietro

1

H	A	I	T	I		C	B	S			P	I	N	A
A	R	T	I	C	U	L	A	T	E		L	O	O	N
M	A	R	T	I	N	A	M	I	S		U	N	I	T
S	L	Y			S	W	A	R	T	H	M	O	R	E
		S	H	E	A				E	S	S			
	B	I	P	A	R	T	I	S	A	N		P	H	D
N	O	C	A	N			M	U	G			H	A	I
A	W	O	R	K	I	N	P	R	O	G	R	E	S	S
D	E	N			D	I	E			E	A	R	T	H
A	D	O		D	O	L	L	A	R	T	R	E	E	
		C	O	O				D	A	Z	E			
M	I	L	K	C	A	R	T	O	N			W	E	B
E	S	A	I		T	H	I	R	D	P	A	R	T	Y
E	L	S	E		M	O	V	E	D	A	P	A	R	T
T	A	T	S			S	O	D		T	E	P	E	E

2

M	G	M		F	E	L	T		S	T	R	A	F	E
E	E	O		O	L	E	O		T	R	I	L	L	O
D	A	N	E	C	O	O	K		R	E	V	L	O	N
I	R	A	N	I			E	L	I		E	U	R	
A	T	M	S		D	A	N	A	C	A	R	V	E	Y
	O	I	L	P	A	N		X	T	C		I	N	E
			A	O	R	T	A			C	O	A	C	T
	D	A	V	E	C	H	A	P	P	E	L	L	E	
T	E	N	E	T			A	H	A	N	D			
A	L	A		I	M	A		A	R	T	F	U	L	
D	I	C	K	C	A	V	E	T	T		O	N	E	A
	M	O	N		T	E	N			O	R	K	I	N
G	E	N	O	M	E		D	C	C	O	M	I	C	S
B	A	D	B	O	Y		A	T	O	Z		N	A	E
S	T	A	S	I	S		T	R	O	Y		D	S	L

3

H	I	G	H		M	E	N	S	A		F	I	L	L
O	N	E	A		A	S	S	A	M		I	D	L	E
C	O	T	T	O	N	S	W	A	B		S	T	A	N
K	I	T		T	E	A		B	I	G	H	A	N	D
	L	O	V	E	D	I	T			L	E	G	O	S
		K	E	R			I	D	E	E	S			
R	U	N	N	I	N	G	M	A	T	E		P	S	I
A	V	O	N		I	N	E	R	T		A	L	A	N
J	A	W		C	R	A	C	K	E	R	J	A	C	K
			P	H	O	T	O			I	A	N		
S	P	O	R	E			P	I	T	C	R	E	W	
P	I	N	E	T	A	R		C	E	E		F	I	G
A	X	I	S		K	O	S	H	E	R	S	A	L	T
R	I	O	T		I	B	E	A	M		A	R	L	O
K	E	N	O		N	E	W	T	S		S	E	A	S

4

M	A	I	A		A	J	A	R		T	H	I	E	F
I	S	B	N		C	O	N	E		C	Y	C	L	O
T	H	E	G	R	E	A	T	P	U	M	P	K	I	N
T	O	L	E	T		D	E	A	N		N	Y	E	T
S	T	I	L	E	S			Y	U	G	O			
		E	A	S	T	L	A		M	O	T	T	O	S
A	T	V			A	A	B	A		B	I	A	L	Y
T	H	E	F	U	N	K	Y	C	H	I	C	K	E	N
M	A	S	A	I		E	S	C	E			E	S	C
S	T	O	L	E	N		S	T	E	F	F	I		
			L	S	A	T			L	I	O	T	T	A
I	S	P	S		V	A	S	E		D	R	E	A	R
T	H	E	F	L	Y	I	N	G	T	O	M	A	T	O
C	A	N	O	E		N	O	G	O		A	S	A	S
H	Y	D	R	A		T	W	O	D		L	Y	R	E

5

S	C	O	O	P		C	R	A	B		A	L	S	O
C	O	N	G	A		R	O	P	E		C	I	A	O
R	O	A	R	S		A	L	E	C		A	M	M	O
A	P	P	E	T	I	Z	E	R	O	R	D	E	R	
P	E	A		O	N	E		T	O	O		R	A	P
E	R	R	O	R	S		B	U	L	B		I	I	I
			S	A	U	C	E	R			A	C	M	E
	B	I	L	L	M	A	Z	E	R	O	S	K	I	
C	O	M	O			L	O	S	E	R	S			
S	T	P		A	W	L	S		F	A	N	N	E	D
I	S	O		O	A	S		L	E	T		A	L	I
	W	U	R	L	I	T	Z	E	R	O	R	G	A	N
Z	A	N	E		T	I	E	D		R	E	S	I	N
I	N	D	O		O	M	N	I		I	N	A	N	E
P	A	S	S		N	E	O	N		O	T	T	E	R

6

C	R	O	P		I	M	A	C		T	I	L	E	D
L	E	C	H		N	A	I	L		E	R	A	S	E
I	D	E	A		G	O	T	O	H	E	A	V	E	N
C	H	A	S	M			C	R	A	T	E			
H	O	N	E	Y	I	M	H	O	M	E		I	F	S
E	T	S		E	G	O		X	M	R	A	D	I	O
			K	Y	O	T	O				D	I	N	O
	T	O	W	E	R	O	F	L	O	N	D	O	N	
M	A	M	A				T	A	P	A	S			
I	P	A	N	E	M	A		D	A	D		F	D	A
T	E	N		K	I	T	T	Y	L	I	T	T	E	R
			O	B	E	S	E			R	E	R	A	N
H	I	D	D	E	N	T	E	X	T		N	O	N	E
A	D	E	E	R		U	N	I	S		D	O	N	S
N	O	M	S	G		D	Y	N	E		S	P	A	S

7

8

S A W T O ■ C A M P ■ L A T H
I M E A N ■ O B O E ■ E U R O
C O B R A ■ R I D E ■ S P A R
■ ■ S P R I N T E R U S A I N
A L I ■ O N E ■ ■ ■ S E I N E
M E T A L F A S T E N E R ■ ■
O N E A L ■ ■ L A L A ■ ■ ■ ■
S A S H ■ A L O O F ■ T C B Y
■ ■ ■ ■ A S I A ■ ■ E R A S E
■ ■ L I G H T N I N G U N I T
S T O N E ■ ■ ■ N E G ■ D X I
L E A V E S U D D E N L Y ■ ■
U L N A ■ T R E E ■ O O M P H
S L E D ■ O G L E ■ G R A C E
H Y D E ■ W E L D ■ S E N S E

9

Q T I P S ■ A P E S ■ G L O B
T O T A L ■ J U M P ■ R O T E
S U C R E ■ A M I R ■ A N T E
■ T H E P U R P L E O N I O N
■ ■ ■ N T H ■ ■ ■ E N D ■ ■ ■
S P A T ■ O P E N S E S A M E
H I S ■ S H A R I ■ R O L E X
E X T R A ■ P I T ■ U N I T E
L E R O I ■ A C T I N ■ B A R
F L O O D P L A I N ■ S I L T
■ ■ ■ T A R ■ ■ ■ C E L ■ ■ ■
T H E W H O L E S H M E A R ■
A U T O ■ B E V Y ■ B A G E L
K E R R ■ E V E N ■ E Z I N E
E Y E D ■ D I S C ■ D E N T S

10

M A W ■ L E C T O R ■ C R O P
A B E ■ A L C O V E ■ A U D I
S R I ■ C L I V E B A R N E S
S I R R E E ■ ■ R A N D D ■ ■
E D D B Y R N E S ■ N O O N E
U G L I ■ ■ O L E O ■ O W E N
R E Y ■ M I L L E B O R N E S
■ ■ ■ D O T ■ ■ ■ I R S ■ ■ ■
D A V I D B I R N E Y ■ R A T
I K E A ■ E A S E ■ ■ C O C O
P A R M A ■ S T B E R N A R D
■ ■ M A R I S ■ ■ L A N D E D
F R O N T B U R N E R ■ M A L
A I N T ■ I M D O N E ■ A G E
N O T E ■ S E A W A R ■ P E R

11

C L A S P S ■ H B O ■ Y O D A
H A C K I T ■ A R P ■ A L I T
E S T A T E ■ N A E ■ M E R V
W E S T V I R G I N I A ■ ■ ■
S R O ■ I N R U N ■ R H E I N
■ S N A P ■ S P I T V A L V E
■ ■ ■ H E M ■ S A O ■ ■ L A W
D I S H R A G ■ C L E M E N S
A S A ■ ■ R O S ■ D X I ■ ■ ■
S P L I T V O T E ■ I G O R ■
H Y E N A ■ D I D S T ■ L A Y
■ ■ ■ A B S O L U T V O D K A
T H A W ■ A M T ■ R I P P E R
V I V A ■ F E E ■ U S E R I D
S P A Y ■ E N D ■ T A L O N S

12

T A L C ■ ■ M E S A ■ A T T A
A R E A ■ E A G E R ■ I R A S
T R A V E L C A R D ■ R I M S
■ ■ ■ I N G ■ D I E ■ F A I T
J E S T E R S ■ O N C A L L ■
A L L Y ■ E T C ■ T A R P ■ ■
B I O ■ S C A R F ■ R E E K S
O T T ■ Z O N E O U T ■ R A W
T E M P E ■ S T O K E ■ I N E
■ ■ A L L S ■ E D U ■ S O Y A
■ S C A L E D ■ S L A N D E R
D A H S ■ L O P ■ E T A ■ ■ ■
E X I T ■ D O U B L E T I M E
C O N E ■ O Z Z I E ■ C O A X
O N E R ■ M Y O B ■ ■ H U G O

13

P	A	W		F	L	O	O	D		I	G	I	V	E
A	H	A		L	A	T	T	E		A	L	O	E	S
R	O	L	L	O	V	E	R	M	I	N	U	T	E	S
T	Y	K	E			L	O	O	P		T	A	S	E
			G	A	O	L		R	O	V	E			
		S	I	T	D	O	W	N	D	I	N	N	E	R
E	N	C	O	R	E		O	A	S	T		O	V	A
P	O	R	N	O		D	R	Y		I	D	T	A	G
I	N	A		P	S	I	S		A	A	R	O	N	S
C	O	M	E	H	E	R	E	O	F	T	E	N		
			L	Y	R	E		B	R	E	A			
P	U	M	A		I	N	E	S			M	A	G	I
S	T	A	Y	O	F	E	X	E	C	U	T	I	O	N
S	A	U	N	A		E	P	S	O	N		D	O	G
T	H	I	E	F		D	O	S	E	S		A	D	E

14

I	B	I	S		C	L	U	E		E	P	S	O	M
S	A	M	M	Y	C	A	H	N		T	R	A	C	E
A	D	M	I	S	S	I	O	N		H	O	S	T	A
S	M	E	L	L		C	H	A	K	A	K	H	A	N
	I	D	E						O	N	E	A	L	S
A	N	I	S	E		M	A	S	K	E	D			
U	T	A		S	H	I	N	T	O		S	M	E	W
T	O	T		C	O	N	G	A	M	E		O	X	O
O	N	E	G		M	I	L	T	O	N		N	I	K
			R	E	E	S	E	S		A	S	S	T	S
E	S	S	E	N	E						O	I	S	
J	A	M	E	S	C	A	A	N		A	L	G	I	D
E	R	I	T	U		F	R	E	E	R	A	N	G	E
C	A	T	E	R		B	I	L	L	Y	C	O	N	N
T	H	E	R	E		S	A	L	K		E	R	S	T

15

A	R	R	R		C	R	O	P			A	P	P	S
N	O	A	H		L	O	V	E	S		R	O	O	T
D	A	V	Y	J	O	N	E	S	L	O	C	K	E	R
I	R	I	S	E	S		R	E	A	M		E	M	U
				L	E	A	S	T		A	V	A	S	T
T	A	L	K	L	I	K	E	A		H	E	R		
A	T	O	I		N	I	E		M	A	G	O	G	
B	A	S	S	O	O	N		P	E	N	G	U	I	N
	D	E	M	O	N		P	A	D		I	N	G	A
		N	E	C		P	I	R	A	T	E	D	A	Y
B	O	O	T	Y		A	N	K	L	E				
A	C	T		T	I	C	K		L	A	A	L	A	A
S	H	I	V	E	R	M	E	T	I	M	B	E	R	S
I	R	M	A		S	A	Y	S	O		B	A	C	H
N	E	E	T			N	E	O	N		A	H	O	Y

16

C	P	U	S		A	P	I	A		L	U	C	A	S
A	L	P	E		N	A	C	L		E	R	O	D	E
B	U	D	G	E	T	C	U	T		A	I	R	E	R
A	R	A		C	O	M			I	N	A	N		
N	A	T	I	O	N	A	L	A	N	T	H	E	M	S
A	L	E	C			N	O	A	H		S	L	A	W
			E	G	G		U	R	A	L		I	R	A
D	O	L	L	A	R	D	I	P	L	O	M	A	C	Y
A	V	E		D	U	E	S		F	L	O			
D	E	F	T		M	A	X	I			J	E	N	A
E	N	T	E	R	P	R	I	S	E	Z	O	N	E	S
		W	H	E	Y			O	X	O		L	A	K
A	K	I	R	A		R	E	N	T	A	C	A	R	S
S	O	N	A	R		A	L	T	O		A	C	T	I
S	I	G	N	S		F	O	O	L		P	E	O	N

17

S	P	A	T		I	T	C	H		S	L	A	S	H
H	E	S	S		N	E	H	I		C	O	P	T	O
A	R	I	A		H	A	I	L		O	A	S	I	S
Q	U	A	R	T	E	R	P	O	U	N	D	E	R	S
				H	R	S			S	E	E			
A	D	M	I	R	E		F	L	U		D	A	T	E
B	U	E	N	O		B	O	A	R		D	U	A	L
H	A	L	F	B	L	O	O	D	P	R	I	N	C	E
O	N	E	I		O	R	L	Y		A	C	T	I	N
R	E	E	D		R	E	S		F	I	E	S	T	A
			E	O	N				P	A	S			
F	U	L	L	M	E	T	A	L	J	A	C	K	E	T
U	S	A	I	N		E	S	A	I		R	A	R	A
D	E	N	T	I		L	E	S	T		A	M	I	S
D	R	A	Y	S		L	A	M	A		B	A	C	K

18

V	I	A	L		T	O	D	D	L	E		M	A	R
A	C	L	U		H	E	R	E	O	N		A	M	I
C	H	I	C	K	E	N	Y	A	R	D		R	I	M
			C	A	W		E	R	N		I	O	N	S
D	I	G	I	T	A	L	Y	E	A	R	B	O	O	K
O	N	O		S	L	I	E	R		E	E	N	S	Y
O	D	O	M		R	N	S		C	P	A			
R	O	P	E	R	U	G		T	O	O	M	A	N	Y
			T	I	S		T	R	U		S	L	A	V
P	I	P	I	T		H	E	I	N	Z		E	S	E
A	N	I	M	A	L	I	N	S	T	I	N	C	T	S
L	U	X	E		E	T	A		R	O	E			
A	R	I		C	A	T	C	H	I	N	A	L	I	E
C	E	E		A	V	E	R	S	E		L	A	M	E
E	D	S		B	E	R	E	T	S		E	X	P	O

19

N	I	N	J	A		A	P	L	U	S		T	A	B
A	R	I	E	S		B	O	O	S	T		E	T	A
G	E	T	S	O	N	E	S	W	A	Y		M	D	S
			U	F	O		S	E	T		C	A	P	S
L	E	N	S		T	H	E	R	O	Y	A	L	W	E
E	P	A		N	E	O			D	E	C	E	N	T
V	I	D	E	O		P	O	P	A	R	T			
I	C	A	N	T	T	E	L	L	Y	O	U	W	H	Y
			A	I	R	S	E	A		U	S	A	G	E
S	C	A	M	P	I			T	N	T		I	T	A
T	A	L	E	S	O	F	W	O	E		A	T	V	S
O	V	A	L		X	I	I		H	E	R			
L	E	S		P	I	T	C	H	I	N	G	W	O	O
I	R	K		E	D	U	C	E		D	U	B	Y	A
D	N	A		R	E	P	A	Y		S	E	A	L	S

20

A	C	D	C		S	P	O	C	K		N	D	A	K
T	H	O	R		T	I	A	R	A		O	I	S	E
T	A	M	E		U	N	T	I	L		I	S	P	Y
N	I	P	S	I	N	T	H	E	B	U	D			
		E	S	L		A	S	S		S	E	E	R	S
S	H	R	I	L	L				L	E	A	N	I	N
P	A	I	D		I	R	O	N	E	D		T	A	I
R	I	G	A		R	E	I	N	A		K	E	L	P
E	R	N		M	A	P	L	E	S		E	R	T	E
A	D	O	R	E	S				E	M	P	T	O	R
D	O	N	E	N		A	C	T		I	T	A		
			J	U	G	G	L	I	N	G	P	I	N	S
M	A	Z	E		A	R	O	M	A		A	N	E	W
A	L	E	C		S	E	W	E	R		C	E	R	A
P	I	N	T		H	E	N	R	Y		E	D	D	Y

21

M	A	R		S	O	B	S			C	O	L	T	S
O	B	I		E	R	R	O	R		A	C	E	I	T
C	I	G	A	R	C	A	S	E		T	H	E	T	A
S	T	O	V	E		C	A	P	E	C	O	R	A	L
		L	E	N	A		D	O	R	A		S	N	L
C	U	E	C	A	R	D			I	L	K			
H	S	T			C	O	A	T	C	L	O	S	E	T
I	S	T	O			U	M	A			S	P	C	A
C	R	O	P	C	I	R	C	L	E			A	R	F
			T	A	D			C	R	E	W	C	I	T
S	H	O		R	O	D	S		A	L	I	E		
C	A	M	E	C	L	E	A	N		E	N	S	U	E
O	S	A	K	A		C	L	A	Y	C	O	U	R	T
O	T	H	E	R		K	A	P	U	T		I	G	O
T	E	A	S	E			D	A	M	S		T	E	N

22

L	A	P	T	O	P		N	E	W	S		R	I	M
O	B	E	Y	E	R		A	C	H	Y		A	L	E
L	O	C	K	D	E	V	I	C	E	S		B	I	N
L	U	K	E		F	E	V	E	R		M	B	A	S
			S	P	A	R	E		E	R	O	I	C	A
A	V	A		R	B	S			T	I	L	T		
C	I	R	C	U	S	A	C	R	O	B	A	T	S	
T	E	C	H	S		C	O	E		C	R	E	P	E
	W	H	I	S	K	E	Y	G	L	A	S	S	E	S
		I	L	I	E			A	I	G		T	D	S
O	U	T	L	A	Y		U	L	C	E	R			
P	R	E	Y		C	U	R	I	E		A	L	A	S
T	I	C		J	A	C	K	A	N	D	J	I	L	L
E	A	T		I	S	L	E		S	C	A	M	P	I
D	H	S		M	E	A	L		E	C	H	O	E	D

23

I	D	E	S		R	A	V	E			R	A	T	S
T	I	L	E		A	T	S	E	A		E	R	A	T
A	V	O	N		N	A	I	L	S		D	O	P	Y
L	A	N	D	M	A	R	X		S	A	D	S	A	X
			S	E	M	I		M	E	L	E	E	S	
	A	D	I	E	U		P	I	T	A	S			
B	L	A	N	K	C	H	E	X		S	T	I	N	T
F	D	R			K	A	P	U	T			D	U	E
F	A	T	W	A		H	Y	P	E	R	L	Y	N	X
			H	U	L	A	S		N	E	I	L	S	
	F	L	A	R	E	S		D	E	A	L			
T	I	E	T	A	X		T	U	M	M	Y	T	U	X
E	R	O	S		U	S	A	G	E		P	O	N	E
N	E	N	A		S	A	T	I	N		A	G	I	N
D	D	A	Y			W	E	N	T		D	A	T	A

24

I	S	L	E		B	A	L	M	Y		T	B	S	P
D	I	E	T		I	L	I	A	D		R	A	T	A
I	N	T	H	E	D	U	M	P	S		I	R	A	S
	T	I	E	R		M	O	O		D	A	R	N	S
P	A	T	R	O	L			U	T	I	L	I	Z	E
A	X	L		D	O	W	N	T	H	E	R	O	A	D
P	E	I		E	P	E	E		E	D	U			
A	S	E	A			B	I	T			N	Y	P	D
			I	A	N		G	R	A	B		O	L	E
O	V	E	R	T	H	E	H	I	L	L		G	E	L
T	E	A	B	A	L	L			F	A	C	I	A	L
O	C	T	A	D		O	H	S		N	A	B	S	
O	T	I	S		U	P	T	H	E	C	R	E	E	K
L	O	N	E		M	E	T	O	O		L	A	D	Y
E	R	G	S		A	S	P	E	N		A	R	O	D

25

S	I	P	S		H	U	S	H		I	N	F	E	R
C	O	A	L		O	H	I	O		N	E	I	G	H
A	N	N	A		N	O	L	O		F	A	R	G	O
M	I	D	N	I	G	H	T	H	O	U	R			
S	C	A	T	S				A	T	T		S	H	A
				M	A	T	T	H	O	U	S	T	O	N
M	A	M	A		R	O	O			R	O	A	S	T
A	P	A	R	T	M	E	N	T	H	O	U	S	E	S
M	I	N	C	E			T	A	E		S	H	A	Y
B	A	S	S	E	T	H	O	U	N	D				
O	N	E		S	H	E				O	U	T	D	O
			W	H	E	R	E	A	R	T	T	H	O	U
C	A	P	R	I		B	L	U	E		U	R	N	S
S	W	E	A	R		A	S	K	S		R	O	U	T
I	N	A	P	T		L	E	S	T		N	E	T	S

26

A	S	A	P		M	E	T	A		A	R	M	O	R
V	A	I	L		A	R	A	B		L	O	U	P	E
A	L	L	A	T	O	N	C	E		I	M	H	I	P
			C	U	R	S	E		S	T	P	A	U	L
F	L	E	A	B	I	T	T	E	N		E	M	M	Y
O	U	T	T	A				R	E	A	R	M		
R	I	P	E		C	A	R	N	E	Y		A	C	E
U	G	H		V	A	M	P	I	R	E		D	I	V
M	I	O		C	R	I	M	E	S		C	A	V	A
		N	O	R	A	S				S	O	L	I	D
B	E	E	S		T	H	I	N	K	T	W	I	C	E
E	T	H	I	C	S		T	O	R	A	H			
A	H	O	R	A		C	A	M	E	R	A	S	H	Y
R	E	M	I	T		C	L	A	M		N	C	A	A
D	R	E	S	S		L	O	N	E		D	I	T	Z

27

S	P	A	S			B	A	G	S		S	P	A	T
W	A	L	K		A	U	R	A	L		N	A	D	A
A	G	E	E		P	S	I	L	O	V	E	Y	O	U
P	E	C	L	A	S	S			B	E	E			
			E	M	O		P	T	B	A	R	N	U	M
	R	I	T	E		S	O	R	E	L		E	N	E
S	E	T	O	N		T	B	A	R		A	B	I	T
C	L	A	N	S		R	O	D		B	R	U	T	E
A	I	L	S		L	U	X	E		A	B	L	E	R
L	E	I		M	I	N	E	R		B	O	A	S	
P	F	C	H	A	N	G	S		O	E	R			
			O	L	D			P	H	L	E	V	E	L
P	G	T	H	I	R	T	E	E	N		T	I	D	Y
O	A	H	U		O	U	T	G	O		U	S	E	R
I	T	E	M		S	E	A	S			M	A	N	E

28

A	B	B	A		F	A	S	C	I	A		B	R	O
F	O	O	L		A	T	H	E	N	A		O	O	F
C	I	N	D	E	R	F	E	L	L	A		S	P	F
		N	E	E			R	E	A		A	T	E	E
B	E	I	N	G	B	O	B	B	Y	B	R	O	W	N
A	B	E	T		A	B	E	S		U	L	N	A	S
R	O	B	E		R	O	T		B	Y	E	B	Y	E
S	N	L		H	E	E		R	A	I	S	A		
		U	R	A	L	S		E	N	T		K	O	I
O	L	E	A	R	Y		A	H	A		V	E	R	T
R	E	B	I	D		E	L	A	N		O	D	E	S
B	O	U	N	C	I	N	G	B	A	B	Y	B	O	Y
I	N	T	S		D	R	E			R	A	E		
T	I	L		F	L	A	B	B	E	R	G	A	S	T
E	N	E		R	E	G	R	E	W		E	N	O	S
D	E	R		I	D	E	A	T	E		R	S	V	P

29

A	S	E	A		A	L	A	M	O		P	O	M	P
S	A	U	D		P	E	T	A	L		S	C	A	R
S	T	R	I	K	E	G	O	L	D		T	A	K	E
A	R	E	N	A		A	M	E	N	D		R	I	T
Y	A	K		R	U	T			I	O	D	I	N	E
S	P	A	R	E	S	O	M	E	C	H	A	N	G	E
			E	N	E		I	R	K		M	A	I	N
W	A	S	P	S		O	L	E		E	A	S	T	S
A	P	I	A		I	O	N		B	U	S			
S	P	L	I	T	T	H	E	J	A	C	K	P	O	T
S	L	I	D	E	S			O	Y	L		E	K	E
A	E	C		N	A	B	O	B		I	S	L	E	T
I	P	O	D		B	O	W	L	E	D	O	V	E	R
L	I	N	E		O	R	E	O	S		F	I	F	I
S	E	E	S		Y	E	N	T	A		A	C	E	S

30

S	T	O	I	C		P	I	N	U	P		K	F	C
S	W	I	R	L		A	N	D	R	E		E	R	E
W	A	L	K	I	N	G	C	A	N	E		Y	I	N
			S	Q	U	E	A	K		P	A	B	S	T
S	P	R	O	U	T	S			S	H	E	I	K	S
T	H	A	M	E	S		F	A	V	O	R	S		
A	L	I	E			A	R	P	E	L		C	O	G
L	O	S		C	O	C	A	I	N	E		A	G	O
L	X	I		O	R	A	N	G			B	Y	R	D
		N	I	M	I	T	Z		B	O	R	N	E	O
R	A	G	T	A	G			D	O	P	I	E	S	T
E	X	C	O	N		S	T	O	N	E	S			
A	L	A		C	I	T	I	Z	E	N	K	A	N	E
P	E	I		H	A	U	T	E		E	L	D	E	R
S	S	N		E	N	D	O	N		R	Y	D	E	R

31

B	B	S	■	I	B	M	P	C	■	A	T	O	M
E	L	O	■	R	A	T	I	O	■	M	A	K	O
D	U	D	E	R	A	N	C	H	■	B	R	O	W
E	T	O	N	■	■	■	K	O	D	I	A	K	S
W	H	I	T	E	R	U	S	S	I	A	N	■	■
■	■	■	S	K	I	S	■	T	A	N	T	E	S
A	R	I	■	C	E	E	S	■	■	C	I	A	O
P	A	R	D	O	N	M	Y	F	R	E	N	C	H
O	B	O	E	■	■	E	N	D	O	■	O	H	O
P	E	N	P	A	L	■	C	I	N	Q	■	■	■
■	■	J	U	L	I	U	S	C	A	E	S	A	R
A	L	A	T	E	E	N	■	■	■	I	A	G	O
K	I	W	I	■	D	R	E	S	S	I	N	G	S
I	D	E	E	■	T	E	V	Y	E	■	D	I	E
N	O	D	S	■	O	P	A	R	T	■	Y	E	S

32

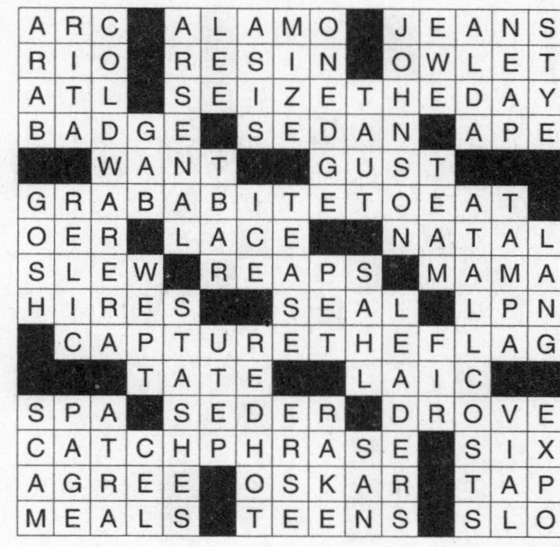

A	R	C	■	A	L	A	M	O	■	J	E	A	N	S
R	I	O	■	R	E	S	I	N	■	O	W	L	E	T
A	T	L	■	S	E	I	Z	E	T	H	E	D	A	Y
B	A	D	G	E	■	S	E	D	A	N	■	A	P	E
■	■	W	A	N	T	■	■	G	U	S	T	■	■	■
G	R	A	B	A	B	I	T	E	T	O	E	A	T	■
O	E	R	■	L	A	C	E	■	■	N	A	T	A	L
S	L	E	W	■	R	E	A	P	S	■	M	A	M	A
H	I	R	E	S	■	■	S	E	A	L	■	L	P	N
■	C	A	P	T	U	R	E	T	H	E	F	L	A	G
■	■	■	T	A	T	E	■	■	L	A	I	C	■	■
S	P	A	■	S	E	D	E	R	■	D	R	O	V	E
C	A	T	C	H	P	H	R	A	S	E	■	S	I	X
A	G	R	E	E	■	O	S	K	A	R	■	T	A	P
M	E	A	L	S	■	T	E	E	N	S	■	S	L	O

33

H	E	P	■	■	S	I	M	P	■	T	E	R	P	S
A	M	I	■	G	E	M	M	A	■	I	D	I	O	T
D	I	E	S	E	L	O	I	L	■	P	I	C	K	Y
J	R	R	T	O	L	K	I	E	N	S	T	H	E	■
■	■	■	I	L	S	A	■	■	E	Y	E	■	■	■
M	A	L	L	■	T	Y	C	H	O	■	D	R	E	D
S	T	E	T	H	O	■	L	A	N	D	■	E	L	I
N	O	T	S	O	■	H	O	W	■	E	G	E	S	T
B	O	G	■	S	E	W	N	■	B	R	A	V	O	S
C	L	O	P	■	B	Y	E	A	R	■	R	E	L	Y
■	■	■	Y	A	R	■	■	T	E	E	M	■	■	■
■	L	O	R	D	O	F	T	H	E	R	I	N	G	S
P	U	R	I	M	■	A	M	A	Z	O	N	A	N	T
D	A	N	T	E	■	V	A	N	E	S	■	D	A	Y
Q	U	E	E	N	■	A	N	D	S	■	■	A	W	E

34

A	R	F	A	R	F	■	A	S	S	■	I	N	R	E
B	U	R	G	E	R	■	E	L	O	■	C	O	O	L
A	S	I	A	G	O	■	R	O	D	■	E	R	O	S
S	T	E	T	S	■	R	O	T	O	■	C	A	K	E
E	S	S	E	■	K	A	C	H	M	I	R	■	■	■
■	■	■	S	T	E	N	O	S	■	R	E	T	R	O
R	O	O	■	R	A	I	L	■	S	O	A	R	E	D
O	I	L	P	A	N	S	■	M	A	N	M	A	D	E
I	N	L	O	V	E	■	D	E	L	I	■	Y	O	S
S	K	A	T	E	■	D	E	T	A	C	H	■	■	■
■	■	■	A	L	A	R	M	E	D	■	A	B	L	E
M	E	A	T	■	D	I	O	R	■	C	L	E	A	R
A	L	T	O	■	O	F	T	■	N	O	V	A	T	O
S	L	O	E	■	R	T	E	■	F	R	A	N	K	S
H	A	M	S	■	E	S	S	■	L	E	S	S	E	E

35

I	N	F	E	R	■	S	C	O	F	F	■	O	W	E
R	O	U	S	E	■	M	O	V	I	E	■	P	O	M
M	E	N	T	A	L	I	M	A	G	E	■	T	O	M
A	L	D	O	■	O	R	A	L	■	D	A	I	L	Y
■	■	■	N	I	C	K	S	■	P	O	B	O	Y	S
G	O	F	I	S	H	■	■	L	I	N	E	N	■	■
O	N	E	A	L	■	S	P	I	N	■	■	P	S	U
T	U	R	N	E	D	T	H	E	T	A	B	L	E	S
H	S	T	■	■	D	A	I	S	■	G	E	A	R	S
■	■	I	D	T	A	G	■	■	B	R	E	Y	E	R
S	A	L	A	R	Y	■	P	I	L	A	F	■	■	■
P	R	I	M	O	■	D	I	N	O	■	S	A	G	A
A	D	Z	■	O	C	E	A	N	B	O	T	T	O	M
D	O	E	■	P	L	A	N	E	■	D	E	N	T	E
E	R	R	■	S	E	N	O	R	■	S	W	O	O	N

36

M	A	T	S	■	M	E	S	A	S	■	A	G	E	S
A	T	R	A	■	A	L	E	R	T	■	R	O	T	E
S	E	A	N	■	D	E	W	A	R	■	L	I	S	A
C	A	N	A	D	I	A	N	B	A	C	O	N	■	■
O	S	C	A	R	S	■	■	S	N	L	■	G	A	T
T	E	E	■	N	O	S	H	■	G	A	D	F	L	Y
■	■	■	M	O	N	T	E	R	E	Y	J	A	C	K
C	O	M	A	■	■	E	R	A	■	■	E	R	S	E
I	T	A	L	I	A	N	B	R	E	A	D	■	■	■
T	I	M	I	N	G	■	S	E	R	F	■	S	P	F
E	S	A	■	N	I	C	■	■	N	A	S	C	A	R
■	■	B	O	S	T	O	N	L	E	T	T	U	C	E
R	U	E	D	■	A	R	I	E	S	■	E	L	K	S
A	T	A	D	■	T	O	L	E	T	■	A	L	E	C
H	E	R	S	■	O	T	E	R	O	■	K	Y	R	A

37

I	N	C	A		B	A	R	D		E	F	L	A	T
N	O	E	L		I	S	A	Y		J	O	Y	C	E
F	U	L	L	H	O	U	S	E		E	U	R	O	S
O	S	T	E	O			P	I	T	C	R	E	W	S
			G	W	E	N		N	O	T	A			
T	H	R	E	E	K	I	N	G	S		C	H	U	M
R	O	O		L	E	N	O		S	M	E	A	R	Y
A	S	S	T	S		O	W	S		A	S	I	G	N
P	E	E	W	E	E		A	W	A	Y		K	E	A
P	A	S	O		R	O	Y	A	L	F	L	U	S	H
			P	A	I	N		B	E	A	U			
I	T	S	A	D	E	A	L			I	T	I	S	I
R	A	P	I	D		P	O	K	E	R	H	A	N	D
E	X	E	R	T		A	L	E	X		E	G	A	L
D	I	D	S	O		R	A	N	T		R	O	P	E

38

I	D	L	E		B	O	S	H			N	O	A	H
R	E	A	D		E	X	P	O		G	E	N	R	E
A	L	B	S		L	E	A	P		E	W	E	R	S
Q	U	E	E	N	A	N	N	E	S	L	A	C	E	
W	I	L	L	I			I	S	P		G	O	S	S
A	S	E		K	I	S	S	O	F	D	E	A	T	H
R	E	D	S		D	O	H			A	N	T	S	Y
			H	E	A	D		B	A	N	D			
F	O	C	A	L			S	O	Y		A	C	C	T
T	R	A	F	F	I	C	C	O	N	E		H	A	I
D	A	R	T		S	O	U			R	E	A	L	M
	C	R	E	A	M	O	F	T	H	E	C	R	O	P
S	L	E	D	S		P	F	U	I		A	G	R	A
H	E	R	B	S		E	L	B	E		R	E	I	N
O	S	A	Y			R	E	E	D		D	R	E	I

39

C	A	L	F		A	R	O	D		B	E	G	I	N
O	R	A	L		N	I	C	E		A	M	A	Z	E
A	L	M	A		Y	V	E	S		R	O	T	O	R
T	O	P	S	T	H	E	L	I	S	T		O	D	D
			K	Y	O	T	O		T	A	D			
D	O	C		P	O	S	T	N	O	B	I	L	L	S
I	N	U	S	E			S	E	M		P	E	A	S
S	T	O	P	O	F	F		O	P	T	S	O	U	T
K	A	M	A		R	U	R			H	O	N	D	A
S	P	O	T	R	E	M	O	V	E	R		E	E	R
			S	A	D		S	I	N	U	S			
J	A	G		P	O	T	S	O	F	M	O	N	E	Y
E	Q	U	I	P		S	I	L	O		C	O	R	E
S	U	A	V	E		A	N	I	L		A	V	O	W
T	A	M	E	R		R	I	N	D		L	A	S	S

40

C	A	J	U	N		L	I	P		P	A	S	T	
O	R	A	T	E		A	M	A		A	C	M	E	S
L	I	K	E	D		S	H	I	P	S	H	A	P	E
E	D	E	N		P	E	E	R	A	T		R	E	A
			S	H	A	R	P	S	H	O	O	T	E	R
A	R	T	I	E	S					R	A	M		
S	H	E	L	L	S	H	O	C	K		F	O	B	S
C	E	L		P	A	R	T	I	I	I		N	E	A
H	A	L	T		S	H	O	R	T	S	H	E	E	T
		M	O	O					E	L	A	Y	N	E
S	H	E	E	P	S	H	E	A	R	E	R			
Y	A	M		T	H	O	R	N	S		D	A	Z	E
S	H	O	E	S	H	I	N	E		S	H	R	E	W
T	A	R	S	I		S	I	R		S	A	C	R	E
	S	E	E	N		T	E	A		E	T	H	O	S

41

I	R	A	Q		M	A	P	L	E		R	I	N	K
N	A	N	U		I	W	I	L	L		O	M	A	N
C	H	I	E	F	T	E	X	A	N		A	P	S	E
		M	E	E	T			M	I	S	D	E	A	L
S	T	A	G	E		G	I	A	N	T	B	I	L	L
E	A	T		L	A	U	D		O	I	L			
R	B	I	S		B	I	O	S		L	O	C	O	S
F	O	O	T	B	A	L	L	M	A	T	C	H	U	P
S	O	N	A	R		T	I	E	R		K	A	T	E
			G	Y	M		Z	A	C	H		M	I	A
J	E	T	P	A	C	K	E	R		U	P	P	E	R
A	R	R	A	N	G	E			P	L	E	A		
R	O	A	R		R	A	M	C	H	A	R	G	E	R
E	D	I	T		A	C	R	I	D		I	N	F	O
D	E	N	Y		W	H	I	G	S		L	E	G	O

42

J	E	T	S			R	I	S	E	N		M	A	P
A	T	O	P		R	E	T	I	N	A		I	L	L
N	E	T	E	A	R	N	I	N	G	S		N	B	A
			E	S	S	E	N			S	L	E	E	T
S	C	U	D	S		W	A	S	T	E	A	R	E	A
C	A	S	S	I	O			H	O	R	N			
A	D	O		G	R	A	D	E	R		A	S	A	P
D	E	F	I	N	I	T	E	A	R	T	I	C	L	E
S	T	A	N		O	S	I	R	I	S		U	L	T
			I	S	L	E			D	E	B	B	I	E
W	Y	A	T	T	E	A	R	P		T	R	A	N	S
H	E	S	S	E			E	R	A	S	E			
E	L	K		P	L	A	N	E	T	E	A	R	T	H
A	L	E		P	O	M	E	L	O		S	U	R	E
T	O	W		E	X	P	E	L			T	E	A	R

43

M	O	R	A	L	■	P	E	W	■	C	H	E	S	S
E	L	O	P	E	■	O	D	E	■	L	E	G	A	L
S	E	L	E	S	■	W	I	L	L	I	N	G	L	Y
H	O	L	D	T	H	E	F	L	O	O	R	■	■	■
■	■	■	■	A	U	R	I	S	T	■	Y	E	A	■
■	H	I	T	T	H	E	C	E	I	L	I	N	G	■
M	I	N	E	■	■	D	E	T	O	X	■	R	E	T
O	T	H	E	R	S	■	■	■	N	I	K	O	N	S
P	E	A	■	P	O	S	S	E	■	■	A	L	T	O
■	C	L	I	M	B	T	H	E	W	A	L	L	S	■
■	H	E	C	■	B	E	A	R	E	R	■	■	■	■
■	■	■	E	X	E	R	C	I	S	E	R	O	O	M
S	U	N	S	T	R	O	K	E	■	N	O	R	M	A
O	N	A	I	R	■	I	L	S	■	A	T	E	A	T
D	O	N	N	A	■	D	E	T	■	S	H	O	N	E

44

L	E	A	P	■	M	C	C	O	O	■	R	E	S	T
O	S	L	O	■	A	R	A	I	L	■	O	T	T	O
C	A	T	S	C	R	A	D	L	E	■	T	H	A	I
H	U	S	T	L	I	N	G	■	■	Q	U	I	L	L
■	■	■	M	O	N	K	E	Y	S	U	N	C	L	E
M	R	H	A	N	E	Y	■	A	T	A	D	■	■	■
B	E	E	N	E	■	■	A	D	A	■	A	F	A	R
A	M	A	■	D	O	G	S	A	G	E	■	A	C	E
S	O	L	O	■	Z	A	P	■	■	Z	A	I	R	E
■	■	■	S	E	M	I	■	U	M	P	I	R	E	D
E	L	E	P	H	A	N	T	S	E	A	R	■	■	■
P	E	A	R	S	■	■	R	E	A	S	S	I	G	N
S	O	R	E	■	L	I	O	N	S	S	H	A	R	E
O	N	L	Y	■	A	R	I	E	L	■	O	G	O	D
M	E	S	S	■	P	A	S	T	Y	■	W	O	W	S

45

R	E	A	C	T	■	O	P	T	E	D	■	T	I	N
A	L	L	A	H	■	L	L	A	N	O	■	H	B	O
P	L	A	N	E	B	O	A	R	D	S	■	I	S	M
T	E	N	■	K	E	R	N	■	■	A	S	S	E	S
■	■	■	M	I	N	D	B	L	O	G	G	I	N	G
S	E	C	A	N	T	■	■	O	D	E	T	S	■	■
P	L	A	N	K	■	E	R	E	I	■	■	T	B	A
C	H	R	I	S	T	M	A	S	C	L	A	R	O	S
A	I	R	■	■	Y	E	N	S	■	A	M	U	S	E
■	■	Y	E	A	R	N	■	■	I	C	I	E	S	T
B	L	O	T	T	E	D	W	A	T	E	R	■	■	■
L	A	N	C	E	■	■	I	T	A	R	■	I	L	E
O	R	B	■	A	D	A	M	S	L	A	N	D	E	R
O	V	A	■	S	N	A	P	E	■	T	I	L	E	S
M	A	G	■	E	A	S	Y	A	■	E	X	E	R	T

46

B	A	T	M	A	N	■	■	R	P	M	■	S	E	E
A	R	O	U	S	E	■	A	E	R	O	■	T	A	X
B	E	N	C	H	W	A	R	M	E	R	■	A	T	A
S	A	S	H	■	■	S	C	A	L	A	■	L	I	L
■	■	■	■	C	A	S	H	P	A	Y	M	E	N	T
S	T	O	P	U	P	■	■	■	T	S	E	■	■	■
M	I	L	L	E	R	L	I	T	E	■	R	A	R	E
U	N	D	I	D	■	E	R	E	■	U	M	I	A	K
T	E	E	N	■	R	I	V	E	R	S	E	D	G	E
■	■	■	T	O	E	■	■	■	T	E	N	S	E	S
N	A	S	H	R	A	M	B	L	E	R	■	■	■	■
I	Z	E	■	C	R	E	E	P	■	■	W	O	K	E
P	U	T	■	H	E	R	E	S	J	O	H	N	N	Y
P	R	O	■	I	N	I	T	■	E	D	I	T	O	R
Y	E	N	■	D	D	T	■	■	D	E	M	O	T	E

47

S	H	E	L	F	■	S	G	T	■	S	N	A	R	E
L	E	V	E	L	■	P	O	E	■	T	O	N	E	S
A	R	E	N	A	■	O	W	E	■	A	S	I	D	E
M	A	R	A	T	H	O	N	M	I	N	I	■	■	■
■	■	■	■	T	A	N	S	■	S	C	R	A	M	S
S	C	A	R	E	D	■	■	E	T	E	■	V	I	E
M	A	R	I	N	E	S	U	B	■	S	M	I	L	E
E	N	C	L	■	S	A	R	A	N	■	C	A	E	N
A	A	H	E	D	■	F	I	N	E	E	X	T	R	A
R	P	I	■	I	S	E	■	■	H	A	L	E	S	T
S	E	E	S	A	W	■	F	O	R	T	■	■	■	■
■	■	■	P	R	E	C	I	O	U	S	S	E	M	I
A	T	A	R	I	■	A	R	M	■	O	I	L	E	D
M	O	V	I	E	■	I	S	P	■	U	T	I	L	E
S	T	A	G	S	■	N	T	H	■	T	E	S	T	S

48

M	A	R	C	■	A	F	R	O	■	L	U	R	E	D
E	L	I	A	■	L	E	I	S	■	E	N	O	L	A
S	T	A	N	D	B	A	C	K	■	T	A	S	E	R
S	O	L	A	R	■	T	H	A	T	S	W	A	C	K
■	■	■	S	I	B	■	■	R	I	T	A	■	■	■
B	R	A	T	P	A	C	K	■	P	A	R	K	A	S
L	I	S	A	■	B	O	O	M	■	L	E	A	S	H
I	F	I	■	C	A	R	J	A	C	K	■	R	P	I
P	L	A	Z	A	■	P	A	I	R	■	E	M	I	R
S	E	N	I	L	E	■	K	N	A	P	S	A	C	K
■	■	■	P	L	A	N	■	■	M	R	T	■	■	■
S	P	I	C	E	R	A	C	K	■	O	A	T	E	S
A	R	M	O	R	■	T	H	U	M	B	T	A	C	K
S	A	U	D	I	■	C	A	R	D	■	E	I	R	E
H	Y	P	E	D	■	H	I	T	S	■	S	L	U	E

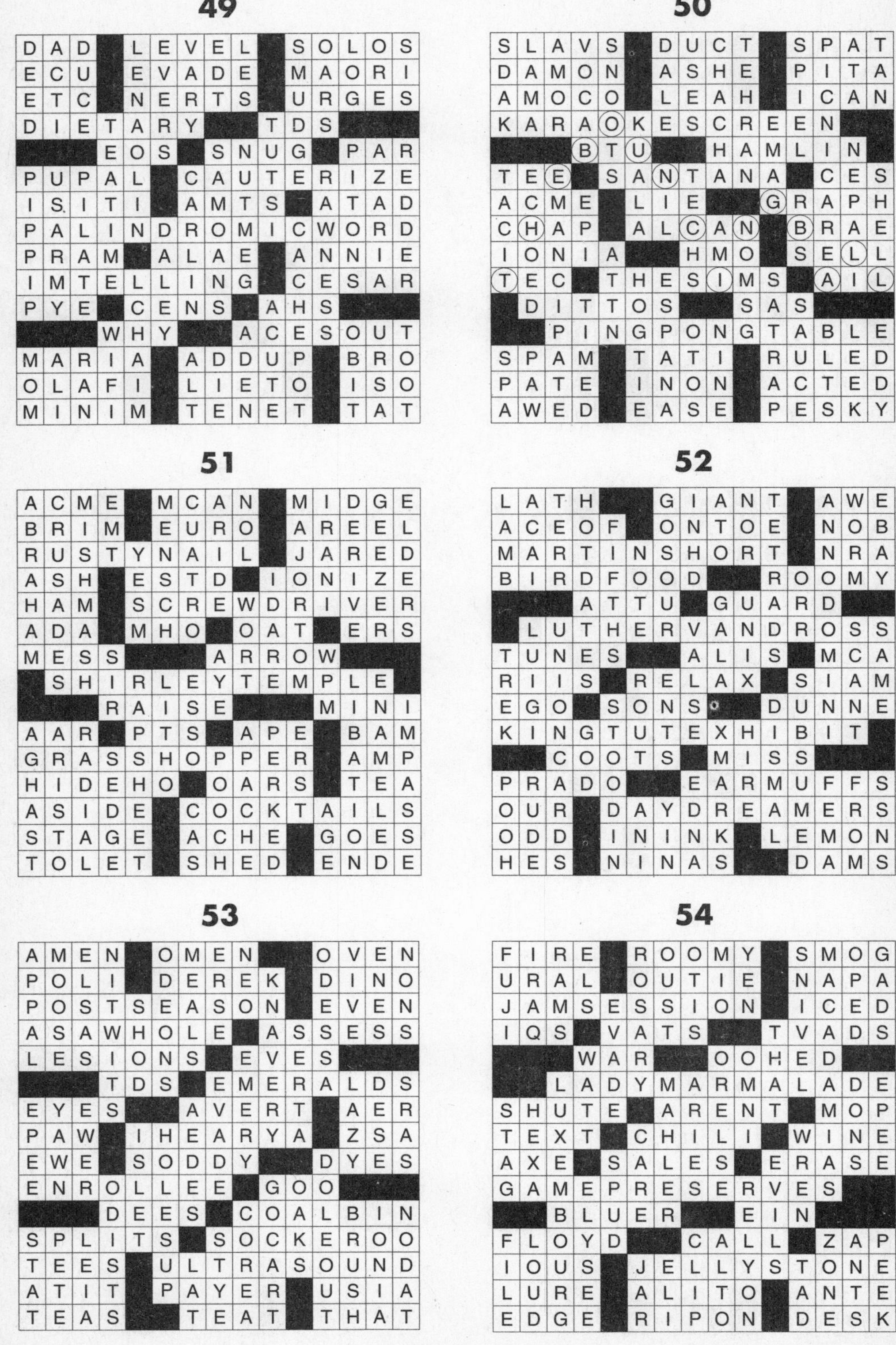

49
DAD LEVEL SOLOS
ECU EVADE MAORI
ETC NERTS URGES
DIETARY TDS
EOS SNUG PAR
PUPAL CAUTERIZE
ISITI AMTS ATAD
PALINDROMICWORD
PRAM ALAE ANNIE
IMTELLING CESAR
PYE CENS AHS
WHY ACESOUT
MARIA ADDUP BRO
OLAFI LIETO ISO
MINIM TENET TAT
50
SLAVS DUCT SPAT
DAMON ASHE PITA
AMOCO LEAH ICAN
KARAOKESCREEN
BTU HAMLIN
TEE SANTANA CES
ACME LIE GRAPH
CHAP ALCAN BRAE
IONIA HMO SELL
TEC THESIMS AIL
DITTOS SAS
PINGPONGTABLE
SPAM TATI RULED
PATE INON ACTED
AWED EASE PESKY
51
ACME MCAN MIDGE
BRIM EURO AREEL
RUSTYNAIL JARED
ASH ESTD IONIZE
HAM SCREWDRIVER
ADA MHO OAT ERS
MESS ARROW
SHIRLEYTEMPLE
RAISE MINI
AAR PTS APE BAM
GRASSHOPPER AMP
HIDEHO OARS TEA
ASIDE COCKTAILS
STAGE ACHE GOES
TOLET SHED ENDE
52
LATH GIANT AWE
ACEOF ONTOE NOB
MARTINSHORT NRA
BIRDFOOD ROOMY
ATTU GUARD
LUTHERVANDROSS
TUNES ALIS MCA
RIIS RELAX SIAM
EGO SONS DUNNE
KINGTUTEXHIBIT
COOTS MISS
PRADO EARMUFFS
OUR DAYDREAMERS
ODD ININK LEMON
HES NINAS DAMS
53
AMEN OMEN OVEN
POLI DEREK DINO
POSTSEASON EVEN
ASAWHOLE ASSESS
LESIONS EVES
TDS EMERALDS
EYES AVERT AER
PAW IHEARYA ZSA
EWE SODDY DYES
ENROLLEE GOO
DEES COALBIN
SPLITS SOCKEROO
TEES ULTRASOUND
ATIT PAYER USIA
TEAS TEAT THAT
54
FIRE ROOMY SMOG
URAL OUTIE NAPA
JAMSESSION ICED
IQS VATS TVADS
WAR OOHED
LADYMARMALADE
SHUTE ARENT MOP
TEXT CHILI WINE
AXE SALES ERASE
GAMEPRESERVES
BLUER EIN
FLOYD CALL ZAP
IOUS JELLYSTONE
LURE ALITO ANTE
EDGE RIPON DESK

55

S	I	C	E	M		T	V	P	G		C	R	A	B
O	C	A	L	A		H	I	R	E		L	A	R	A
S	E	V	I	L	L	E	E	E	L	L	I	V	E	S
A	T	E		L	O	F	T			A	N	I	S	E
			A	R	E	A		S	O	N	G			
W	A	R	S	A	W	N	U	N	W	A	S	R	A	W
A	W	A	I	T			M	I	N	I		A	L	A
G	A	M	S		S	H	I	P	S		A	B	I	T
E	K	E		C	H	I	A			D	R	I	V	E
R	E	N	O	R	O	C	K	C	O	R	O	N	E	R
			R	E	E	K		I	R	O	N			
I	L	I	A	D			S	N	A	P		A	R	A
B	O	S	T	O	N	D	I	D	N	O	T	S	O	B
I	D	L	E		O	O	Z	E		F	A	T	A	L
S	E	E	S		D	E	E	R		F	R	A	M	E

56

S	L	I	N	G		E	D	G	E		C	P	A	S
L	A	N	A	I		N	E	A	R		A	L	I	T
A	U	N	T	J	E	M	I	M	A		L	A	M	A
M	D	S		O	M	I	T			N	I	N	E	R
			B	E	T	T	Y	C	R	O	C	K	E	R
D	E	B	U	S	S	Y		L	I	M	O			
E	T	A	L				H	U	E	S		J	A	I
J	O	L	L	Y	G	R	E	E	N	G	I	A	N	T
A	N	D		O	O	O	H				S	I	T	S
			O	R	G	S		B	E	D	E	L	I	A
C	H	E	F	B	O	Y	A	R	D	E	E			
H	O	F	F	A			P	O	U	F		S	A	S
E	L	L	E		C	A	P	N	C	R	U	N	C	H
W	E	A	R		B	O	L	T		A	N	I	M	E
S	S	T	S		S	K	E	E		Y	I	P	E	S

57

P	S	H	A	W		R	I	C	H		A	T	U	B
I	R	A	Q	I		E	R	M	A		L	O	N	E
M	I	N	U	T	E	M	A	I	D		T	U	B	A
		D	A	C	C	A			J	A	I	L	E	R
A	B	M		H	O	P	E	D	I	A	M	O	N	D
D	U	A	L			S	R	O		R	A	N	T	S
O	L	D	S	O	D		N	O	L	O				
	B	E	D	S	I	D	E	M	A	N	N	E	R	
				A	X	E	S		G	S	E	V	E	N
N	O	M	S	G		E	T	A			W	E	P	T
A	D	I	M	E	A	D	O	Z	E	N		N	O	H
P	O	L	I	S	H			T	N	O	T	E		
L	U	L	L		M	I	X	E	D	M	E	D	I	A
E	L	E	E		E	L	E	C		A	R	U	B	A
S	S	T	S		D	A	D	S		R	I	P	E	R

58

P	E	C	K		C	H	A	P		F	S	T	O	P
O	S	H	A		B	O	R	E		A	T	A	R	I
S	T	A	T		S	T	I	R	F	R	Y	I	N	G
T	U	L	I	P			S	K	I	M		L	A	P
W	A	K	E	F	O	R	E	S	T		D	O	T	E
A	R	I		C	R	O				S	I	R	E	N
R	Y	E	S		A	T	T	A	C	K	S			
		R	O	L	L	O	V	E	R	A	C	D		
			L	I	B	R	A	R	Y		O	A	F	S
G	E	N	I	E				I	P	O		Y	O	W
A	X	E	D		S	T	R	E	T	C	H	B	R	A
U	P	C		A	R	I	A			T	A	R	O	T
G	E	T	U	P	A	N	D	G	O		L	E	N	T
E	R	A	S	E		T	I	N	Y		L	A	C	E
S	T	R	A	D		S	O	U	L		E	K	E	D

59

A	R	A	L			J	U	A	N			D	A	T
R	A	R	E		P	U	R	D	U	E		R	B	I
M	I	S	S	M	A	N	N	E	R	S		A	R	E
	D	E	L	A	N	O			S	T	A	G	E	D
D	E	N	I	E	D		O	R	E	A	S	S	A	Y
E	R	I	E		O	G	R	E	S		H	O	S	E
E	S	C		T	R	A	P	P		K	E	N	T	S
				W	A	S	H	R	A	G				
A	R	E	N	A		P	E	O	N	S		P	O	T
N	E	N	E		S	E	U	S	S		D	E	L	I
I	L	L	W	I	N	D	S		W	E	I	R	D	O
M	A	I	T	R	E			S	E	T	O	U	T	
A	B	S		M	A	S	S	T	R	A	N	S	I	T
T	E	T		A	K	I	T	A	S		N	A	M	E
E	L	S			Y	S	E	R			E	L	E	M

60

B	A	L	M		M	A	C			B	R	A	V	O
A	R	E	A		I	C	E	S		R	E	V	E	L
I	C	A	N	T	S	T	O	P	L	O	V	I	N	G
T	S	H	I	R	T	S		R	A	W		S	T	A
			L	O	A		A	I	M	S				
I	M	W	A	L	K	I	N	G	B	E	H	I	N	D
D	I	E		L	E	N	D			S	U	R	E	R
T	A	B	S		S	K	I	L	L		B	A	S	E
A	M	E	N	D			R	O	U	T		Q	T	S
G	I	R	L	I	M	G	O	N	N	A	M	I	S	S
				S	O	O	N		C	H	E			
B	A	G		O	N	O		C	H	O	O	S	E	S
O	N	L	Y	W	A	N	N	A	B	E	W	I	T	H
O	N	I	O	N		S	I	L	O		E	T	T	U
R	E	B	U	S			B	M	X		D	E	A	N

61

M	A	C	H	U		S	T	U	B		R	O	M	A
A	L	O	O	F		A	O	N	E		O	L	E	G
C	O	M	M	O	N	K	N	O	W	L	E	D	G	E
S	T	A	B		A	S	S		A	E	N	E	A	S
			R	E	V			T	R	O	T			
	A	V	E	R	A	G	E	H	E	I	G	H	T	
C	D	I		A	H	O	L	E		V	E	E	R	S
D	I	E	T		O	B	I	T	S		N	A	I	L
S	E	W	O	N		U	H	A	U	L		R	O	Y
	U	S	U	A	L	S	U	S	P	E	C	T	S	
			L	S	A	T			E	X	O			
O	H	I	O	A	N		E	R	R		L	O	A	D
R	E	G	U	L	A	R	G	A	S	O	L	I	N	E
E	R	O	S		I	B	A	R		F	A	N	T	A
S	O	R	E		S	I	D	E		A	R	K	I	N

62

W	A	D	S		G	A	R	P		A	B	U	S	E
A	L	E	C		O	D	E	R		T	O	N	E	R
R	O	S	A		K	E	N	O		A	N	D	E	S
P	H	I	N	E	A	S	T	B	A	R	N	U	M	
S	A	L		M	R	T		O	R	I	E	L		
		U	N	I	T	E	D	W	E	S	T	A	N	D
			E	T	S		I	L	S			N	A	T
Z	E	S	T	S		A	D	S		T	O	T	E	S
A	R	T			H	Q	S		B	A	R			
G	R	O	S	S	O	U	T	H	U	M	O	R		
		P	A	P	U	A		E	S	P		E	V	A
	H	O	N	O	R	T	H	Y	F	A	T	H	E	R
C	O	V	E	R		I	A	M	A		H	E	R	R
B	L	E	S	T		C	Z	A	R		I	M	N	O
C	E	R	T	S		S	Y	N	E		N	S	E	W

63

D	O	G	G		H	E	M	P		C	H	U	R	L
D	I	E	U		O	D	I	E		H	O	S	E	A
E	L	L	E	W	O	O	D	S		A	G	U	A	S
			S	O	D		S	T	A	R	W	A	R	S
J	E	T	S	K	I		T	O	D		A	L	S	O
U	L	Y	S	S	E	S			I	D	S			
K	A	R	O			T	I	M	E	S	H	A	R	E
E	T	O		S	P	I	N	O	U	T		L	O	T
S	E	L	F	W	O	R	T	H			R	A	S	H
			R	E	P			S	I	B	E	R	I	A
E	P	E	E		U	H	S		M	A	D	M	E	N
M	O	N	E	Y	P	I	T		P	E	W			
B	L	A	Z	E		M	A	G	A	Z	I	N	E	S
E	A	T	E	N		O	V	A	L		N	I	L	E
D	R	E	S	S		M	E	G	A		E	X	I	T

64

G	A	G	A		R	E	F	E	R		D	A	D	A
O	W	E	N		A	L	I	V	E		O	N	I	T
W	A	R	Y		T	A	T	A	F	O	R	N	O	W
N	Y	M	P	H	E	T	S			H	E	A	R	T
			L	O	D	E		Z	O	O	M			
M	A	M	A	C	A	S	S	E	L	L	I	O	T	
A	B	A	C	K			L	A	D	Y		C	O	B
A	B	L	E		J	A	I	L	S		L	U	R	E
M	E	T		T	E	R	M			B	A	L	S	A
	Y	A	Y	A	S	I	S	T	E	R	H	O	O	D
			A	N	T	Z		I	D	E	D			
E	N	E	M	Y			T	E	A	R	I	N	T	O
B	A	B	A	A	U	R	H	U	M		D	O	E	S
O	P	A	H		G	O	A	P	E		A	R	C	H
N	A	N	A		H	E	I	S	S		H	A	H	A

65

M	E	W	S		P	L	A	N		S	C	A	D	S
A	M	A	H		T	O	M	E		H	A	R	E	M
N	A	S	A		A	C	U	T	E	A	N	G	L	E
T	I	T	H	E		A	S	S	A	M		O	I	L
A	L	E		V	O	T	E	A	G	A	I	N	S	T
		A	D	E	L	E		L	E	N	D			
L	O	W	E	N	D		P	E	R		E	S	P	Y
A	V	A	S	T		Q	T	S		C	A	P	E	R
M	A	Y	I		B	U	S		P	U	T	O	N	S
			R	H	E	A		E	G	R	E	T		
L	A	T	E	A	R	R	I	V	A	L		O	B	I
I	C	I		V	E	R	S	E		S	A	F	E	S
R	A	B	B	I	T	E	A	R	S		I	T	L	L
A	L	I	E	N		L	A	S	E		M	E	T	E
S	L	A	N	G		S	C	O	W		S	A	S	S

66

E	T	A	I	L		T	E	S	H		N	A	T	O
A	E	T	N	A		A	N	T	E		A	L	I	T
S	L	E	E	T		P	T	A	S		F	O	N	T
T	E	M	P	O	R	A	R	Y	T	A	T	T	O	O
			T	Y	E			I	O	T	A			
A	L	T		A	N	T	E	N	N	A		S	T	A
R	I	O	T		T	O	V			R	I	T	A	S
T	E	N	N	E	S	S	E	E	T	I	T	A	N	S
S	U	E	T	S			N	T	H		S	T	Y	E
Y	T	D		T	E	E	T	H	E	S		S	A	T
			S	E	T	A			F	T	D			
T	E	E	T	E	R	T	O	T	T	E	R	I	N	G
H	T	T	P		A	S	T	O		P	O	S	I	T
A	T	T	A		D	A	R	T		P	I	N	T	O
T	A	U	T		E	T	A	S		E	T	T	E	S

67

U P S ■ S T A S I S ■ E S P Y
Z O O ■ P I N A T A ■ D A R E
I N F I E L D S I N ■ G L E S
■ D A N C E R ■ ■ D R Y ■ ■ ■
■ ■ ■ S T R E E T P I ■ A N O
A I R E R S ■ G A I T ■ D O R
S C O R E ■ N O L T E ■ D E A
S E C T ■ M E T E S ■ G A L T
E C K ■ B O A R S ■ F O Y L E
S A C ■ A N T I ■ T O S S E D
S P A ■ C E O P E R A S ■ ■ ■
■ ■ ■ S K Y ■ ■ T I M I N G ■
W E N T ■ B A R H O P P I N G
D A D A ■ A R M A D A ■ N A E
S T Y X ■ G I N N E D ■ E W E

68

W E E B ■ T B A R ■ E P S O M
U C L A ■ H O R A ■ M I N G O
S T E A M R O O M ■ I G O R S
S O M B R E R O ■ A L L W E T
■ ■ ■ A S E ■ ■ B R E A ■ ■ ■
S C R A P P A P E R ■ T V A D
T R E ■ E M I R S ■ L I E T O
R O L F E ■ R O T ■ O N R E D
I W I L L ■ W O O E R ■ S I G
P E T A ■ W A F F L E C O N E
■ ■ ■ T H E Y ■ ■ E L O ■ ■ ■
A B A S E D ■ L O V E R B O Y
B U X O M ■ F I V E I R O N S
B R E D A ■ A M I N ■ A D E E
A L L A N ■ D A D S ■ L E A R

69

R O S E ■ Z E L D A ■ E M T S
O R E M ■ E M A I L ■ P E S T
X S Q U A R E D P L U S T W O
Y O U ■ B O N E S ■ N O R A D
■ ■ E M B E D ■ ■ L I N I N G
A N N O Y S ■ G U A C ■ C A Y
L O C O ■ ■ F I S H E R ■ ■ ■
T W E N T Y O V E R F I V E X
■ ■ ■ S H O R E S ■ ■ G A T E
C A M ■ E D E N ■ J E E R E D
A R A B I A ■ ■ M I L L I ■ ■
T R I E S ■ S T O N E ■ A K A
N I N E M I N U S X C U B E D
I V E S ■ R I N S E ■ S L E D
P E R T ■ S P A Y S ■ B E N S

70

C H E N ■ M A R S ■ P S H A W
R O T A ■ A T O P ■ I P A N A
I W A S ■ N C A A ■ X A N A X
M A L L E T O R C L A W ■ ■ ■
E R I ■ Q A S ■ E A R N I N G
A D I E U ■ T A M I ■ ■ N O M
■ ■ ■ R A J ■ P E R I O D I C
W R I G L E Y A N D C O O R S
A E R O S T A R ■ S I N ■ ■ ■
I N A ■ ■ S R T A ■ C A B I N
F E E L B A D ■ R E L ■ A N Y
■ ■ ■ L I M A O R L E N T I L
M Y B A D ■ R B I S ■ O H T O
B E A M E ■ M O V E ■ R E I N
A W M A N ■ S E E S ■ A D O S

71

O B I ■ I M A C S ■ C R A Z E D
P A C ■ C A BFA R E ■ D E N I R O
T H E H O B B I T ■ S L A MBA N G
■ ■ MA I N E ■ E A P ■ A R L E S
O N K P ■ L T R ■ A N I M I S T
A G E N A ■ I S O P O D ■ S T A
F O R E S E E ■ R E F ■ BA T O R
■ ■ ■ S I X D E G R E E S ■ ■ ■
S E T S ■ C I R ■ B E A S T I E
C MD R ■ M O N A C O ■ T H R O W
R A I M E N T ■ R Y E ■ O U S E
A S T E R ■ O V O ■ N E R D ■ ■
W H E N C E ■ JD S A L I N G E R
L E S S E R ■ A S L A N ■ E P I
S S T A R S ■ Y E T I S ■ R A G

72

X M A S ■ R A D A R S ■ P A T
R A I L ■ U N C L E S ■ O R E
A T R O P H Y C A S E ■ R T E
Y A B B E R ■ A M I ■ A T I T
L H A S A ■ E B O N Y F I S H
A A S ■ L A V ■ ■ ■ E L A T E
B R E A ■ C A R D I A C ■ ■ ■
■ I S L A N D E R T R I A L ■
■ ■ ■ C R E E P I N ■ O L E O
A L L O T ■ ■ ■ F O G ■ E A R
O L I V E B A I T ■ M A U N A
L A T E ■ A N D ■ W A N T O N
E M T ■ U N I T P I C K I N G
R A E ■ R E M A I N ■ L A M E
S S R ■ U S A G E S ■ E N E S

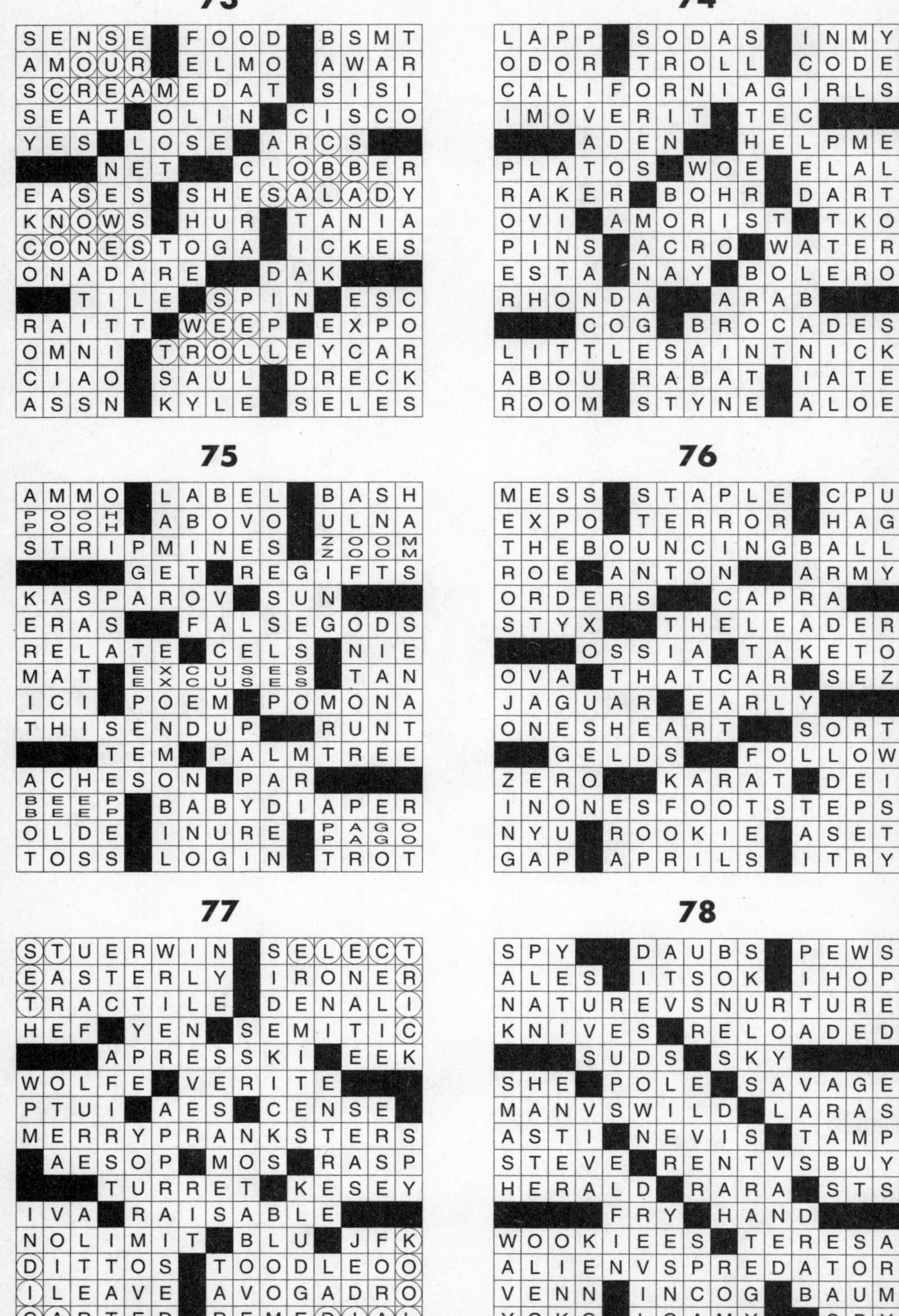
73
SENSE FOOD BSMT
AMOUR ELMO AWAR
SCREAMEDAT SISI
SEAT OLIN CISCO
YES LOSE ARCS
NET CLOBBER
EASES SHESALADY
KNOWS HUR TANIA
CONESTOGA ICKES
ONADARE DAK
TILE SPIN ESC
RAITT WEEP EXPO
OMNI TROLLEYCAR
CIAO SAUL DRECK
ASSN KYLE SELES
74
LAPP SODAS INMY
ODOR TROLL CODE
CALIFORNIAGIRLS
IMOVERIT TEC
ADEN HELPME
PLATOS WOE ELAL
RAKER BOHR DART
OVI AMORIST TKO
PINS ACRO WATER
ESTA NAY BOLERO
RHONDA ARAB
COG BROCADES
LITTLESAINTNICK
ABOU RABAT IATE
ROOM STYNE ALOE
75
AMMO LABEL BASH
POOH POOH ABOVO ULNA
STRIPMINES ZOOM ZOOM
GET REGIFTS
KASPAROV SUN
ERAS FALSEGODS
RELATE CELS NIE
MAT EXCUSES EXCUSES TAN
ICI POEM POMONA
THISENDUP RUNT
TEM PALMTREE
ACHESON PAR
BEEP BEEP BABYDIAPER
OLDE INURE PAGO PAGO
TOSS LOGIN TROT
76
MESS STAPLE CPU
EXPO TERROR HAG
THEBOUNCINGBALL
ROE ANTON ARMY
ORDERS CAPRA
STYX THELEADER
OSSIA TAKETO
OVA THATCAR SEZ
JAGUAR EARLY
ONESHEART SORT
GELDS FOLLOW
ZERO KARAT DEI
INONESFOOTSTEPS
NYU ROOKIE ASET
GAP APRILS ITRY
77
STUERWIN SELECT
EASTERLY IRONER
TRACTILE DENALI
HEF YEN SEMITIC
APRESSKI EEK
WOLFE VERITE
PTUI AES CENSE
MERRYPRANKSTERS
AESOP MOS RASP
TURRET KESEY
IVA RAISABLE
NOLIMIT BLU JFK
DITTOS TOODLEOO
ILEAVE AVOGADRO
CARTED REMEDIAL
78
SPY DAUBS PEWS
ALES ITSOK IHOP
NATUREVSNURTURE
KNIVES RELOADED
SUDS SKY
SHE POLE SAVAGE
MANVSWILD LARAS
ASTI NEVIS TAMP
STEVE RENTVSBUY
HERALD RARA STS
FRY HAND
WOOKIEES TERESA
ALIENVSPREDATOR
VENN INCOG BAUM
YOKO LOAMY SPY

79

(1)	A	R	R	E	S	T		A	N	I	M	A	L	(3)
B	R	E	A	D	T	H		R	I	B	E	Y	E	S
R	E	S	T	O	R	E		C	H	I	A	N	T	I
O	C	T		M	I	O		H	I	D		R	S	T
K	I	S	S		A	N	S	E	L		W	A	L	T
E	B	O	A	T		I	E	R		A	R	N	I	E
N	O	N	U	N	I	O	N		A	B	I	D	E	R
			C	O	R	N	E	R	L	O	T			
C	O	S	E	T	S		C	U	L	D	E	S	A	C
L	U	C	R	E		C	A	N		E	I	E	I	O
E	T	E	S		B	A	S	A	L		N	E	R	F
A	L	P		C	E	N		W	I	S		I	M	F
N	O	T	T	H	A	T		A	L	U	M	N	A	E
S	O	R	I	A	N	O		Y	A	C	H	T	I	E
(2)	K	E	E	P	E	R		S	C	H	O	O	L	(4)

80

Z	E	B	U		A	R	Y	A	N	S		M	C	A
I	R	A	N		R	E	E	D	I	T		I	A	N
G	A	R	D	E	N	G	R	O	V	E		D	V	D
			E	L	O	I			E	R	A	S	E	R
P	U	R	R	S		O	C	E	A	N	S	I	D	E
E	M	U	S		I	N	O	N			U	Z	I	S
U	P	B	E	A	T		R	U	M	P		E	N	S
		B	A	K	E	R	S	F	I	E	L	D		
O	P	E		A	M	I	E		S	A	U	C	E	S
F	I	R	S			C	T	R	S		N	A	S	H
S	A	N	T	A	R	O	S	A		T	E	R	S	E
O	N	E	D	G	E			M	A	R	T			
R	I	C		I	N	N	E	R	C	I	T	I	E	S
T	S	K		L	I	E	S	O	N		E	T	T	A
S	T	S		E	N	C	O	D	E		S	T	A	X

81

S	T	A	R	F	R	U	I	T		W	E	B	B	S
E	S	P	E	R	A	N	T	O		A	L	E	U	T
D	A	I	L	Y	M	A	I	L		M	I	N	D	Y
E	R	N	S		P	B	S			P	A	S	S	
R	S	T		D	E	L	I	C	O	U	N	T	E	R
			T	I	D	E		A	R	M		E	L	M
		F	A	A			B	R	A		R	I	I	S
	D	I	L	L	Y	D	A	L	L	Y	I	N	G	
T	Y	N	E		E	A	R			A	B	S		
A	N	A		L	L	D		A	P	R	S			
D	O	L	L	Y	P	A	R	T	O	N		S	N	L
	M	E	A	T			A	T	L		B	A	I	O
F	I	X	I	T		D	U	L	Y	N	O	T	E	D
I	T	A	L	O		I	C	E	P	A	L	A	C	E
R	E	M	A	N		T	H	E	S	T	O	N	E	S

82

P	E	A	C	E		B	O	I	S		E	B	A	Y
A	T	L	A	S		O	N	C	E		M	I	N	E
T	H	E	T	A		S	T	E	T		A	C	O	W
E	A	R	C	U	T	S	O	L	U	T	I	O	N	
	N	T	H		D	E	P		P	O	L	A		
			A	S	S	D	I	S	M	I	S	S	E	D
A	M	O	L	E			C	P	A			T	Z	E
D	U	L	L	A	R	D		A	N	T	F	A	R	M
I	N	D			E	R	R			K	O	L	A	S
A	I	M	S	A	D	J	U	S	T	O	R			
		A	A	N	D		S	E	N		E	D	O	
	A	S	H	O	F	T	H	E	T	I	T	A	N	S
A	C	T	A		O	R	D	S		N	O	F	E	E
B	R	E	R		X	I	I	I		C	L	O	U	T
S	E	R	A		X	M	E	N		A	D	E	P	T

83

P	O	P	U	P		P	I	S	A		O	N	E	L
I	R	E	N	E		R	O	A	R		D	I	R	E
G	R	A	D	E	B	O	N	U	S		D	C	I	V
				R	A	F		S	E	M		E	T	E
C	U	P	C	A	K	E		A	N	T	I	Q	U	E
S	T	O	O	G	E	S		G	I	N	S	U		
P	E	S	T	E	R	S		E	C	S	T	A	S	Y
A	R	I										L	I	E
N	O	T	E	P	A	D		T	H	E	S	I	M	S
		I	R	A	T	E		R	O	P	E	T	O	W
S	A	V	A	N	T	S		A	N	O	D	Y	N	E
N	A	E		T	I	P		S	E	N				
A	R	E	A		M	A	T	H	S	Y	M	B	O	L
F	O	N	D		E	I	R	E		M	A	O	R	I
U	N	D	O		S	R	A	S		S	T	A	B	S

84

A	S	H		V	I	S	T	A	S		E	L	A	N
C	E	O		A	T	T	I	L	A		N	A	L	A
C	AA	N		R	E	P	E	A	L		T	R	A	P
R	I	D	D	E	R		A	N	AA	L	I	C	I	A
A	R	O	U	S	A	L		I	M	E	T			
			S	E	T	U	P	S		O	L	D	I	E
O	B	I	T		I	L	A		S	N	E	E	Z	Y
S	AA	B		D	O	U	B	L	E	A		S	AA	R
H	E	I	D	E	N		L	E	G		P	I	K	E
A	D	D	E	R		H	O	A	R	S	E			
			N	E	M	O		N	E	O	N	A	T	E
A	F	R	I	K	AA	N	S		G	U	N	N	E	R
Q	U	I	Z		L	I	A	N	A	S		N	AA	N
U	R	G	E		O	N	L	A	T	E		I	C	I
A	L	A	N		X	G	A	M	E	S		E	T	E

85

Y	A	W		I	N	N	A	T	E		B	A	S	K
A	L	I		P	E	O	R	I	A		A	N	T	I
D	I	D	Y	O	U	H	E	A	R	A	B	O	U	T
A	S	T	I		M	O	A		P	R	Y	N	N	E
	T	H	E	L	A	W	S	U	I	T	S			
			L	A	N			R	E	S	I	D	U	E
M	A	N	D	M		A	T	I	C		T	E	S	T
A	G	O		B	E	T	W	E	E	N		M	E	T
R	U	T	H		V	I	A	L		E	R	O	D	E
S	E	V	E	N	A	M			I	R	A			
			H	A	N	E	S	A	N	D	B	V	D	
M	A	S	H	I	E		T	O	D		B	A	R	E
B	R	I	E	F	S	W	E	R	E	F	I	L	E	D
A	M	A	H		C	A	N	T	B	E		E	G	G
S	Y	M	S		E	R	S	A	T	Z		T	S	E

86

M	A	M	A		S	T	A	B		R	A	F	T	S
O	P	A	L		T	O	R	A		A	L	L	A	H
S	P	L	I	T	A	G	U	T		G	L	A	R	Y
H	A	W		A	R	A	B	I	C		O	R	T	S
I	R	A		B	R	E	A	K	A	S	W	E	A	T
N	E	R	D						I	N	S	U	R	E
G	L	E	E	M		P	L	A	N	A		P	E	R
			C	U	T	A	C	H	E	C	K			
I	C	E		Z	E	L	D	A		K	E	A	T	S
P	O	L	E	A	X						G	L	E	E
C	R	A	C	K	A	S	M	I	L	E		A	L	P
R	O	T	H		S	O	O	N	E	R		M	A	T
E	L	I	O	T		B	U	S	T	A	M	O	V	E
S	L	O	E	S		A	S	T	I		E	D	I	T
S	A	N	D	P		D	E	R	N		R	E	V	S

87

R	A	C	E	D		F	A	T	H	O	M		G	D	P
A	P	A	C	E		O	N	A	U	T	O		L	E	A
D	O	T	H	E	B	R	I	G	H	T	T	H	I	N	G
I	S	A	O		I	B	M				I	O	N	I	A
O	T	C			B	E	A	S	T	O	F	E	D	E	N
A	L	O	F	T		S	L	U	R	P		D	A	D	S
D	E	M	O	N	S			L	E	E	K				
		B	O	U	T	O	F	A	F	R	I	C	A		
				T	O	I	L			A	D	L	I	B	S
C	I	T	Y		O	L	A	F	I		D	E	R	M	A
H	O	W	A	R	D	S	B	E	N	D			P	O	T
A	D	A	N	O				S	C	I		D	L	V	I
S	I	N	G	I	N	I	N	T	H	E	B	R	A	I	N
E	N	G		D	E	C	R	E	E		R	A	N	E	E
R	E	Y		S	W	E	A	R	S		A	T	E	S	T

88

U	R	I		A	B	L	E		A	T	H	E	N	A
S	E	C		S	A	I	L		M	A	U	L	E	D
U	P	I	N	A	R	M	S		E	L	B	O	W	S
R	E	C	A	P		B	I	B	L	E				
P	A	L	S			S	E	E	I	N	G	R	E	D
S	T	E	A	M	S			R	E	T	A	I	N	S
				C	A	B	A	L			P	A	U	L
	B	E	S	I	D	E	H	I	M	S	E	L	F	
P	E	T	E			R	A	N	U	P				
H	I	T	L	I	S	T			G	A	S	B	A	G
I	N	A	L	A	T	H	E	R			P	I	L	L
				M	E	A	D	E		V	I	S	T	A
D	R	O	W	S	E		I	N	C	E	N	S	E	D
U	N	R	E	A	D		F	E	A	T		A	R	E
H	A	R	E	M	S		Y	E	W	S		U	S	S

89

S	P	A	S			B	B	C			BW	N	E	R
L	A	M	P	BW		A	R	A	B		B	E	D	E
A	L	O	R	S		B	A	N	A	N	A	O	I	L
B	E	S	E	A	T	E	D		C	A	R	N	E	Y
			A	L	A	S		S	K	I	T			
BW	A	D	D	E	R		V	E	I	L		A	L	L
W	I	R	E	S		T	E	E	N	S		L	E	I
A	M	O	R		BW	A	N	D	BW		F	O	A	L
S	E	W		S	M	I	T	S		V	I	N	N	Y
H	E	N		P	A	L	S		K	A	R	E	N	BW
			J	U	T	S		D	I	N	E			
A	S	L	A	N	T		B	E	A	N	T	R	E	E
C	L	O	C	K	E	D	I	N		A	R	O	M	A
H	U	N	K		R	A	T	S		BW	A	N	T	S
E	G	G	BW			B	E	E			P	A	S	T

90

A	G	A	P	E		A	D	Z	E		A	G	A	S
S	O	L	O	S		D	R	E	S	S	R	A	C	K
S	T	O	P	P	E	D	O	N	A	P	E	N	N	Y
O	T	O			X	I	S			A	W	G	E	E
C	A	P	T	A	I	N	S	D	I	M	E	S		
			A	F	T			A	M	S		I	C	I
H	O	O	H	A		V	E	R	A		E	G	A	D
I	N	C	O	R	R	E	C	T	C	H	A	N	G	E
L	U	C	E		E	R	O	S		A	T	S	E	A
L	S	U		O	A	S			S	H	E			
		P	U	M	P	E	R	Q	U	A	R	T	E	R
A	M	A	N	A			O	A	F			I	L	E
P	I	N	C	H	I	N	G	N	I	C	K	E	L	S
A	C	C	L	A	I	M	E	D		E	E	R	I	E
R	A	Y	E		N	I	T	A		O	N	S	E	T

91

PALEASA(3) INBIG
EATINGOUT WHENI
ADAPTEDTO OLAFV
USDA WAN NAE
RUR TNT SITU
(1)WRITERS FREEUP
OOO ADEUX ATBAT
FOG HAUNTED ATH
ADELA PARED BEE
CYRANO MARLEYS(4)
HAEC AHI YET
ALB UFO RAUL
NLERS LHASAAPSO
CERTS YESINDEED
ENTER (2)BUSTERS

(1) GHOST (2) GHOST (3) GHOST (4) GHOST

92

CARL SEMI RASPY
OBOE TRAC ICHAT
TODIVORCE GUARD
SUE OOOH CARR
TOPULLUPSTAKES
ASS APO SLO
ASAP SARAN KEW
SPLITINFINITIVE
SIL ROUTS ONED
ERI INF ALF
TOGOFIFTYFIFTY
AREA HAGS AID
ATTIC TOSHATTER
SHOOT ASIA HALE
LORNA BERN USDA

93

LAVA ABODE SMOG
ALEG SAVOR QEII
SIRE CLARA URNS
HAYNEEDLESTACK
DON MEAT
CANDYKIDSTORE
ICE SEEN KENYA
MALL DWEEB REAR
ASLOW LEES UNS
CHINABULLSHOP
GRAS TEN
HANDHELLBASKET
JOKE ADIEU ANTE
EPIC MUTED LENA
MINK APERS EXAM

94

GMAN MSRP SOHIO
ROLO OTOE OPART
OPENTOALL FIRST
WINNINGFOOTED
DECAFS SDS HOO
ISO FINNISHTANK
MTNS GIE OATES
INNKEEPER
GUANO DNA AIMS
SINNINGSONG TAL
TEA SUE TOASTY
GUINNESSAGAIN
TERRE INAUDIBLE
CRAGS ANTI LEDS
UNMET LEST ETAS

95

INUIT ISTO PSIS
KINDA NEIN LENA
EXCEL WEAKLINKS
LAKEINSPANISH
CIO EST WYLIE
ACTORCHANEY END
LAHR DOSED
FLEESFROMPRISON
STRAP AHME
TSP PASTURELAND
ALONE SIX GIS
CAPITALLETTER
OYSTERBED ABUTS
MEIR GAIT NAGAT
ARNO ORSO TYSON

96

BOTH FIT NEVADA
INNOTIME UNISEX
NETPROFS COSINE
OER TEL TATS
TENNESSEETANS
PAL TLC LIE
ABET LAM ASTRO
NOVISORSALLOWED
ERECT NCO TOGO
AIG TWP AIR
LEARNERSPERMS
BARB JOE IRA
EUROPE CUTITOUT
ERODES UNCLELEO
PARENT RAH RAYS

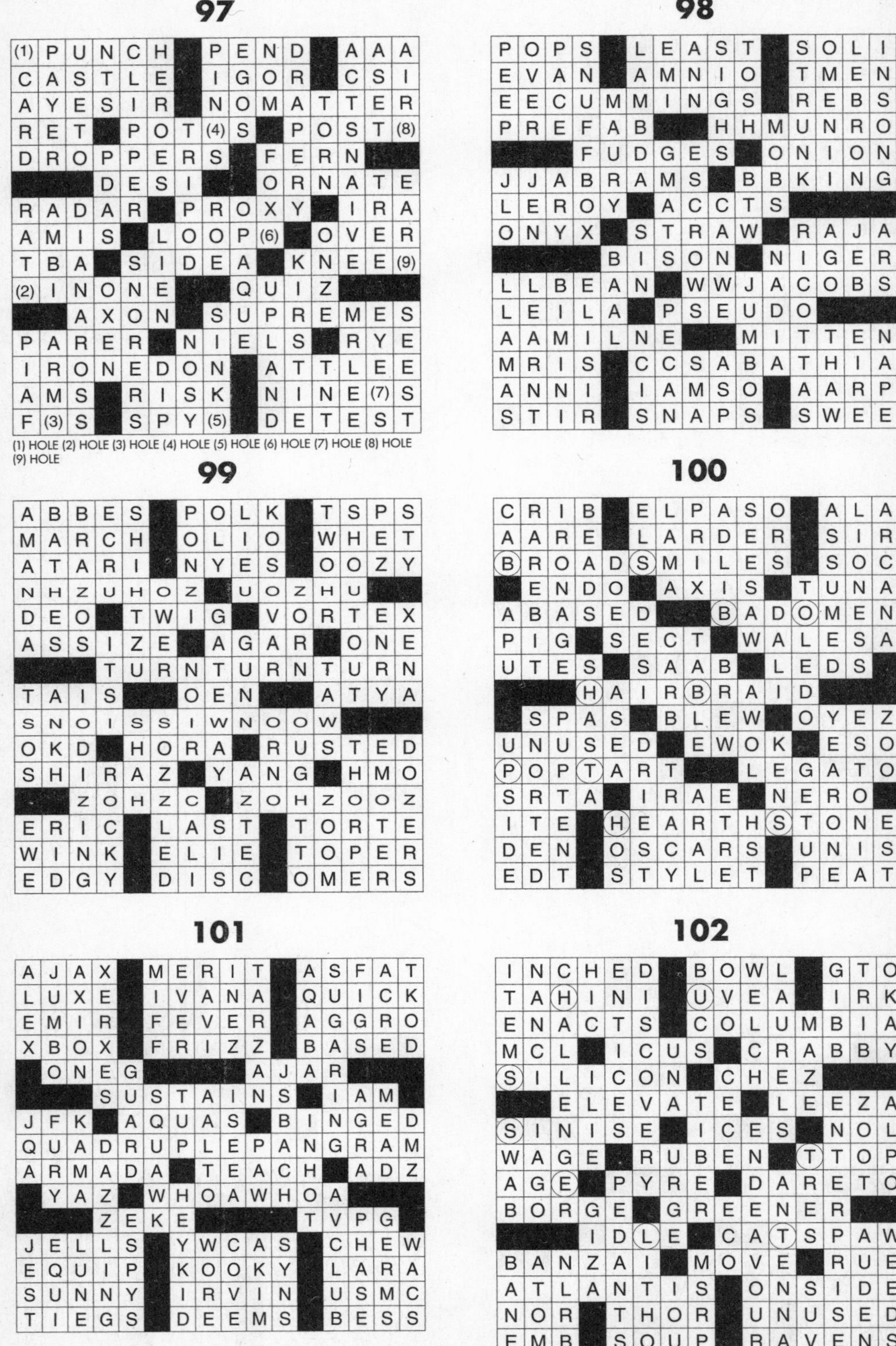
97
(1) PUNCH PEND AAA
CASTLE IGOR CSI
AYESIR NOMATTER
RET POT (4) S POST (8)
DROPPERS FERN
DESI ORNATE
RADAR PROXY IRA
AMIS LOOP (6) OVER
TBA SIDEA KNEE (9)
(2) INONE QUIZ
AXON SUPREMES
PARER NIELS RYE
IRONEDON ATTLEE
AMS RISK NINE (7) S
F (3) S SPY (5) DETEST
(1) HOLE (2) HOLE (3) HOLE (4) HOLE (5) HOLE (6) HOLE (7) HOLE (8) HOLE (9) HOLE
98
POPS LEAST SOLI
EVAN AMNIO TMEN
EECUMMINGS REBS
PREFAB HHMUNRO
FUDGES ONION
JJABRAMS BBKING
LEROY ACCTS
ONYX STRAW RAJA
BISON NIGER
LLBEAN WWJACOBS
LEILA PSEUDO
AAMILNE MITTEN
MRIS CCSABATHIA
ANNI IAMSO AARP
STIR SNAPS SWEE
99
ABBES POLK TSPS
MARCH OLIO WHET
ATARI NYES OOZY
NHZUHOZ UOZHU
DEO TWIG VORTEX
ASSIZE AGAR ONE
TURNTURNTURNTURN
TAIS OEN ATYA
SNOISSIWNOOW
OKD HORA RUSTED
SHIRAZ YANG HMO
ZOHZC ZOHZOOZ
ERIC LAST TORTE
WINK ELIE TOPER
EDGY DISC OMERS
100
CRIB ELPASO ALA
AARE LARDER SIR
BROADSMILES SOC
ENDO AXIS TUNA
ABASED BADOMEN
PIG SECT WALESA
UTES SAAB LEDS
HAIRBRAID
SPAS BLEW OYEZ
UNUSED EWOK ESO
POPTART LEGATO
SRTA IRAE NERO
ITE HEARTHSTONE
DEN OSCARS UNIS
EDT STYLET PEAT
101
AJAX MERIT ASFAT
LUXE IVANA QUICK
EMIR FEVER AGGRO
XBOX FRIZZ BASED
ONEG AJAR
SUSTAINS IAM
JFK AQUAS BINGED
QUADRUPLEPANGRAM
ARMADA TEACH ADZ
YAZ WHOAWHOA
ZEKE TVPG
JELLS YWCAS CHEW
EQUIP KOOKY LARA
SUNNY IRVIN USMC
TIEGS DEEMS BESS
102
INCHED BOWL GTO
TAHINI UVEA IRK
ENACTS COLUMBIA
MCL ICUS CRABBY
SILICON CHEZ
ELEVATE LEEZA
SINISE ICES NOL
WAGE RUBEN TTOP
AGE PYRE DARETO
BORGE GREENER
IDLE CATSPAW
BANZAI MOVE RUE
ATLANTIS ONSIDE
NOR THOR UNUSED
EMB SOUP RAVENS

103

D	I	O		S	W	I	T		G	O	T	O	I	T
A	N	G	E	L	I	N	A		E	T	H	Y	N	E
M	A	L	C	O	L	M	X		T	O	R	E	A	T
A	N	I	T		L	A	C	S			O	Z	M	A
G	E	N	O	A		T	O	N	A	L		O	O	N
E	R	G		V	E	E		O	N	L	Y	Y	O	U
			K	E	R		S	U	C	C	E	E	D	S
		G	E	N	E	R	A	T	I	O	N	Z		
F	E	R	G	U	S	O	N		E	O	S			
T	E	A	S	E	T	S		S	N	L		S	S	R
M	L	S		Q	U	A	I	L		J	E	T	T	A
E	S	P	O			S	T	I	R		L	R	O	N
A	K	I	M	B	O		S	P	E	C	I	A	L	K
D	I	N	N	E	R		M	U	S	C	A	T	E	L
E	N	G	I	N	E		E	P	P	S		O	N	E

104

W	O	O	D	Y		B	E	A		M	A	T	C	H
A	S	I	R	E	C	A	L	L		S	T	O	L	A
R	A	D	I	O	D	A	Y	S		R	O	M	A	S
				M	I	S	S	T	E	P		C	S	T
A	L	I	C	E			I	O	N		B	A	S	E
R	A	M	O	N		M	A	N	H	A	T	T	A	N
A	M	A	H		K	A	N		A	W	W			
B	A	N	A	N	A	S		S	L	E	E	P	E	R
			B	A	T		A	N	O		L	A	L	A
A	N	N	I	E	H	A	L	L		A	V	I	O	N
A	O	U	T		I	D	I			Z	E	L	I	G
A	N	C		P	E	R	G	O	L	A				
M	O	L	T	O		I	N	T	E	R	I	O	R	S
A	N	E	A	R		F	E	B	R	I	L	I	T	Y
P	O	I	N	T		T	D	S		A	L	L	E	N

105

F	A	R	E	A	S	T		S	I	T	U	A	T	E
A	V	I	A	T	O	R		O	N	E	S	P	O	T
D	E	G	R	A	D	E		B	E	N	E	A	T	H
E	R	A		L	O	S	E	S			U	T	E	S
			A	L	I	S	T		S	T	P			
S	E	W	S				D	O	P	E		A	B	C
P	R	O	N	O	U	N		N	U	M	E	R	A	L
E	N	T	E	N	T	E		E	M	P	A	T	H	Y
W	E	A	R	O	U	T		R	E	T	R	E	A	D
S	S	N		U	R	S	A				P	L	I	E
			E	R	N		S	N	A	G	S			
S	L	A	W			S	A	Y	S	O		B	A	H
L	I	B	E	R	A	L		A	T	L	A	R	G	E
A	V	E	R	A	G	E		S	I	G	N	I	F	Y
G	E	T	S	M	A	D		A	R	I	S	T	A	S

106

J	A	D	E		O	S	H	A		W	A	S	N	T
A	P	O	P		R	A	T	S		A	L	T	A	R
Y	P	S	I	L	A	N	T	I		R	E	A	T	A
			C	A	L	Y	P	S	O	M	U	S	I	C
A	C	T		I	L	O			V	O	T	I	V	E
G	O	A	W	R	Y		S	L	A	V		S	E	R
A	M	M	O			C	O	O	L	I	O			
	A	P	O	C	A	L	Y	P	S	E	N	O	W	
			F	A	M	O	U	S			E	N	I	D
A	T	V		L	U	T	Z		K	P	D	U	T	Y
S	H	A	W	L	S			L	A	I		S	H	E
S	E	C	R	E	T	A	G	E	N	T	S			
U	S	A	I	R		G	Y	P	S	Y	M	O	T	H
C	E	N	T	I		A	R	E	A		O	W	I	E
H	A	T	E	D		R	O	W	S		G	E	N	X

107

P	L	O	D		S	C	A	M	S		P	S	A	T
E	L	H	I		H	O	V	E	L		O	C	T	O
R	A	Y	E		E	M	I	L	E		T	R	O	Y
C	N	O	T	E		B	L	O	W	O	P	E	N	
H	O	U	S	E	B	O	A	T		L	I	E		
			O	L	A	V		T	A	L	E	N	T	S
B	A	W	D		N	E	W		N	A	S	D	A	Q
O	S	H	A		D	R	A	M	A	S		O	S	U
M	C	I		M	A	S	C	O	T		S	O	S	A
B	I	T	T	E	N		O	R	O		P	R	O	D
S	I	E	R	R	A	S		A	L	I	I			
		T	I	L		H	O	L	Y	C	R	O	S	S
	F	R	E	E	B	I	R	D		H	I	M	O	M
Y	E	A	S		A	N	G	U	S		T	A	R	O
A	M	S	O		S	T	A	T	E		O	N	E	K
Z	A	H	N		S	O	N	Y	A		F	I	R	E

108

K	I	T	H		F	L	E	X		A	T	B	A	Y
A	B	R	A		L	A	V	E		S	H	U	T	E
N	O	I	R		O	D	I	N		S	E	R	T	A
J	O	C	K	F	U	L	L	O	N	U	T	S		
I	K	E		O	N	E	S		A	M	A	T	O	L
			T	L	C			W	I	E		O	R	A
J	E	E	R	L	E	A	D	E	R		S	P	I	T
A	L	L	E	Y		Q	U	E		S	C	E	N	T
M	I	T	E		J	U	M	P	C	H	A	N	G	E
U	S	O		M	I	A			H	A	M			
P	E	N	P	A	L		G	L	A	D		S	T	P
		J	E	S	T	P	R	O	T	E	C	T	O	R
B	R	O	N	C		O	O	R	T		A	L	P	O
E	T	H	N	O		P	U	C	E		P	E	A	L
T	E	N	E	T		S	T	A	R		O	O	Z	E

109

110

FAVOR PALM OTIS
READE ASIA OHNO
OILED CHER LEFT
GOODTIME SNAFU
SUR ANA ABELARD
FINN LARAMIE
SMALLS CERF IAT
CADY ONE ALTE
ACA BTEN SPRYER
LAYDOWN SURF
ARSENIO PLO FRO
TWEEN YOURHEAD
SHOR KHAN AERIE
PURE LUNG TEAMO
ARKS EDGY ALLIN

111

112

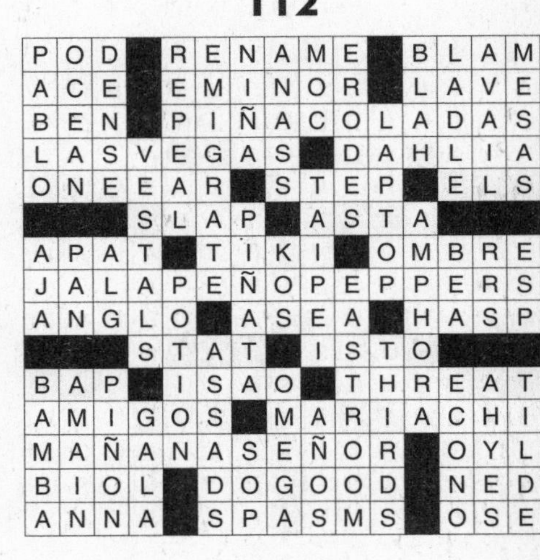

113

ASH SLO PIANO
CHAR TERM EMBER
OUSE ATCO CALEB
PLAN TMAN AGER
STEVIE ORNO
WIN ETAS TER
JAPES AVOW ARNO
OPERA TIN GROOM
KIAS OTAY AMPLE
EAR THAN GEL
FISC OOLONG
FORT HERE CORD
NONET EMMA KWAI
NOTRE SPAS SING
ELVER TNT NTS

114

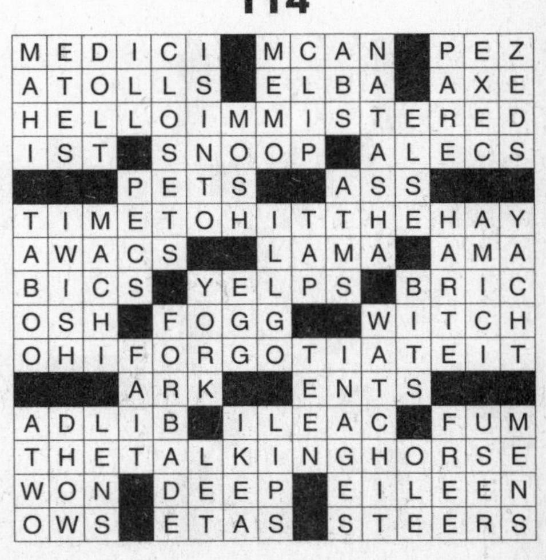

115

W	A	W	A		J	I	N	X		B	R	E	A	K
I	M	A	Y		A	C	E	R		A	A	N	D	E
P	E	R	C	A	P	I	T	A	I	N	C	O	M	E
E	X	H	A	L	E		W	Y	O		K	T	E	L
		A	R	A		P	O	E	T		S	E	N	S
A	M	M	A	N	J	O	R	D	A	N				
H	A	M	M		A	R	K			M	I	S	D	O
E	Y	E	B	A	N	K		B	R	I	T	P	O	P
M	O	R	A	L			I	O	U		S	L	U	E
				P	E	R	C	E	N	T	S	I	G	N
T	O	R	I		L	E	E	R		H	I	T		
A	C	A	T		E	L	F		S	A	M	P	L	E
M	A	R	S	H	M	A	L	L	O	W	P	E	E	P
E	L	I	O	T		Y	O	Y	O		L	A	N	E
R	A	N	K	S		S	E	E	N		E	S	T	E

116

(1)	B	A	K	E	D		B	U	S		O	N	E	(5)
T	E	X	A	C	O		A	N	A		W	I	N	N
R	A	I	N	O	N		N	O	W		E	C	C	E
U	T	A			E	R	G		E	R	R	O	L	L
T	O	L	U	E	N	E		R	D	A		L	O	S
H	U	L	K	S		S	T	O	I	C		E	S	O
	T	Y	R	E		T	O	A	N	Y		T	E	N
					(3)	A	N	D	(4)					
B	R	A		S	H	I	E	S		N	Y	P	D	
E	A	R		H	E	N	R	I		P	A	R	E	O
T	V	A		O	A	S		D	A	R	K	E	S	T
T	E	L	L	E	R		B	E	D			N	E	H
E	L	S	A		T	A	O		O	H	S	U	R	E
R	E	E	D		E	L	F		L	A	U	P	E	R
(2)	D	A	Y		D	E	F		F	I	R	S	T	(6)

(1) HALF (2) HALF (3) HALF (4) HALF (5) HALF (6) HALF

117

G	U	F	F		A	G	H	A		F	E	M	M	E
I	S	E	E		F	R	O	N	T	R	O	O	M	S
M	U	R	D	E	R	O	N	T	H	E	N	I	L	E
M	A	M	I	E			E	L	I	E				
E	L	I	N	N	O	R	D	E	G	R	E	N		
			T	Y	R	O		R	H	E	N	I	S	H
O	L	E	O		C	U	E			I	G	O	T	O
N	U	N		T	A	X	L	I	E	N		B	I	O
E	N	D	O	W			M	T	A		S	E	R	F
S	K	I	D	O	O	S		E	T	A	T			
		N	E	I	L	A	R	M	S	T	R	O	N	G
				R	I	F	E			M	O	B	I	L
G	O	E	S	O	V	E	R	T	H	E	L	I	N	E
B	A	N	A	N	A	C	A	K	E		L	E	E	S
S	T	A	Y	S		O	N	O	R		S	S	R	S

118

S	H	A	L	T		M	A	S	T		A	B	B	Y
L	I	M	O	S		A	R	E	A		I	L	I	A
A	M	A	Z	E		G	M	A	I	L	R	O	O	M
N	O	N	E		A	N	O			I	D	O	L	S
G	M	A	N	O	V	E	R	B	O	A	R	D		
			G	N	A	T		U	N	R	O	L	L	S
A	G	R	E	E			O	S	E		P	U	P	A
L	E	A		G	E	E	W	H	I	Z		S	G	T
D	R	I	B		M	S	N			A	C	T	A	S
A	M	N	E	S	I	A		A	R	C	H			
		G	S	T	R	I	N	G	T	H	E	O	R	Y
O	V	A	T	E			A	L	E		E	L	E	E
G	S	U	I	T	C	A	S	E		D	R	I	L	L
R	I	G	A		F	R	A	T		R	I	V	A	L
E	X	E	L		O	I	L	S		J	O	E	Y	S

119

A	G	O	R	A		D	M	V		V	O	D	K	A
B	O	S	O	N		I	I	I		O	P	A	R	T
C	E	S	T	A		A	S	S		G	E	T	A	T
	S	O	C	I	A	L	S	E	C	U	R	I	T	Y
C	O	B		S	H	U	I		H	E	A	V	E	S
O	V	U	M		A	P	N	E	A		S	E	R	
D	E	C	A	F			G	A	F	F	E			
	R	O	Y	A	L	A	I	R	F	O	R	C	E	
			O	R	I	O	N			G	I	A	N	T
	O	R	C		P	L	A	N	A		A	R	G	O
T	H	E	L	I	P		C	O	D	A		L	I	E
A	D	M	I	N	I	S	T	R	A	T	I	O	N	
S	E	A	N	S		A	I	M		A	T	R	E	E
S	A	D	I	E		K	O	A		R	E	F	E	R
E	R	E	C	T		S	N	L		I	N	F	R	A

120

N	E	A	R		A	C	L	U		B	E	N	C	H
A	B	R	A		C	H	I	N		O	M	A	H	A
T	O	R	T		C	A	N	I		R	I	P	E	N
C	L	O	S	E	E	N	C	O	U	N	T	E	R	S
H	A	W		T	N	T		N	N	E				
			B	U	T	S	E	R	I	O	U	S	L	Y
S	A	L	A	D	S		L	E	S		S	O	U	S
E	R	A	S	E		P	E	P		D	I	N	G	E
A	L	P	S		F	A	N		L	O	N	G	E	R
N	O	S	O	L	I	C	I	T	I	N	G			
				A	L	I		A	A	H		D	E	B
C	I	G	A	R	A	F	I	C	I	O	N	A	D	O
H	O	A	R	Y		I	N	K	S		O	L	I	N
A	N	T	O	N		S	L	O	E		R	A	T	E
D	E	T	O	X		T	A	N	S		M	I	S	S

121

M	U	S	E		J	E	R	R	Y		R	I	S	E
I	N	I	T		A	T	H	O	S		I	N	T	L
D	I	R	T	Y	C	H	O	K	E		S	T	A	Y
S	T	R	E	A	K	Y			R	A	K	E	R	
T	E	E		S	O	L	F	A		L	Y	N	C	H
	D	E	M	I			L	U	P	E		T	H	O
			O	R	T	H	O	D	O	X	C	H	E	W
O	R	T	O		Y	O	W	I	E		E	S	S	E
C	O	U	R	T	C	H	E	S	T	E	R			
H	U	N		S	O	U	R			N	A	P	S	
O	S	A	K	A		M	S	N	B	C		E	E	K
	S	M	A	R	T			B	A	Y	A	R	E	A
M	E	E	T		B	R	O	A	D	C	H	U	M	P
M	A	L	I		S	T	E	E	L		E	S	T	O
M	U	T	E		P	E	R	R	Y		M	E	O	W

122

L	A	S	T			B	L	U	E		D	R	O	P
O	T	T	I	S		R	A	N	D		R	E	P	S
B	E	A	L	L		A	S	H	E	S	S	H	E	S
B	A	R	T	A	B			A	M	A		A	N	T
E	S	T	A	T	E	S	S	T	A	T	E	S		
R	E	S	T		T	A	U	S			A	H	I	T
				S	I	G	N		E	G	R	E	T	S
I	S	L	A	N	D	E	R	S	L	A	N	D	E	R
S	T	I	L	L	E		I	A	M	B				
M	A	C	E			E	S	S	E		S	O	L	A
		O	R	A	N	G	E	S	R	A	N	G	E	S
J	A	R		L	O	O			S	M	O	L	T	S
U	S	I	N	G	S	I	N	G		A	R	E	T	E
T	A	C	O		I	S	N	T		H	E	R	E	S
S	P	E	D		R	T	E	S			S	S	R	S

123

R	A	K	E	S		M	O	W	S		A	A	R	E
A	D	O	U	T		I	C	E	E		P	O	O	L
B	O	R	N	E		L	A	T	E		E	N	O	S
B	L	E	U		B	L	T	S		A	R	E	T	E
I	F	A	C	L	U	E		P	F	F	T			
			H	E	R		P	O	L	L	U	T	E	S
T	U	E		I	N	S	A	N	A		R	O	C	K
I	S	M	I	S	S	I	N	G	U	S	E	T	H	E
E	D	I	T		I	N	D	E	N	T		S	O	W
R	A	T	S	T	A	I	L		T	Y	S			
			S	U	N	S		N	E	X	T	O	N	E
S	C	O	O	T		T	E	A	R		A	V	O	N
R	O	W	S		O	R	T	S		A	T	E	I	T
I	D	E	A		W	A	N	T		C	U	R	S	E
S	E	N	D		S	L	A	Y		E	S	T	E	R

124

C	A	R	Y			G	E	S	S	O		T	A	T
A	L	O	E		B	U	R	T	O	N		E	C	O
T	O	Y	S	U	R	P	R	I	S	E		N	R	A
C	H	A		D	E	T	E	R		A	C	N	E	D
H	A	L	F	D	E	A	D		B	R	A	E		
			L	E	D			S	I	M	P	S	O	N
A	T	T	A	R		F	L	A	G		I	S	N	O
N	E	W	T	S		E	A	R		S	T	E	E	L
N	E	E	T		S	E	M	I		T	A	E	B	O
O	M	N	I	B	U	S			V	A	L			
		T	R	U	E		S	K	I	P	J	A	C	K
B	A	Y	E	D		W	E	I	L	L		W	O	N
R	H	O		G	R	I	D	D	L	E	C	A	K	E
I	O	N		E	T	R	A	D	E		O	R	E	L
E	Y	E		T	E	E	N	Y			B	E	S	T

125

M	O	M		I	T	S	W	A	R			M	A	C
A	C	E		F	A	C	I	L	E		S	A	S	H
D	O	N	N	A	K	A	R	A	N		C	I	T	I
E	N	T	O		E	L	E	N	A	K	A	G	A	N
I	N	E	R	T	I	A			M	E	R	R	I	E
R	E	E	D	I	T		G	R	I	P	P	E	R	S
A	R	S	I	S		F	E	I	N	T		T	E	E
			C	A	R	L	S	A	G	A	N			
J	A	R		P	E	A	T	S		T	E	S	S	A
E	M	A	C	I	A	T	E		P	I	T	T	E	D
R	I	G	H	T	S			S	E	T	T	E	R	S
K	A	T	E	Y	S	A	G	A	L		L	I	R	A
I	B	I	S		E	R	I	C	H	S	E	G	A	L
E	L	M	S		S	I	R	R	A	H		E	N	E
R	Y	E			S	A	L	O	M	E		R	O	S

126

A	N	E	L	E		G	A	S	H		H	E	S	S
R	E	N	E	S		O	S	L	O		A	L	O	T
T	V	G	A	M	E	S	H	O	W		G	I	L	A
H	A	R	P	E	R	S			S	I	G	N	A	L
U	D	A	Y		N	I	N	E	O	C	L	O	C	K
R	A	V	E	S		P	O	L		H	E	R	E	
S	N	E	A	K	S		M	A	L					
		D	R	I	N	K	I	N	G	A	G	E		
					L	E	N		E	C	A	R	T	E
	B	A	I	T		R	E	B		A	T	O	W	N
J	U	M	P	S	T	R	E	E	T		O	T	I	C
A	L	T	H	E	A			T	S	A	R	I	N	A
M	O	R	O		B	L	A	C	K	J	A	C	K	S
E	V	A	N		B	A	C	H		A	D	A	L	E
S	A	K	E		Y	M	C	A		R	E	L	E	D

127

W	H	A		A	R	M	A	D	A		T	T	O	P
H	I	C		S	E	E	N	I	T		H	I	V	E
A	K	A		H	A	N	D	S	O	M	E	R	E	D
M	E	D	A	L			G	A	M	E	D	E	N	S
		E	X	A	C	T	O	R		N	O	D	S	
C	O	M	E	N	O	W		M	I	S	O			
A	N	Y		D	R	E	W		C	A	R	F	A	X
L	E	A	P		P	E	A	C	E		S	L	E	D
M	A	D	R	A	S		R	I	S	E		A	R	I
			E	V	E	S		T	A	L	K	S	O	N
	C	A	T	E		T	H	E	W	A	S	H		
B	U	Y	E	R	B	E	E			P	U	F	F	S
A	R	R	E	S	T	R	A	N	T	S		O	L	E
L	I	E	N		E	N	R	O	B	E		R	E	X
M	O	S	S		N	O	T	B	A	D		D	A	Y

128

A	G	A	S	P		H	A	T		A	B	H	O	R
L	O	T	T	O		I	W	O		R	O	O	N	E
E	T	T	A	S		L	O	N		F	A	M	E	D
C	H	A	N	T	I	L	L	Y	L	A	C	E		
S	I	C		T	O	E		S	I	R		I	A	N
	C	H	A	I	N	L	I	N	K	F	E	N	C	E
			U	M	A		M	O	E		L	O	N	E
R	A	N	G	E		L	O	W		L	I	N	E	D
I	S	E	E		O	O	F		K	E	A			
C	H	U	R	C	H	O	F	F	R	A	N	C	E	
H	E	R		A	O	K		L	O	S		A	X	L
		O	U	T	S	I	D	E	C	H	A	N	C	E
M	A	S	T	S		N	I	X		L	A	D	E	N
B	L	I	N	I		T	K	O		A	R	L	E	N
A	S	S	E	T		O	E	R		W	E	E	D	Y

129

G	N	A	T		G	L	A	D		I	N	A	P	T
R	A	V	E		R	A	V	I		N	O	R	A	H
O	M	I	T		A	K	I	N		A	F	I	R	E
W	E	A	R	E	D	E	V	O		W	E	A	R	Y
N	O	T	A	T	E				P	H	E	N	O	L
U	N	I		C	A	M	P	A	R	I		A	T	L
P	E	O	N			O	R	I	O	L	E			
		N	O	U	N	D	E	R	W	E	A	R		
			S	P	O	U	S	E			R	E	P	S
A	L	P		R	O	S	S	S	E	A		H	E	T
W	E	A	R	I	N				I	S	W	E	A	R
N	O	T	U	S		G	O	L	D	P	I	A	N	O
I	V	A	N	I		O	B	O	E		D	R	U	B
N	I	K	O	N		N	E	A	R		E	S	T	E
G	I	I	N	G		G	Y	M	S		N	E	S	S

130

N	O	R	M		O	S	A	K	A		H	A	L	E
C	R	E	E		U	N	F	E	D		U	B	E	R
A	F	A	R	E	T	O	R	E	M	E	M	B	E	R
A	F	L		A	A	R	O	N		U	M	A	S	S
			M	T	G	E			C	L	E			
	A	C	O	M	E	D	Y	O	F	E	R	A	S	
O	L	I	V	E			I	V	O	R		T	O	N
J	I	V	E		A	R	E	A	S		Z	O	L	A
O	B	I		A	X	E	L			C	A	L	V	E
	I	C	Y	D	E	A	D	P	E	O	P	L	E	
			O	L	D			R	A	M	S			
S	A	U	D	I		S	W	A	R	M		U	R	I
L	U	K	E	B	A	C	K	I	N	A	N	G	E	R
O	R	E	L		P	A	R	S	E		E	L	I	A
B	A	S	S		U	M	P	E	D		C	I	N	Q

131

F	O	R	T	M	C	H	E	N	R	Y		D	E	C
I	D	A	H	O	P	O	T	A	T	O		E	L	L
N	O	T	E	L	L	M	O	T	E	L		C	E	O
A	R	F		D	U	E			S	K	U	L	K	S
L	O	I	S		S	E	W	S		S	P	A	T	E
S	U	N	N	Y		C	R	A	G		T	I	R	O
	S	K	O	A	L		I	A	M	W	O	M	A	N
			W	R	I	S	T	B	A	N	D			
A	N	E	C	D	O	T	E		N	E	A	P	S	
P	I	E	R		N	A	T	O		T	T	O	P	S
P	C	L	A	B		N	O	H	O		E	R	L	E
L	E	S	B	O	S			O	L	E		T	I	N
A	O	K		S	O	U	T	H	A	F	R	I	C	A
U	N	I		C	A	S	E	O	F	F	I	C	E	R
D	E	N		O	R	A	L	H	I	S	T	O	R	Y

132

A	S	P	I	R	E	S		C	I	T	A	D	E	L
T	H	E	D	E	E	P		A	N	A	T	O	L	E
H	I	T	B	E	L	O	W	T	H	E	B	E	L	T
E	P	E	E	S		O	H	S	O		A	S	I	S
A	P	R		E	I	N	E		M	O	R	A	S	S
R	E	C	E	S	S		N	O	E	L		D	O	E
T	R	O	T		T	A	P	E		A	S	O	N	E
		T	H	E	S	W	I	N	E	F	L	U		
D	I	T	S	Y		O	G	O	D		A	B	E	T
E	G	O		R	E	L	S		G	A	G	L	A	W
C	O	N	G	E	R		F	I	E	F		E	T	O
E	T	T	U		A	L	L	S		F	I	T	O	F
I	C	A	N	T	S	A	Y	A	S	I	H	A	V	E
T	H	I	N	K	E	R		A	L	R	O	K	E	R
S	A	L	S	O	D	A		C	A	M	P	E	R	S

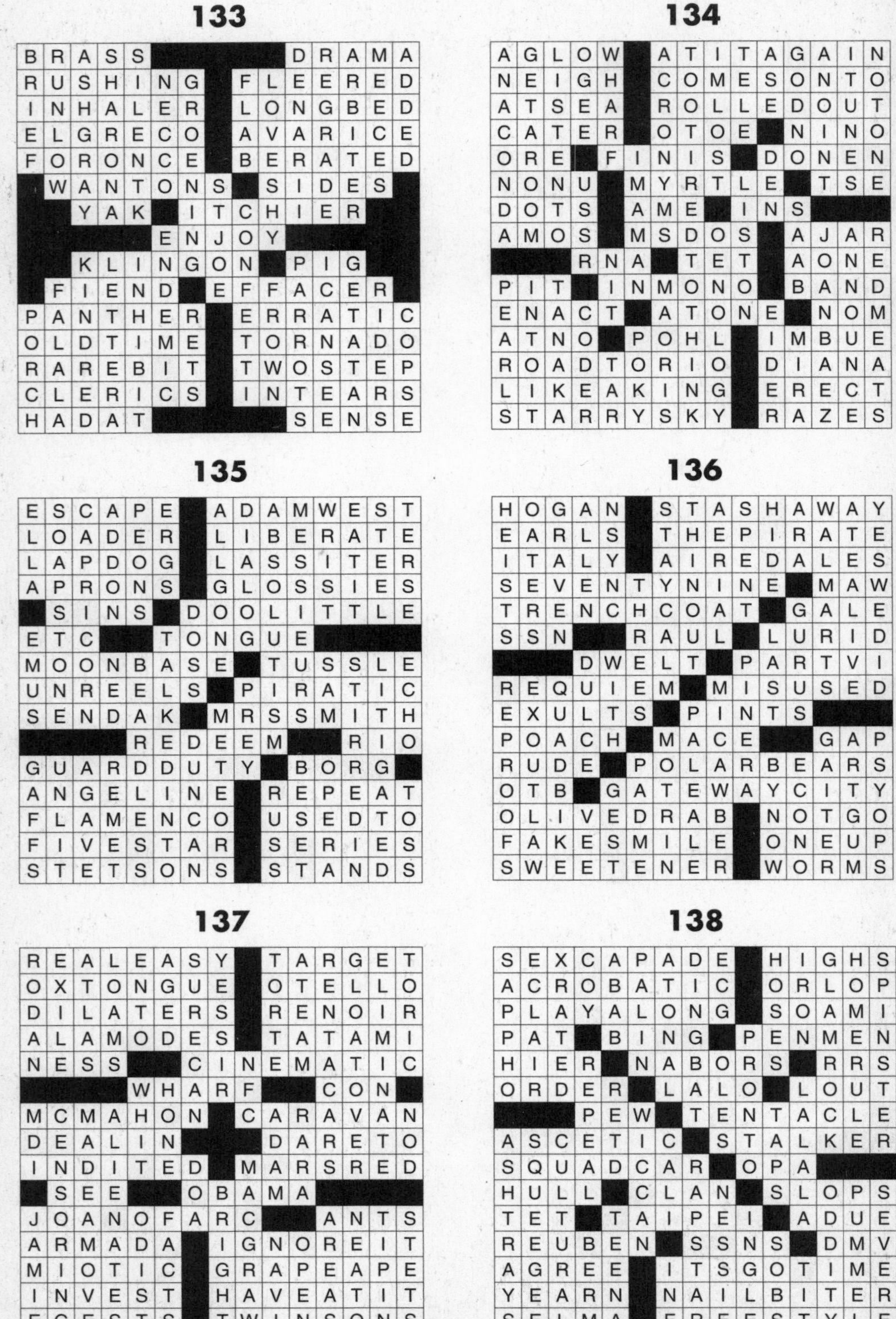

133

BRASS DRAMA
RUSHING FLEERED
INHALER LONGBED
ELGRECO AVARICE
FORONCE BERATED
WANTONS SIDES
YAK ITCHIER
ENJOY
KLINGON PIG
FIEND EFFACER
PANTHER ERRATIC
OLDTIME TORNADO
RAREBIT TWOSTEP
CLERICS INTEARS
HADAT SENSE

134

AGLOW ATITAGAIN
NEIGH COMESONTO
ATSEA ROLLEDOUT
CATER OTOE NINO
ORE FINIS DONEN
NONU MYRTLE TSE
DOTS AME INS
AMOS MSDOS AJAR
RNA TET AONE
PIT INMONO BAND
ENACT ATONE NOM
ATNO POHL IMBUE
ROADTORIO DIANA
LIKEAKING ERECT
STARRYSKY RAZES

135

ESCAPE ADAMWEST
LOADER LIBERATE
LAPDOG LASSITER
APRONS GLOSSIES
SINS DOOLITTLE
ETC TONGUE
MOONBASE TUSSLE
UNREELS PIRATIC
SENDAK MRSSMITH
REDEEM RIO
GUARDDUTY BORG
ANGELINE REPEAT
FLAMENCO USEDTO
FIVESTAR SERIES
STETSONS STANDS

136

HOGAN STASHAWAY
EARLS THEPIRATE
ITALY AIREDALES
SEVENTYNINE MAW
TRENCHCOAT GALE
SSN RAUL LURID
DWELT PARTVI
REQUIEM MISUSED
EXULTS PINTS
POACH MACE GAP
RUDE POLARBEARS
OTB GATEWAYCITY
OLIVEDRAB NOTGO
FAKESMILE ONEUP
SWEETENER WORMS

137

REALEASY TARGET
OXTONGUE OTELLO
DILATERS RENOIR
ALAMODES TATAMI
NESS CINEMATIC
WHARF CON
MCMAHON CARAVAN
DEALIN DARETO
INDITED MARSRED
SEE OBAMA
JOANOFARC ANTS
ARMADA IGNOREIT
MIOTIC GRAPEAPE
INVEST HAVEATIT
EGESTS TWINSONS

138

SEXCAPADE HIGHS
ACROBATIC ORLOP
PLAYALONG SOAMI
PAT BING PENMEN
HIER NABORS RRS
ORDER LALO LOUT
PEW TENTACLE
ASCETIC STALKER
SQUADCAR OPA
HULL CLAN SLOPS
TET TAIPEI ADUE
REUBEN SSNS DMV
AGREE ITSGOTIME
YEARN NAILBITER
SELMA FREESTYLE

139

N	E	E	D	T	O	K	N	O	W	B	A	S	I	S
E	D	U	C	A	T	I	O	N	A	L	F	I	L	M
A	G	R	E	E	T	O	D	I	S	A	G	R	E	E
T	E	A	L	■	O	S	S	O	■	S	H	O	R	E
■	S	I	L	T	■	K	A	N	■	T	A	C	■	■
■	■	L	S	A	T	■	T	R	S	■	N	C	A	R
■	■	■	■	P	H	D	■	O	N	E	I	O	T	A
I	S	A	D	O	R	A	■	L	E	T	S	S	E	E
S	I	S	E	N	O	R	■	L	E	A	■	■	■	■
O	T	I	C	■	E	T	C	■	R	I	N	G	■	■
■	■	T	R	E	■	A	R	P	■	L	A	R	D	■
R	A	W	E	R	■	G	A	I	A	■	S	E	A	M
C	L	E	A	R	A	N	D	P	R	E	S	E	N	T
P	E	R	S	O	N	A	L	E	F	F	E	C	T	S
T	R	E	E	L	I	N	E	D	S	T	R	E	E	T

140

J	A	B	B	A	■	K	I	T	K	A	T	B	A	R
C	R	O	O	N	■	I	N	A	G	R	O	O	V	E
C	R	O	C	K	■	D	V	D	B	U	R	N	E	R
H	O	K	K	A	I	D	O	■	■	M	E	A	D	E
A	W	W	■	■	V	O	L	T	A	■	■	M	O	A
S	K	O	P	J	E	■	V	I	T	A	M	I	N	D
E	E	R	I	E	■	S	E	Z	W	H	O	■	■	■
Z	Y	M	U	R	G	Y	■	Z	O	O	C	R	E	W
■	■	■	S	K	U	N	K	Y	■	O	H	A	R	E
M	R	M	I	Y	A	G	I	■	S	T	A	D	I	A
O	E	O	■	■	M	E	N	L	O	■	■	I	C	K
H	A	R	U	M	■	■	F	A	T	H	E	A	D	S
A	G	I	T	A	T	I	O	N	■	O	N	T	A	P
W	A	T	E	R	H	O	L	E	■	A	D	E	N	O
K	N	A	P	S	A	C	K	S	■	R	E	S	E	T

141

F	I	S	H	E	R	M	A	N	S	W	H	A	R	F
A	L	T	E	R	N	A	T	E	R	O	U	T	E	S
C	L	A	S	S	A	C	T	I	O	N	S	U	I	T
E	G	G	■	■	■	R	E	G	■	■	■	N	C	O
T	O	S	S	I	N	O	N	E	S	S	L	E	E	P
■	■	■	I	L	L	■	■	■	A	P	E	■	■	■
S	C	A	R	L	E	T	T	A	N	A	G	E	R	S
H	A	R	E	B	R	A	I	N	E	D	I	D	E	A
I	N	O	N	E	S	S	P	A	R	E	T	I	M	E
P	A	S	■	■	■	T	I	S	■	■	■	T	I	N
S	L	E	E	P	L	E	S	S	N	I	G	H	T	S
■	■	■	L	O	A	■	■	■	A	T	O	■	■	■
A	S	B	U	S	Y	A	S	A	B	E	A	V	E	R
S	T	A	T	E	U	N	I	V	E	R	S	I	T	Y
U	N	D	E	R	P	A	R	I	S	S	K	I	E	S

142

L	A	B	A	M	B	A	■	H	U	M	P	D	A	Y
A	S	A	T	E	A	M	■	O	B	S	E	R	V	E
C	A	T	E	R	T	O	■	T	O	G	G	L	E	S
E	G	G	■	L	O	S	T	C	A	T	■	A	R	I
U	R	I	S	■	R	O	B	O	T	■	H	U	T	S
P	A	R	E	S	■	Z	A	C	■	A	G	R	E	E
S	Y	L	V	A	N	■	R	O	E	V	W	A	D	E
■	■	■	E	L	E	V	■	A	R	I	E	■	■	■
S	I	G	N	O	V	E	R	■	A	L	L	O	W	S
A	R	R	A	N	■	R	A	J	■	A	L	O	H	A
L	O	O	M	■	N	A	I	A	D	■	S	H	A	D
U	N	U	■	M	I	N	D	S	E	T	■	L	U	C
T	O	P	S	E	E	D	■	O	C	A	N	A	D	A
E	R	O	T	I	C	A	■	N	O	R	U	L	E	S
S	E	N	O	R	E	S	■	X	Y	P	L	A	N	E

143

S	T	R	I	P	D	O	W	N	■	P	S	S	S	T
T	H	E	R	O	O	K	I	E	■	O	N	A	I	R
R	I	S	K	P	R	O	N	E	■	T	A	L	L	Y
I	N	C	■	A	S	K	E	D	■	S	P	I	E	S
N	O	A	M	■	■	■	S	S	E	■	P	E	N	T
G	U	L	P	I	N	G	■	A	L	D	E	N	T	E
S	T	E	G	N	E	R	■	P	I	R	A	T	E	D
■	■	■	■	T	W	A	■	U	S	A	■	■	■	■
H	E	I	N	O	U	S	■	S	H	I	N	D	I	G
E	L	F	O	W	L	S	■	H	A	N	S	O	L	O
S	L	O	T	■	M	F	G	■	■	■	W	I	L	T
B	A	R	E	R	■	R	E	C	U	R	■	D	E	W
A	M	O	V	E	■	O	N	A	V	E	R	A	G	E
C	A	N	E	D	■	G	O	N	E	V	I	R	A	L
K	E	E	N	S	■	S	A	T	A	S	P	E	L	L

144

P	A	T	T	I	■	M	E	D	■	S	T	R	A	P
A	L	I	E	N	A	B	D	U	C	T	I	O	N	S
V	O	L	K	S	W	A	G	E	N	J	E	T	T	A
E	T	E	■	E	A	S	E	■	N	U	D	I	S	T
■	■	S	O	C	K	■	R	O	N	D	O	■	■	■
S	C	E	N	T	E	D	■	R	E	E	N	T	E	R
H	A	T	E	S	■	C	L	A	W	S	■	O	T	O
E	S	T	S	■	F	A	I	T	S	■	D	R	A	W
A	T	E	■	C	U	R	S	E	■	E	E	R	I	E
F	E	R	R	U	L	E	■	S	E	X	C	E	L	L
■	■	■	A	T	L	A	S	■	R	E	I	N	■	■
A	W	H	I	L	E	■	P	L	U	M	■	T	A	M
P	A	I	D	A	S	T	E	E	P	P	R	I	C	E
I	N	V	E	S	T	M	E	N	T	T	E	A	M	S
A	G	E	R	S	■	I	D	S	■	S	O	L	E	S

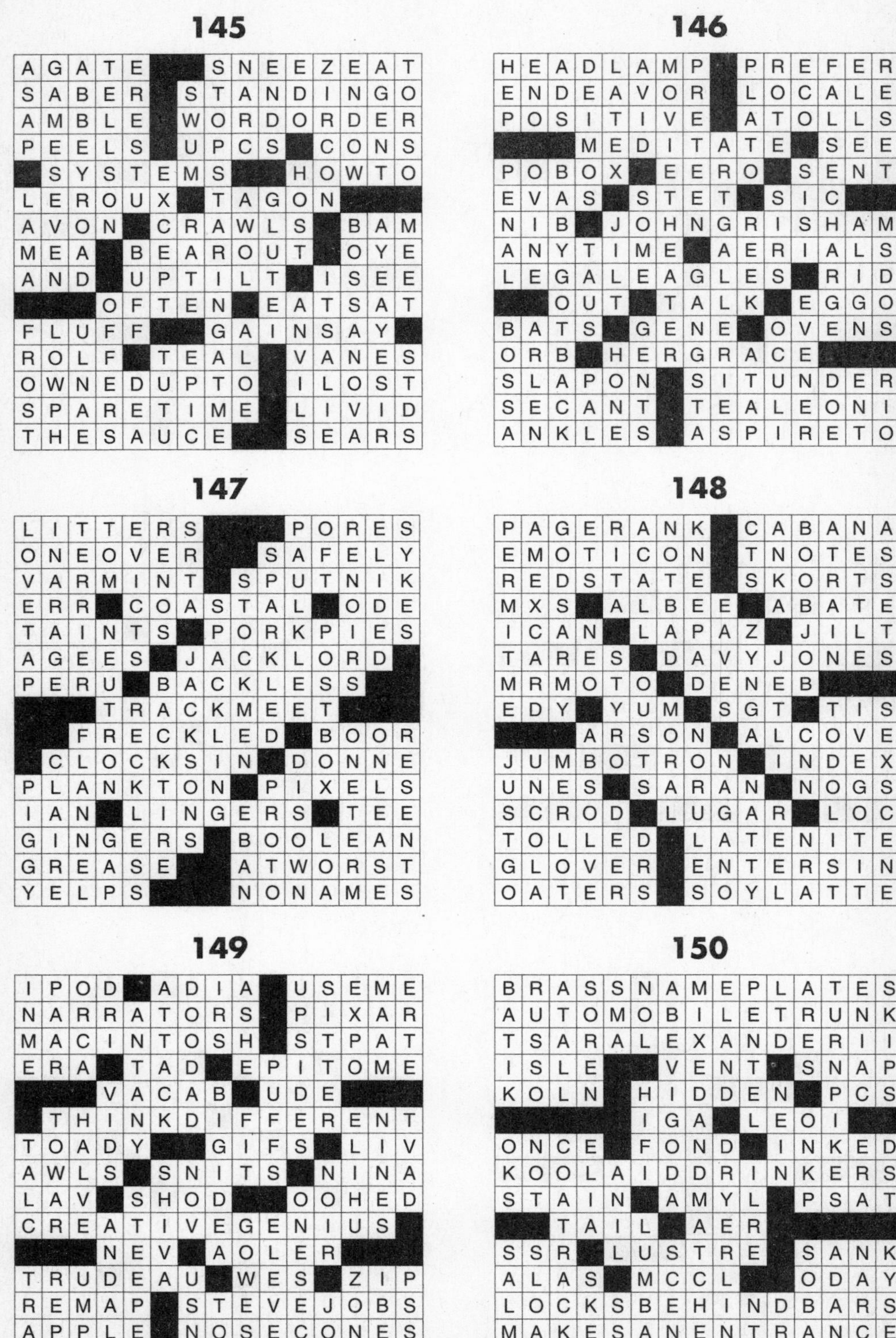

145
146
147
148
149
150

151

I	T	A	L	I	A		A	B	E	T		N	I	B
C	E	S	A	R	R	O	M	E	R	O		O	F	A
K	R	I	S	T	E	N	W	I	I	G		S	Y	R
E	R	A	S		S	T	A	G	E	A	C	T	O	R
S	A	N	E	R		A	Y	E			A	A	U	
			S	A	A	R		S	H	A	L	L	W	E
C	P	A		B	L	I	P		I	D	I	G	I	T
F	A	C	E	B	O	O	K	P	R	O	F	I	L	E
C	R	O	N	I	N		G	E	E	R		A	L	S
S	T	U	N	T	E	D		T	E	E	S			
	I	S	U			E	M	U		D	E	B	R	A
M	A	T	I	N	G	C	A	L	L		A	R	A	M
E	L	I		A	E	O	L	I	A	N	H	A	R	P
E	T	C		V	A	C	L	A	V	H	A	V	E	L
K	O	S		E	R	T	E		A	L	G	O	R	E

152

K	N	I	C	K	K	N	A	C	K		S	M	U	G
V	A	M	P	I	R	E	B	A	T		T	I	N	O
E	S	C	A	L	A	T	O	R	S		O	N	C	E
T	H	O		O	U	T	R	E		F	A	I	L	S
C	U	L	L		T	E	T	E		E	S	S	E	N
H	A	D	O	N		D	E	N	S	E		T	S	U
			P	O	L		D	E	A	D	M	E	A	T
C	H	E	E	T	O	S		D	I	S	A	R	M	S
Z	A	N	Z	I	B	A	R		L	O	G			
O	R	S		C	E	L	E	B		N	I	P	A	T
L	A	N	C	E		E	L	I	N		C	A	L	S
G	N	A	R	S		S	L	O	O	P		S	T	K
O	G	R	E		A	M	E	N	T	O	T	H	A	T
S	U	E	S		S	E	N	I	O	R	I	T	I	S
Z	E	S	T		K	N	O	C	K	K	N	O	C	K

153

J	A	C	K	B	L	A	C	K		E	Q	U	U	S
I	N	H	E	R	I	T	O	R		S	U	P	P	E
G	A	R	G	A	N	T	U	A		N	E	G	R	I
G	T	O		S	E	A	R	A	C	E		R	I	N
L	O	N	G	S		G	A	L	A		E	A	V	E
E	M	I	L		B	I	G	S	P	E	N	D	E	R
S	Y	C	A	M	O	R	E			I	C	E	R	S
			Z	E	A	L		R	O	N	A			
U	P	P	E	D			F	O	R	E	S	T	E	R
S	H	A	R	O	N	T	A	T	E		E	E	R	O
T	O	N	S		B	O	S	H		A	D	A	N	A
I	N	T		P	A	R	T	I	A	L		L	E	D
N	E	L	L	Y		P	O	R	T	L	I	E	S	T
O	N	E	I	L		I	N	A	M	O	R	A	T	A
V	O	G	U	E		D	E	S	E	R	T	F	O	X

154

U	S	S	R			A	R	A	B		P	A	P	A
N	A	T	E		A	M	A	N	A		A	B	E	D
A	R	O	D		F	A	I	N	T		I	O	T	A
P	A	N	E	L	I	S	T		T	A	N	D	E	M
T	H	E	F	I	R	S	T	L	E	T	T	E	R	S
		W	I	F	E			A	R	M	S			
S	L	A	N	T		P	I	N	E	S		D	J	S
P	A	L	E		S	H	O	E	D		B	E	A	K
A	W	L		S	P	A	N	S		W	E	L	B	Y
			G	U	Y	S			A	A	A	A		
F	I	L	L	E	V	E	R	Y	C	I	R	C	L	E
A	L	E	U	T	S		A	I	R	F	A	R	E	S
R	I	O	T		S	P	R	E	E		B	O	A	T
S	A	N	E		P	E	E	L	S		L	I	V	E
I	D	E	S		Y	A	R	D			E	X	E	S

155

S	O	C	I	A	L	D	A	R	W	I	N	I	S	M
A	R	U	N	F	O	R	T	H	E	M	O	N	E	Y
F	O	R	G	I	V	E	M	E	F	A	T	H	E	R
E	Z	R		T	E	A	S	E	T	S		E	N	O
R	C	A	S								B	E	A	N
	O	N	E	S	T	A	R	H	O	T	E	L	S	
		T	A	L	E	B	E	A	R	E	R	S		
			G	O	R	A	N	G	E	R	S			
		B	R	A	I	N	T	E	A	S	E	R		
	T	R	A	N	S	G	E	N	D	E	R	E	D	
B	R	A	M								K	T	E	L
A	A	H		A	N	T	I	G	U	N		A	C	A
A	C	M	E	C	O	R	P	O	R	A	T	I	O	N
L	E	A	S	T	R	E	S	I	S	T	A	N	C	E
S	Y	S	T	E	M	S	A	N	A	L	Y	S	T	S

156

W	I	F	I	H	O	T	S	P	O	T		P	B	S
A	C	T	S	O	N	E	S	A	G	E		I	R	A
R	O	M	A	N	C	A	N	D	L	E		G	A	L
N	N	E		G	U	M			E	N	D	S	I	T
I	C	A	N		E	U	R	O		A	I	O	L	I
N	U	D	E	S		P	A	G	O		R	U	L	E
G	R	E	W	U	P		M	R	K	O	T	T	E	R
			B	E	E	F	J	E	R	K	Y			
S	H	O	E	T	R	E	E		A	I	R	I	E	R
T	Y	R	A		E	M	T	S		E	A	R	L	Y
E	D	I	T	S		A	S	C	H		T	O	N	E
P	R	E	S	T	O			R	O	D		N	O	B
H	O	N		I	L	T	R	O	V	A	T	O	R	E
E	X	T		P	A	R	A	D	E	R	O	U	T	E
N	Y	S		E	N	E	W	S	L	E	T	T	E	R

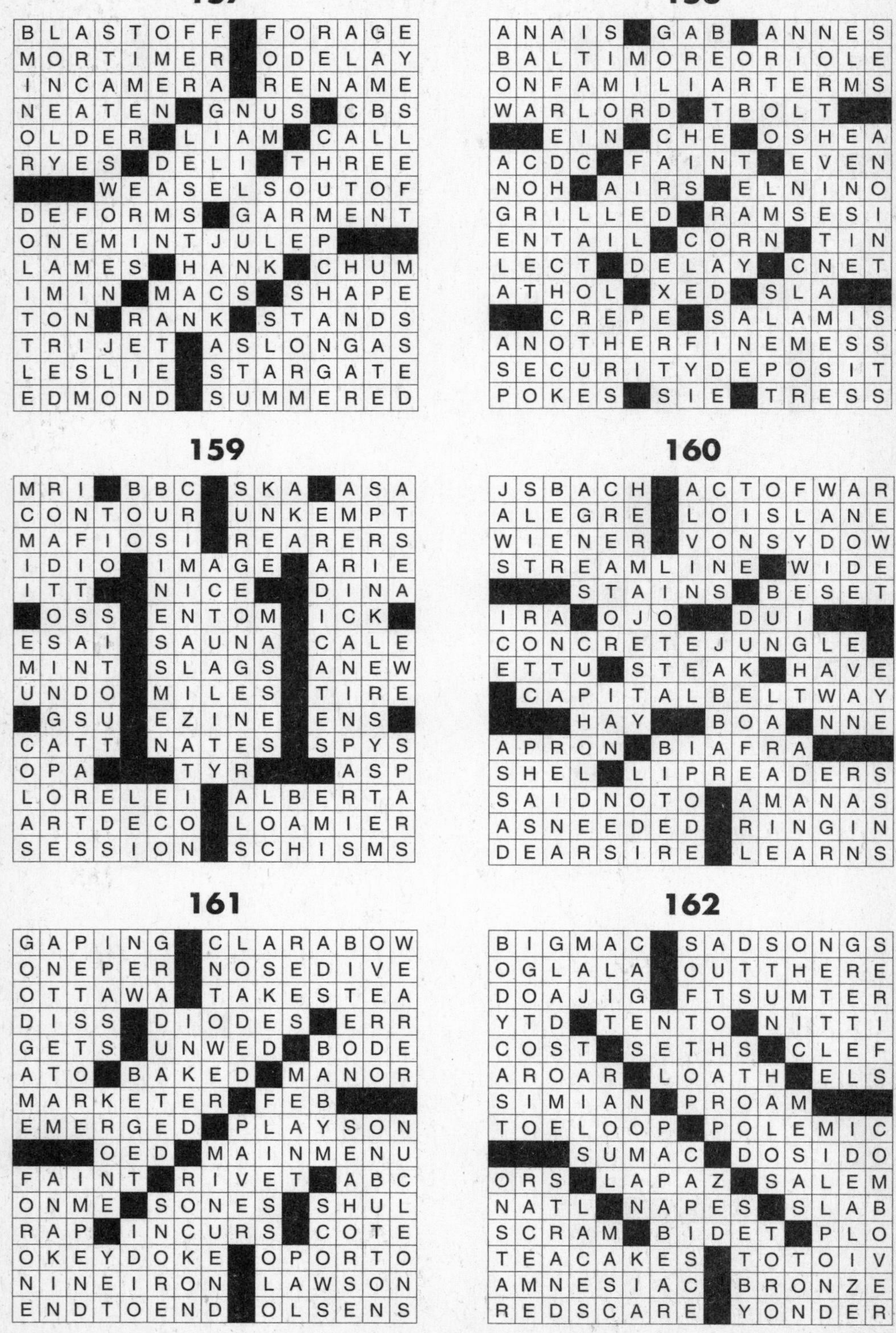
157
158
159
160
161
162

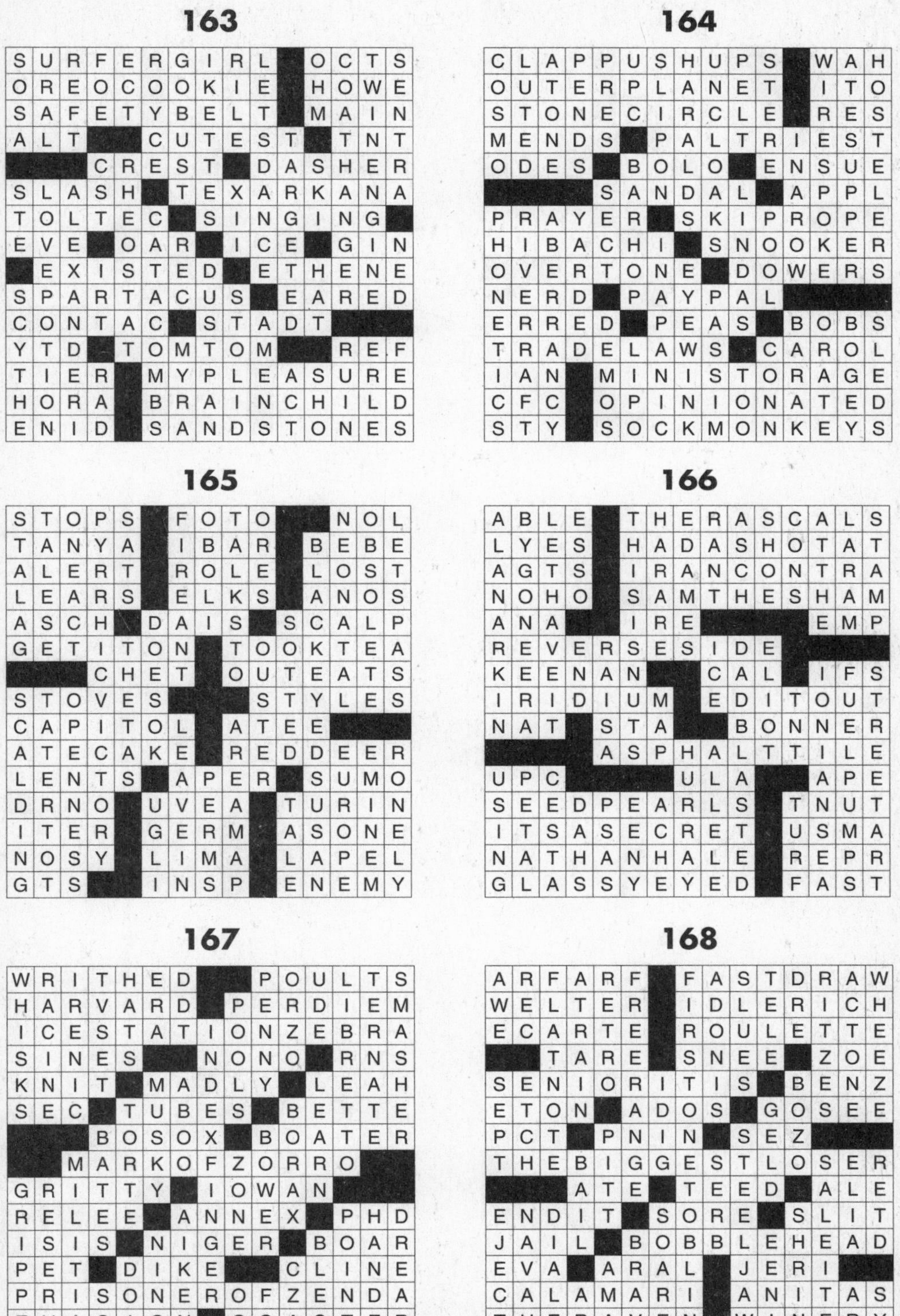
163
SURFERGIRL OCTS
OREOCOOKIE HOWE
SAFETYBELT MAIN
ALT CUTEST TNT
CREST DASHER
SLASH TEXARKANA
TOLTEC SINGING
EVE OAR ICE GIN
EXISTED ETHENE
SPARTACUS EARED
CONTAC STADT
YTD TOMTOM REF
TIER MYPLEASURE
HORA BRAINCHILD
ENID SANDSTONES
164
CLAPPUSHUPS WAH
OUTERPLANET ITO
STONECIRCLE RES
MENDS PALTRIEST
ODES BOLO ENSUE
SANDAL APPL
PRAYER SKIPROPE
HIBACHI SNOOKER
OVERTONE DOWERS
NERD PAYPAL
ERRED PEAS BOBS
TRADELAWS CAROL
IAN MINISTORAGE
CFC OPINIONATED
STY SOCKMONKEYS
165
STOPS FOTO NOL
TANYA IBAR BEBE
ALERT ROLE LOST
LEARS ELKS ANOS
ASCH DAIS SCALP
GETITON TOOKTEA
CHET OUTEATS
STOVES STYLES
CAPITOL ATEE
ATECAKE REDDEER
LENTS APER SUMO
DRNO UVEA TURIN
ITER GERM ASONE
NOSY LIMA LAPEL
GTS INSP ENEMY
166
ABLE THERASCALS
LYES HADASHOTAT
AGTS IRANCONTRA
NOHO SAMTHESHAM
ANA IRE EMP
REVERSESIDE
KEENAN CAL IFS
IRIDIUM EDITOUT
NAT STA BONNER
ASPHALTTILE
UPC ULA APE
SEEDPEARLS TNUT
ITSASECRET USMA
NATHANHALE REPR
GLASSYEYED FAST
167
WRITHED POULTS
HARVARD PERDIEM
ICESTATIONZEBRA
SINES NONO RNS
KNIT MADLY LEAH
SEC TUBES BETTE
BOSOX BOATER
MARKOFZORRO
GRITTY IOWAN
RELEE ANNEX PHD
ISIS NIGER BOAR
PET DIKE CLINE
PRISONEROFZENDA
EVASION COASTER
RESETS TERSELY
168
ARFARF FASTDRAW
WELTER IDLERICH
ECARTE ROULETTE
TARE SNEE ZOE
SENIORITIS BENZ
ETON ADOS GOSEE
PCT PNIN SEZ
THEBIGGESTLOSER
ATE TEED ALE
ENDIT SORE SLIT
JAIL BOBBLEHEAD
EVA ARAL JERI
CALAMARI ANITAS
THERAVEN WINERY
SODAJERK SEEMED

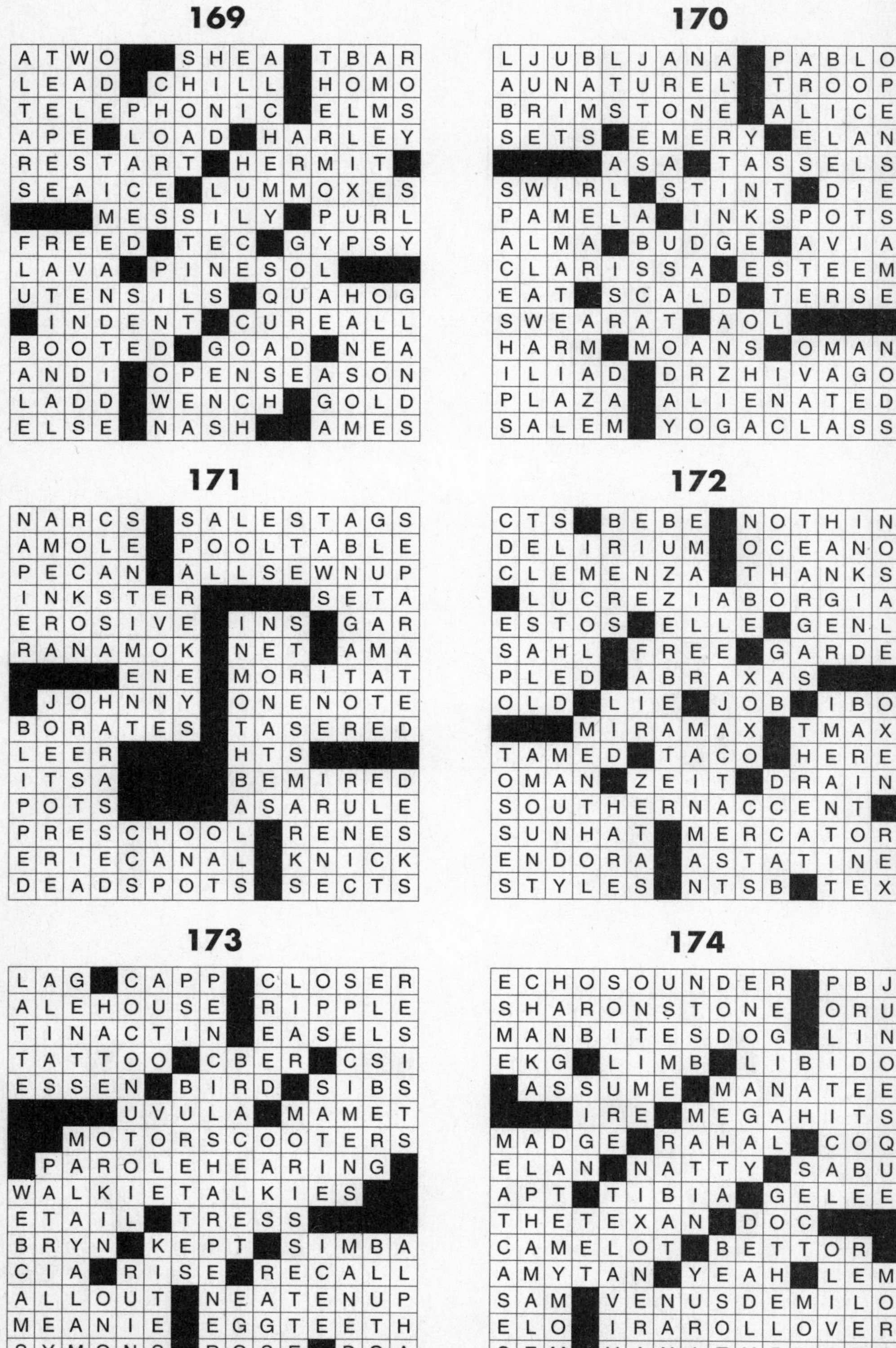
169
ATWO SHEA TBAR
LEAD CHILL HOMO
TELEPHONIC ELMS
APE LOAD HARLEY
RESTART HERMIT
SEAICE LUMMOXES
MESSILY PURL
FREED TEC GYPSY
LAVA PINESOL
UTENSILS QUAHOG
INDENT CUREALL
BOOTED GOAD NEA
ANDI OPENSEASON
LADD WENCH GOLD
ELSE NASH AMES
170
LJUBLJANA PABLO
AUNATUREL TROOP
BRIMSTONE ALICE
SETS EMERY ELAN
ASA TASSELS
SWIRL STINT DIE
PAMELA INKSPOTS
ALMA BUDGE AVIA
CLARISSA ESTEEM
EAT SCALD TERSE
SWEARAT AOL
HARM MOANS OMAN
ILIAD DRZHIVAGO
PLAZA ALIENATED
SALEM YOGACLASS
171
NARCS SALESTAGS
AMOLE POOLTABLE
PECAN ALLSEWNUP
INKSTER SETA
EROSIVE INS GAR
RANAMOK NET AMA
ENE MORITAT
JOHNNY ONENOTE
BORATES TASERED
LEER HTS
ITSA BEMIRED
POTS ASARULE
PRESCHOOL RENES
ERIECANAL KNICK
DEADSPOTS SECTS
172
CTS BEBE NOTHIN
DELIRIUM OCEANO
CLEMENZA THANKS
LUCREZIABORGIA
ESTOS ELLE GENL
SAHL FREE GARDE
PLED ABRAXAS
OLD LIE JOB IBO
MIRAMAX TMAX
TAMED TACO HERE
OMAN ZEIT DRAIN
SOUTHERNACCENT
SUNHAT MERCATOR
ENDORA ASTATINE
STYLES NTSB TEX
173
LAG CAPP CLOSER
ALEHOUSE RIPPLE
TINACTIN EASELS
TATTOO CBER CSI
ESSEN BIRD SIBS
UVULA MAMET
MOTORSCOOTERS
PAROLEHEARING
WALKIETALKIES
ETAIL TRESS
BRYN KEPT SIMBA
CIA RISE RECALL
ALLOUT NEATENUP
MEANIE EGGTEETH
SYMONS ROSE DOA
174
ECHOSOUNDER PBJ
SHARONSTONE ORU
MANBITESDOG LIN
EKG LIMB LIBIDO
ASSUME MANATEE
IRE MEGAHITS
MADGE RAHAL COQ
ELAN NATTY SABU
APT TIBIA GELEE
THETEXAN DOC
CAMELOT BETTOR
AMYTAN YEAH LEM
SAM VENUSDEMILO
ELO IRAROLLOVER
SEM VANITYPLATE

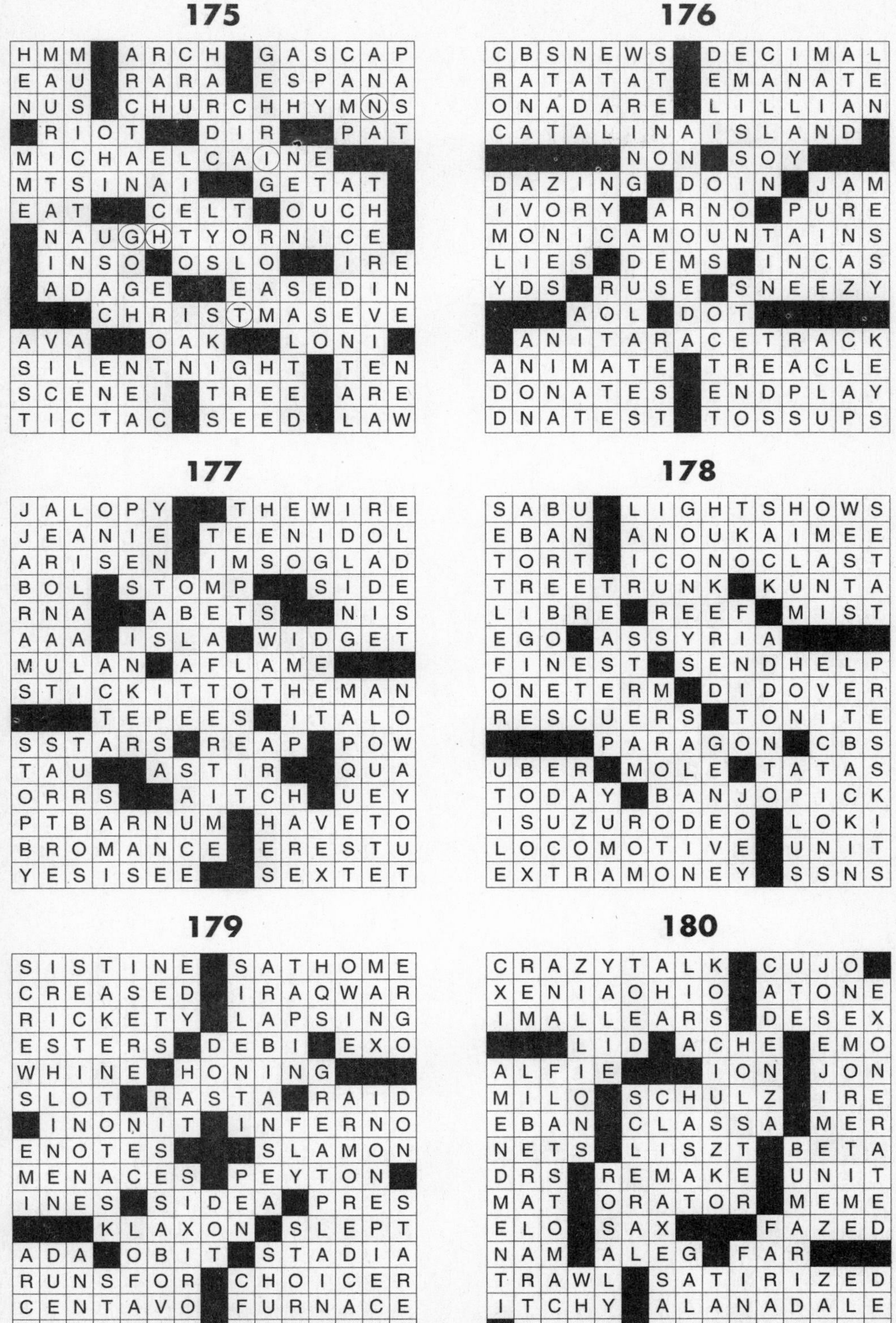
175
HMM ARCH GASCAP
EAU RARA ESPANA
NUS CHURCHHYMNS
RIOT DIR PAT
MICHAELCAINE
MTSINAI GETAT
EAT CELT OUCH
NAUGHTYORNICE
INSO OSLO IRE
ADAGE EASEDIN
CHRISTMASEVE
AVA OAK LONI
SILENTNIGHT TEN
SCENEI TREE ARE
TICTAC SEED LAW
176
CBSNEWS DECIMAL
RATATAT EMANATE
ONADARE LILLIAN
CATALINAISLAND
NON SOY
DAZING DOIN JAM
IVORY ARNO PURE
MONICAMOUNTAINS
LIES DEMS INCAS
YDS RUSE SNEEZY
AOL DOT
ANITARACETRACK
ANIMATE TREACLE
DONATES ENDPLAY
DNATEST TOSSUPS
177
JALOPY THEWIRE
JEANIE TEENIDOL
ARISEN IMSOGLAD
BOL STOMP SIDE
RNA ABETS NIS
AAA ISLA WIDGET
MULAN AFLAME
STICKITTOTHEMAN
TEPEES ITALO
SSTARS REAP POW
TAU ASTIR QUA
ORRS AITCH UEY
PTBARNUM HAVETO
BROMANCE ERESTU
YESISEE SEXTET
178
SABU LIGHTSHOWS
EBAN ANOUKAIMEE
TORT ICONOCLAST
TREETRUNK KUNTA
LIBRE REEF MIST
EGO ASSYRIA
FINEST SENDHELP
ONETERM DIDOVER
RESCUERS TONITE
PARAGON CBS
UBER MOLE TATAS
TODAY BANJOPICK
ISUZURODEO LOKI
LOCOMOTIVE UNIT
EXTRAMONEY SSNS
179
SISTINE SATHOME
CREASED IRAQWAR
RICKETY LAPSING
ESTERS DEBI EXO
WHINE HONING
SLOT RASTA RAID
INONIT INFERNO
ENOTES SLAMON
MENACES PEYTON
INES SIDEA PRES
KLAXON SLEPT
ADA OBIT STADIA
RUNSFOR CHOICER
CENTAVO FURNACE
STOUTEN SEESRED
180
CRAZYTALK CUJO
XENIAOHIO ATONE
IMALLEARS DESEX
LID ACHE EMO
ALFIE ION JON
MILO SCHULZ IRE
EBAN CLASSA MER
NETS LISZT BETA
DRS REMAKE UNIT
MAT ORATOR MEME
ELO SAX FAZED
NAM ALEG FAR
TRAWL SATIRIZED
ITCHY ALANADALE
SHAN TAPEDECKS

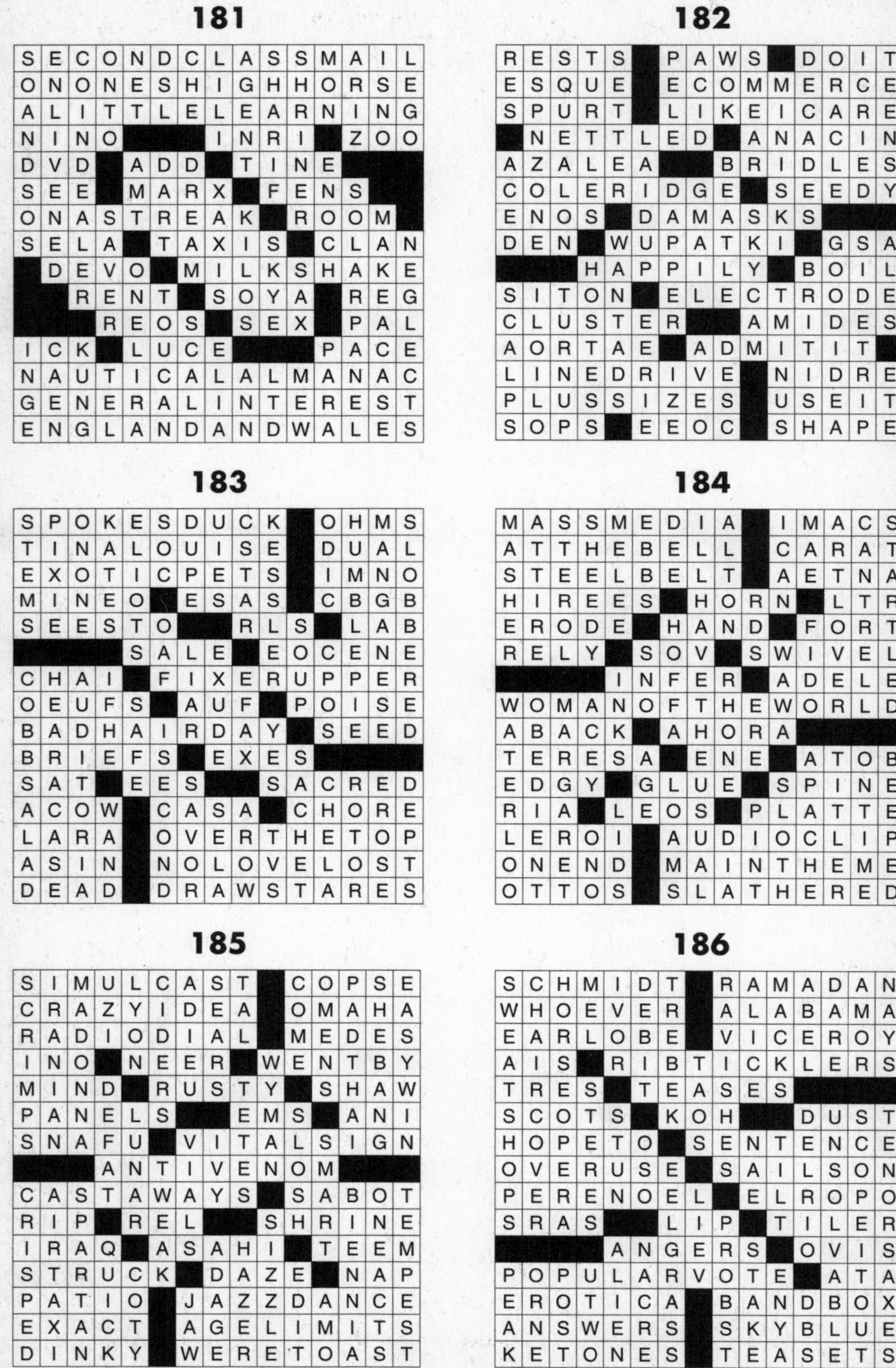

181
SECONDCLASSMAIL
ONONESHIGHHORSE
ALITTLELEARNING
NINO INRI ZOO
DVD ADD TINE
SEE MARX FENS
ONASTREAK ROOM
SELA TAXIS CLAN
DEVO MILKSHAKE
RENT SOYA REG
REOS SEX PAL
ICK LUCE PACE
NAUTICALALMANAC
GENERALINTEREST
ENGLANDANDWALES
182
RESTS PAWS DOIT
ESQUE ECOMMERCE
SPURT LIKEICARE
NETTLED ANACIN
AZALEA BRIDLES
COLERIDGE SEEDY
ENOS DAMASKS
DEN WUPATKI GSA
HAPPILY BOIL
SITON ELECTRODE
CLUSTER AMIDES
AORTAE ADMITIT
LINEDRIVE NIDRE
PLUSSIZES USEIT
SOPS EEOC SHAPE
183
SPOKESDUCK OHMS
TINALOUISE DUAL
EXOTICPETS IMNO
MINEO ESAS CBGB
SEESTO RLS LAB
SALE EOCENE
CHAI FIXERUPPER
OEUFS AUF POISE
BADHAIRDAY SEED
BRIEFS EXES
SAT EES SACRED
ACOW CASA CHORE
LARA OVERTHETOP
ASIN NOLOVELOST
DEAD DRAWSTARES
184
MASSMEDIA IMACS
ATTHEBELL CARAT
STEELBELT AETNA
HIREES HORN LTR
ERODE HAND FORT
RELY SOV SWIVEL
INFER ADELE
WOMANOFTHEWORLD
ABACK AHORA
TERESA ENE ATOB
EDGY GLUE SPINE
RIA LEOS PLATTE
LEROI AUDIOCLIP
ONEND MAINTHEME
OTTOS SLATHERED
185
SIMULCAST COPSE
CRAZYIDEA OMAHA
RADIODIAL MEDES
INO NEER WENTBY
MIND RUSTY SHAW
PANELS EMS ANI
SNAFU VITALSIGN
ANTIVENOM
CASTAWAYS SABOT
RIP REL SHRINE
IRAQ ASAHI TEEM
STRUCK DAZE NAP
PATIO JAZZDANCE
EXACT AGELIMITS
DINKY WERETOAST
186
SCHMIDT RAMADAN
WHOEVER ALABAMA
EARLOBE VICEROY
AIS RIBTICKLERS
TRES TEASES
SCOTS KOH DUST
HOPETO SENTENCE
OVERUSE SAILSON
PERENOEL ELROPO
SRAS LIP TILER
ANGERS OVIS
POPULARVOTE ATA
EROTICA BANDBOX
ANSWERS SKYBLUE
KETONES TEASETS

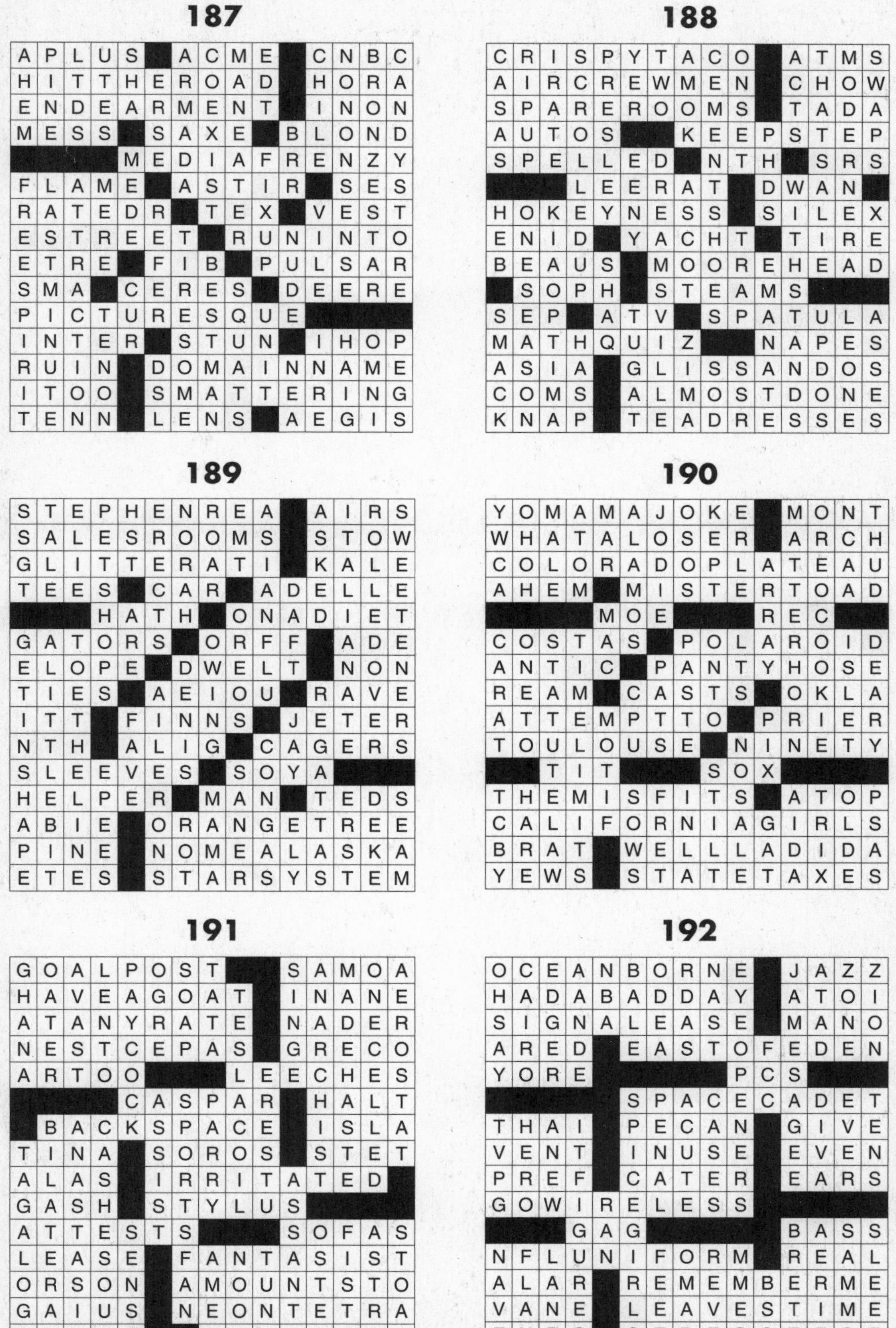
187
APLUS ACME CNBC
HITTHEROAD HORA
ENDEARMENT INON
MESS SAXE BLOND
MEDIAFRENZY
FLAME ASTIR SES
RATEDR TEX VEST
ESTREET RUNINTO
ETRE FIB PULSAR
SMA CERES DEERE
PICTURESQUE
INTER STUN IHOP
RUIN DOMAINNAME
ITOO SMATTERING
TENN LENS AEGIS
188
CRISPYTACO ATMS
AIRCREWMEN CHOW
SPAREROOMS TADA
AUTOS KEEPSTEP
SPELLED NTH SRS
LEERAT DWAN
HOKEYNESS SILEX
ENID YACHT TIRE
BEAUS MOOREHEAD
SOPH STEAMS
SEP ATV SPATULA
MATHQUIZ NAPES
ASIA GLISSANDOS
COMS ALMOSTDONE
KNAP TEADRESSES
189
STEPHENREA AIRS
SALESROOMS STOW
GLITTERATI KALE
TEES CAR ADELLE
HATH ONADIET
GATORS ORFF ADE
ELOPE DWELT NON
TIES AEIOU RAVE
ITT FINNS JETER
NTH ALIG CAGERS
SLEEVES SOYA
HELPER MAN TEDS
ABIE ORANGETREE
PINE NOMEALASKA
ETES STARSYSTEM
190
YOMAMAJOKE MONT
WHATALOSER ARCH
COLORADOPLATEAU
AHEM MISTERTOAD
MOE REC
COSTAS POLAROID
ANTIC PANTYHOSE
REAM CASTS OKLA
ATTEMPTTO PRIER
TOULOUSE NINETY
TIT SOX
THEMISFITS ATOP
CALIFORNIAGIRLS
BRAT WELLLADIDA
YEWS STATETAXES
191
GOALPOST SAMOA
HAVEAGOAT INANE
ATANYRATE NADER
NESTCEPAS GRECO
ARTOO LEECHES
CASPAR HALT
BACKSPACE ISLA
TINA SOROS STET
ALAS IRRITATED
GASH STYLUS
ATTESTS SOFAS
LEASE FANTASIST
ORSON AMOUNTSTO
GAIUS NEONTETRA
SLATE SNEERSAT
192
OCEANBORNE JAZZ
HADABADDAY ATOI
SIGNALEASE MANO
ARED EASTOFEDEN
YORE PCS
SPACECADET
THAI PECAN GIVE
VENT INUSE EVEN
PREF CATER EARS
GOWIRELESS
GAG BASS
NFLUNIFORM REAL
ALAR REMEMBERME
VANE LEAVESTIME
EXES STRESSTEST

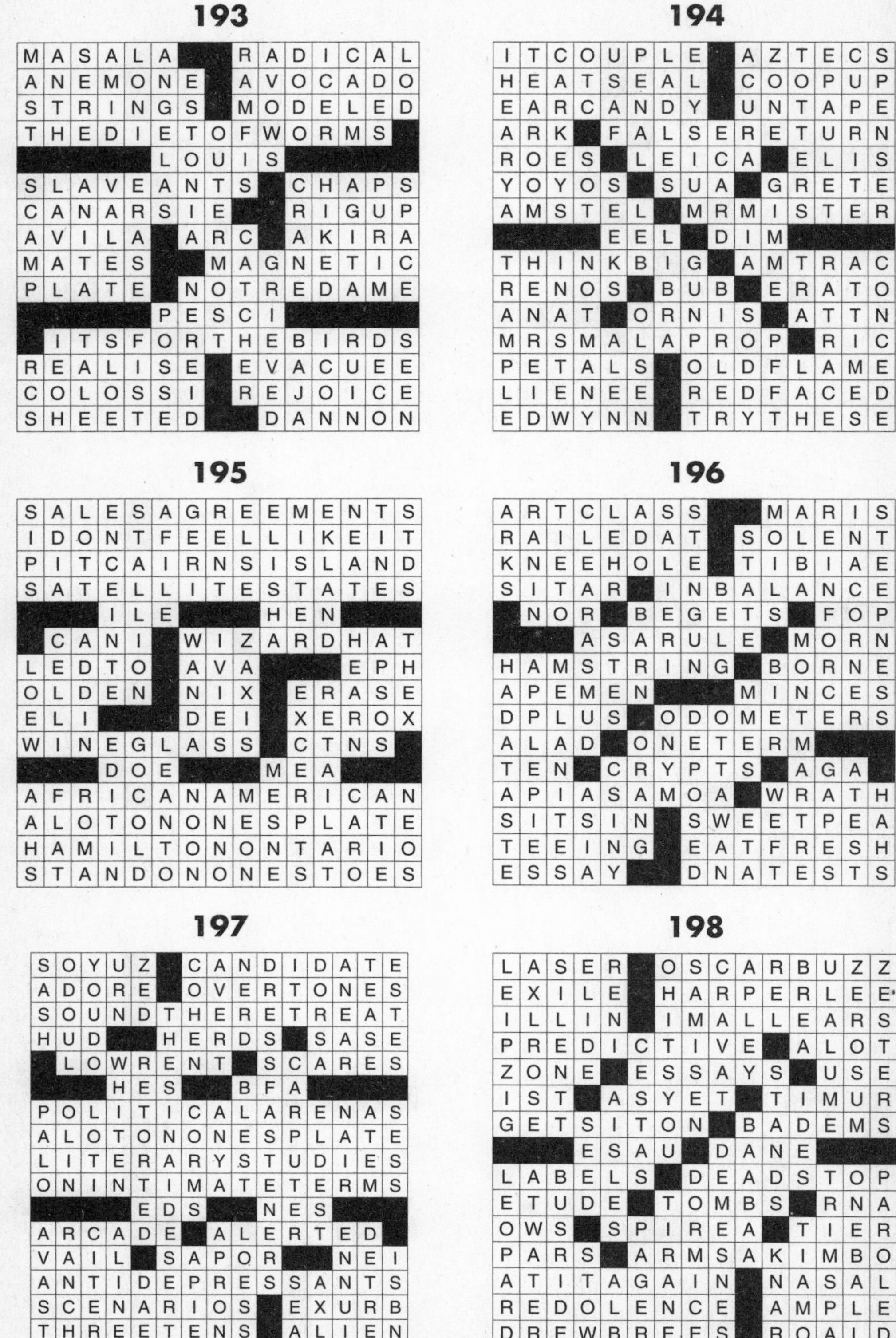

193

MASALA RADICAL
ANEMONE AVOCADO
STRINGS MODELED
THEDIETOFWORMS
LOUIS
SLAVEANTS CHAPS
CANARSIE RIGUP
AVILA ARC AKIRA
MATES MAGNETIC
PLATE NOTREDAME
PESCI
ITSFORTHEBIRDS
REALISE EVACUEE
COLOSSI REJOICE
SHEETED DANNON

194

ITCOUPLE AZTECS
HEATSEAL COOPUP
EARCANDY UNTAPE
ARK FALSERETURN
ROES LEICA ELIS
YOYOS SUA GRETE
AMSTEL MRMISTER
EEL DIM
THINKBIG AMTRAC
RENOS BUB ERATO
ANAT ORNIS ATTN
MRSMALAPROP RIC
PETALS OLDFLAME
LIENEE REDFACED
EDWYNN TRYTHESE

195

SALESAGREEMENTS
IDONTFEELLIKEIT
PITCAIRNSISLAND
SATELLITESTATES
ILE HEN
CANI WIZARDHAT
LEDTO AVA EPH
OLDEN NIX ERASE
ELI DEI XEROX
WINEGLASS CTNS
DOE MEA
AFRICANAMERICAN
ALOTONONESPLATE
HAMILTONONTARIO
STANDONONESTOES

196

ARTCLASS MARIS
RAILEDAT SOLENT
KNEEHOLE TIBIAE
SITAR INBALANCE
NOR BEGETS FOP
ASARULE MORN
HAMSTRING BORNE
APEMEN MINCES
DPLUS ODOMETERS
ALAD ONETERM
TEN CRYPTS AGA
APIASAMOA WRATH
SITSIN SWEETPEA
TEEING EATFRESH
ESSAY DNATESTS

197

SOYUZ CANDIDATE
ADORE OVERTONES
SOUNDTHERETREAT
HUD HERDS SASE
LOWRENT SCARES
HES BFA
POLITICALARENAS
ALOTONONESPLATE
LITERARYSTUDIES
ONINTIMATETERMS
EDS NES
ARCADE ALERTED
VAIL SAPOR NEI
ANTIDEPRESSANTS
SCENARIOS EXURB
THREETENS ALIEN

198

LASER OSCARBUZZ
EXILE HARPERLEE
ILLIN IMALLEARS
PREDICTIVE ALOT
ZONE ESSAYS USE
IST ASYET TIMUR
GETSITON BADEMS
ESAU DANE
LABELS DEADSTOP
ETUDE TOMBS RNA
OWS SPIREA TIER
PARS ARMSAKIMBO
ATITAGAIN NASAL
REDOLENCE AMPLE
DREWBREES ROALD

199

R	A	W	F	I	S	H		B	E	S	T	M	A	N
T	R	A	L	A	L	A		A	K	I	H	I	T	O
S	E	N	A	T	O	R		L	E	E	R	S	A	T
			N	E	W	A	G	E			I	S	L	E
A	C	H	S		N	R	A		B	E	L	I	E	D
U	R	I		K	E	E	L	H	A	U	L	S		
R	E	G	R	O	W		L	E	G	R	E	S	T	S
A	M	H	E	R	S	T		C	H	A	R	I	O	T
L	E	A	N	E	D	O	N		D	I	S	P	E	L
		S	E	A	A	N	I	M	A	L		P	I	E
B	R	A	W	N	Y		N	E	D		G	I	N	O
E	E	K	A			R	A	T	I	T	E			
A	M	I	B	L	U	E		I	R	O	N	O	U	T
R	A	T	L	I	K	E		M	A	F	I	O	S	I
S	N	E	E	Z	E	D		E	Q	U	I	N	O	X

200

S	L	E	U	T	H		C	A	R	B	O	M	B	S
T	O	U	P	E	E		I	T	O	L	D	Y	O	U
O	R	G	A	N	S		R	E	S	T	S	T	O	P
O	D	E	S		S	E	R	I	E	S		H	M	S
D	I	N				R	U	N	T					
A	T	E	M		M	A	S	T	I	C		J	E	T
P	O	L	I	C	E	S		O	N	L	E	A	V	E
A	V	E	R	T	S				T	E	X	M	E	X
R	E	V	E	R	S	I		D	E	F	I	A	N	T
T	R	Y		L	A	N	C	E	D		T	I	M	E
					G	A	L	A				C	O	D
A	I	R		V	E	R	O	N	A		B	A	R	I
C	R	E	P	E	P	A	N		C	L	A	R	E	T
A	A	V	E	R	A	G	E		C	A	R	U	S	O
I	N	S	P	A	D	E	S		T	R	E	M	O	R

The New York Times

Crossword Puzzles

The #1 Name in Crosswords

Available at your local bookstore or online at nytimes.com/nytstore

Coming Soon!

Title	ISBN
ABCs of Crosswords	978-1-250-00922-7
Best of Monday Crosswords	978-1-250-00926-5
Best of Tuesday Crosswords	978-1-250-00927-2
Sunday in the Surf Crosswords	978-1-250-00924-1
Dreaming of Crosswords	978-1-250-00930-2
Mad About Crosswords	978-1-250-00923-4
Crossword Getaway	978-1-250-00928-9
All the Crosswords that Are Fit to Print	978-1-250-00925-8
Easy Crossword Puzzle Omnibus Vol. 8	978-1-250-00929-6

Special Editions

Title	ISBN
Will Shortz Picks His Favorite Puzzles	978-0-312-64550-2
Crosswords for the Holidays	978-0-312-64544-1
Crossword Lovers Only: Easy Puzzles	978-0-312-54619-9
Crossword Lovers Only: Easy to Hard Puzzles	978-0-312-68139-5
Little Pink Book of Crosswords	978-0-312-65421-4
Little Black & White Book of Holiday Crosswords	978-0-312-65424-5
Little Black (and White) Book of Sunday Crosswords	978-0-312-59003-1
Will Shortz's Wittiest, Wackiest Crosswords	978-0-312-59034-5
Crosswords to Keep Your Brain Young	0-312-37658-8
Little Black (and White) Book of Crosswords	0-312-36105-X
Little Red and Green Book of Crosswords	0-312-37661-8
Little Flip Book of Crosswords	0-312-37043-1
How to Conquer the *New York Times* Crossword Puzzle	0-312-36554-3
Will Shortz's Favorite Crossword Puzzles	0-312-30613-X
Will Shortz's Favorite Sunday Crossword Puzzles	0-312-32488-X
Will Shortz's Greatest Hits	0-312-34242-X
Will Shortz Presents Crosswords for 365 Days	0-312-36121-1
Will Shortz's Funniest Crossword Puzzles Vol. 2	0-312-33960-7
Will Shortz's Funniest Crossword Puzzles	0-312-32489-8
Will Shortz's Xtreme Xwords	0-312-35203-4

Easy Crosswords

Title	ISBN
Easy Crossword Puzzles Vol. 13	978-1-250-00403-1
Easy Crossword Puzzles Vol. 12	978-0-312-68137-1

Volumes 2–11 also available

Tough Crosswords

Title	ISBN
Tough Crossword Puzzles Vol. 13	0-312-34240-3
Tough Crossword Puzzles Vol. 12	0-312-32442-1

Volumes 9–11 also available

Sunday Crosswords

Title	ISBN
Simply Sundays	978-1-250-00390-4
Fireside Sunday Crosswords	978-0-312-64546-5
Snuggle Up Sunday Crosswords	978-0-312-59057-4
Stay in Bed Sunday Crosswords	978-0-312-68144-9
Relaxing Sunday Crosswords	978-0-312-65429-0
Finally Sunday Crosswords	978-0-312-64113-9
Crosswords for a Lazy Sunday	978-0-312-60820-0
Sunday's Best	0-312-37637-5
Sunday at Home Crosswords	0-312-37834-3
Sunday Crossword Puzzles Vol.37	978-0-312-64549-6

Omnibus

Title	ISBN
Easy to Not-So-Easy Crossword Puzzle Omnibus Vol. 6	978-1-250-00402-4
Day at the Beach Crossword Puzzle Omnibus	978-0-312-58843-4
Easy to Not-So-Easy Crossword Puzzle Omnibus Vol. 5	978-0-312-68138-8
Garden Party Crossword Puzzles	978-0-312-60824-8
Lazy Day Crossword Puzzle Omnibus	0-312-56532-1
Weekend in the Country	0-312-38270-7
Crosswords for Two	0-312-37830-0
Crosswords for a Relaxing Weekend	0-312-37829-7
Crosswords for a Lazy Afternoon	0-312-33108-8
Lazy Weekend Crossword Puzzle Omnibus	0-312-34247-0
Lazy Sunday Crossword Puzzle Omnibus	0-312-35279-4
Ultimate Crossword Omnibus	0-312-31622-4
Tough Crossword Puzzle Omnibus Vol. 1	0-312-32441-3
Crossword Challenge	0-312-33951-8
Crosswords for a Weekend Getaway	0-312-35198-4
Easy Crossword Puzzle Omnibus Vol. 7	978-0-312-59058-1
Crossword Puzzle Omnibus Vol. 16	0-312-36104-1
Sunday Crossword Omnibus Vol. 10	0-312-59006-7

Previous volumes also available

Portable Size Format

Title	ISBN
Picnic Blanket Crosswords	978-1-250-00391-1
Scrumptiously Simple Crosswords	978-1-250-00393-5
Deliciously Doable Crosswords	978-1-250-00394-2
Delightfully Difficult Crosswords	978-1-250-00395-9
Huge Book of Easy Crosswords	978-1-250-00399-7
Springtime Solving Crosswords	978-1-250-00400-0
Cunning Crosswords	978-0-312-64543-4
Little Book of Lots of Crosswords	978-0-312-64548-9
Effortlessly Easy Crossword Puzzles	978-0-312-64545-8
Big, Bad Book of Crosswords	978-0-312-58841-0
Midsummer Night's Crosswords	978-0-312-58842-7
Early Morning Crosswords	978-0-312-58840-3
Pop Culture Crosswords	978-0-312-59059-8
Mad Hatter Crosswords	978-0-312-58847-2
Crosswords to Unwind Your Mind	978-0-312-68135-7
Keep Calm and Crossword On	978-0-312-68141-8
Light and Easy Crosswords	978-0-312-68142-5
Hot and Steamy Crosswords	978-0-312-68140-1
Big and Bold Crosswords	978-0-312-68134-0
Weekends with Will	978-0-312-65668-3
Every Day with Crosswords	978-0-312-65426-9
Clever Crosswords	978-0-312-65425-2
Everyday Easy Crosswords	978-0-312-64115-3
Puzzle Doctor Presents Crossword Fever	978-0-312-64110-8
Poolside Puzzles	978-0-312-64114-6
Sunny Crosswords	978-0-312-61446-0
Mild Crosswords	978-0-312-64117-7
Mellow Crosswords	978-0-312-64118-4
Mischievous Crosswords	978-0-312-64119-1
Wake Up with Crosswords	978-0-312-60819-4
Simply Soothing Crosswords	978-0-312-60823-1
Simply Satisfying Crosswords	978-0-312-60822-4
Simply Sneaky Crosswords	978-0-312-60821-7
Tame Crosswords	0-312-54168-6
Wild Crosswords	0-312-54169-4
Ferocious Crosswords	0-312-54170-8
Ready, Set, Solve! Crosswords	0-312-38623-0
Favorite Day Crosswords: Tuesday	0-312-37072-5
Favorite Day Crosswords: Monday	0-312-36556-X
Big Book of Easy Crosswords	0-312-38268-5
Real Simple Crosswords	0-312-38254-5

Other volumes also available

St. Martin's Griffin